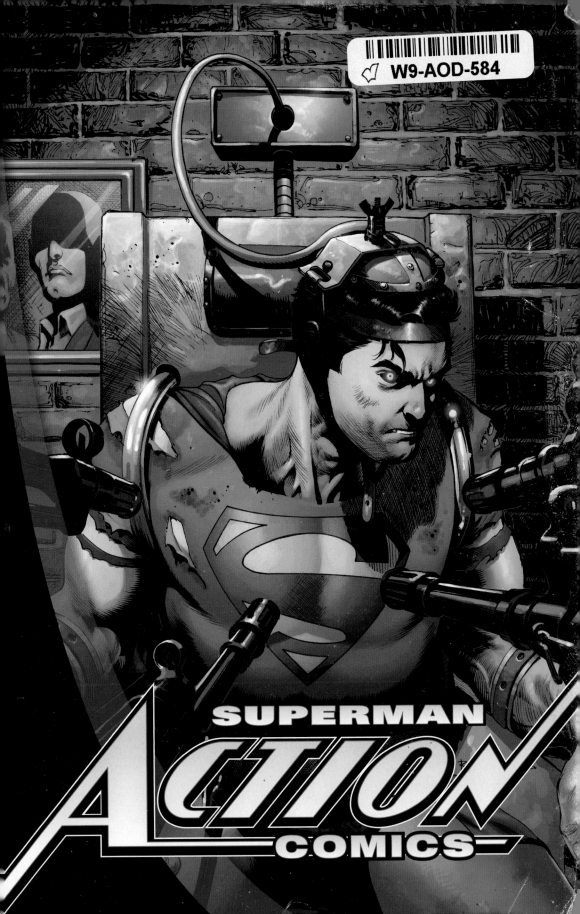

W9-AOD-584

SUPERMAN
ACTION
COMICS

VOLUME 1 SUPERMAN AND THE MEN OF STEEL

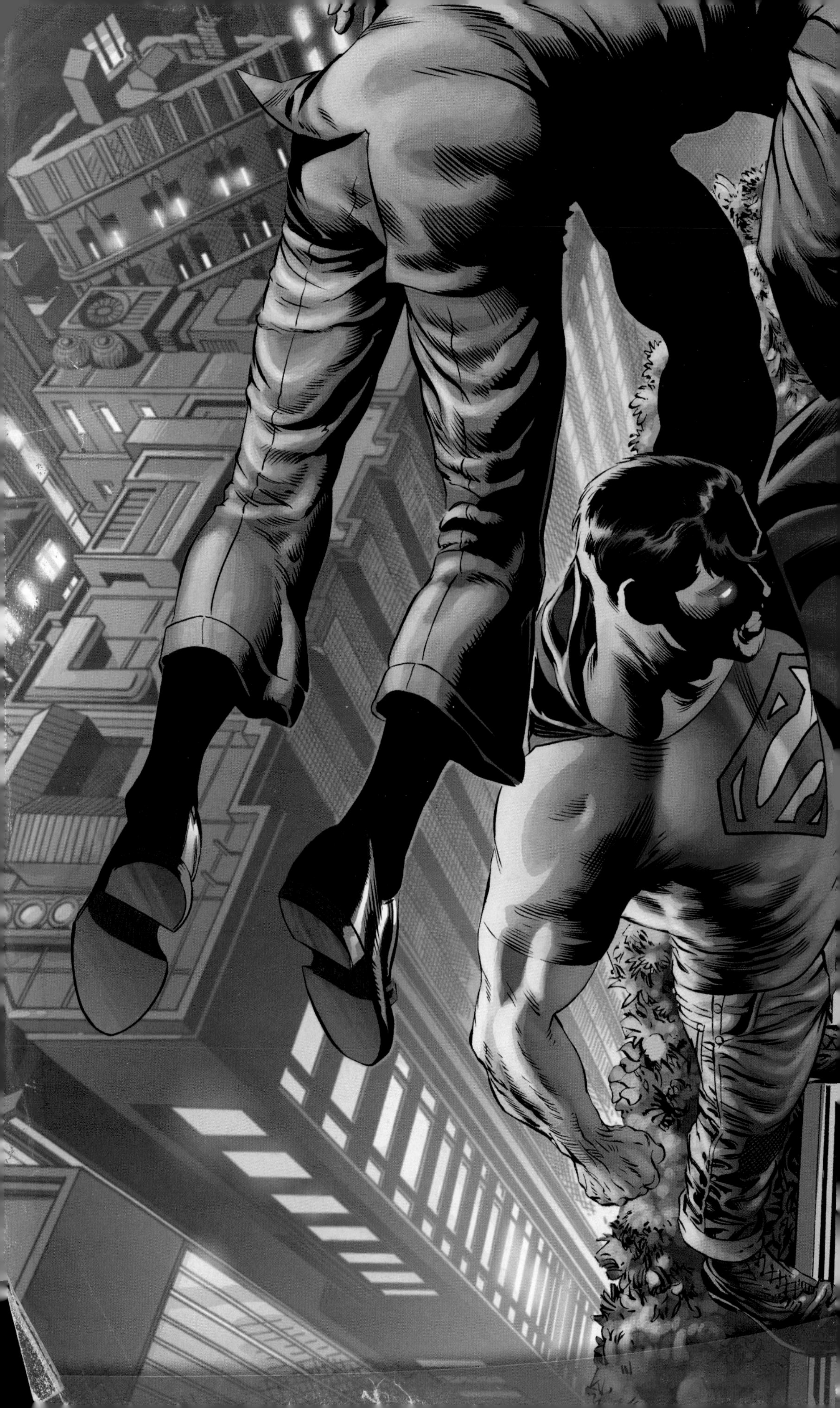

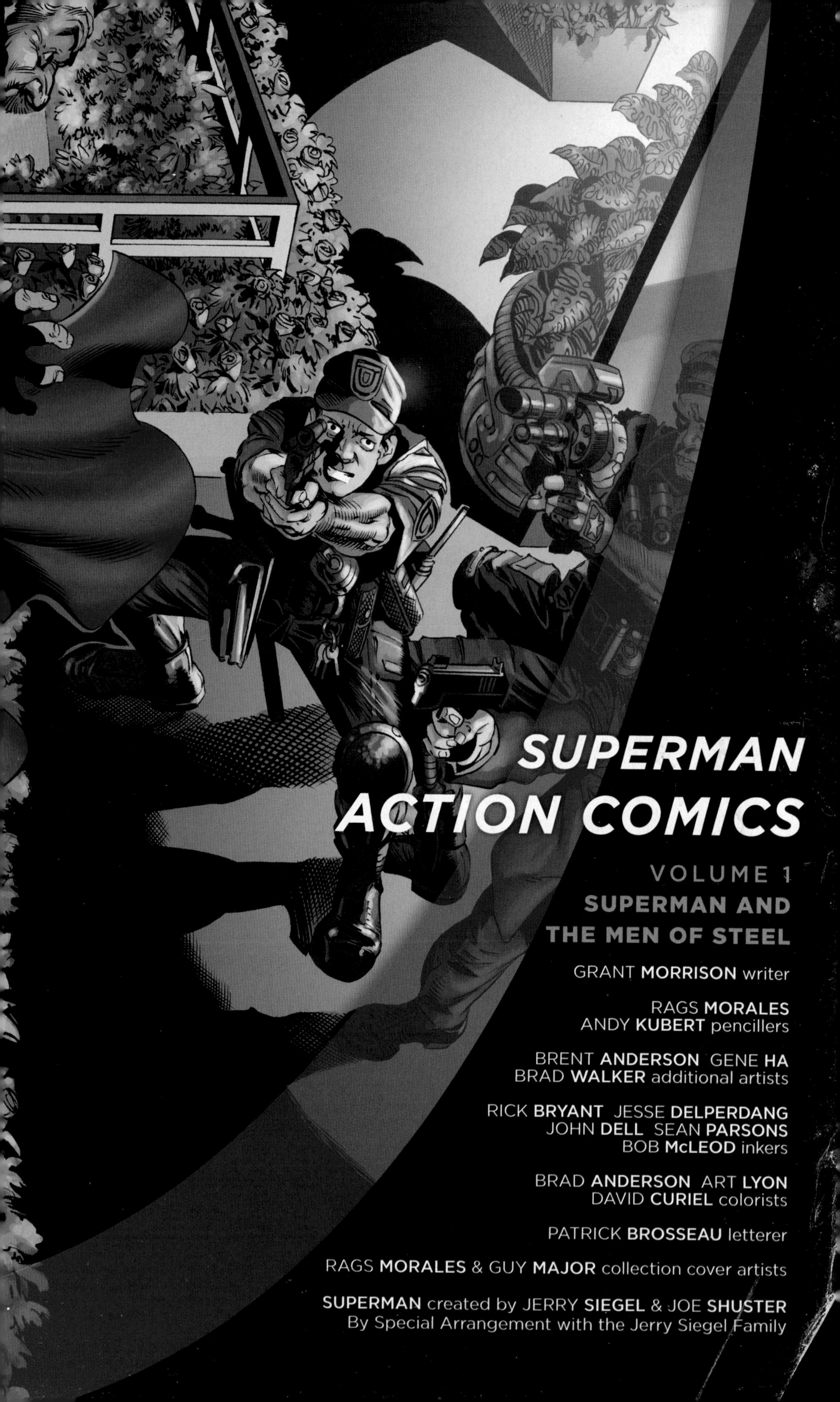

SUPERMAN ACTION COMICS

VOLUME 1

SUPERMAN AND THE MEN OF STEEL

GRANT **MORRISON** writer

RAGS **MORALES**
ANDY **KUBERT** pencillers

BRENT **ANDERSON** GENE **HA**
BRAD **WALKER** additional artists

RICK **BRYANT** JESSE **DELPERDANG**
JOHN **DELL** SEAN **PARSONS**
BOB **McLEOD** inkers

BRAD **ANDERSON** ART **LYON**
DAVID **CURIEL** colorists

PATRICK **BROSSEAU** letterer

RAGS **MORALES** & GUY **MAJOR** collection cover artists

SUPERMAN created by JERRY **SIEGEL** & JOE **SHUSTER**
By Special Arrangement with the Jerry Siegel Family

MATT IDELSON Editor – Original Series WIL MOSS Associate Editor – Original Series PETER HAMBOUSSI Editor
ROBBIN BROSTERMAN Design Director – Books ROBBIE BIEDERMAN Publication Design

BOB HARRAS Senior VP – Editor-in-Chief, DC Comics

DIANE NELSON President DAN DIDIO and JIM LEE Co-Publishers
GEOFF JOHNS Chief Creative Officer
JOHN ROOD Executive VP – Sales, Marketing & Business Development
AMY GENKINS Senior VP – Business & Legal Affairs NAIRI GARDINER Senior VP – Finance
JEFF BOISON VP – Publishing Planning MARK CHIARELLO VP – Art Direction & Design
JOHN CUNNINGHAM VP – Marketing TERRI CUNNINGHAM VP – Editorial Administration
ALISON GILL Senior VP – Manufacturing & Operations HANK KANALZ Senior VP – Vertigo & Integrated Publishing
JAY KOGAN VP – Business & Legal Affairs, Publishing JACK MAHAN VP – Business Affairs, Talent
NICK NAPOLITANO VP – Manufacturing Administration SUE POHJA VP – Book Sales
COURTNEY SIMMONS Senior VP – Publicity BOB WAYNE Senior VP – Sales

SUPERMAN — ACTION COMICS VOLUME 1: SUPERMAN AND THE MEN OF STEEL

Published by DC Comics. Cover and compilation Copyright © 2012 DC Comics. All Rights Reserved.

Originally published in single magazine form in ACTION COMICS 1-8 Copyright © 2011, 2012 DC Comics.
All Rights Reserved. All characters, their distinctive likenesses and related elements featured in
this publication are trademarks of DC Comics. The stories, characters and incidents featured in this publication
are entirely fictional. DC Comics does not read or accept unsolicited ideas, stories or artwork.

DC Comics, 1700 Broadway, New York, NY 10019
A Warner Bros. Entertainment Company.
Printed by RR Donnelley, Salem, VA, USA. 6/7/13. Second Printing.
ISBN: 978-1-4012-3547-5

SUSTAINABLE
FORESTRY
INITIATIVE

Certified Chain of Custody
At Least 20% Certified Forest Content
www.sfiprogram.org
SFI-01042
APPLIES TO TEXT STOCK ONLY

Library of Congress Cataloging-in-Publication Data

Morrison, Grant.
Superman - Action Comics. Volume 1, Superman and the men of steel / Grant Morrison, Rags Morales, Andy Kubert.
p. cm.
"Originally published in single magazine form in ACTION COMICS 1-8" – T.p. verso.
ISBN 978-1-4012-3546-8
1. Graphic novels. I. Morales, Rags. II. Kubert, Andy. III. Title. IV. Title: Superman and the men of steel.
PN6728.S9M73 2012
741.5'9411 – dc23
2012010313

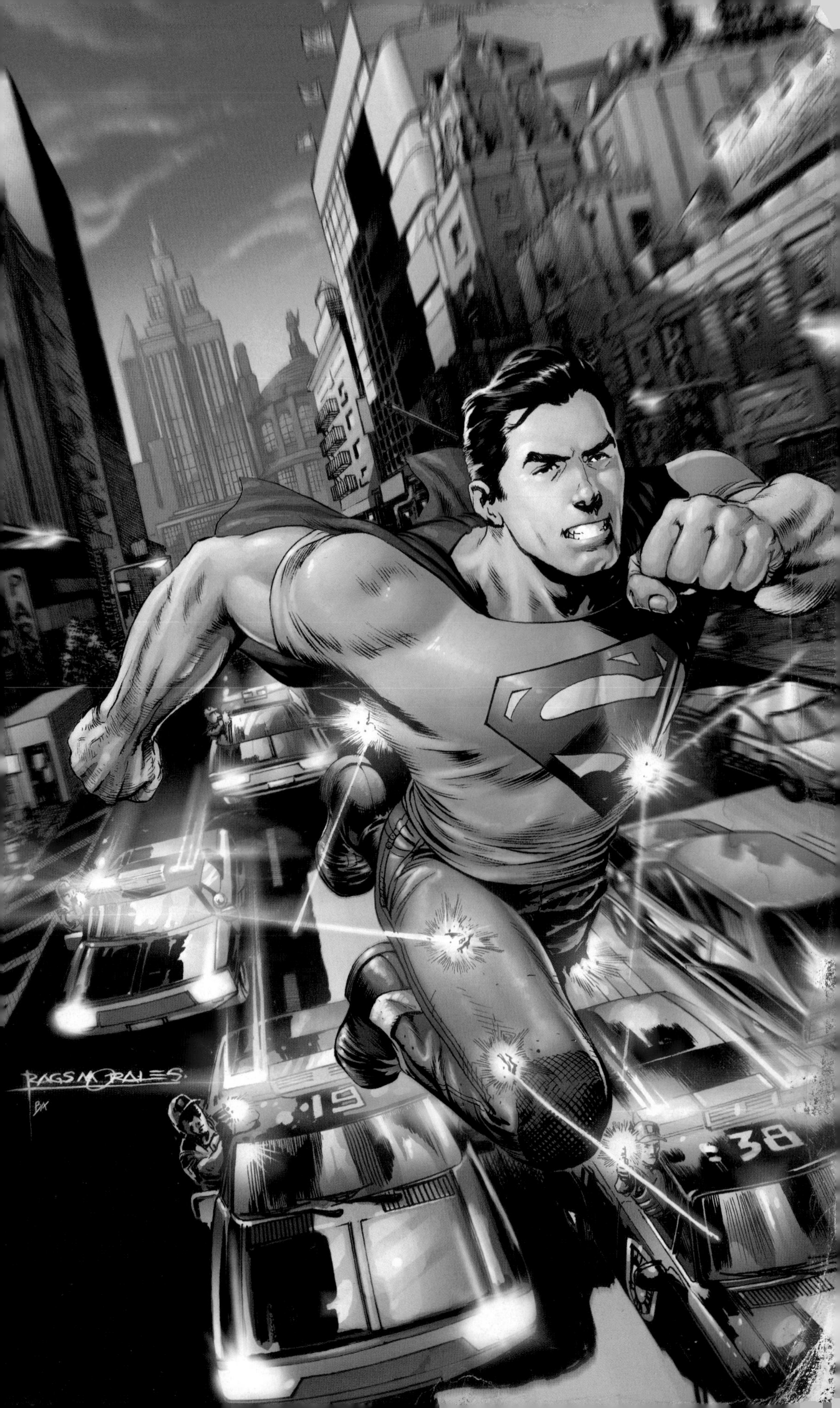
RAGS MORALES
BIX
19
38

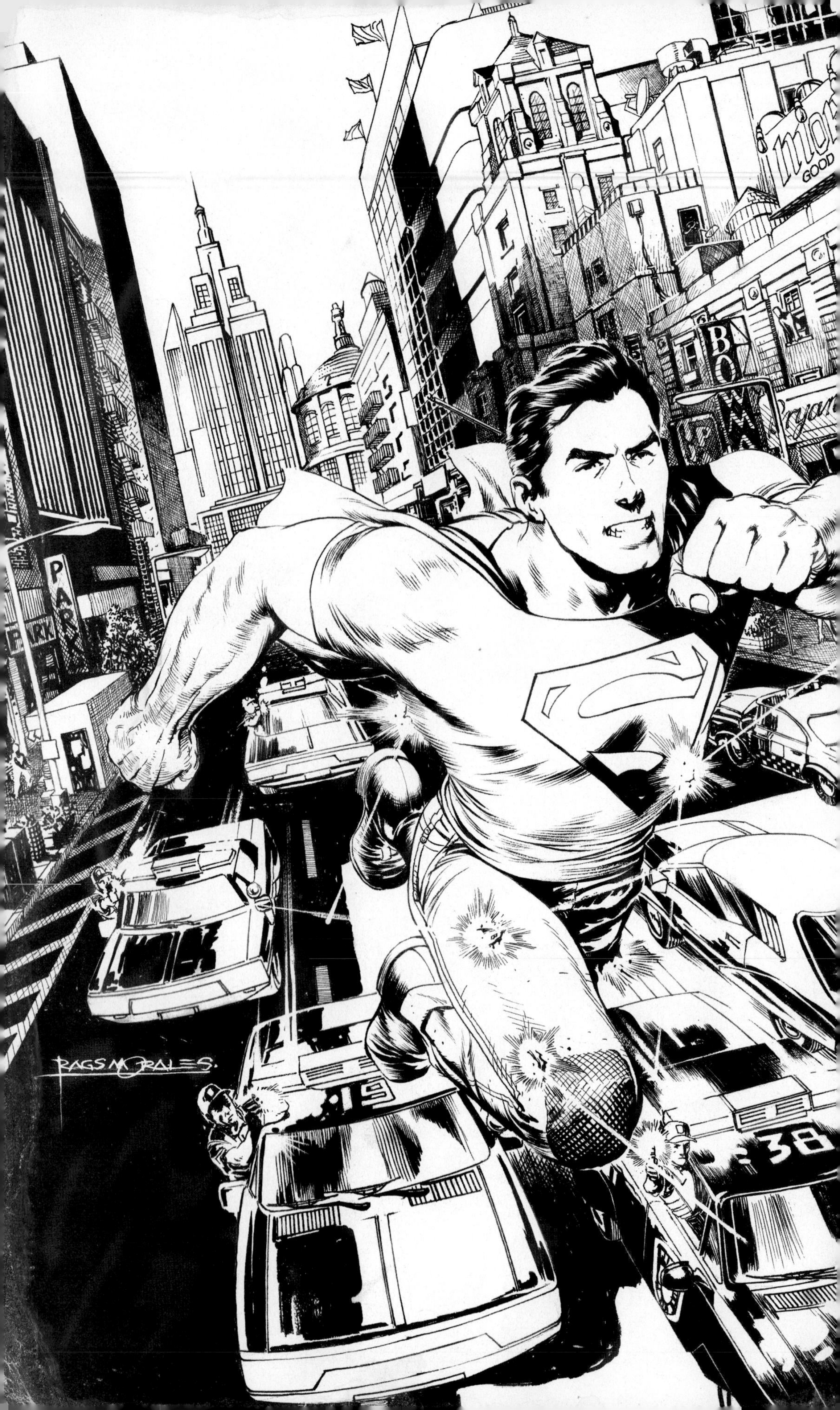
PARK
GOOD
RAGS MORALES.
19
38

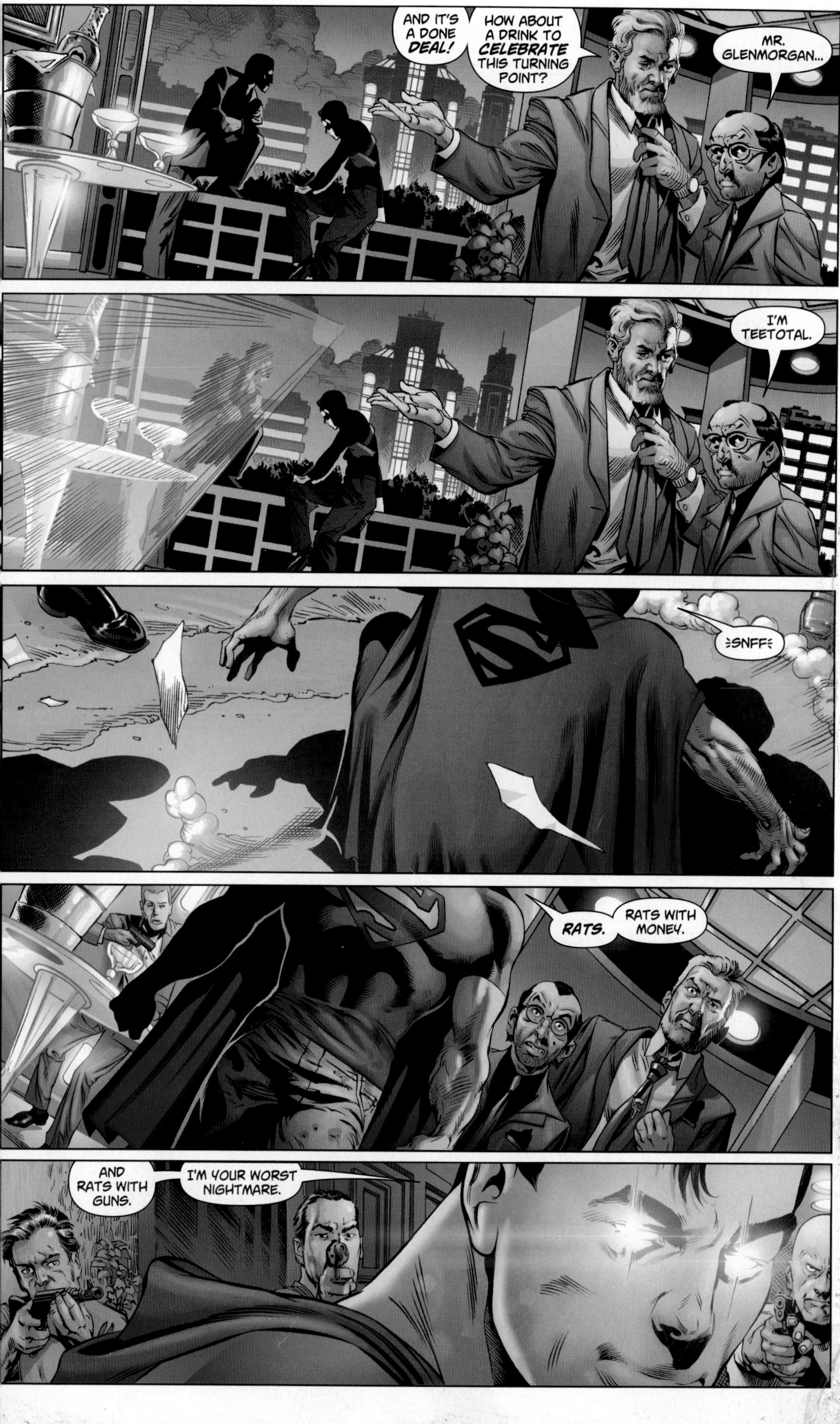
AND IT'S A DONE DEAL!
HOW ABOUT A DRINK TO CELEBRATE THIS TURNING POINT?
MR. GLENMORGAN...
I'M TEETOTAL.
SNFF
RATS.
RATS WITH MONEY.
AND RATS WITH GUNS.
I'M YOUR WORST NIGHTMARE.

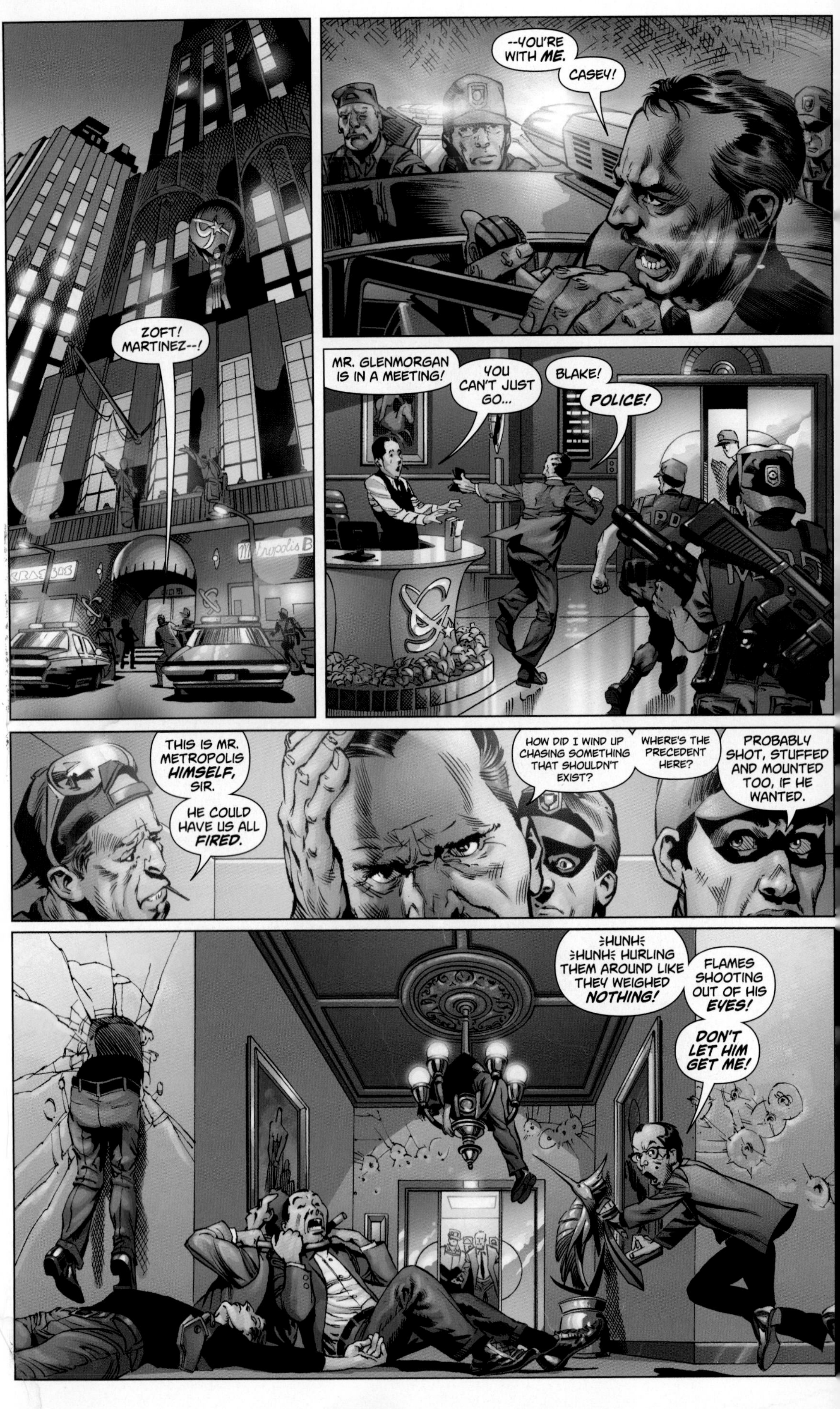

ZOFT! MARTINEZ--!
--YOU'RE WITH ME.
CASEY!
MR. GLENMORGAN IS IN A MEETING!
YOU CAN'T JUST GO...
BLAKE!
POLICE!
THIS IS MR. METROPOLIS HIMSELF, SIR.
HE COULD HAVE US ALL FIRED.
HOW DID I WIND UP CHASING SOMETHING THAT SHOULDN'T EXIST?
WHERE'S THE PRECEDENT HERE?
PROBABLY SHOT, STUFFED AND MOUNTED TOO, IF HE WANTED.
HUNH HUNH HURLING THEM AROUND LIKE THEY WEIGHED NOTHING!
FLAMES SHOOTING OUT OF HIS EYES!
DON'T LET HIM GET ME!

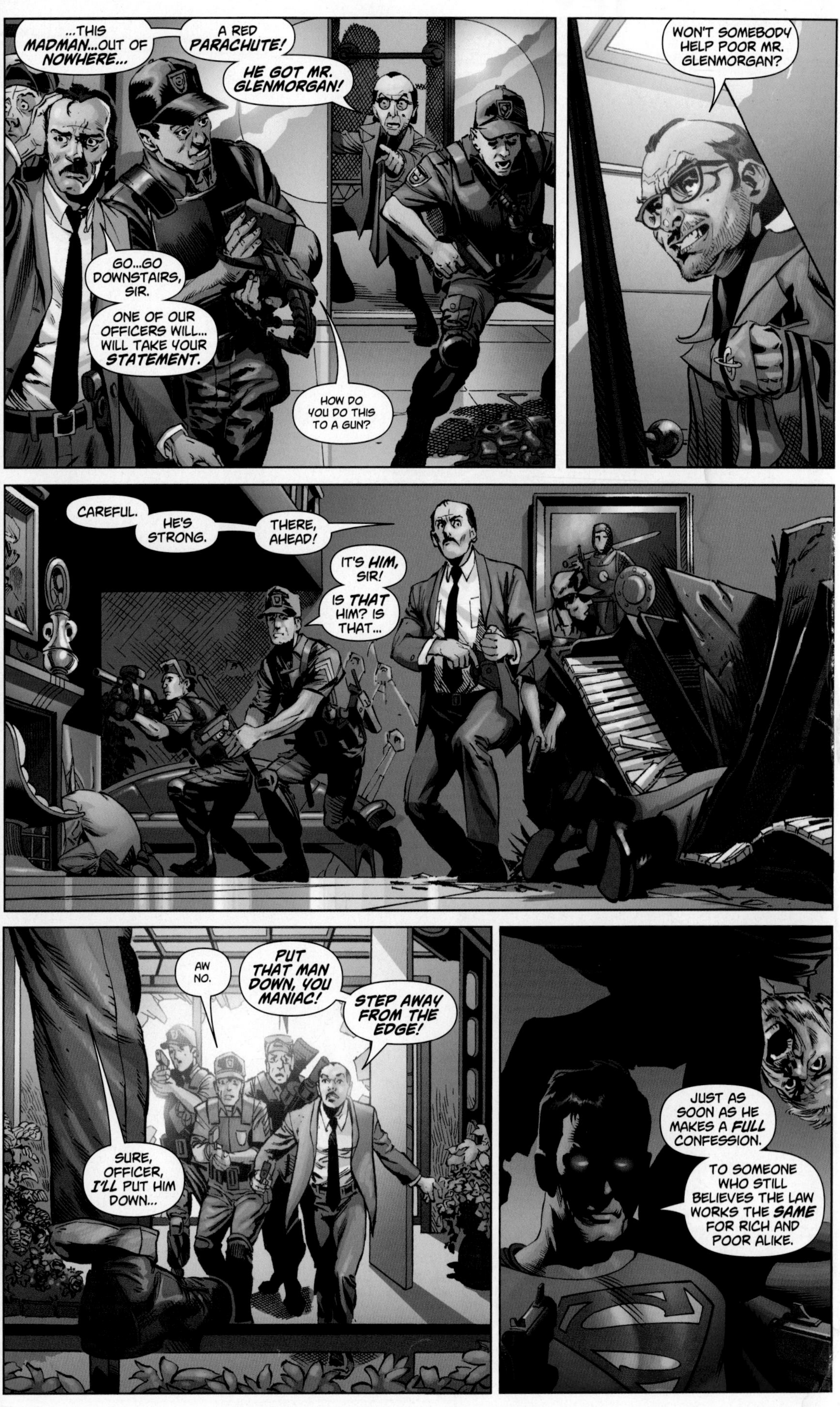
...THIS MADMAN...OUT OF NOWHERE...
A RED PARACHUTE!
HE GOT MR. GLENMORGAN!
GO...GO DOWNSTAIRS, SIR.
ONE OF OUR OFFICERS WILL... WILL TAKE YOUR STATEMENT.
HOW DO YOU DO THIS TO A GUN?
WON'T SOMEBODY HELP POOR MR. GLENMORGAN?
CAREFUL.
HE'S STRONG.
THERE, AHEAD!
IT'S HIM, SIR!
IS THAT HIM? IS THAT...
AW NO.
PUT THAT MAN DOWN, YOU MANIAC!
STEP AWAY FROM THE EDGE!
SURE, OFFICER, I'LL PUT HIM DOWN...
JUST AS SOON AS HE MAKES A FULL CONFESSION.
TO SOMEONE WHO STILL BELIEVES THE LAW WORKS THE SAME FOR RICH AND POOR ALIKE.

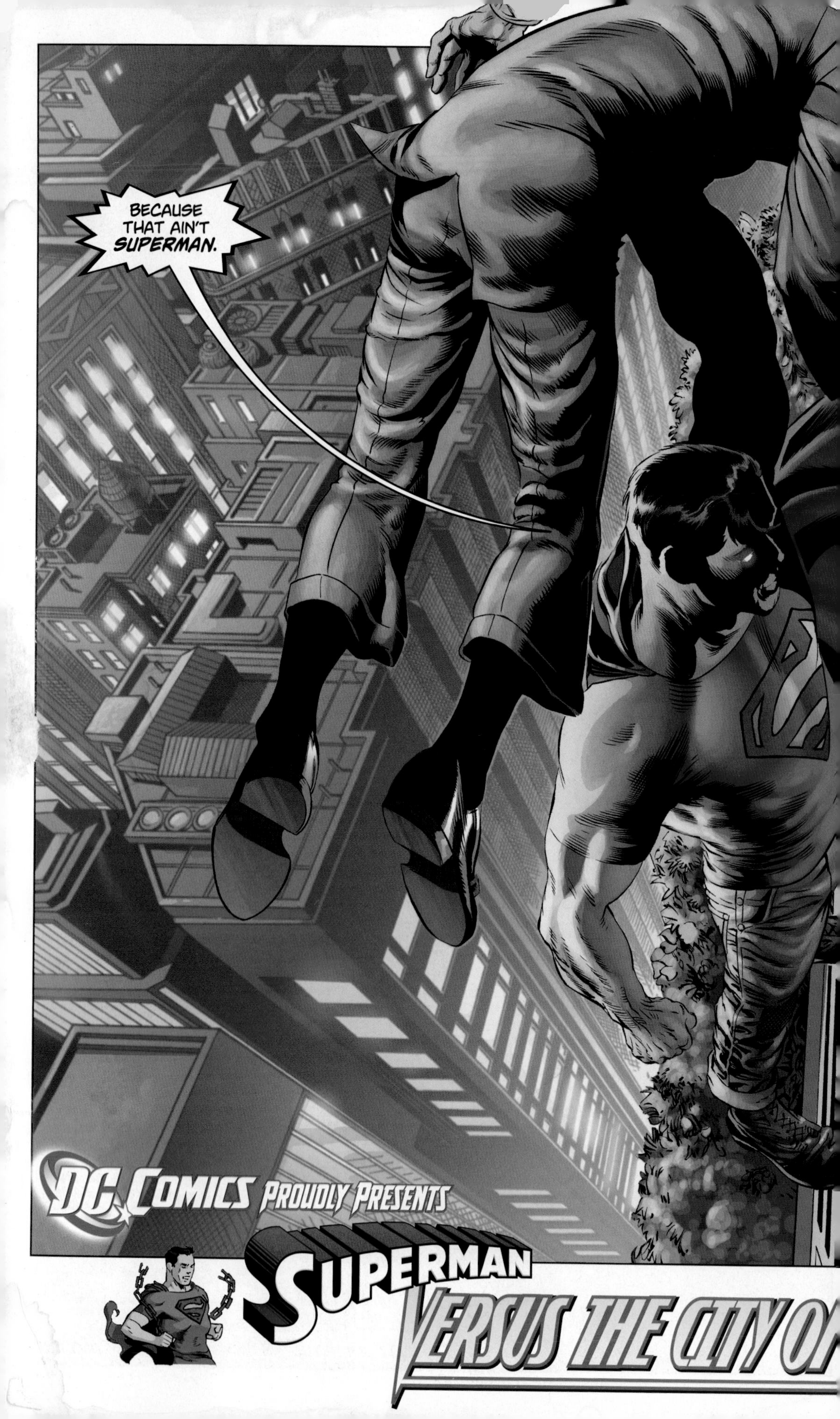
BECAUSE THAT AIN'T SUPERMAN.
DC COMICS PROUDLY PRESENTS
SUPERMAN

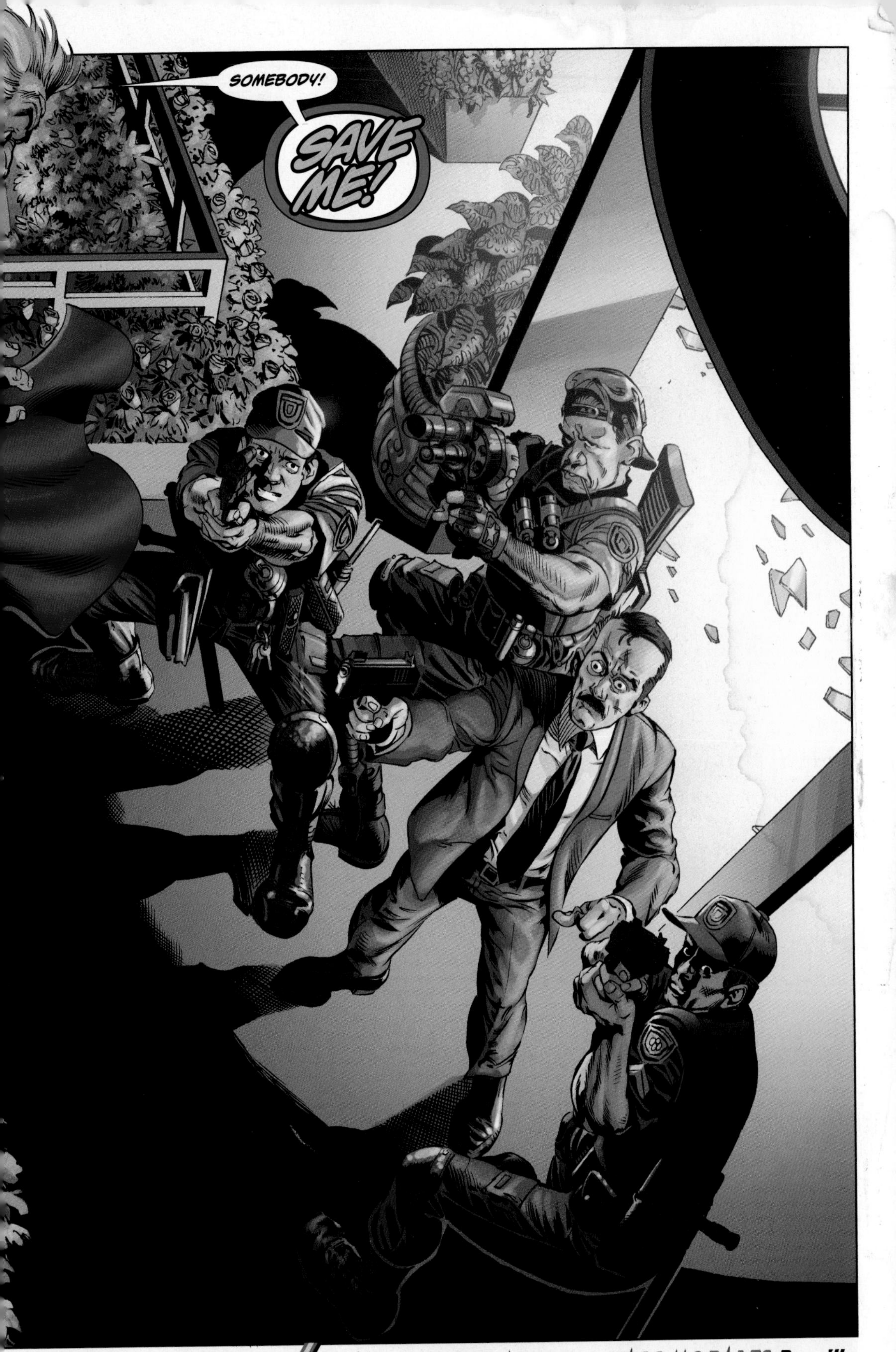
SOMEBODY!
SAVE ME!

TOMORROW

GRANT MORRISON Writer RAGS MORALES Penciller
RICK BRYANT Inker BRAD ANDERSON Colorist PATRICK BROSSEAU Letterer
RAGS MORALES & BRAD ANDERSON Cover JIM LEE, SCOTT WILLIAMS & ALEX SINCLAIR Variant Cover
WIL MOSS Associate Editor MATT IDELSON Editor SUPERMAN Created by JERRY SIEGEL & JOE SHUSTER

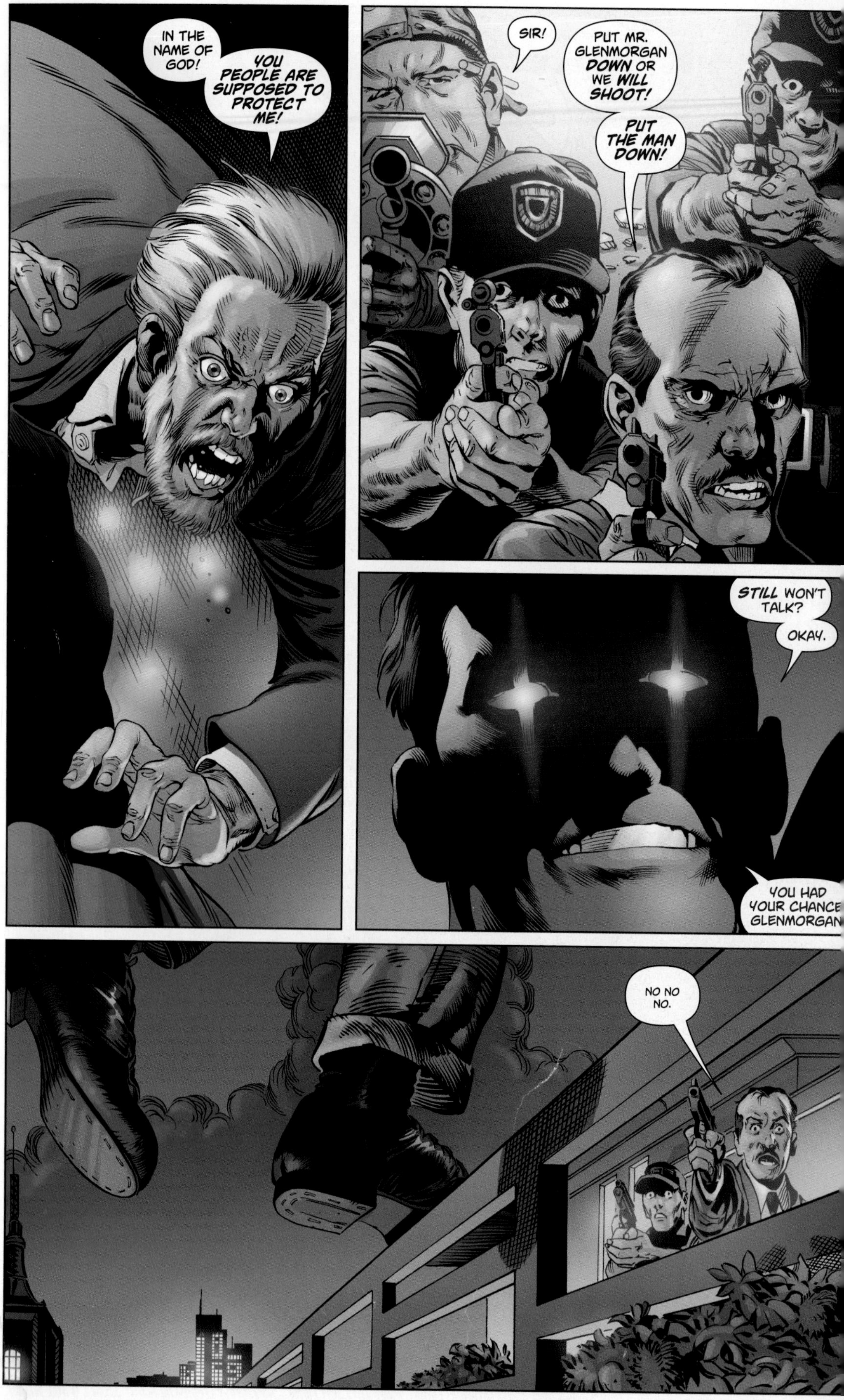

IN THE NAME OF GOD!
YOU PEOPLE ARE SUPPOSED TO PROTECT ME!
SIR!
PUT MR. GLENMORGAN DOWN OR WE WILL SHOOT!
PUT THE MAN DOWN!
STILL WON'T TALK?
OKAY.
YOU HAD YOUR CHANCE GLENMORGAN
NO NO NO.

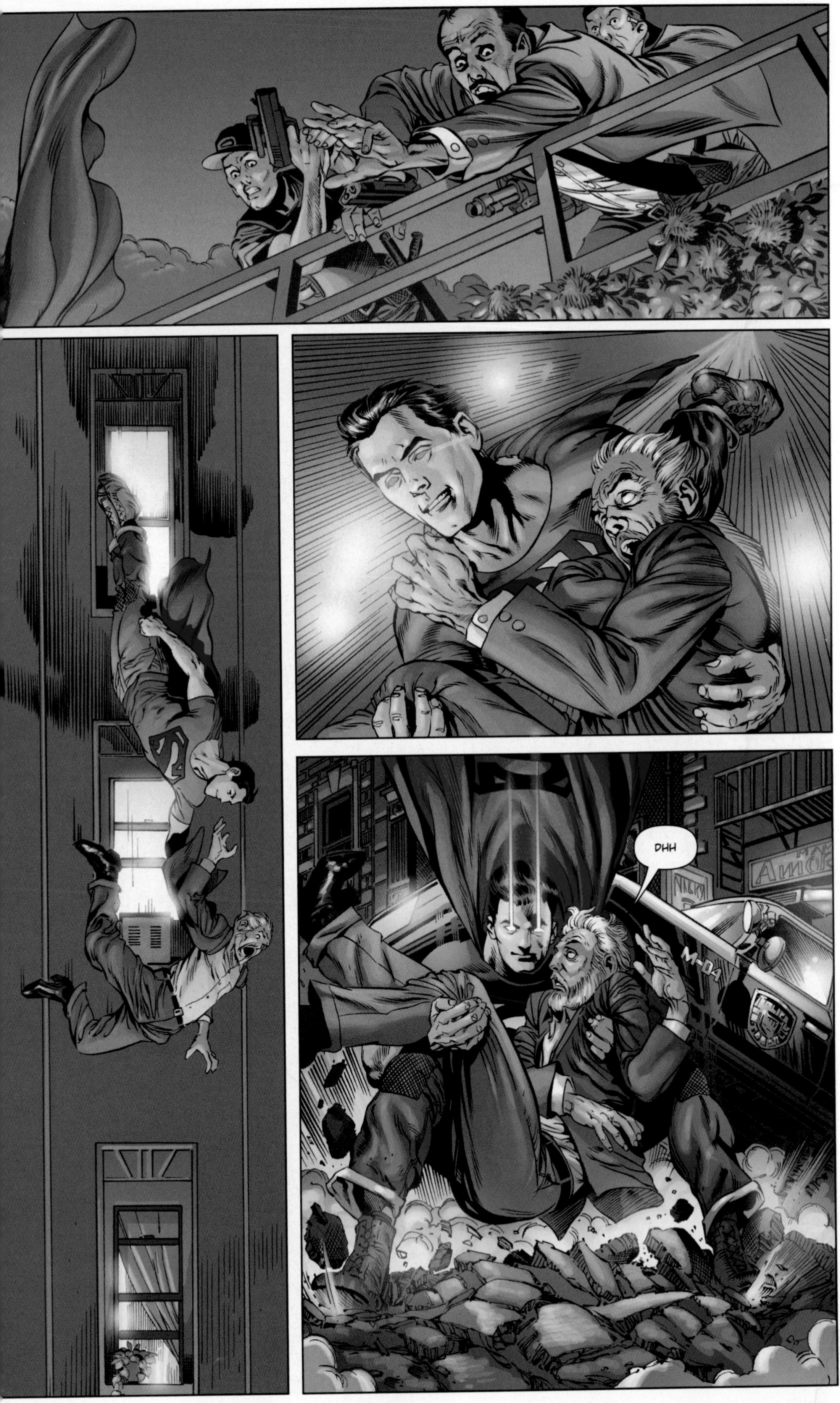
DHH

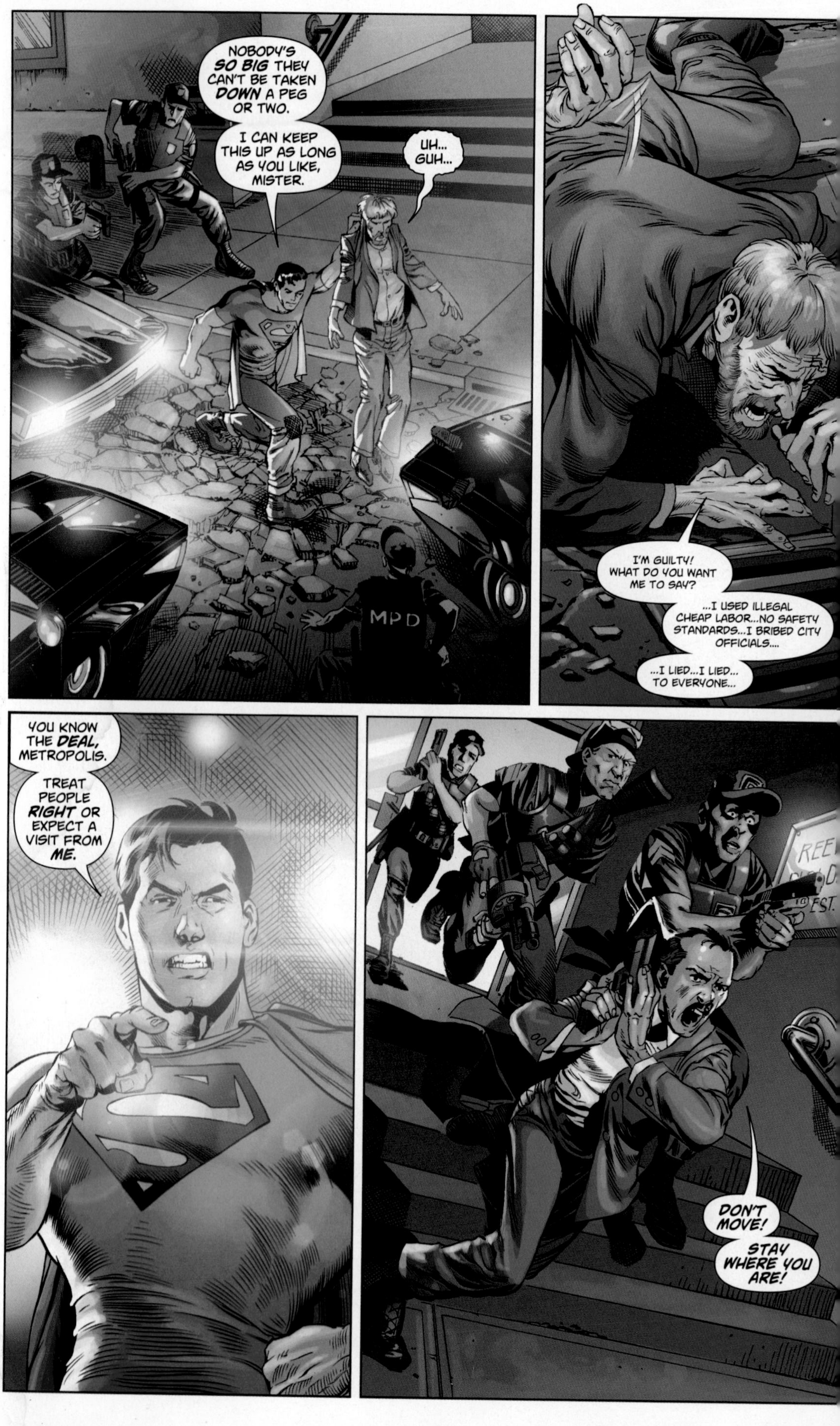

NOBODY'S SO BIG THEY CAN'T BE TAKEN DOWN A PEG OR TWO.
I CAN KEEP THIS UP AS LONG AS YOU LIKE, MISTER.
UH... GUH...
MPD
I'M GUILTY! WHAT DO YOU WANT ME TO SAY?
...I USED ILLEGAL CHEAP LABOR...NO SAFETY STANDARDS...I BRIBED CITY OFFICIALS....
...I LIED...I LIED... TO EVERYONE...
YOU KNOW THE DEAL, METROPOLIS.
TREAT PEOPLE RIGHT OR EXPECT A VISIT FROM ME.
DON'T MOVE!
STAY WHERE YOU ARE!

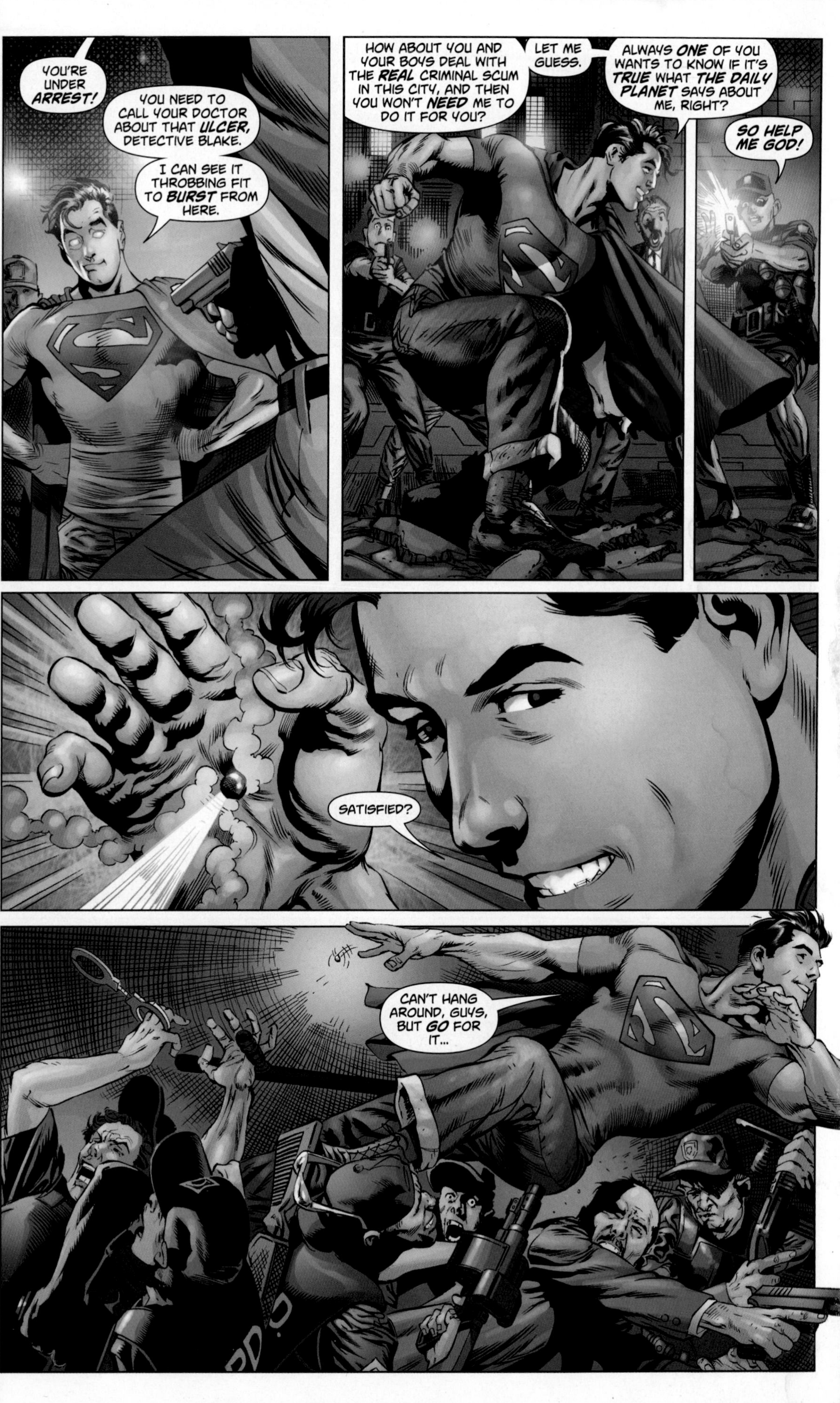

YOU'RE UNDER ARREST!
YOU NEED TO CALL YOUR DOCTOR ABOUT THAT ULCER, DETECTIVE BLAKE.
I CAN SEE IT THROBBING FIT TO BURST FROM HERE.
HOW ABOUT YOU AND YOUR BOYS DEAL WITH THE REAL CRIMINAL SCUM IN THIS CITY, AND THEN YOU WON'T NEED ME TO DO IT FOR YOU?
LET ME GUESS.
ALWAYS ONE OF YOU WANTS TO KNOW IF IT'S TRUE WHAT THE DAILY PLANET SAYS ABOUT ME, RIGHT?
SO HELP ME GOD!
SATISFIED?
CAN'T HANG AROUND, GUYS, BUT GO FOR IT...

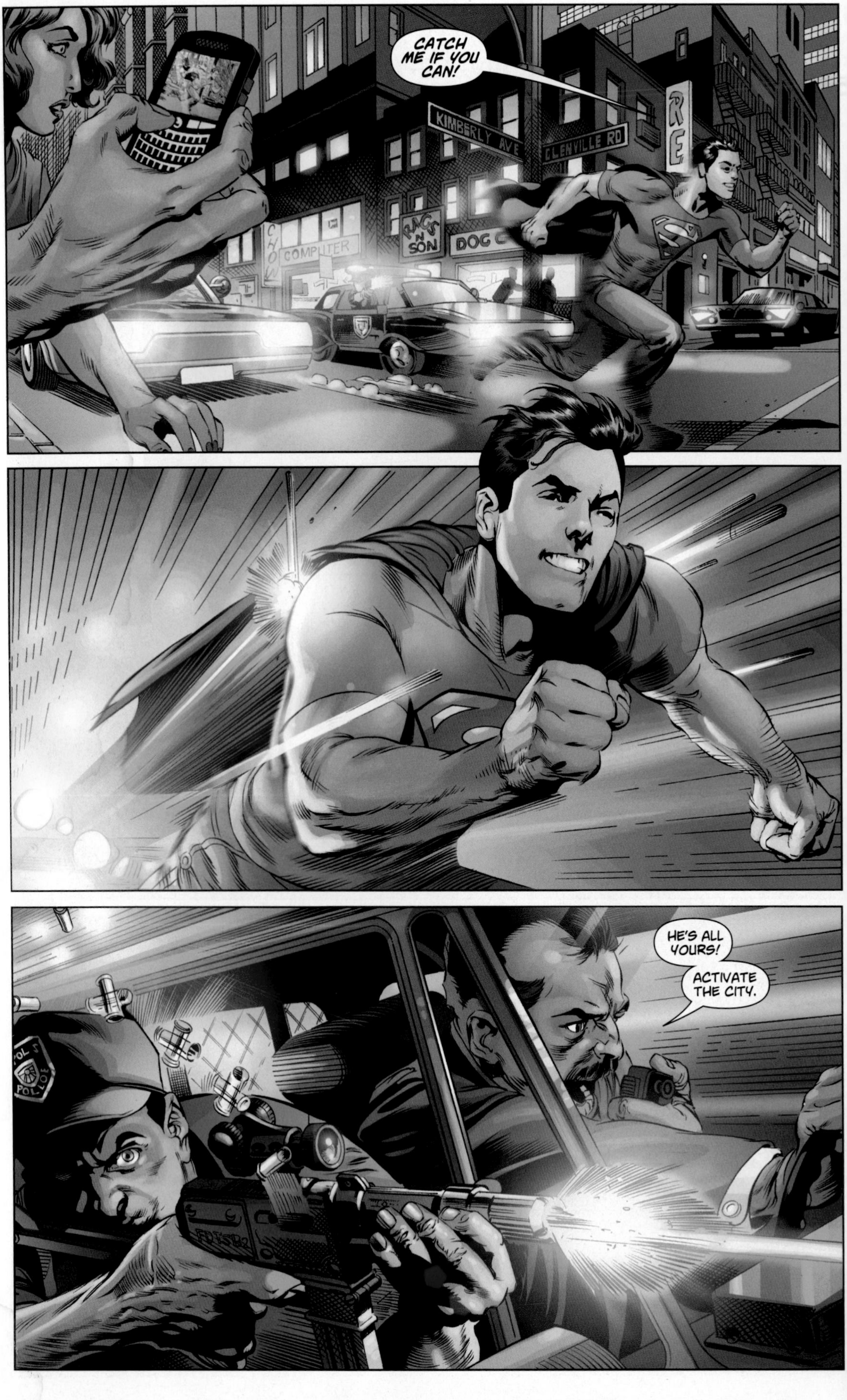
CATCH ME IF YOU CAN!
KIMBERLY AVE
GLENVILLE RD
RE
RAGS N SON
CHOW
COMPUTER
DOG C
HE'S ALL YOURS!
ACTIVATE THE CITY.

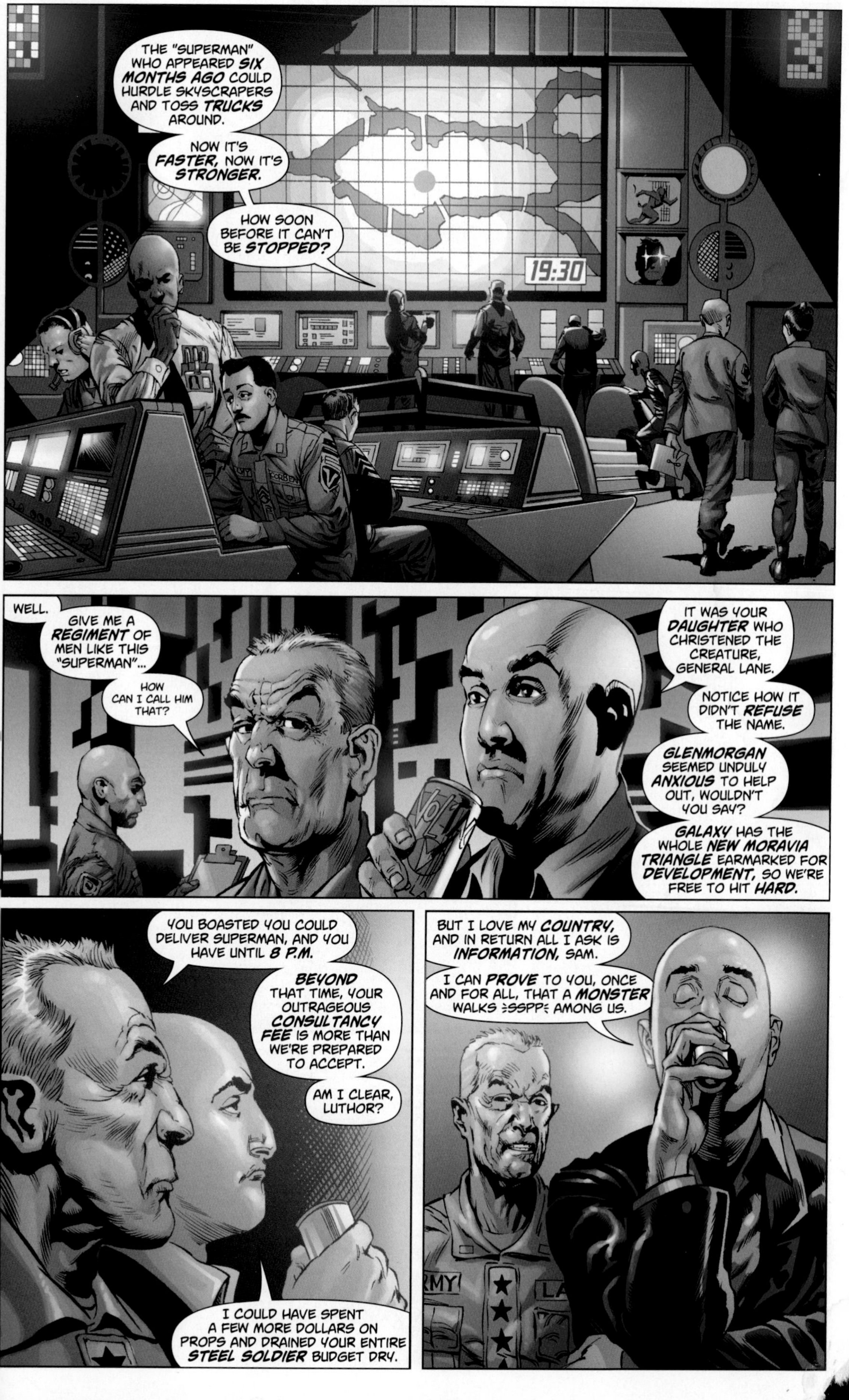
THE "SUPERMAN" WHO APPEARED SIX MONTHS AGO COULD HURDLE SKYSCRAPERS AND TOSS TRUCKS AROUND.
NOW IT'S FASTER, NOW IT'S STRONGER.
HOW SOON BEFORE IT CAN'T BE STOPPED?
19:30
WELL.
GIVE ME A REGIMENT OF MEN LIKE THIS "SUPERMAN"...
HOW CAN I CALL HIM THAT?
IT WAS YOUR DAUGHTER WHO CHRISTENED THE CREATURE, GENERAL LANE.
NOTICE HOW IT DIDN'T REFUSE THE NAME.
GLENMORGAN SEEMED UNDULY ANXIOUS TO HELP OUT, WOULDN'T YOU SAY?
GALAXY HAS THE WHOLE NEW MORAVIA TRIANGLE EARMARKED FOR DEVELOPMENT, SO WE'RE FREE TO HIT HARD.
YOU BOASTED YOU COULD DELIVER SUPERMAN, AND YOU HAVE UNTIL 8 P.M.
BEYOND THAT TIME, YOUR OUTRAGEOUS CONSULTANCY FEE IS MORE THAN WE'RE PREPARED TO ACCEPT.
AM I CLEAR, LUTHOR?
I COULD HAVE SPENT A FEW MORE DOLLARS ON PROPS AND DRAINED YOUR ENTIRE STEEL SOLDIER BUDGET DRY.
BUT I LOVE MY COUNTRY, AND IN RETURN ALL I ASK IS INFORMATION, SAM.
I CAN PROVE TO YOU, ONCE AND FOR ALL, THAT A MONSTER WALKS SSPP AMONG US.

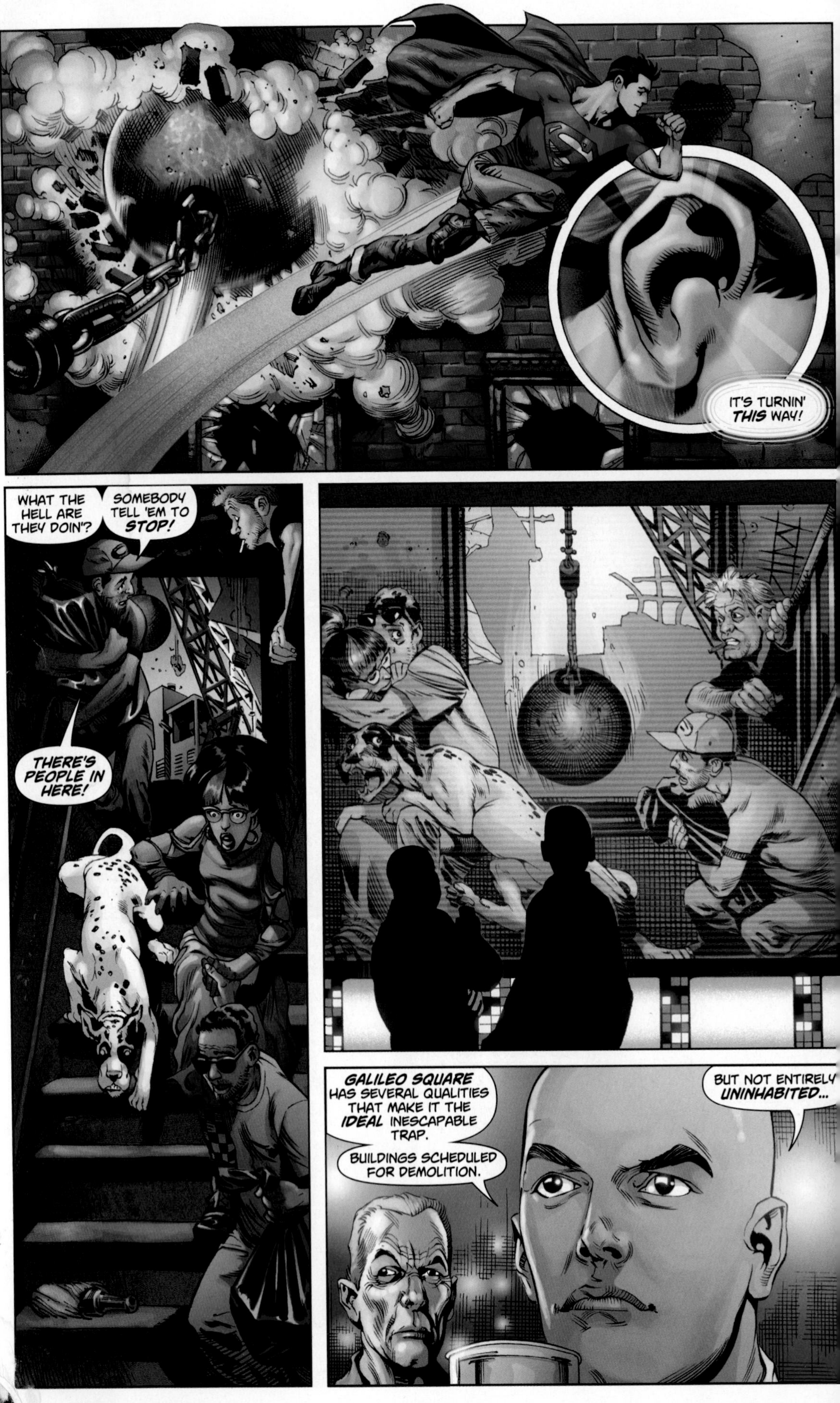
IT'S TURNIN' THIS WAY!
WHAT THE HELL ARE THEY DOIN'?
SOMEBODY TELL 'EM TO STOP!
THERE'S PEOPLE IN HERE!
GALILEO SQUARE HAS SEVERAL QUALITIES THAT MAKE IT THE IDEAL INESCAPABLE TRAP.
BUILDINGS SCHEDULED FOR DEMOLITION.
BUT NOT ENTIRELY UNINHABITED...

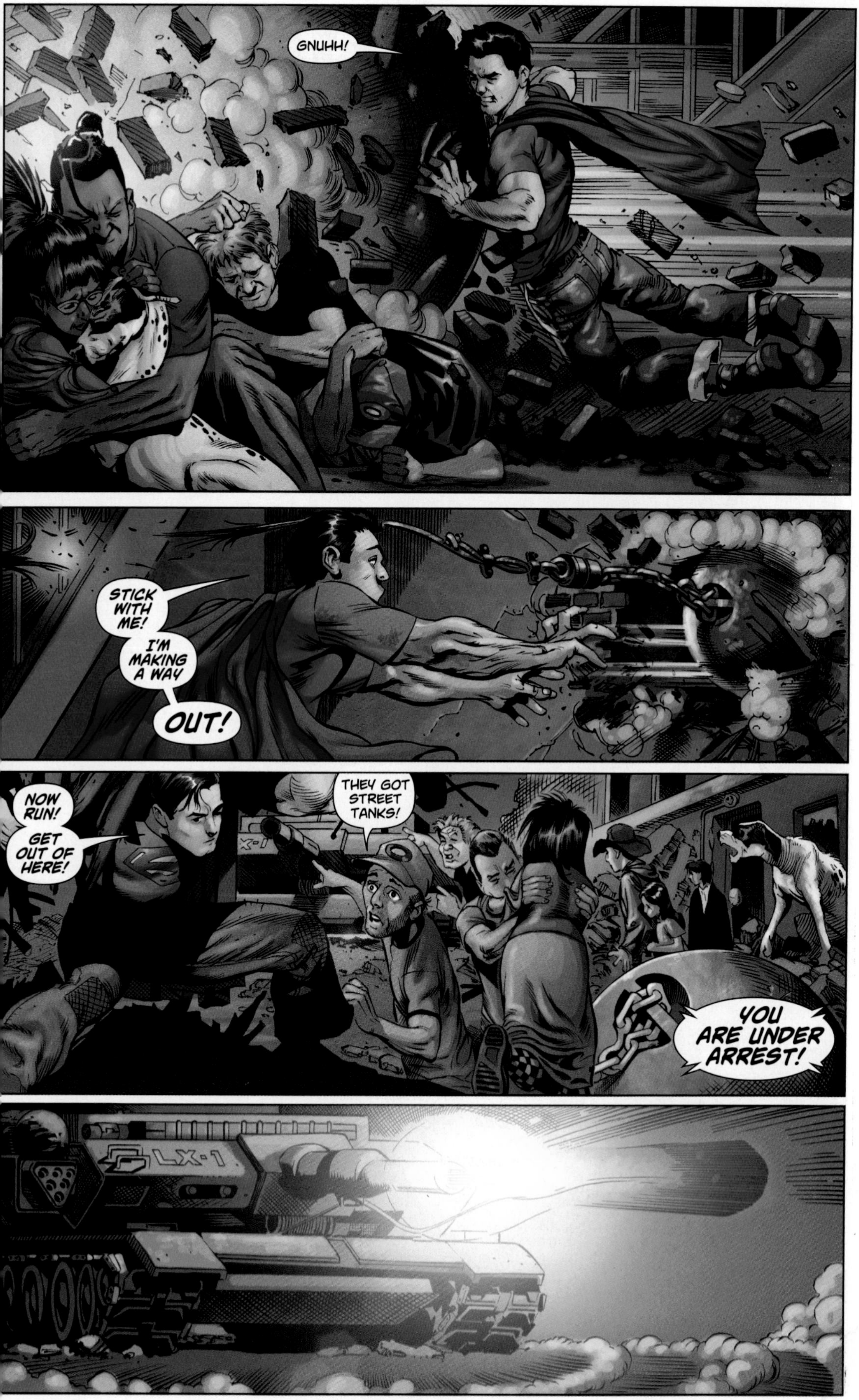
GNUHH!
STICK WITH ME!
I'M MAKING A WAY
OUT!
NOW RUN!
GET OUT OF HERE!
THEY GOT STREET TANKS!
YOU ARE UNDER ARREST!
LX-1

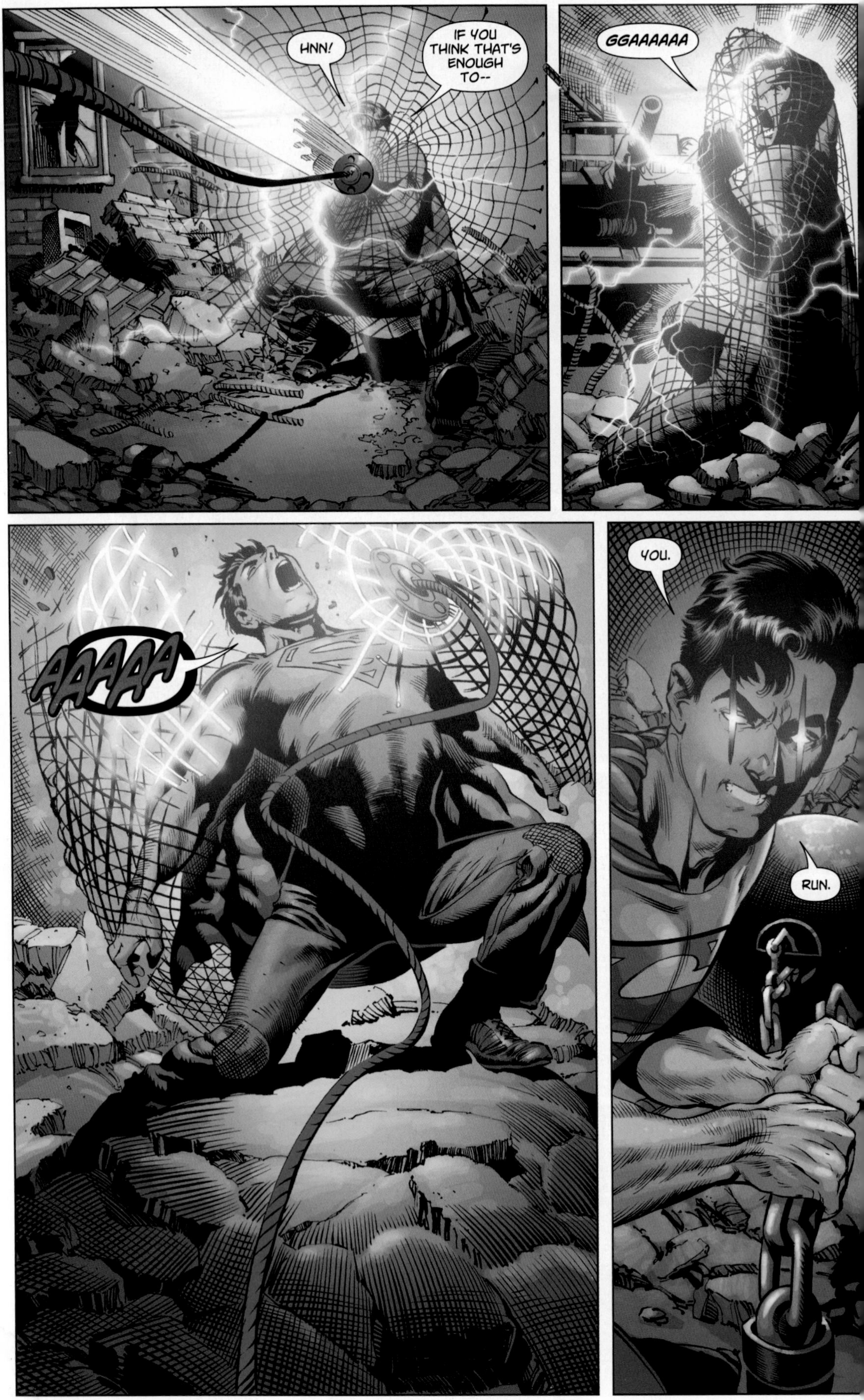
HNN!
IF YOU THINK THAT'S ENOUGH TO--
GGAAAAAA
AAAAA
YOU.
RUN.

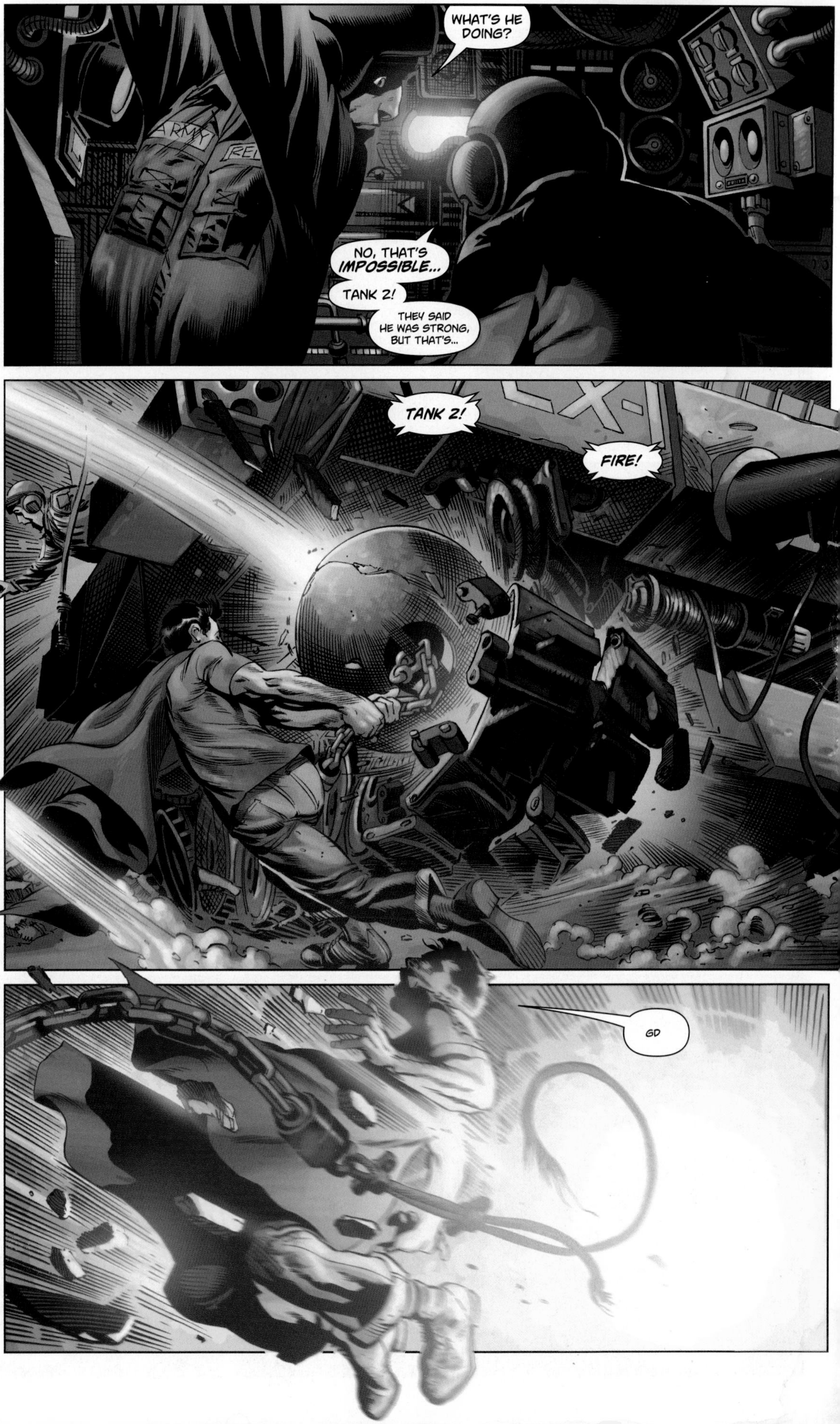

WHAT'S HE DOING?
NO, THAT'S IMPOSSIBLE...
TANK 2!
THEY SAID HE WAS STRONG, BUT THAT'S...
TANK 2!
FIRE!
GD

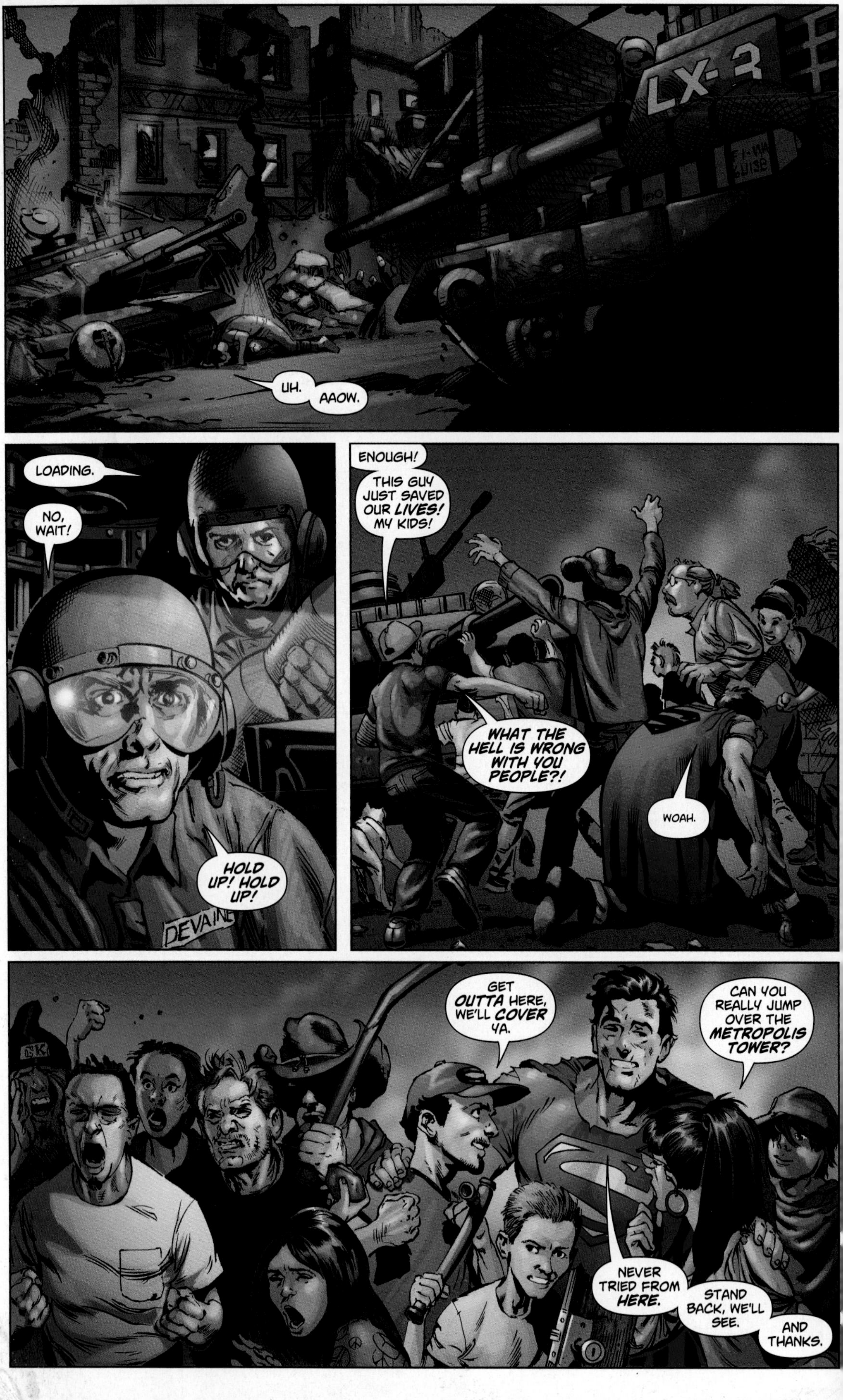

LX-3
UH.
AAOW.
LOADING.
NO, WAIT!
HOLD UP! HOLD UP!
DEVAINE
ENOUGH!
THIS GUY JUST SAVED OUR *LIVES!* MY KIDS!
WHAT THE HELL IS WRONG WITH YOU PEOPLE?!
WOAH.
GET *OUTTA* HERE, WE'LL *COVER* YA.
CAN YOU REALLY JUMP OVER THE ***METROPOLIS TOWER?***
NEVER TRIED FROM ***HERE.***
STAND BACK, WE'LL SEE.
AND THANKS.

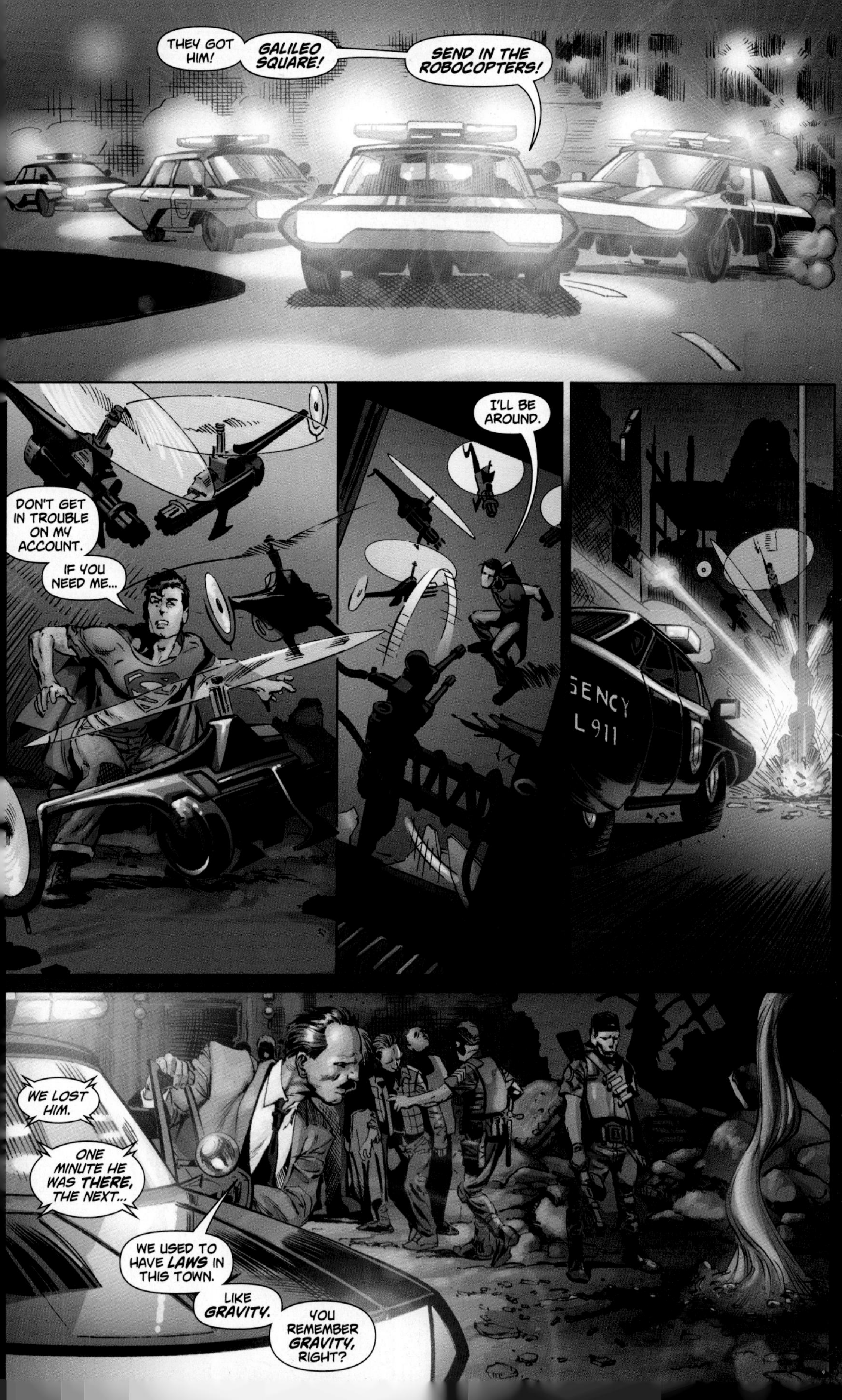

THEY GOT HIM!
GALILEO SQUARE!
SEND IN THE ROBOCOPTERS!
DON'T GET IN TROUBLE ON MY ACCOUNT.
IF YOU NEED ME...
I'LL BE AROUND.
GENCY
L911
WE LOST HIM.
ONE MINUTE HE WAS THERE, THE NEXT...
WE USED TO HAVE LAWS IN THIS TOWN.
LIKE GRAVITY.
YOU REMEMBER GRAVITY, RIGHT?

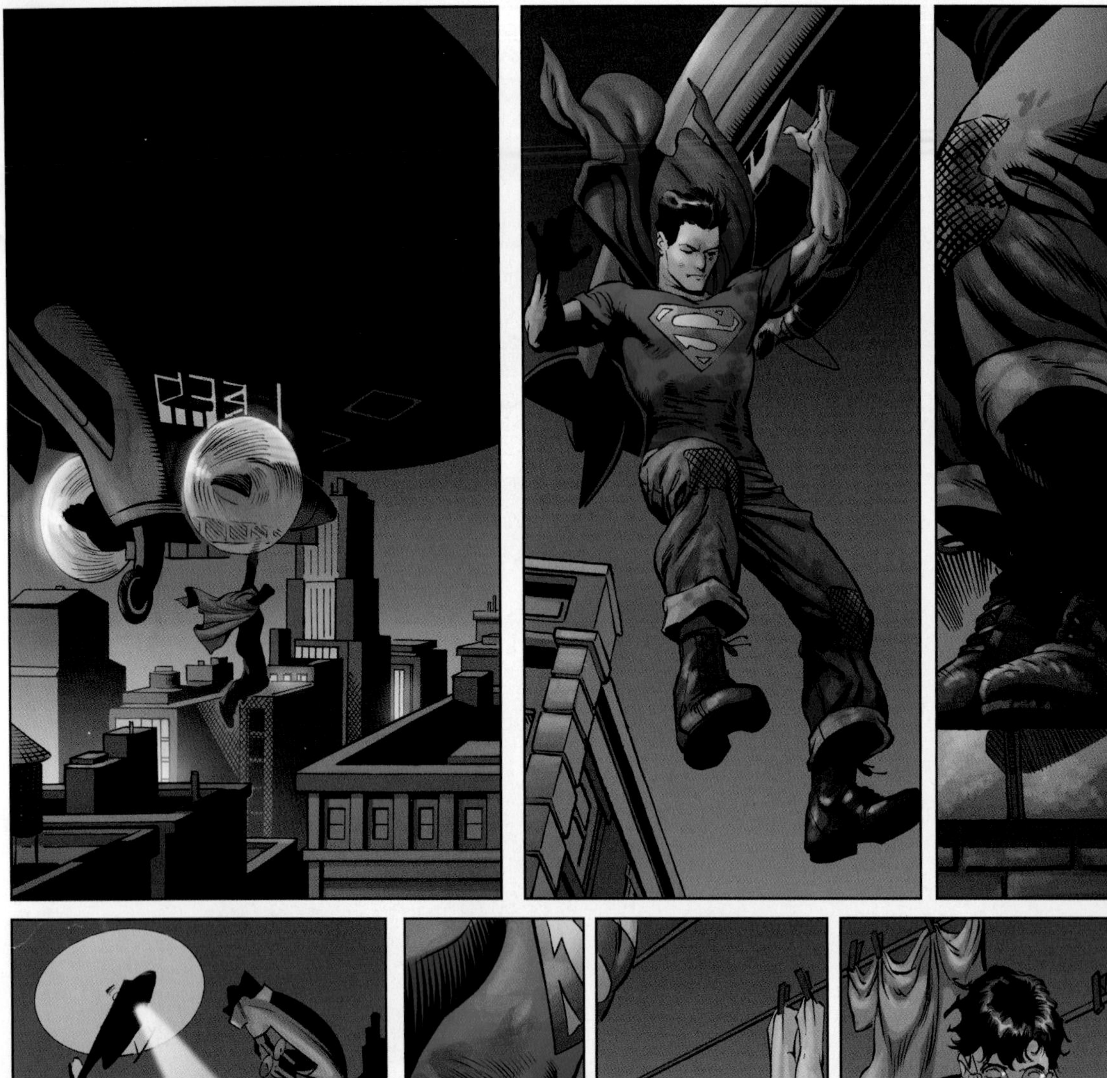

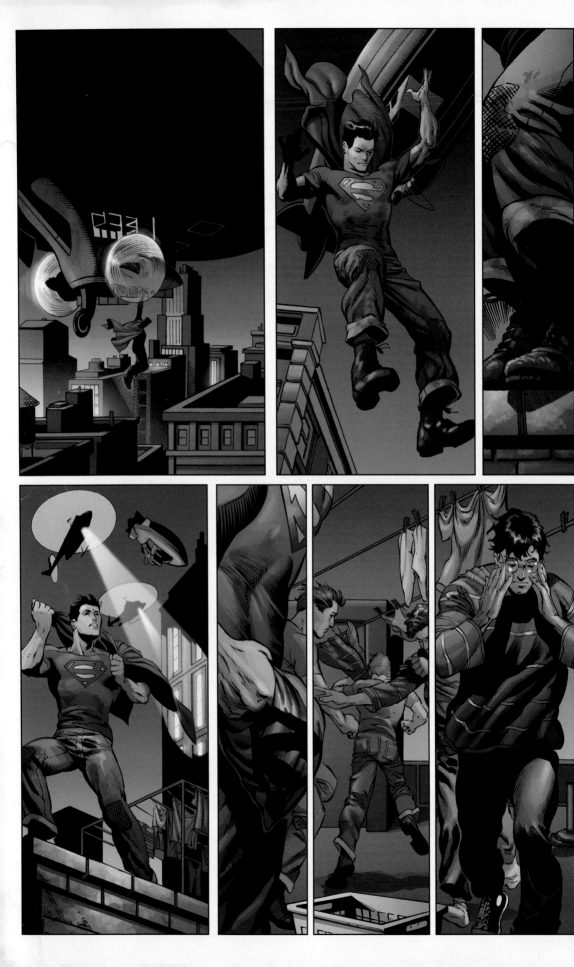

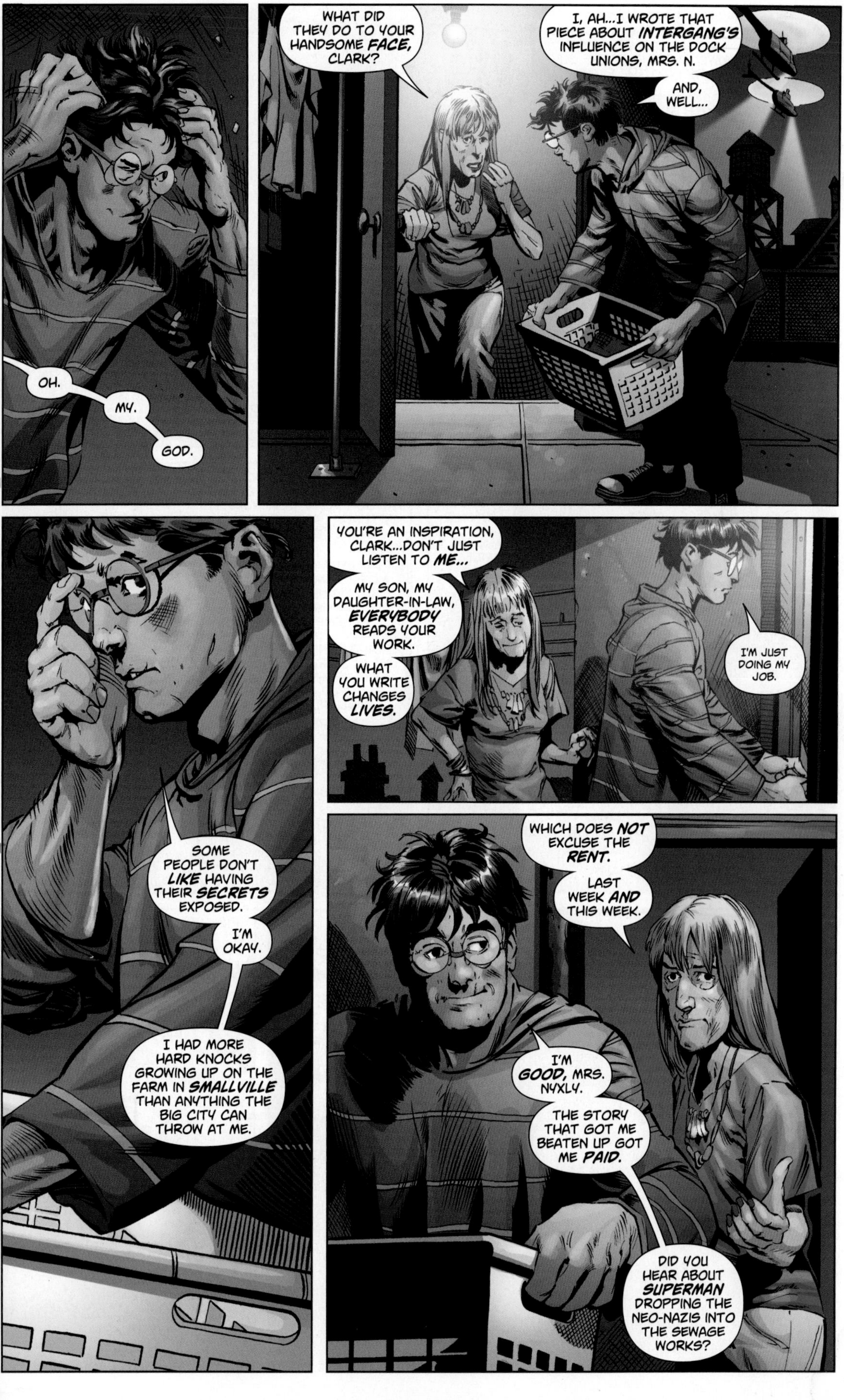
OH.
MY.
GOD.
WHAT DID THEY DO TO YOUR HANDSOME FACE, CLARK?
I, AH...I WROTE THAT PIECE ABOUT INTERGANG'S INFLUENCE ON THE DOCK UNIONS, MRS. N.
AND, WELL...
SOME PEOPLE DON'T LIKE HAVING THEIR SECRETS EXPOSED.
I'M OKAY.
I HAD MORE HARD KNOCKS GROWING UP ON THE FARM IN SMALLVILLE THAN ANYTHING THE BIG CITY CAN THROW AT ME.
YOU'RE AN INSPIRATION, CLARK...DON'T JUST LISTEN TO ME...
MY SON, MY DAUGHTER-IN-LAW, EVERYBODY READS YOUR WORK.
WHAT YOU WRITE CHANGES LIVES.
I'M JUST DOING MY JOB.
WHICH DOES NOT EXCUSE THE RENT.
LAST WEEK AND THIS WEEK.
I'M GOOD, MRS. NYXLY.
THE STORY THAT GOT ME BEATEN UP GOT ME PAID.
DID YOU HEAR ABOUT SUPERMAN DROPPING THE NEO-NAZIS INTO THE SEWAGE WORKS?

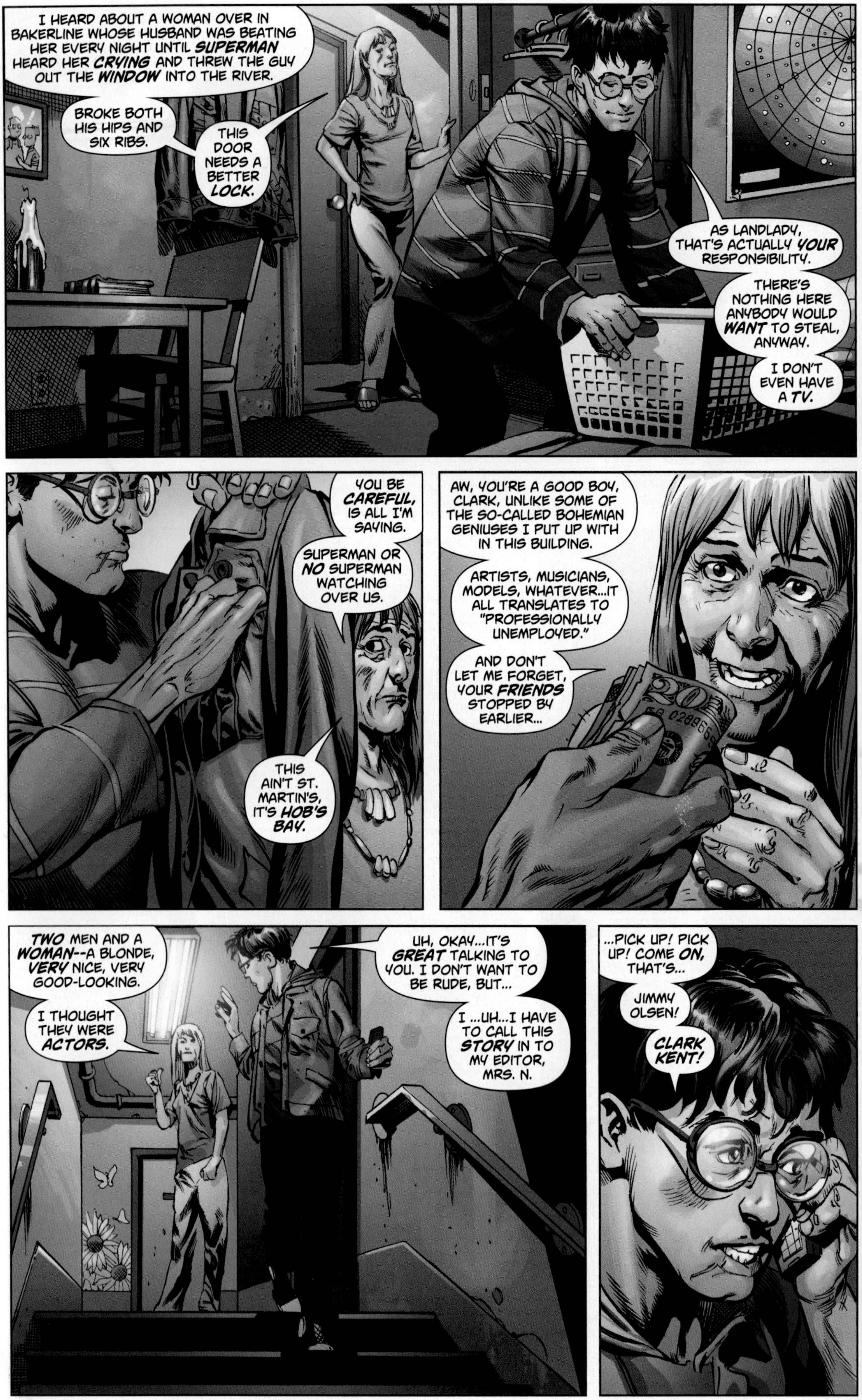
I HEARD ABOUT A WOMAN OVER IN BAKERLINE WHOSE HUSBAND WAS BEATING HER EVERY NIGHT UNTIL SUPERMAN HEARD HER CRYING AND THREW THE GUY OUT THE WINDOW INTO THE RIVER.
BROKE BOTH HIS HIPS AND SIX RIBS.
THIS DOOR NEEDS A BETTER LOCK.
AS LANDLADY, THAT'S ACTUALLY YOUR RESPONSIBILITY.
THERE'S NOTHING HERE ANYBODY WOULD WANT TO STEAL, ANYWAY.
I DON'T EVEN HAVE A TV.
YOU BE CAREFUL, IS ALL I'M SAYING.
SUPERMAN OR NO SUPERMAN WATCHING OVER US.
THIS AIN'T ST. MARTIN'S, IT'S HOB'S BAY.
AW, YOU'RE A GOOD BOY, CLARK, UNLIKE SOME OF THE SO-CALLED BOHEMIAN GENIUSES I PUT UP WITH IN THIS BUILDING.
ARTISTS, MUSICIANS, MODELS, WHATEVER...IT ALL TRANSLATES TO "PROFESSIONALLY UNEMPLOYED."
AND DON'T LET ME FORGET, YOUR FRIENDS STOPPED BY EARLIER...
TWO MEN AND A WOMAN--A BLONDE, VERY NICE, VERY GOOD-LOOKING.
I THOUGHT THEY WERE ACTORS.
UH, OKAY...IT'S GREAT TALKING TO YOU. I DON'T WANT TO BE RUDE, BUT...
I ...UH...I HAVE TO CALL THIS STORY IN TO MY EDITOR, MRS. N.
...PICK UP! PICK UP! COME ON, THAT'S...
JIMMY OLSEN!
CLARK KENT!

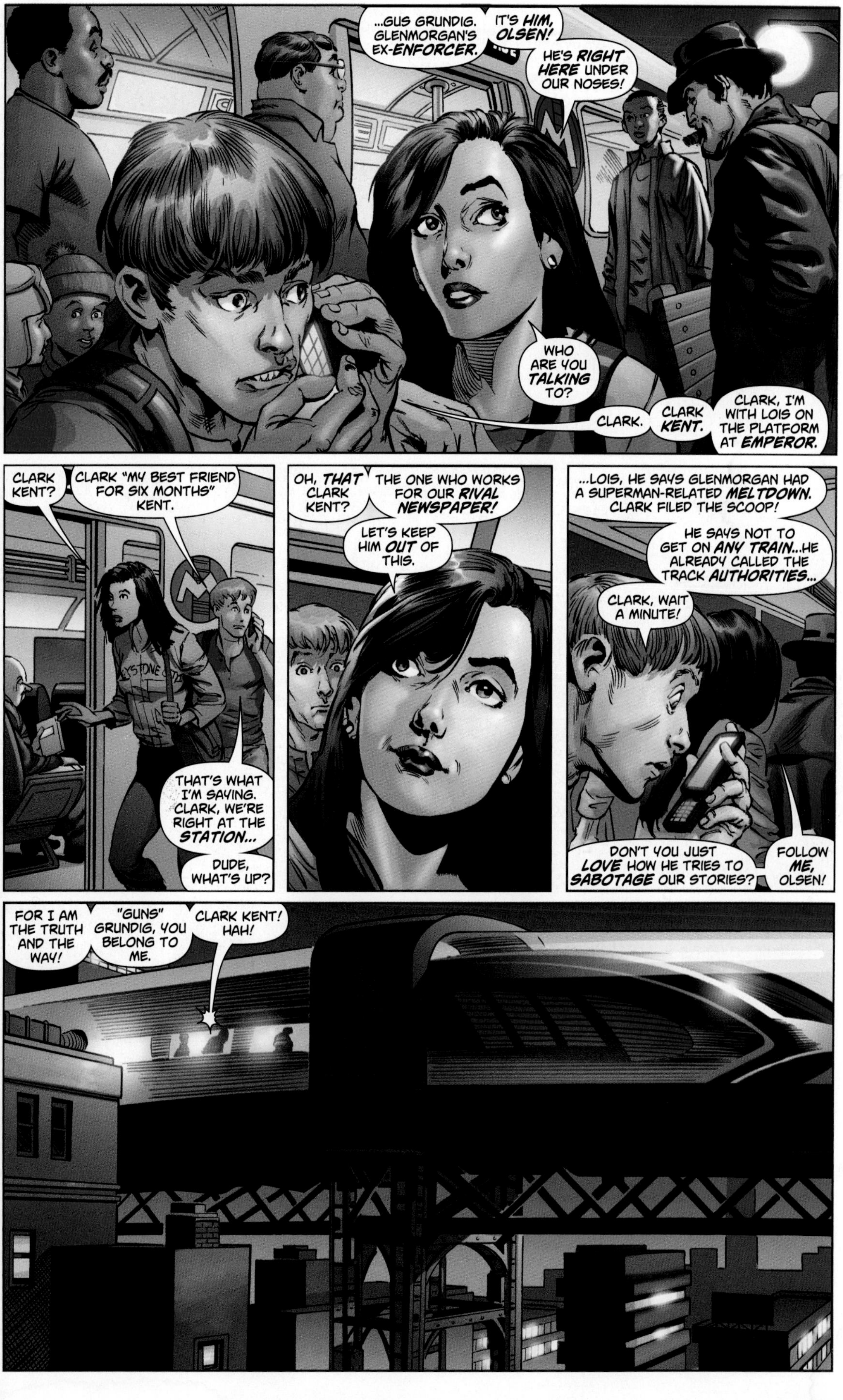

...GUS GRUNDIG. GLENMORGAN'S EX-ENFORCER.
IT'S HIM, OLSEN!
HE'S RIGHT HERE UNDER OUR NOSES!
WHO ARE YOU TALKING TO?
CLARK.
CLARK KENT.
CLARK, I'M WITH LOIS ON THE PLATFORM AT EMPEROR.
CLARK KENT?
CLARK "MY BEST FRIEND FOR SIX MONTHS" KENT.
THAT'S WHAT I'M SAYING. CLARK, WE'RE RIGHT AT THE STATION...
DUDE, WHAT'S UP?
OH, THAT CLARK KENT?
THE ONE WHO WORKS FOR OUR RIVAL NEWSPAPER!
LET'S KEEP HIM OUT OF THIS.
...LOIS, HE SAYS GLENMORGAN HAD A SUPERMAN-RELATED MELTDOWN. CLARK FILED THE SCOOP!
HE SAYS NOT TO GET ON ANY TRAIN...HE ALREADY CALLED THE TRACK AUTHORITIES...
CLARK, WAIT A MINUTE!
DON'T YOU JUST LOVE HOW HE TRIES TO SABOTAGE OUR STORIES?
FOLLOW ME, OLSEN!
FOR I AM THE TRUTH AND THE WAY!
"GUNS" GRUNDIG, YOU BELONG TO ME.
CLARK KENT! HAH!

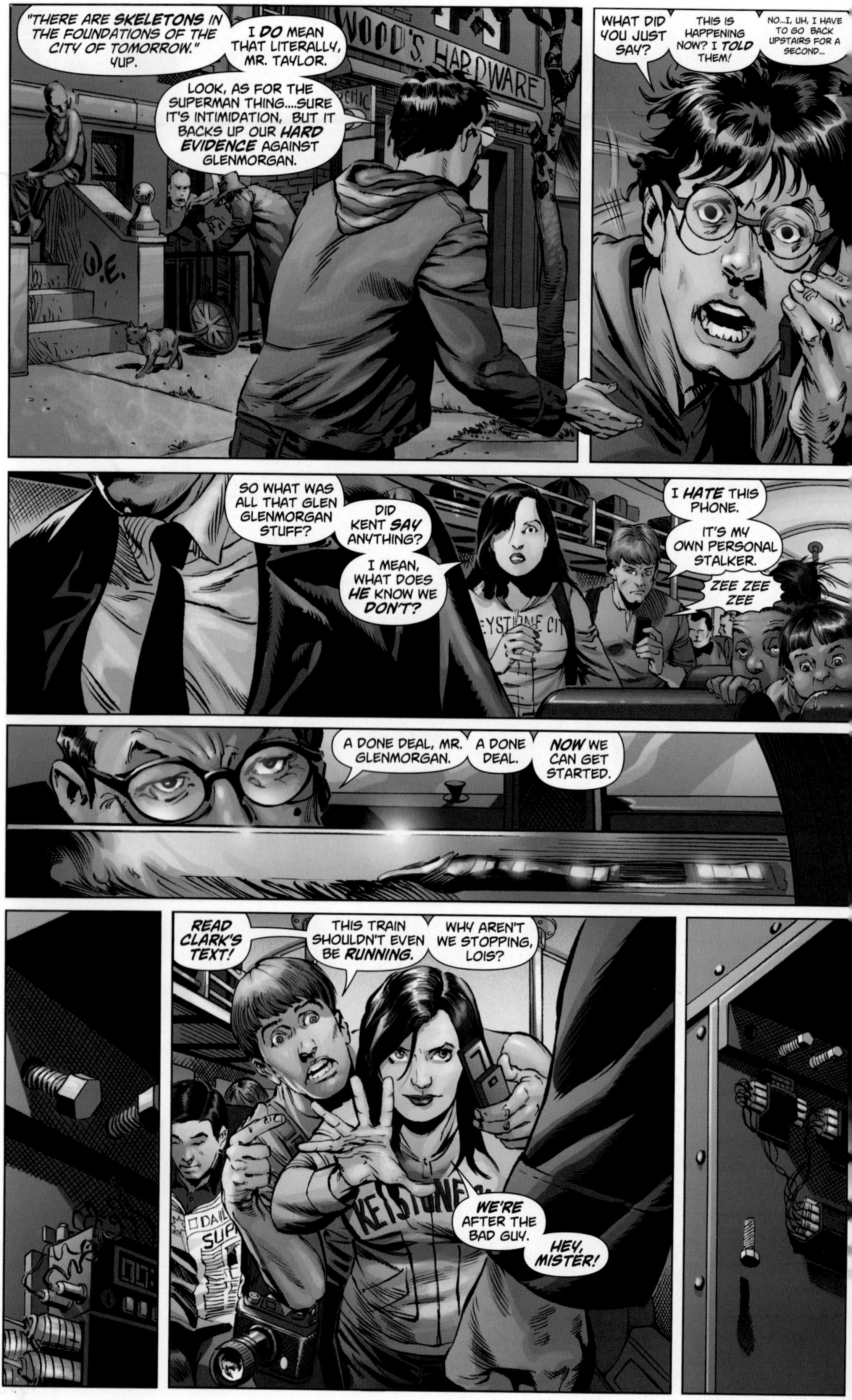
"THERE ARE SKELETONS IN THE FOUNDATIONS OF THE CITY OF TOMORROW." YUP.
I DO MEAN THAT LITERALLY, MR. TAYLOR.
LOOK, AS FOR THE SUPERMAN THING....SURE IT'S INTIMIDATION, BUT IT BACKS UP OUR HARD EVIDENCE AGAINST GLENMORGAN.
WOOD'S HARDWARE
WHAT DID YOU JUST SAY?
THIS IS HAPPENING NOW? I TOLD THEM!
NO...I, UH, I HAVE TO GO BACK UPSTAIRS FOR A SECOND...
SO WHAT WAS ALL THAT GLEN GLENMORGAN STUFF?
DID KENT SAY ANYTHING?
I MEAN, WHAT DOES HE KNOW WE DON'T?
I HATE THIS PHONE.
IT'S MY OWN PERSONAL STALKER.
ZEE ZEE ZEE
A DONE DEAL, MR. GLENMORGAN.
A DONE DEAL.
NOW WE CAN GET STARTED.
READ CLARK'S TEXT!
THIS TRAIN SHOULDN'T EVEN BE RUNNING.
WHY AREN'T WE STOPPING, LOIS?
WE'RE AFTER THE BAD GUY.
HEY, MISTER!

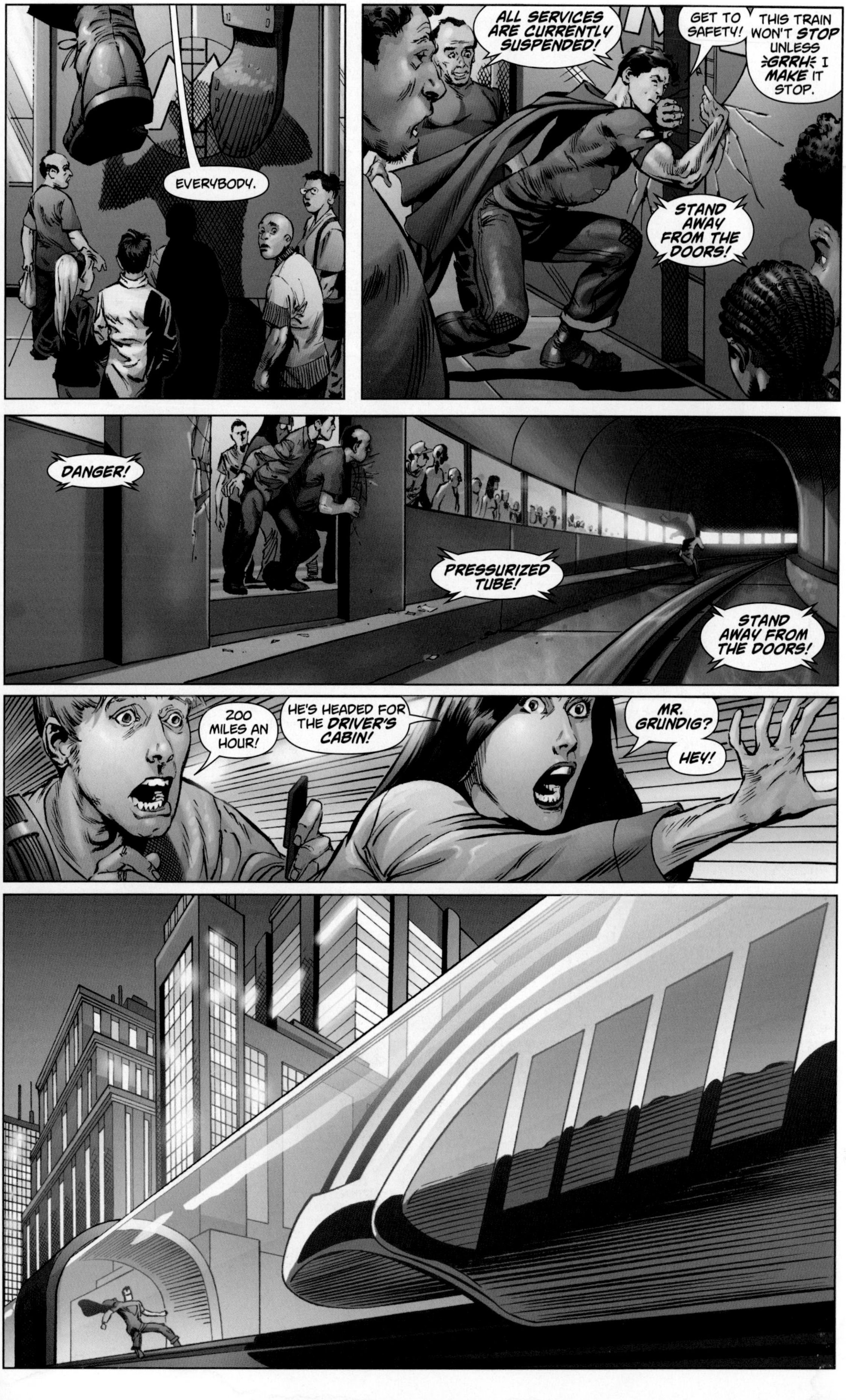
EVERYBODY.
ALL SERVICES ARE CURRENTLY SUSPENDED!
GET TO SAFETY!
THIS TRAIN WON'T STOP UNLESS GRRH I MAKE IT STOP.
STAND AWAY FROM THE DOORS!
DANGER!
PRESSURIZED TUBE!
STAND AWAY FROM THE DOORS!
ZOO MILES AN HOUR!
HE'S HEADED FOR THE DRIVER'S CABIN!
MR. GRUNDIG?
HEY!

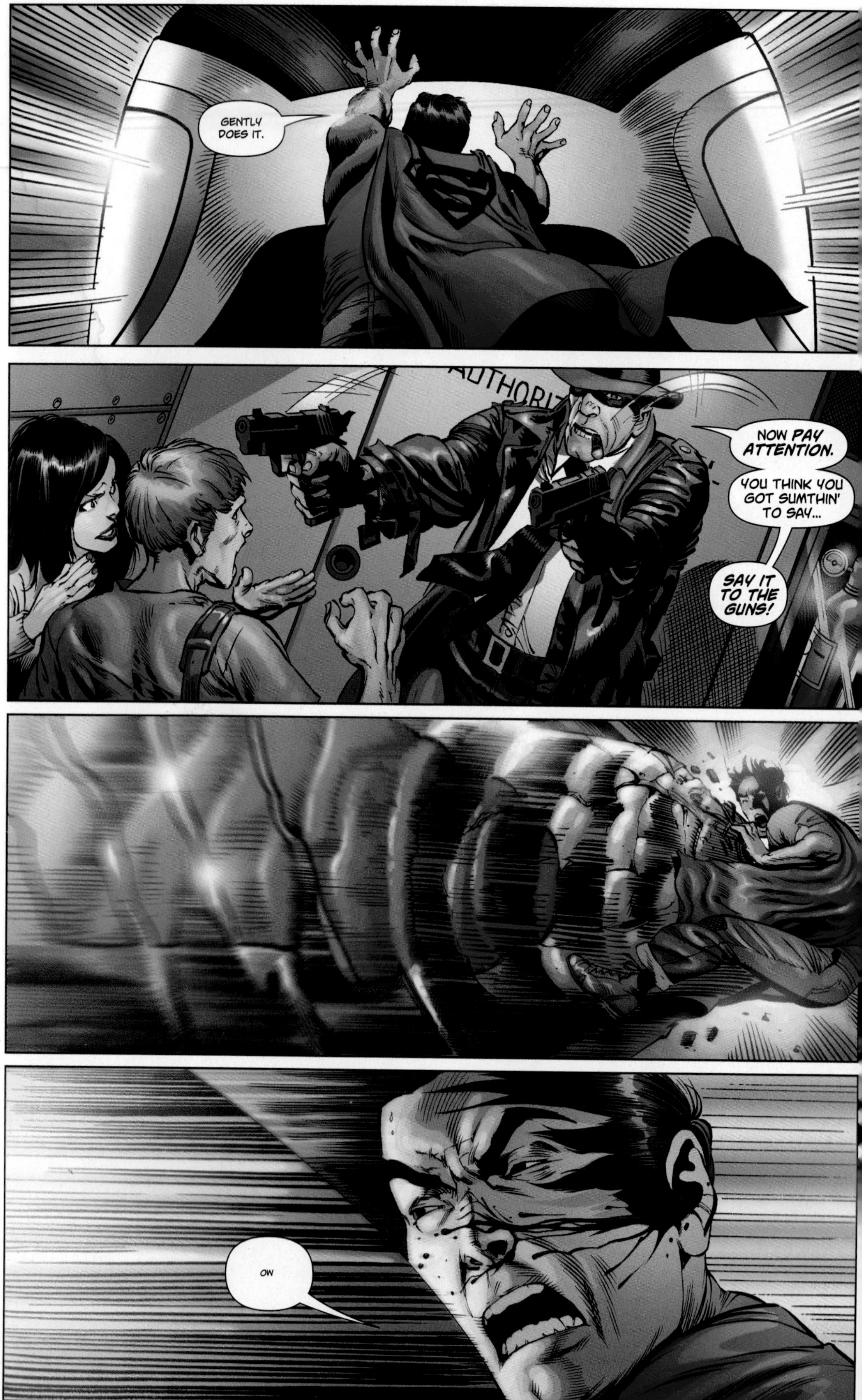
GENTLY DOES IT.
AUTHORIT
NOW PAY ATTENTION.
YOU THINK YOU GOT SUMTHIN' TO SAY...
SAY IT TO THE GUNS!
OW

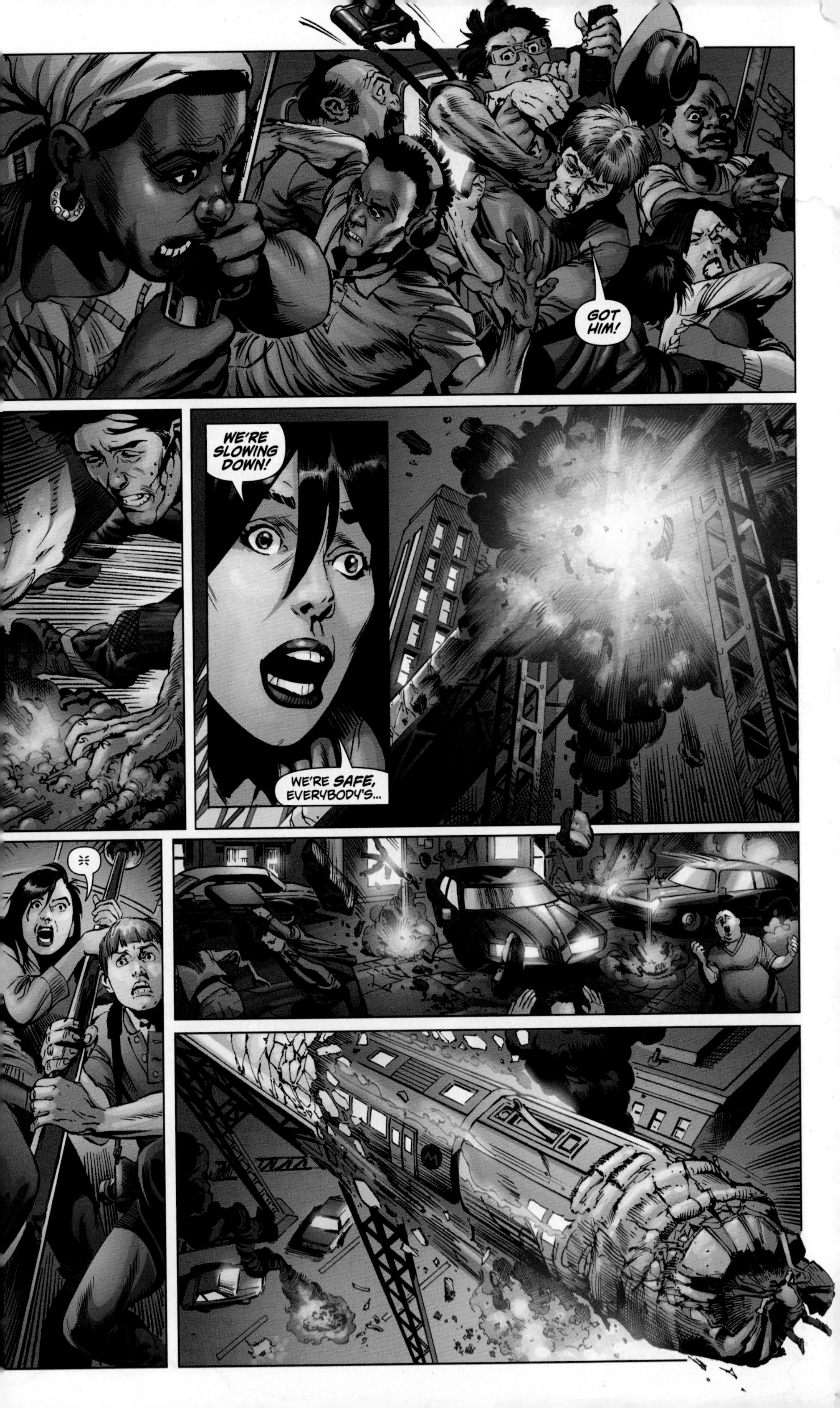
GOT HIM!
WE'RE SLOWING DOWN!
WE'RE SAFE, EVERYBODY'S...

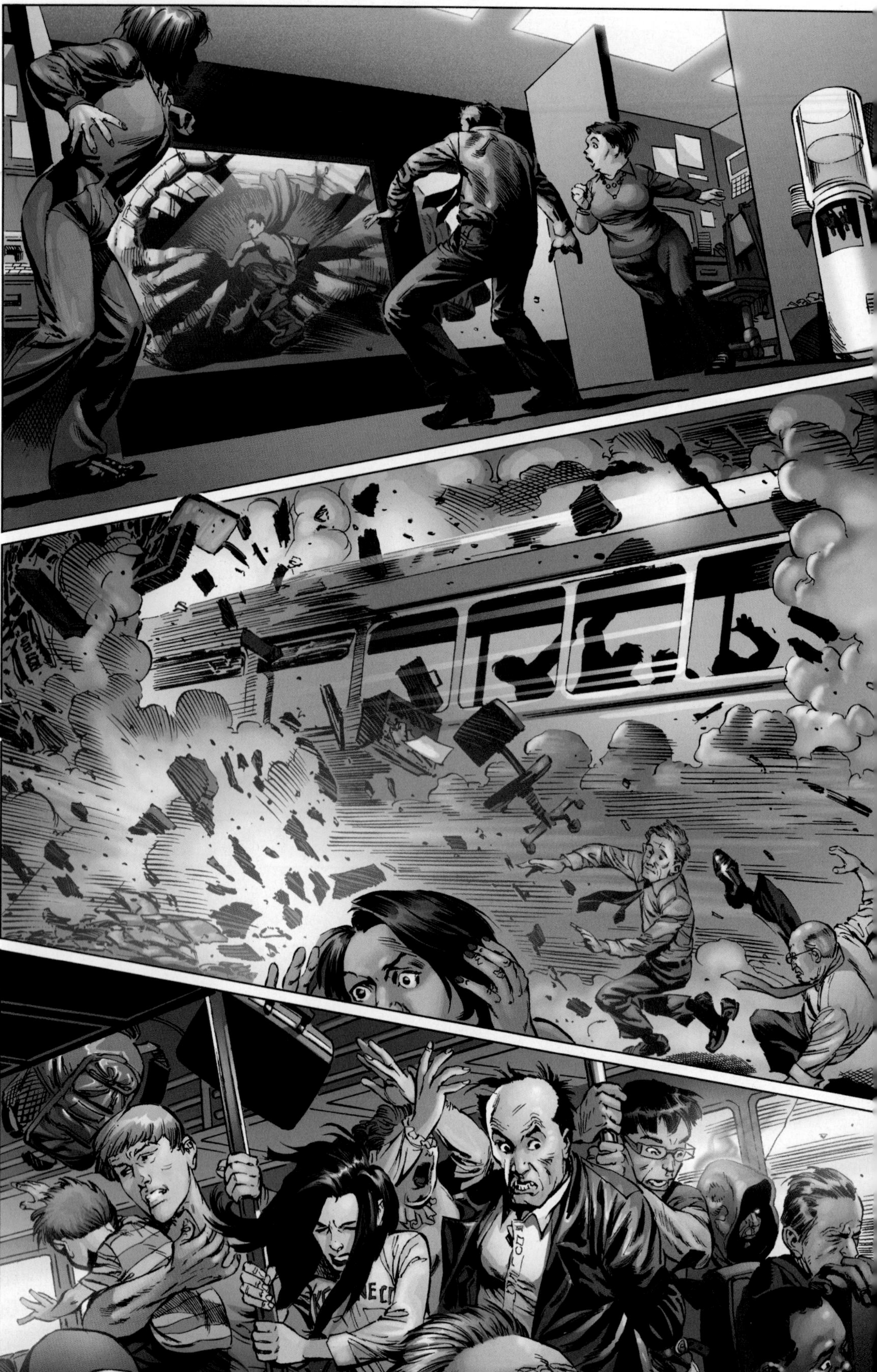

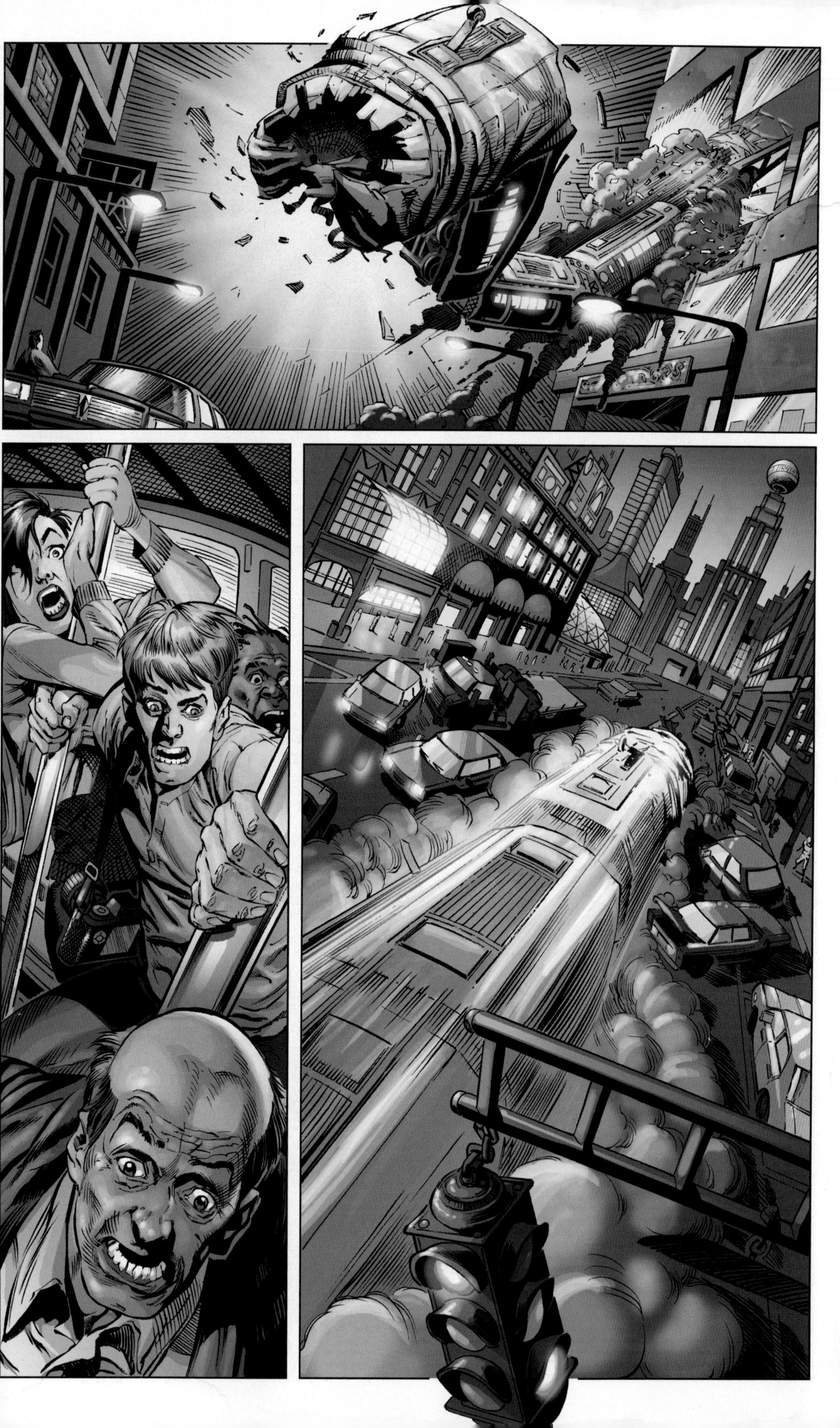

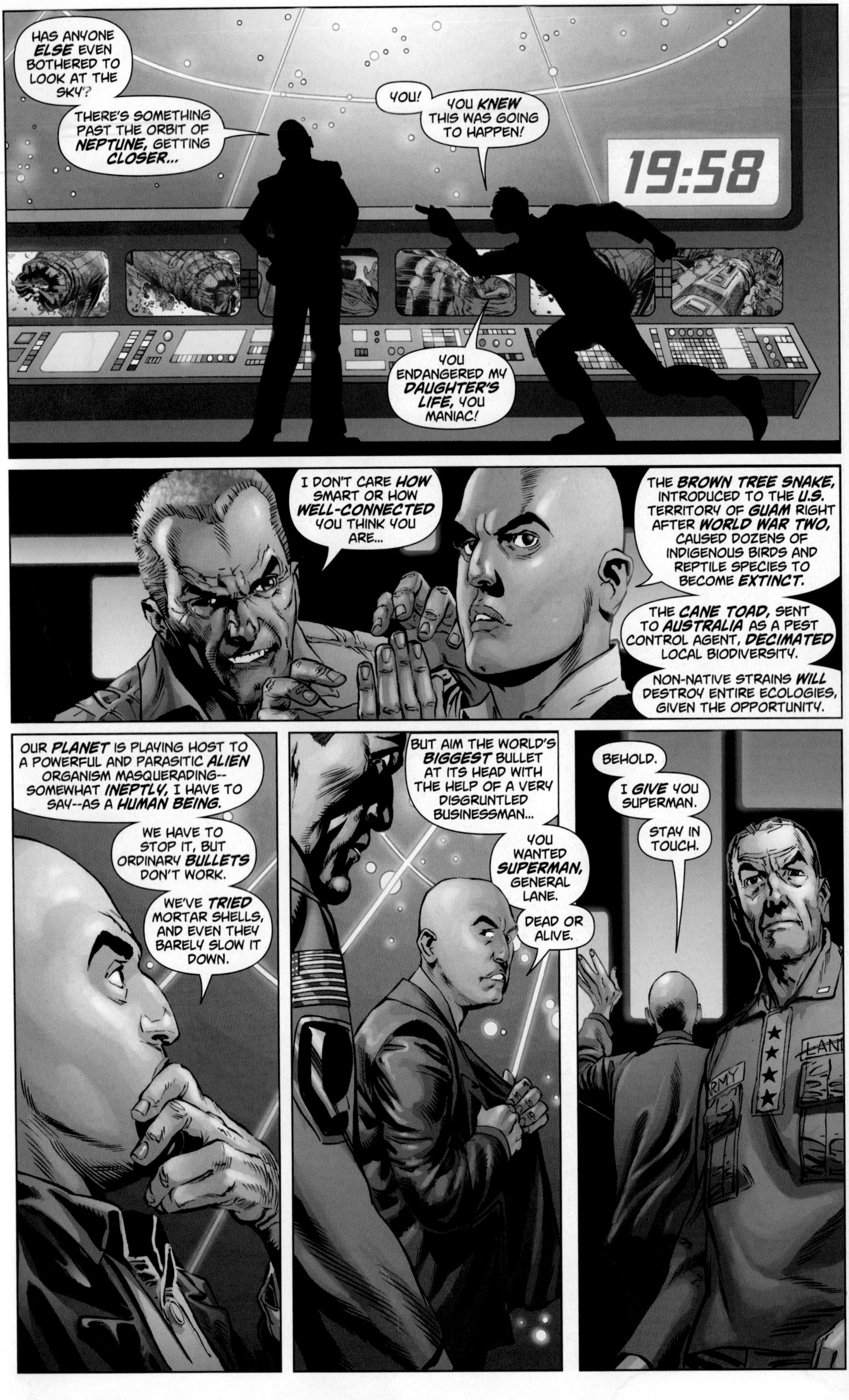

HAS ANYONE ELSE EVEN BOTHERED TO LOOK AT THE SKY?
THERE'S SOMETHING PAST THE ORBIT OF NEPTUNE, GETTING CLOSER...
YOU!
YOU KNEW THIS WAS GOING TO HAPPEN!
19:58
YOU ENDANGERED MY DAUGHTER'S LIFE, YOU MANIAC!
I DON'T CARE HOW SMART OR HOW WELL-CONNECTED YOU THINK YOU ARE...
THE BROWN TREE SNAKE, INTRODUCED TO THE U.S. TERRITORY OF GUAM RIGHT AFTER WORLD WAR TWO, CAUSED DOZENS OF INDIGENOUS BIRDS AND REPTILE SPECIES TO BECOME EXTINCT.
THE CANE TOAD, SENT TO AUSTRALIA AS A PEST CONTROL AGENT, DECIMATED LOCAL BIODIVERSITY.
NON-NATIVE STRAINS WILL DESTROY ENTIRE ECOLOGIES, GIVEN THE OPPORTUNITY.
OUR PLANET IS PLAYING HOST TO A POWERFUL AND PARASITIC ALIEN ORGANISM MASQUERADING--SOMEWHAT INEPTLY, I HAVE TO SAY--AS A HUMAN BEING.
WE HAVE TO STOP IT, BUT ORDINARY BULLETS DON'T WORK.
WE'VE TRIED MORTAR SHELLS, AND EVEN THEY BARELY SLOW IT DOWN.
BUT AIM THE WORLD'S BIGGEST BULLET AT ITS HEAD WITH THE HELP OF A VERY DISGRUNTLED BUSINESSMAN...
YOU WANTED SUPERMAN, GENERAL LANE.
DEAD OR ALIVE.
BEHOLD.
I GIVE YOU SUPERMAN.
STAY IN TOUCH.

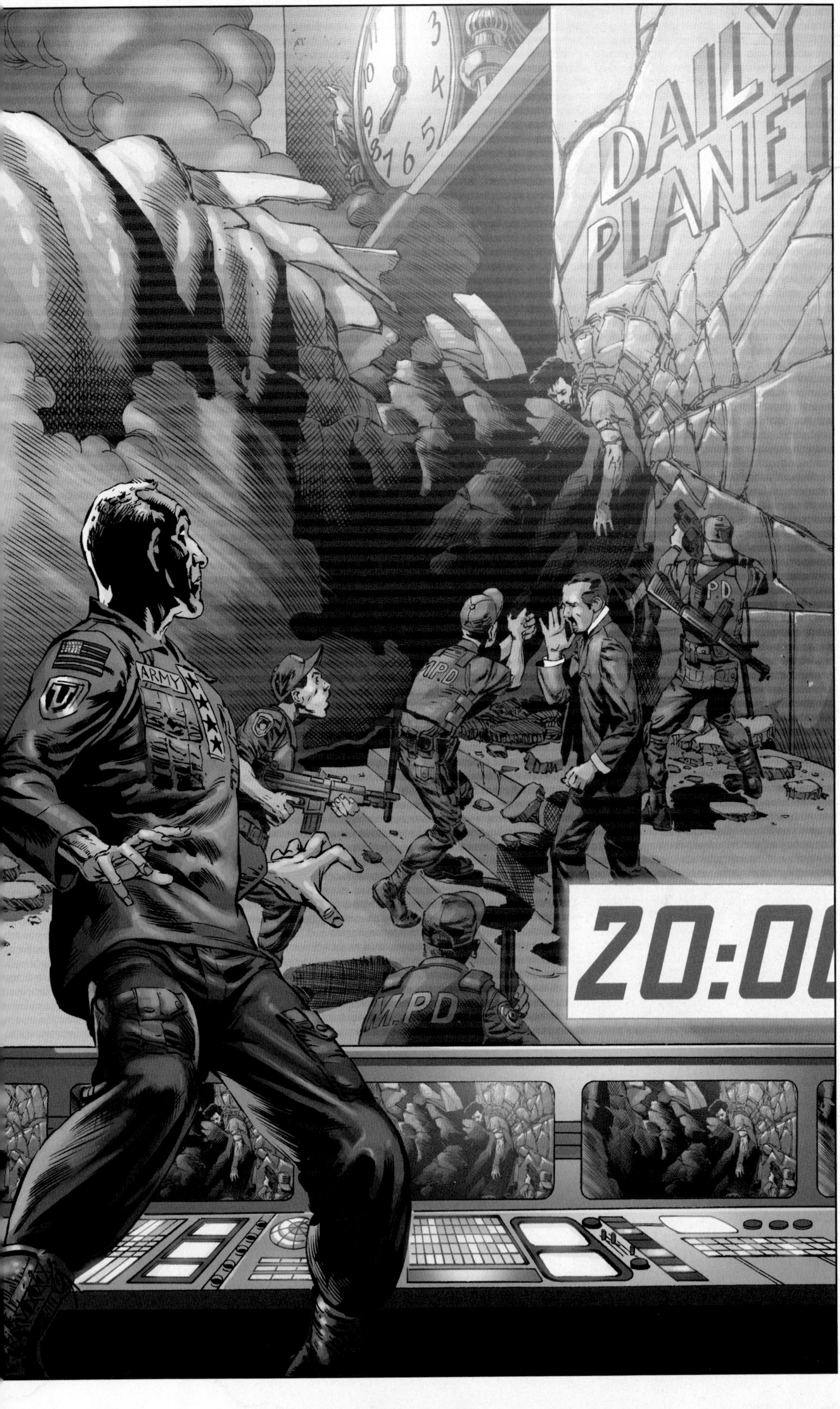

DAILY PLANET
ARMY
M.P.D.
P.D.
M.P.D.
20:00

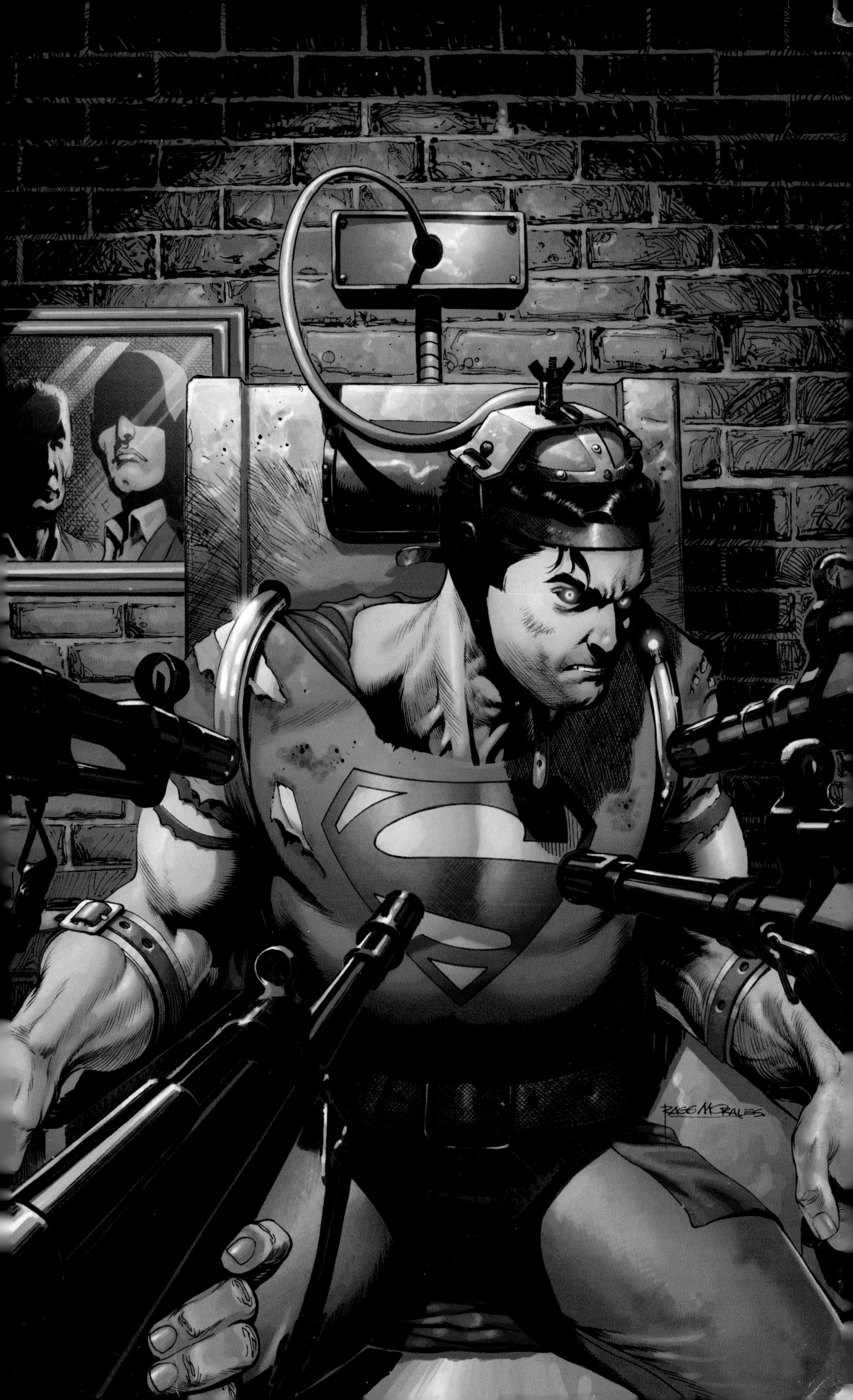
RAGS MORALES

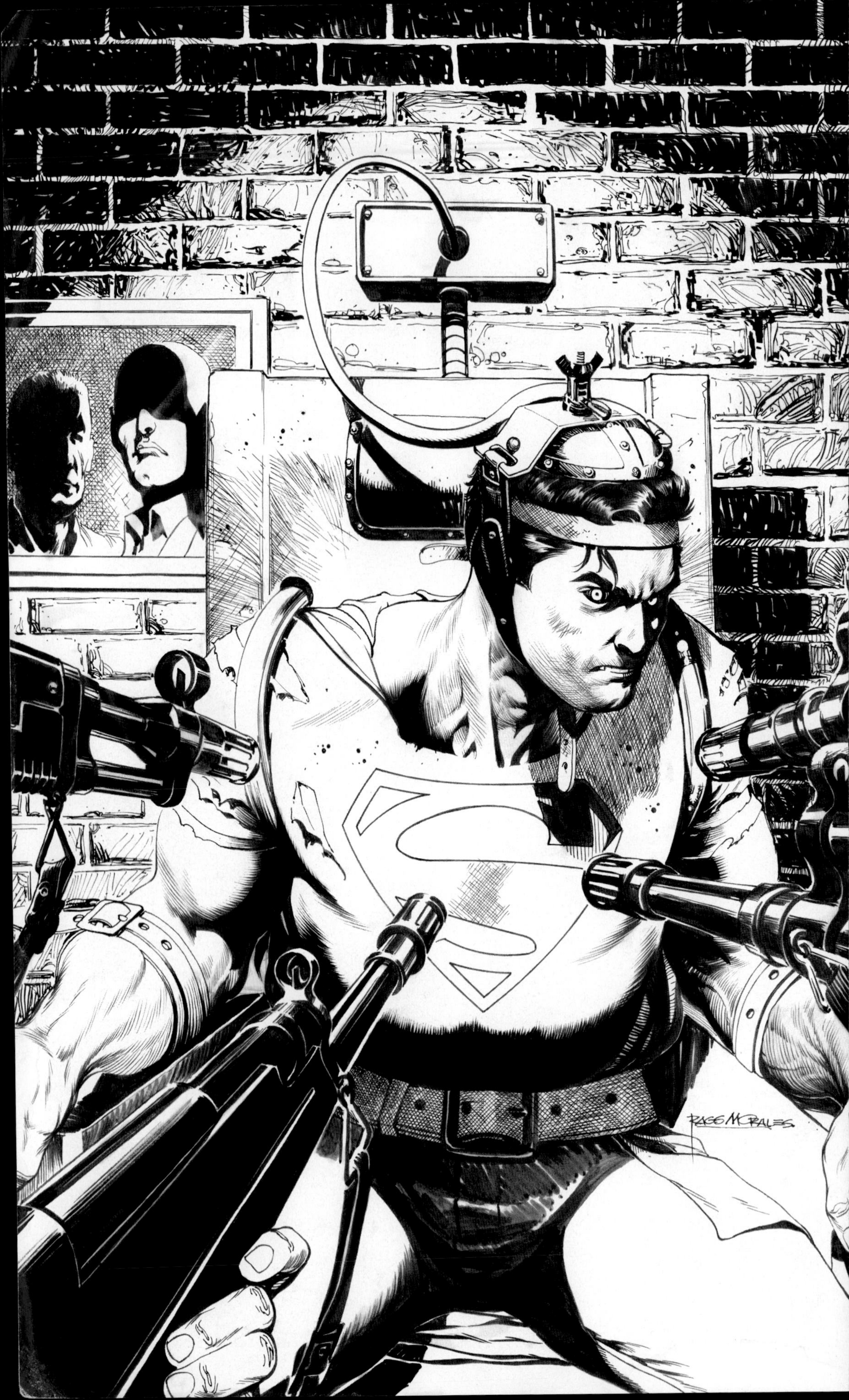
RAGS MORALES

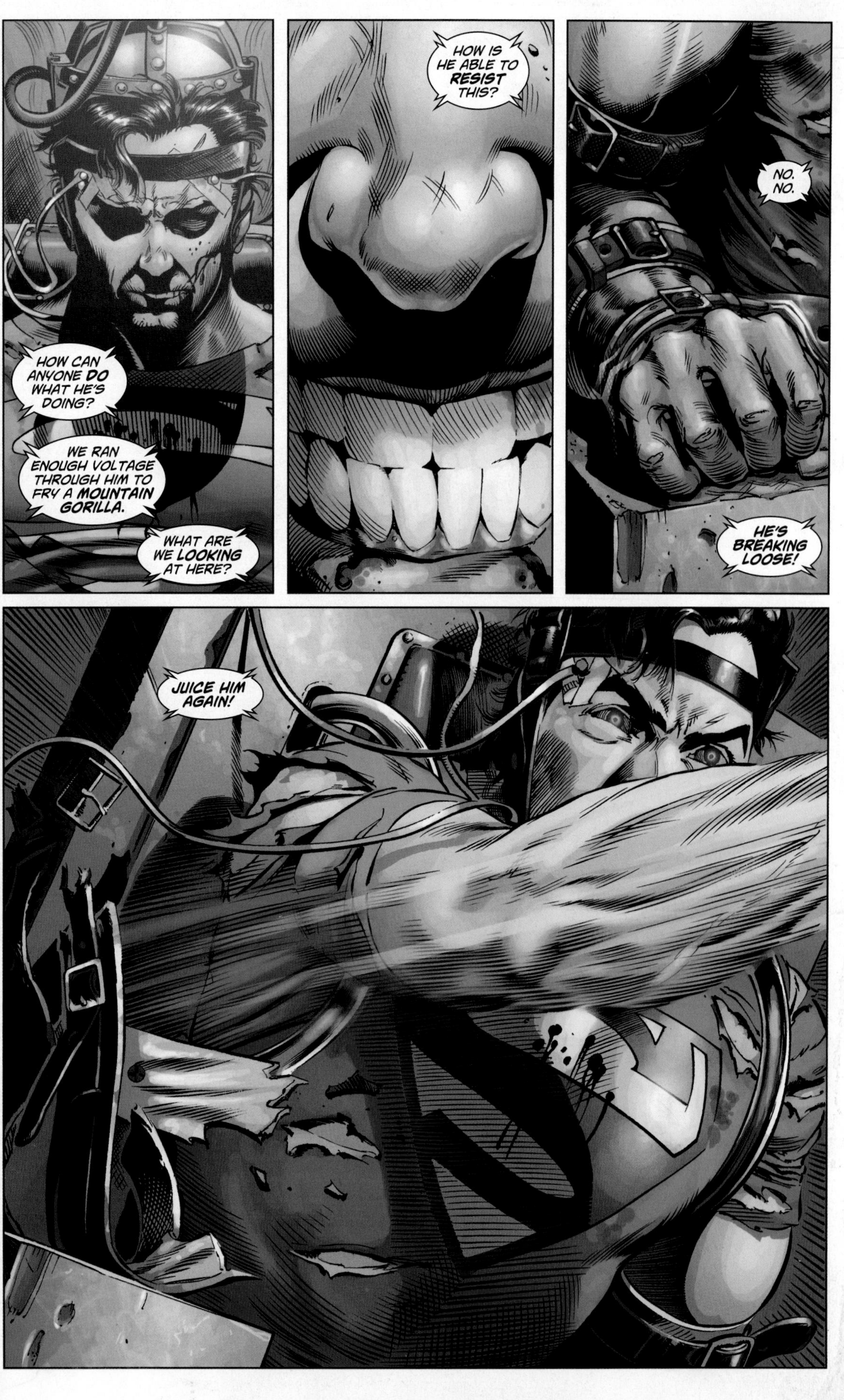
HOW CAN ANYONE DO WHAT HE'S DOING?
WE RAN ENOUGH VOLTAGE THROUGH HIM TO FRY A MOUNTAIN GORILLA.
WHAT ARE WE LOOKING AT HERE?
HOW IS HE ABLE TO RESIST THIS?
NO. NO.
HE'S BREAKING LOOSE!
JUICE HIM AGAIN!

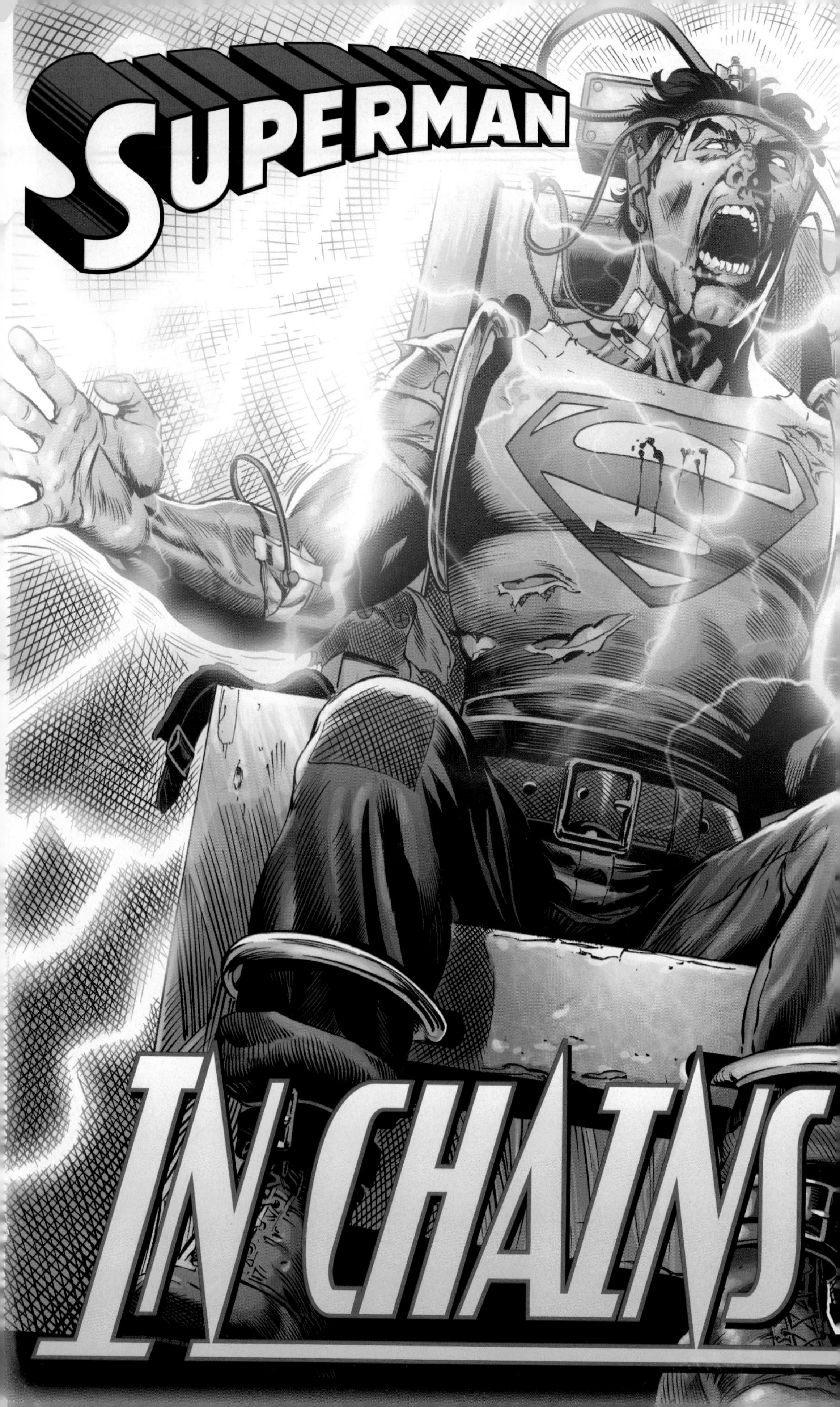
SUPERMAN
IN CHAINS

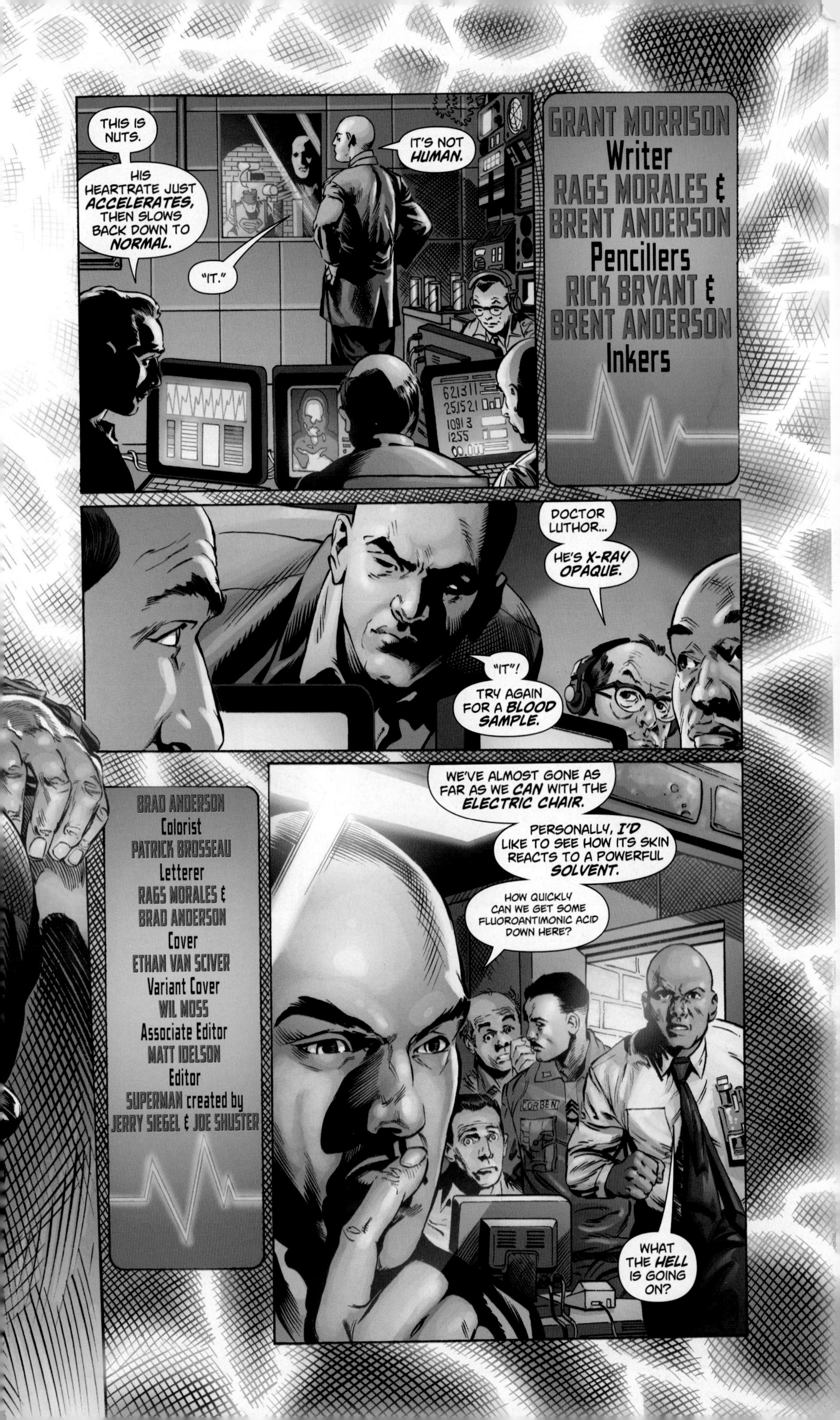
THIS IS NUTS.
HIS HEARTRATE JUST ACCELERATES, THEN SLOWS BACK DOWN TO NORMAL.
IT'S NOT HUMAN.
"IT."
GRANT MORRISON Writer
RAGS MORALES & BRENT ANDERSON Pencillers
RICK BRYANT & BRENT ANDERSON Inkers
DOCTOR LUTHOR...
HE'S X-RAY OPAQUE.
"IT"!
TRY AGAIN FOR A BLOOD SAMPLE.
BRAD ANDERSON Colorist
PATRICK BROSSEAU Letterer
RAGS MORALES & BRAD ANDERSON Cover
ETHAN VAN SCIVER Variant Cover
WIL MOSS Associate Editor
MATT IDELSON Editor
SUPERMAN created by JERRY SIEGEL & JOE SHUSTER
WE'VE ALMOST GONE AS FAR AS WE CAN WITH THE ELECTRIC CHAIR.
PERSONALLY, I'D LIKE TO SEE HOW ITS SKIN REACTS TO A POWERFUL SOLVENT.
HOW QUICKLY CAN WE GET SOME FLUOROANTIMONIC ACID DOWN HERE?
CORBEN
WHAT THE HELL IS GOING ON?

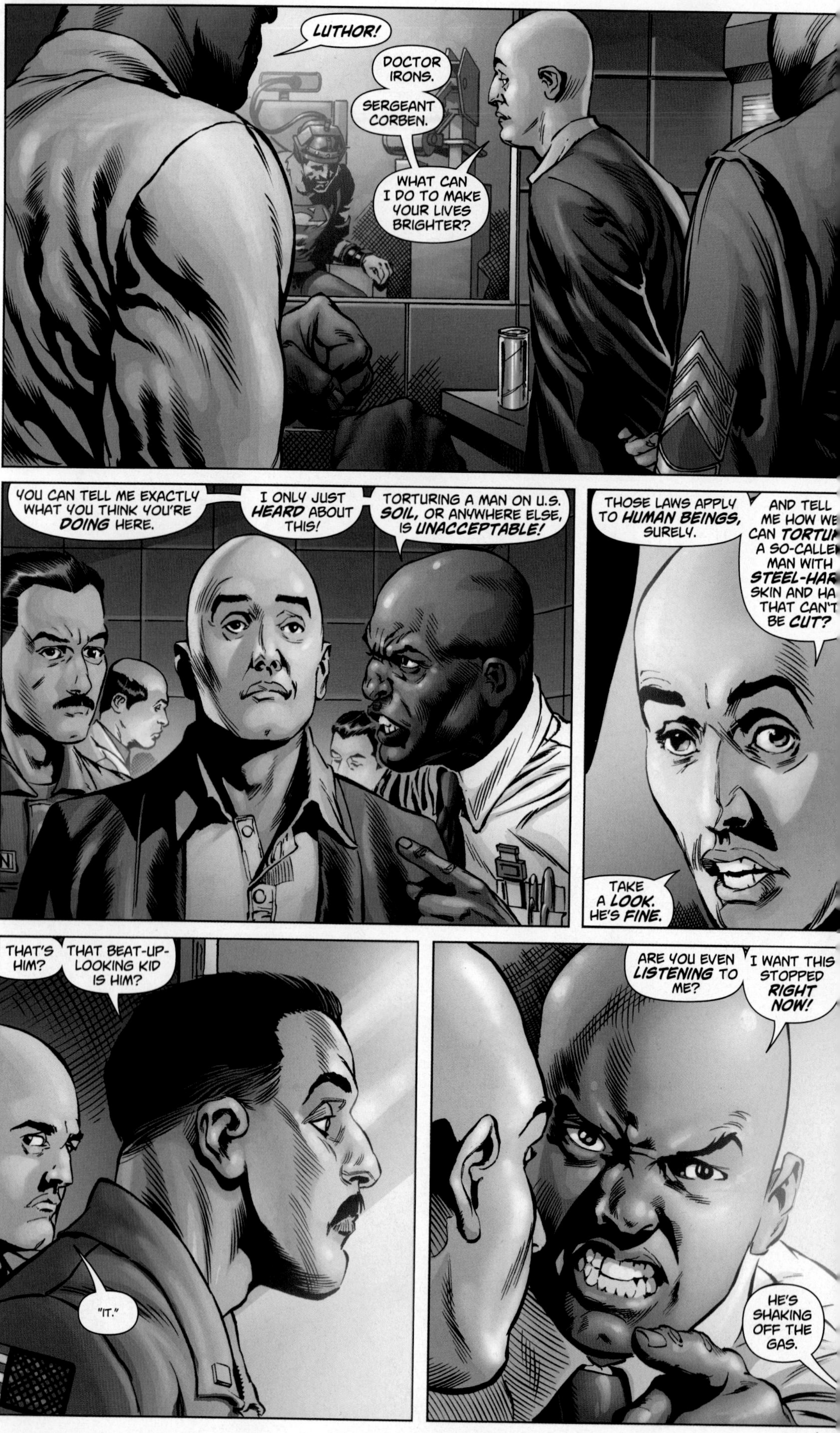
LUTHOR!
DOCTOR IRONS.
SERGEANT CORBEN.
WHAT CAN I DO TO MAKE YOUR LIVES BRIGHTER?
YOU CAN TELL ME EXACTLY WHAT YOU THINK YOU'RE DOING HERE.
I ONLY JUST HEARD ABOUT THIS!
TORTURING A MAN ON U.S. SOIL, OR ANYWHERE ELSE, IS UNACCEPTABLE!
THOSE LAWS APPLY TO HUMAN BEINGS, SURELY.
AND TELL ME HOW WE CAN TORTU A SO-CALLE MAN WITH STEEL-HAR SKIN AND HA THAT CAN'T BE CUT?
TAKE A LOOK. HE'S FINE.
THAT'S HIM?
THAT BEAT-UP-LOOKING KID IS HIM?
"IT."
ARE YOU EVEN LISTENING TO ME?
I WANT THIS STOPPED RIGHT NOW!
HE'S SHAKING OFF THE GAS.

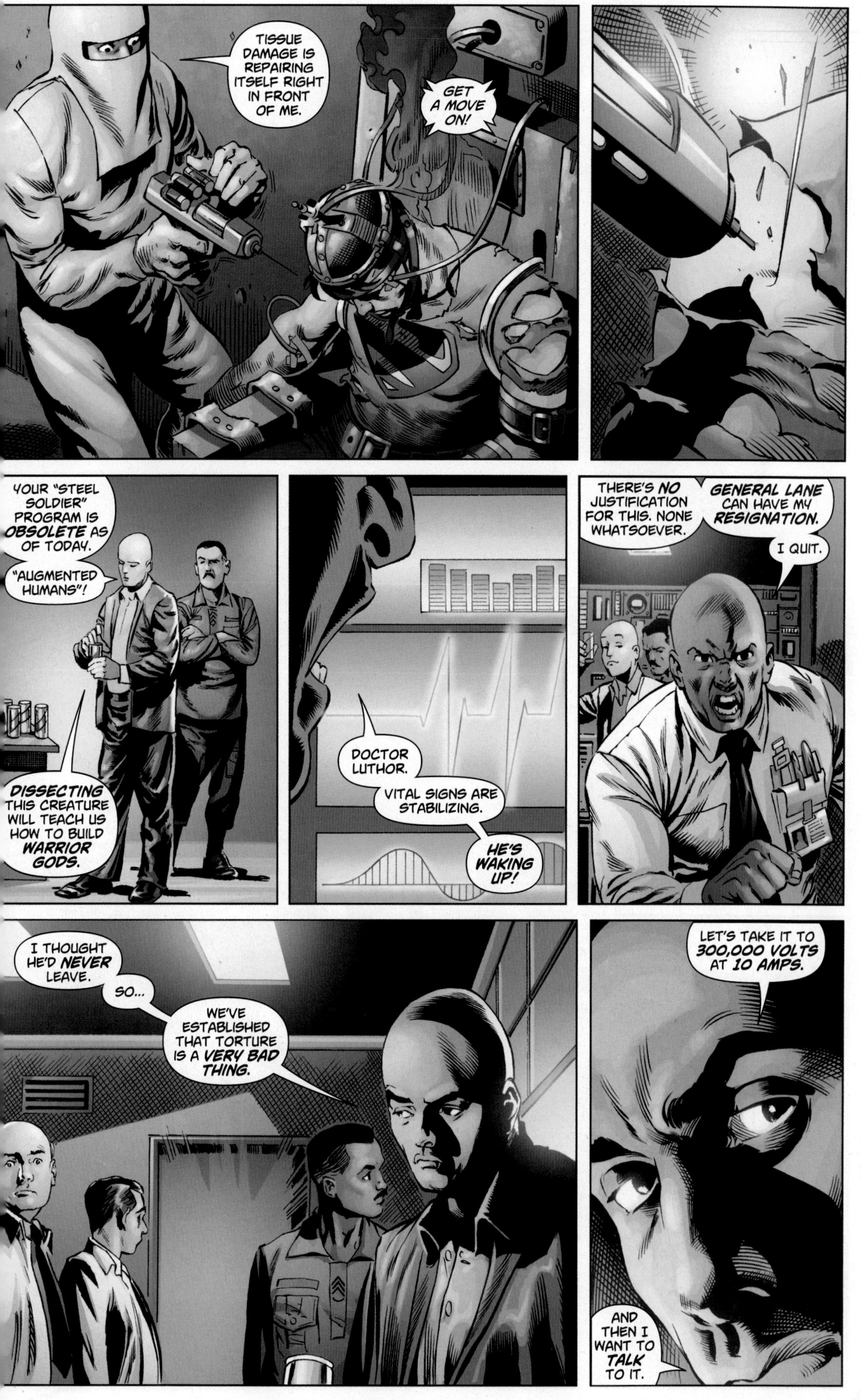
TISSUE DAMAGE IS REPAIRING ITSELF RIGHT IN FRONT OF ME.
GET A MOVE ON!
YOUR "STEEL SOLDIER" PROGRAM IS OBSOLETE AS OF TODAY.
"AUGMENTED HUMANS"!
DISSECTING THIS CREATURE WILL TEACH US HOW TO BUILD WARRIOR GODS.
DOCTOR LUTHOR.
VITAL SIGNS ARE STABILIZING.
HE'S WAKING UP!
THERE'S NO JUSTIFICATION FOR THIS. NONE WHATSOEVER.
GENERAL LANE CAN HAVE MY RESIGNATION.
I QUIT.
I THOUGHT HE'D NEVER LEAVE.
SO...
WE'VE ESTABLISHED THAT TORTURE IS A VERY BAD THING.
LET'S TAKE IT TO 300,000 VOLTS AT 10 AMPS.
AND THEN I WANT TO TALK TO IT.

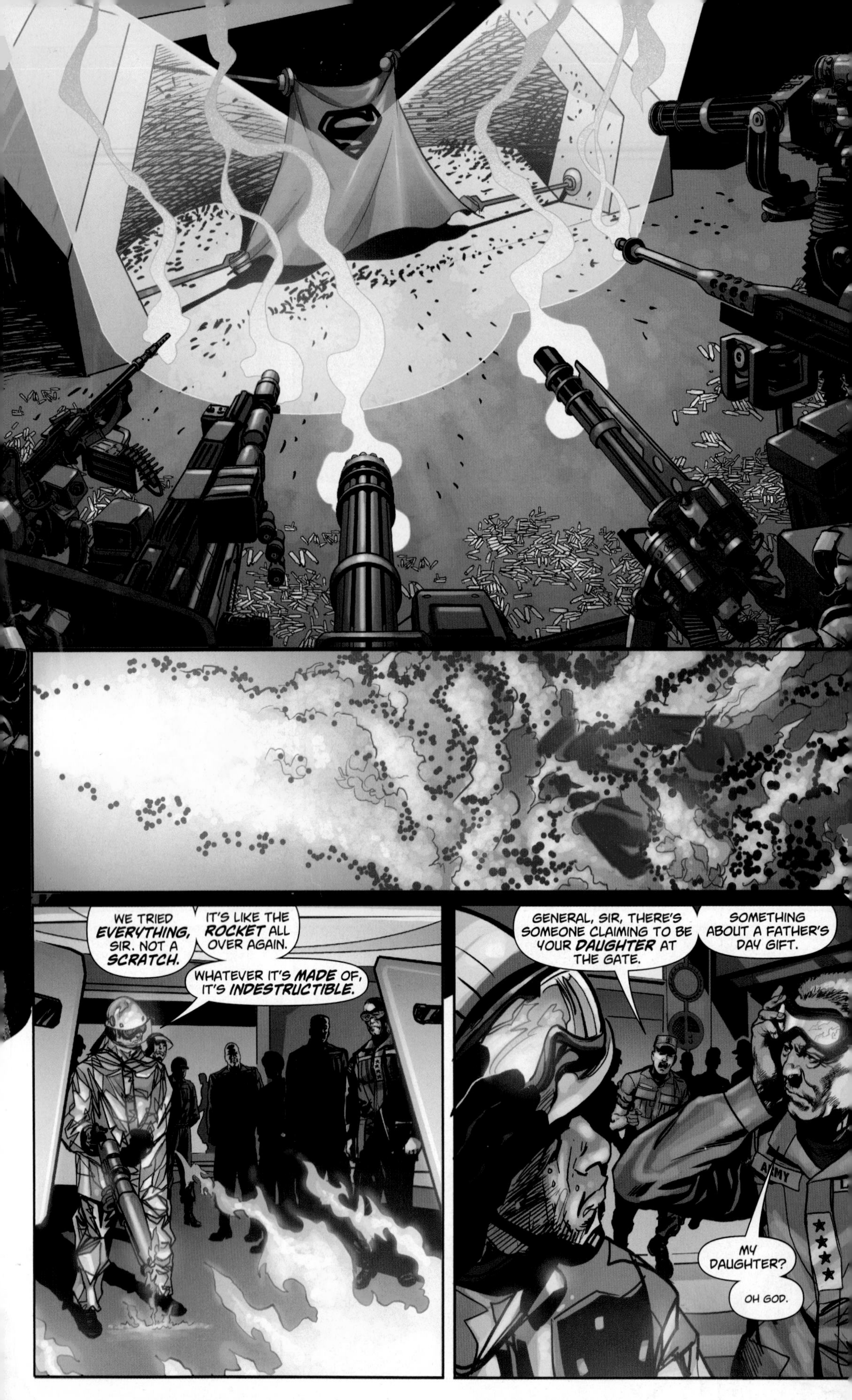
WE TRIED EVERYTHING, SIR. NOT A SCRATCH.
IT'S LIKE THE ROCKET ALL OVER AGAIN.
WHATEVER IT'S MADE OF, IT'S INDESTRUCTIBLE.
GENERAL, SIR, THERE'S SOMEONE CLAIMING TO BE YOUR DAUGHTER AT THE GATE.
SOMETHING ABOUT A FATHER'S DAY GIFT.
MY DAUGHTER?
OH GOD.
ARMY

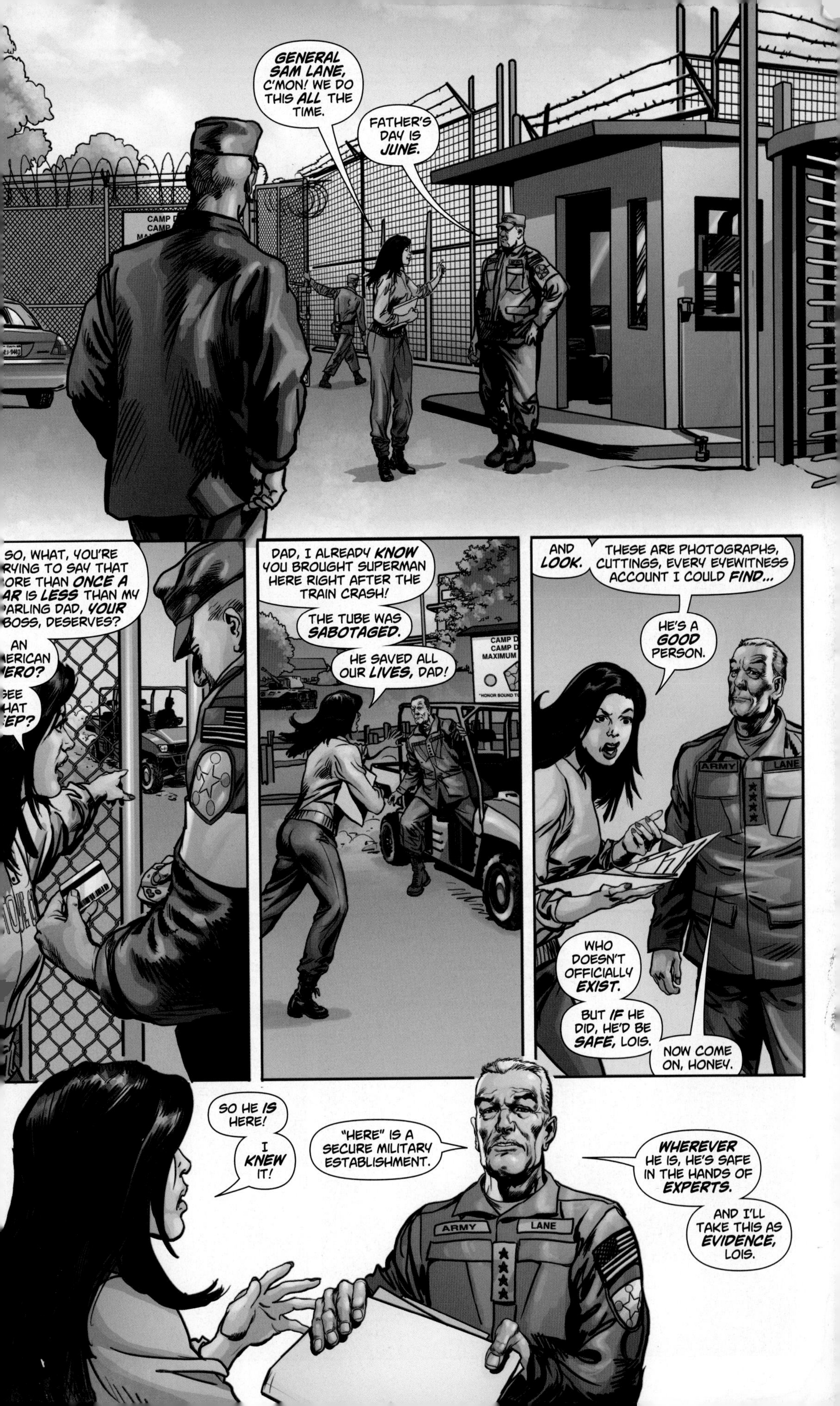

GENERAL SAM LANE, C'MON! WE DO THIS ALL THE TIME.
FATHER'S DAY IS JUNE.
SO, WHAT, YOU'RE RYING TO SAY THAT ORE THAN ONCE A AR IS LESS THAN MY PARLING DAD, YOUR BOSS, DESERVES?
AN ERICAN ERO?
GEE HAT EP?
DAD, I ALREADY KNOW YOU BROUGHT SUPERMAN HERE RIGHT AFTER THE TRAIN CRASH!
THE TUBE WAS SABOTAGED.
HE SAVED ALL OUR LIVES, DAD!
CAMP D
CAMP D
MAXIMUM
AND LOOK.
THESE ARE PHOTOGRAPHS, CUTTINGS, EVERY EYEWITNESS ACCOUNT I COULD FIND...
HE'S A GOOD PERSON.
ARMY
LANE
WHO DOESN'T OFFICIALLY EXIST.
BUT IF HE DID, HE'D BE SAFE, LOIS.
NOW COME ON, HONEY.
SO HE IS HERE!
I KNEW IT!
"HERE" IS A SECURE MILITARY ESTABLISHMENT.
WHEREVER HE IS, HE'S SAFE IN THE HANDS OF EXPERTS.
AND I'LL TAKE THIS AS EVIDENCE, LOIS.
ARMY
LANE

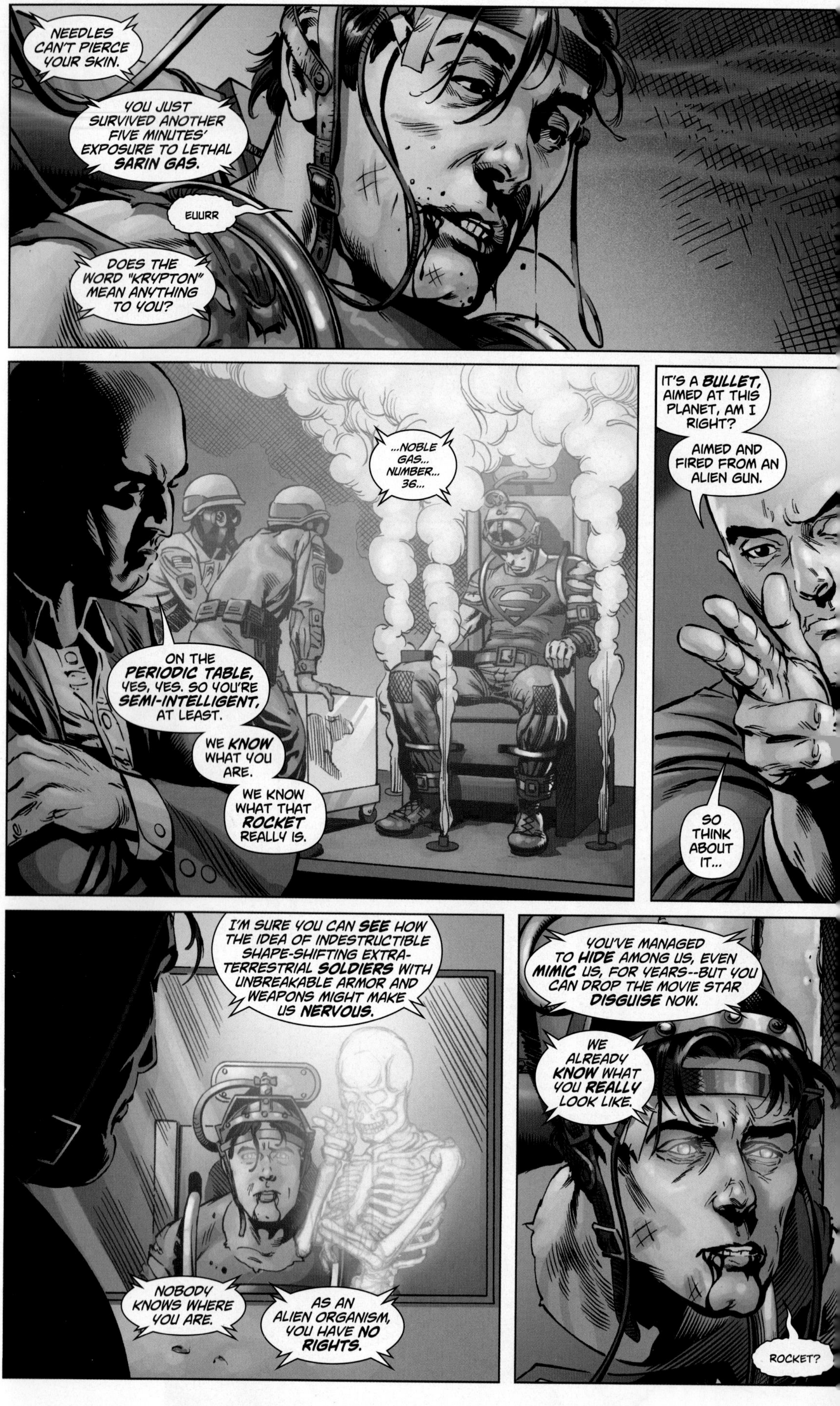
NEEDLES CAN'T PIERCE YOUR SKIN.
YOU JUST SURVIVED ANOTHER FIVE MINUTES' EXPOSURE TO LETHAL SARIN GAS.
EUURR
DOES THE WORD "KRYPTON" MEAN ANYTHING TO YOU?
...NOBLE GAS... NUMBER... 36...
ON THE PERIODIC TABLE, YES, YES. SO YOU'RE SEMI-INTELLIGENT, AT LEAST.
WE KNOW WHAT YOU ARE.
WE KNOW WHAT THAT ROCKET REALLY IS.
IT'S A BULLET, AIMED AT THIS PLANET, AM I RIGHT?
AIMED AND FIRED FROM AN ALIEN GUN.
SO THINK ABOUT IT...
I'M SURE YOU CAN SEE HOW THE IDEA OF INDESTRUCTIBLE SHAPE-SHIFTING EXTRA-TERRESTRIAL SOLDIERS WITH UNBREAKABLE ARMOR AND WEAPONS MIGHT MAKE US NERVOUS.
NOBODY KNOWS WHERE YOU ARE.
AS AN ALIEN ORGANISM, YOU HAVE NO RIGHTS.
YOU'VE MANAGED TO HIDE AMONG US, EVEN MIMIC US, FOR YEARS--BUT YOU CAN DROP THE MOVIE STAR DISGUISE NOW.
WE ALREADY KNOW WHAT YOU REALLY LOOK LIKE.
ROCKET?

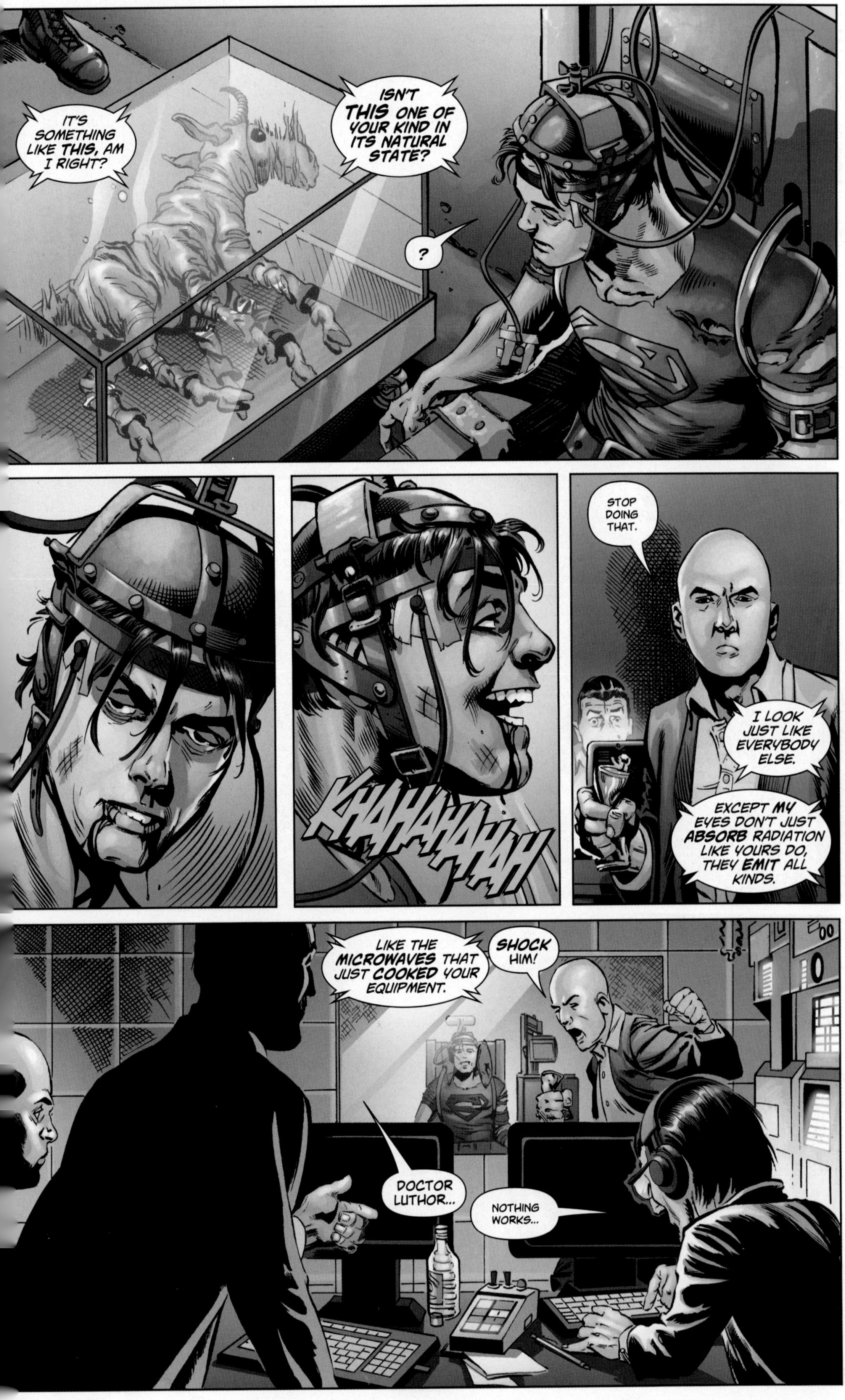
IT'S SOMETHING LIKE THIS, AM I RIGHT?
ISN'T THIS ONE OF YOUR KIND IN ITS NATURAL STATE?
?
KHAHAHAHAHAH
STOP DOING THAT.
I LOOK JUST LIKE EVERYBODY ELSE.
EXCEPT MY EYES DON'T JUST ABSORB RADIATION LIKE YOURS DO, THEY EMIT ALL KINDS.
LIKE THE MICROWAVES THAT JUST COOKED YOUR EQUIPMENT.
SHOCK HIM!
DOCTOR LUTHOR...
NOTHING WORKS...

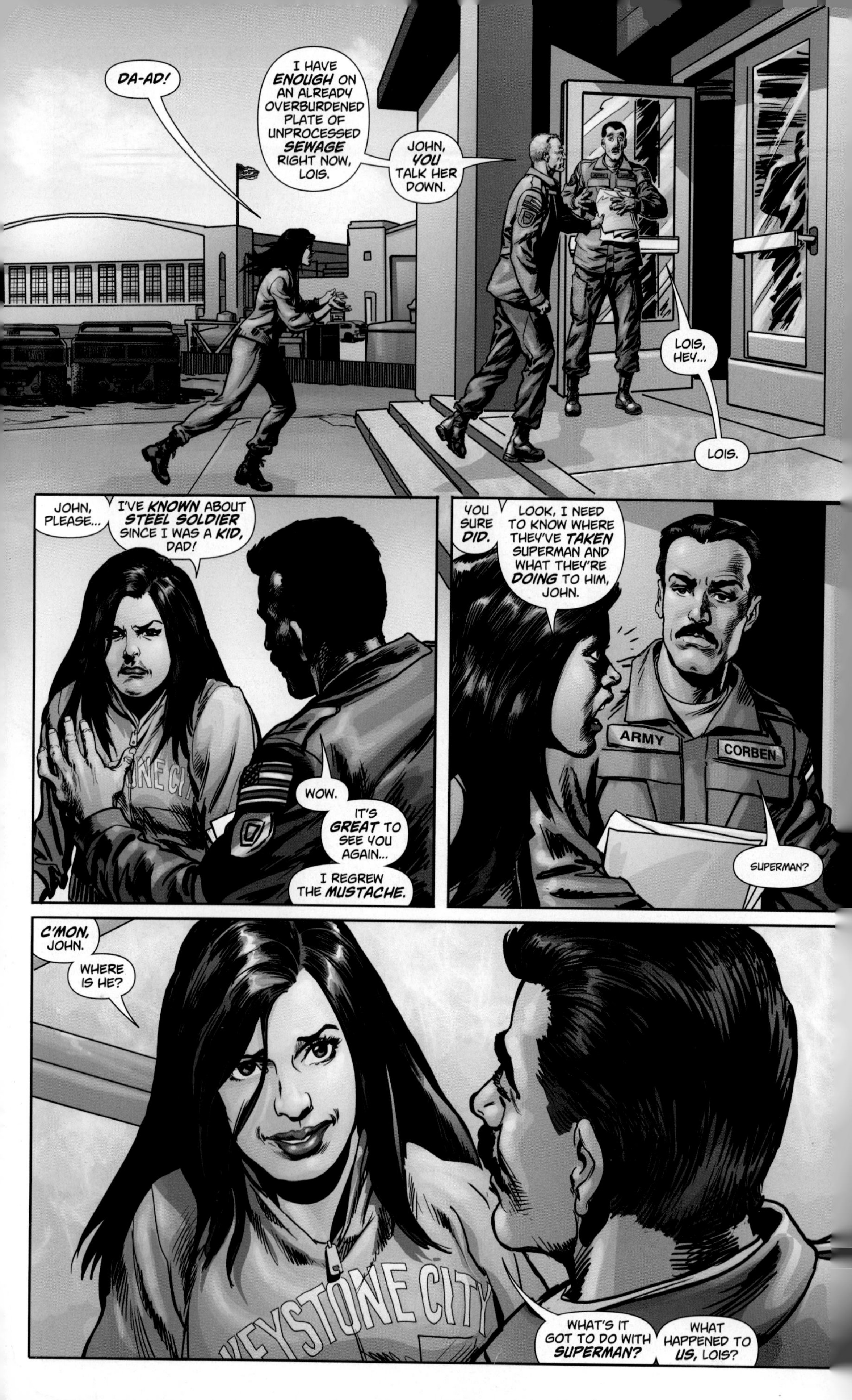
DA-AD!
I HAVE ENOUGH ON AN ALREADY OVERBURDENED PLATE OF UNPROCESSED SEWAGE RIGHT NOW, LOIS.
JOHN, YOU TALK HER DOWN.
LOIS, HEY...
LOIS.
JOHN, PLEASE...
I'VE KNOWN ABOUT STEEL SOLDIER SINCE I WAS A KID, DAD!
WOW.
IT'S GREAT TO SEE YOU AGAIN...
I REGREW THE MUSTACHE.
YOU SURE DID.
LOOK, I NEED TO KNOW WHERE THEY'VE TAKEN SUPERMAN AND WHAT THEY'RE DOING TO HIM, JOHN.
ARMY
CORBEN
SUPERMAN?
C'MON, JOHN.
WHERE IS HE?
KEYSTONE CITY
WHAT'S IT GOT TO DO WITH SUPERMAN?
WHAT HAPPENED TO US, LOIS?

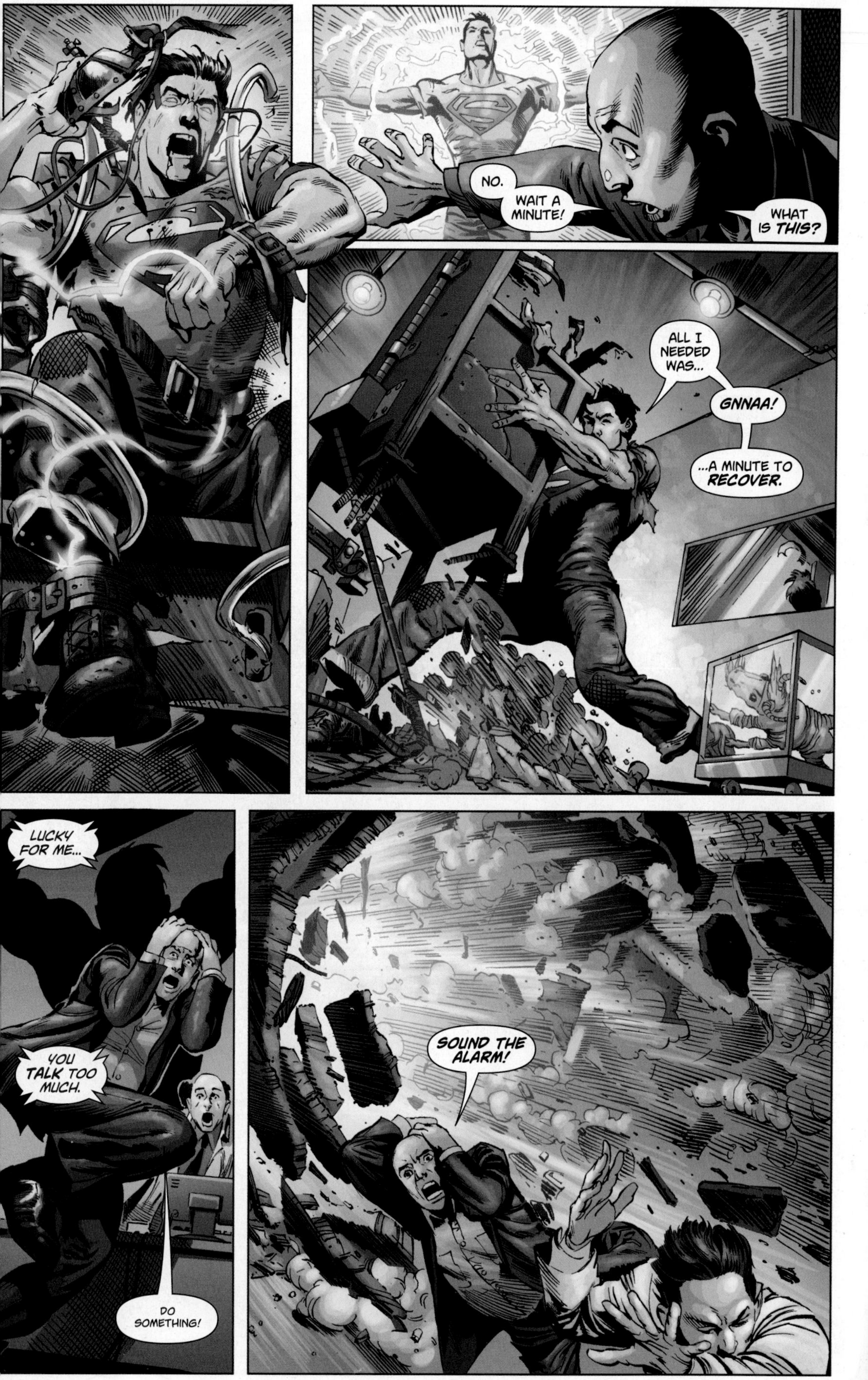
NO.
WAIT A MINUTE!
WHAT IS THIS?
ALL I NEEDED WAS...
GNNAA!
...A MINUTE TO RECOVER.
LUCKY FOR ME...
YOU TALK TOO MUCH.
DO SOMETHING!
SOUND THE ALARM!

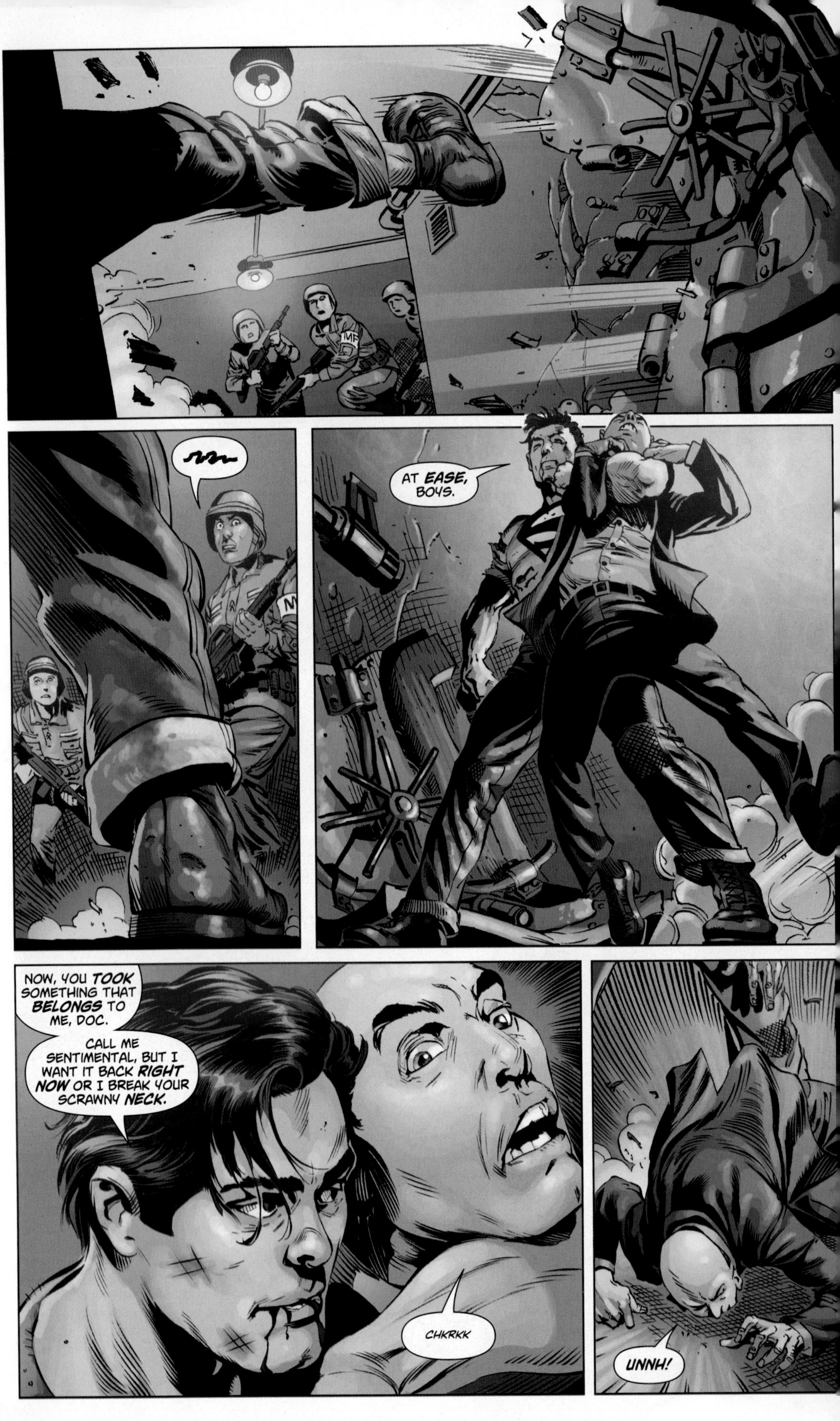

AT EASE, BOYS.
NOW, YOU TOOK SOMETHING THAT BELONGS TO ME, DOC.
CALL ME SENTIMENTAL, BUT I WANT IT BACK RIGHT NOW OR I BREAK YOUR SCRAWNY NECK.
CHKRKK
UNNH!

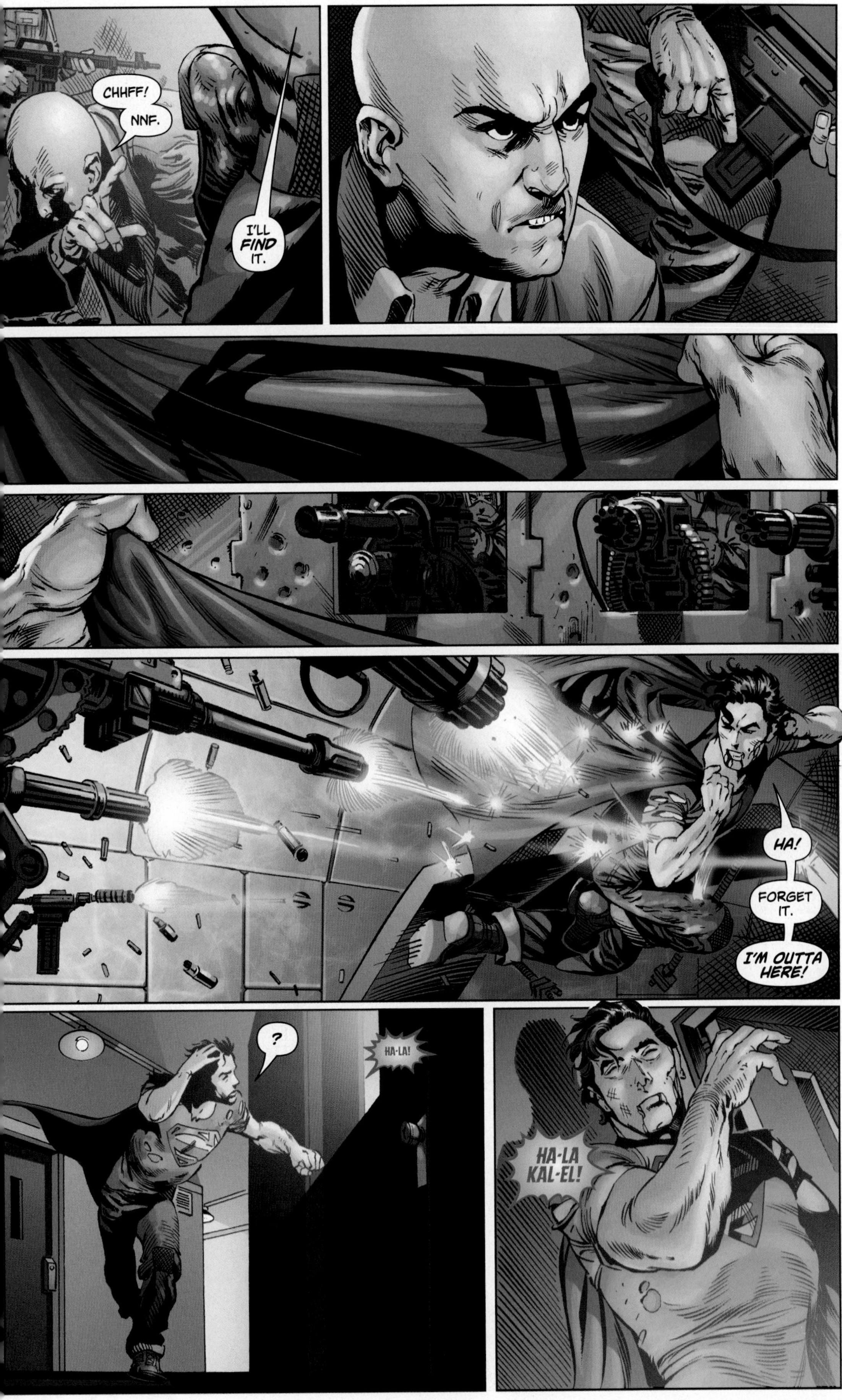
CHHFF!
NNF.
I'LL FIND IT.
HA!
FORGET IT.
I'M OUTTA HERE!
?
HA-LA!
HA-LA KAL-EL!

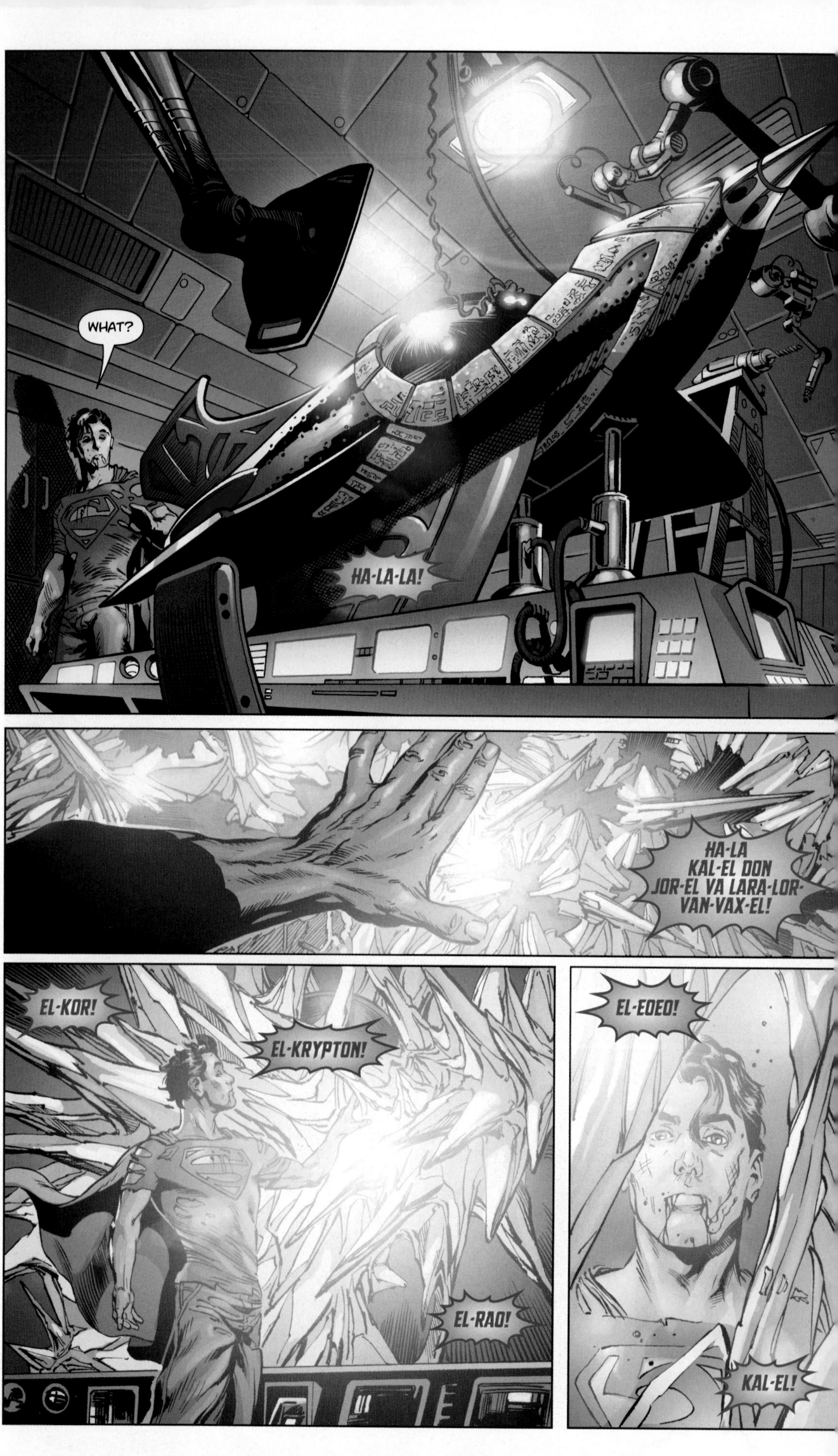
WHAT?
HA-LA-LA!
HA-LA KAL-EL DON JOR-EL VA LARA-LOR-VAN-VAX-EL!
EL-KOR!
EL-KRYPTON!
EL-RAO!
EL-EOEO!
KAL-EL!

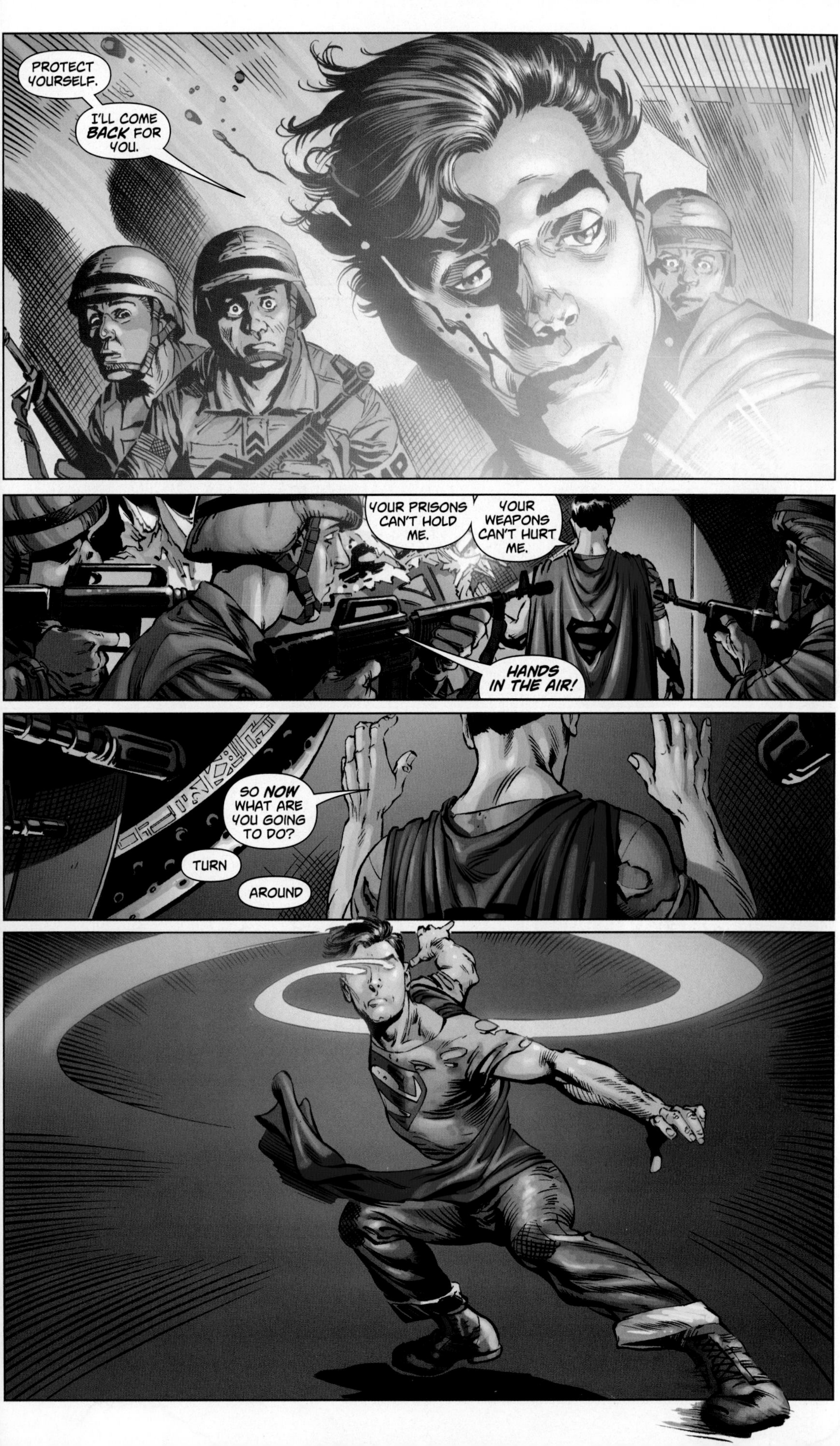
PROTECT YOURSELF.
I'LL COME BACK FOR YOU.
YOUR PRISONS CAN'T HOLD ME.
YOUR WEAPONS CAN'T HURT ME.
HANDS IN THE AIR!
SO NOW WHAT ARE YOU GOING TO DO?
TURN
AROUND

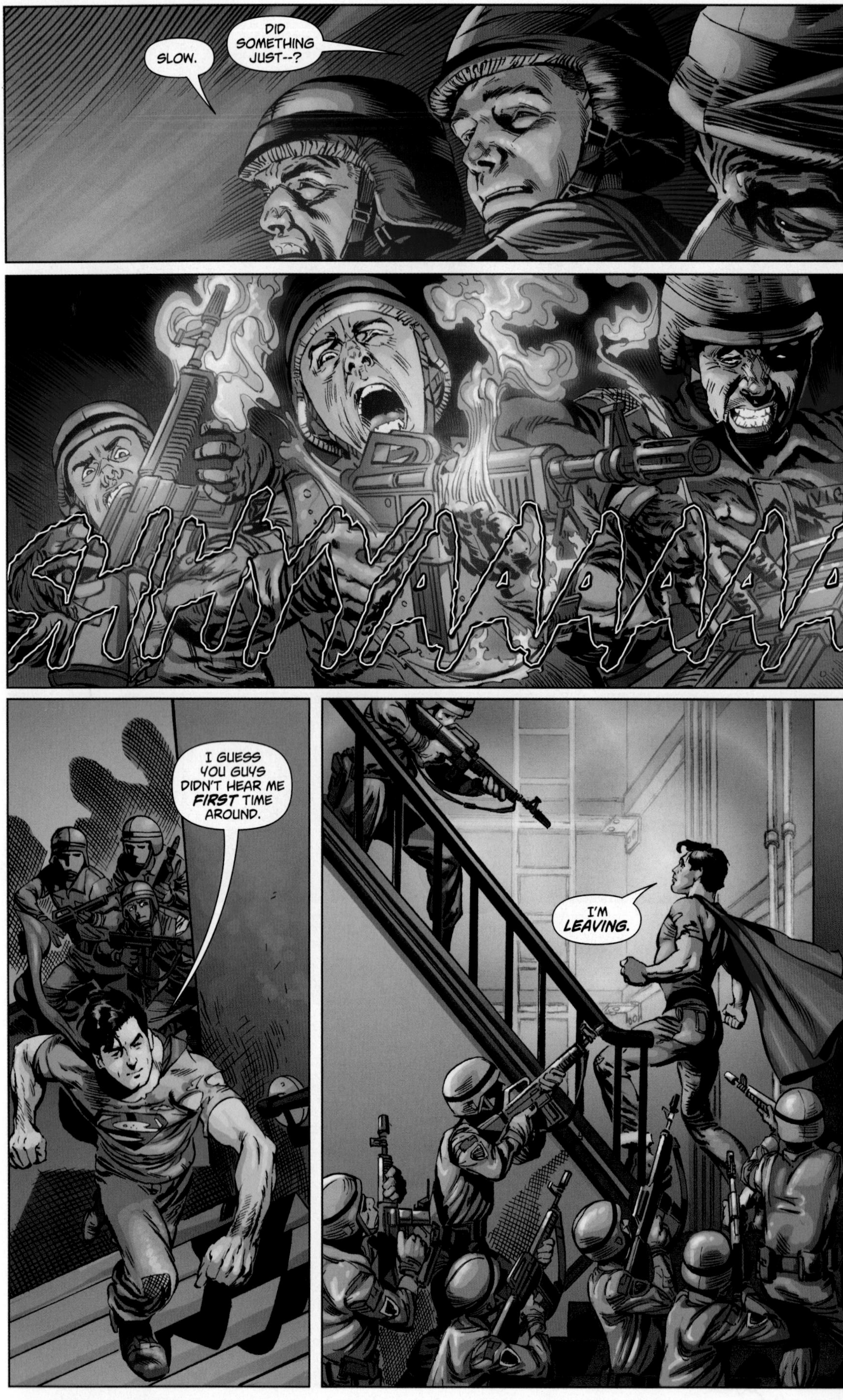
DID SOMETHING JUST--?
SLOW.
SHHHMMMMAAAAA
I GUESS YOU GUYS DIDN'T HEAR ME *FIRST* TIME AROUND.
I'M *LEAVING*.

HE'S IN THE SHAFT!

HM.

HE'S ON THE LOOSE!

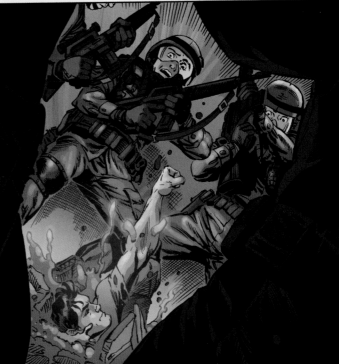

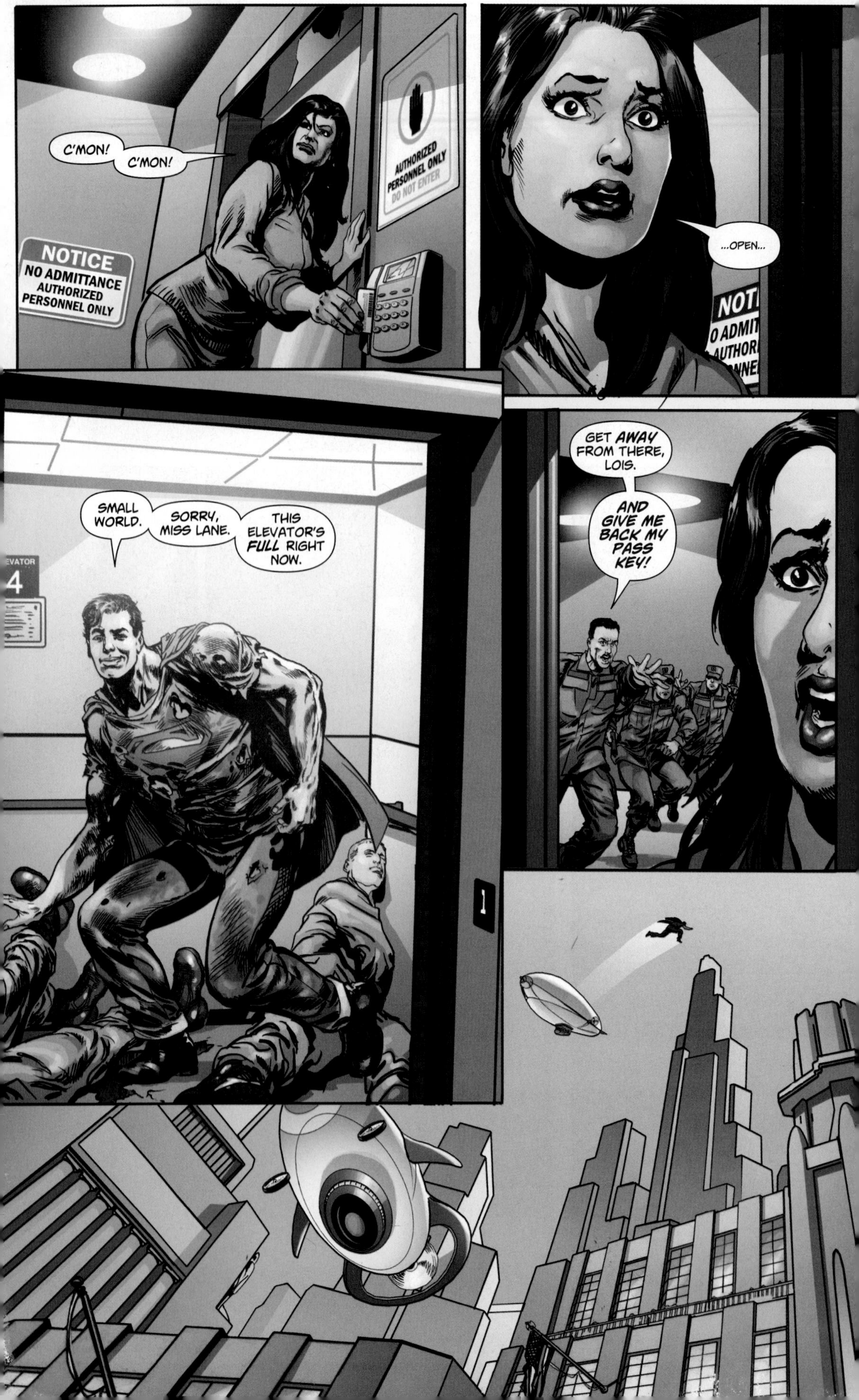
C'MON!
C'MON!
AUTHORIZED PERSONNEL ONLY
DO NOT ENTER
NOTICE
NO ADMITTANCE
AUTHORIZED
PERSONNEL ONLY
...OPEN...
SMALL WORLD.
SORRY, MISS LANE.
THIS ELEVATOR'S ***FULL*** RIGHT NOW.
4
1
GET ***AWAY*** FROM THERE, LOIS.
AND GIVE ME BACK MY PASS KEY!

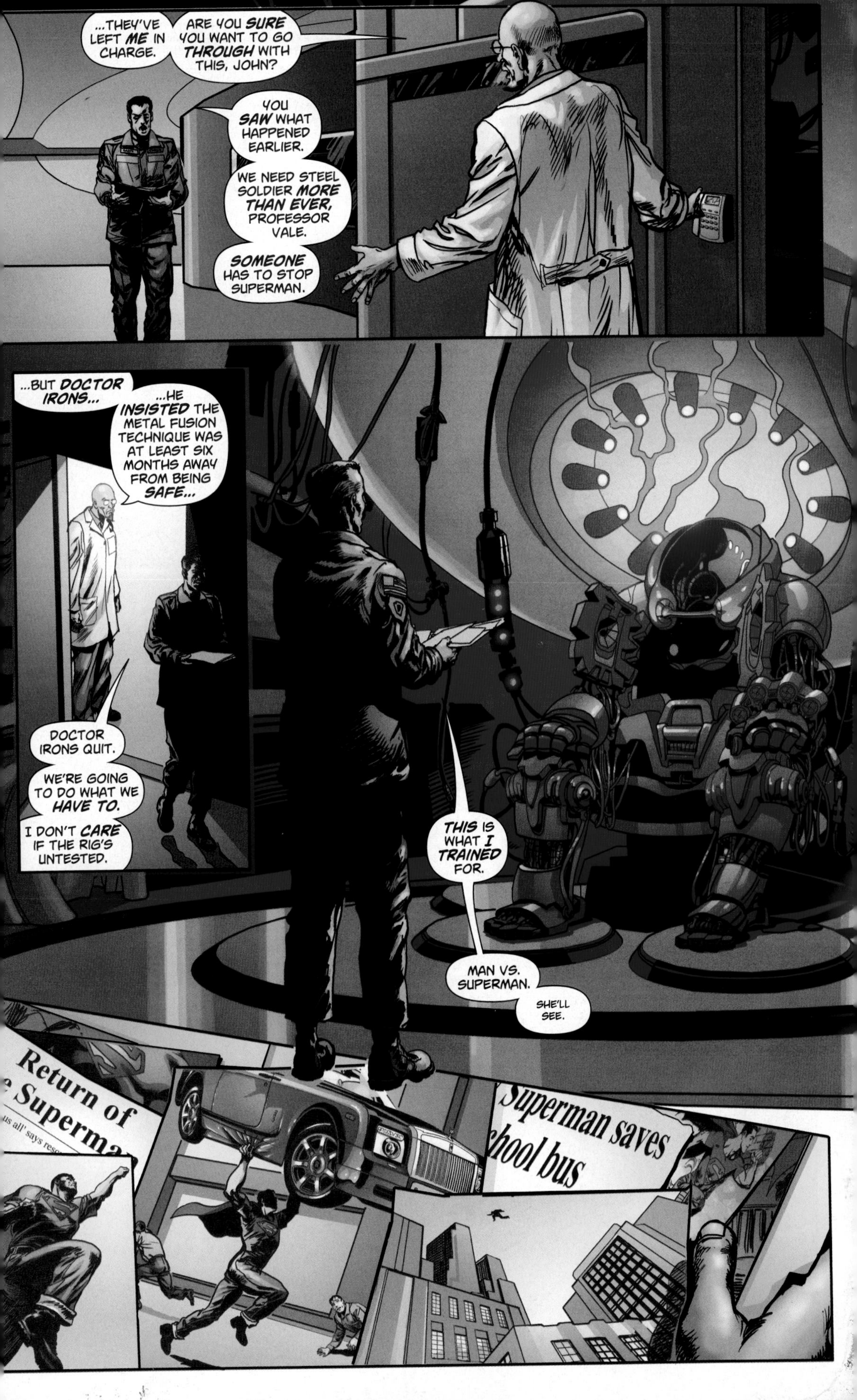

...THEY'VE LEFT ME IN CHARGE.
ARE YOU SURE YOU WANT TO GO THROUGH WITH THIS, JOHN?
YOU SAW WHAT HAPPENED EARLIER.
WE NEED STEEL SOLDIER MORE THAN EVER, PROFESSOR VALE.
SOMEONE HAS TO STOP SUPERMAN.
...BUT DOCTOR IRONS...
...HE INSISTED THE METAL FUSION TECHNIQUE WAS AT LEAST SIX MONTHS AWAY FROM BEING SAFE...
DOCTOR IRONS QUIT.
WE'RE GOING TO DO WHAT WE HAVE TO.
I DON'T CARE IF THE RIG'S UNTESTED.
THIS IS WHAT I TRAINED FOR.
MAN VS. SUPERMAN.
SHE'LL SEE.
Return of
e Superma
Superman saves
hool bus

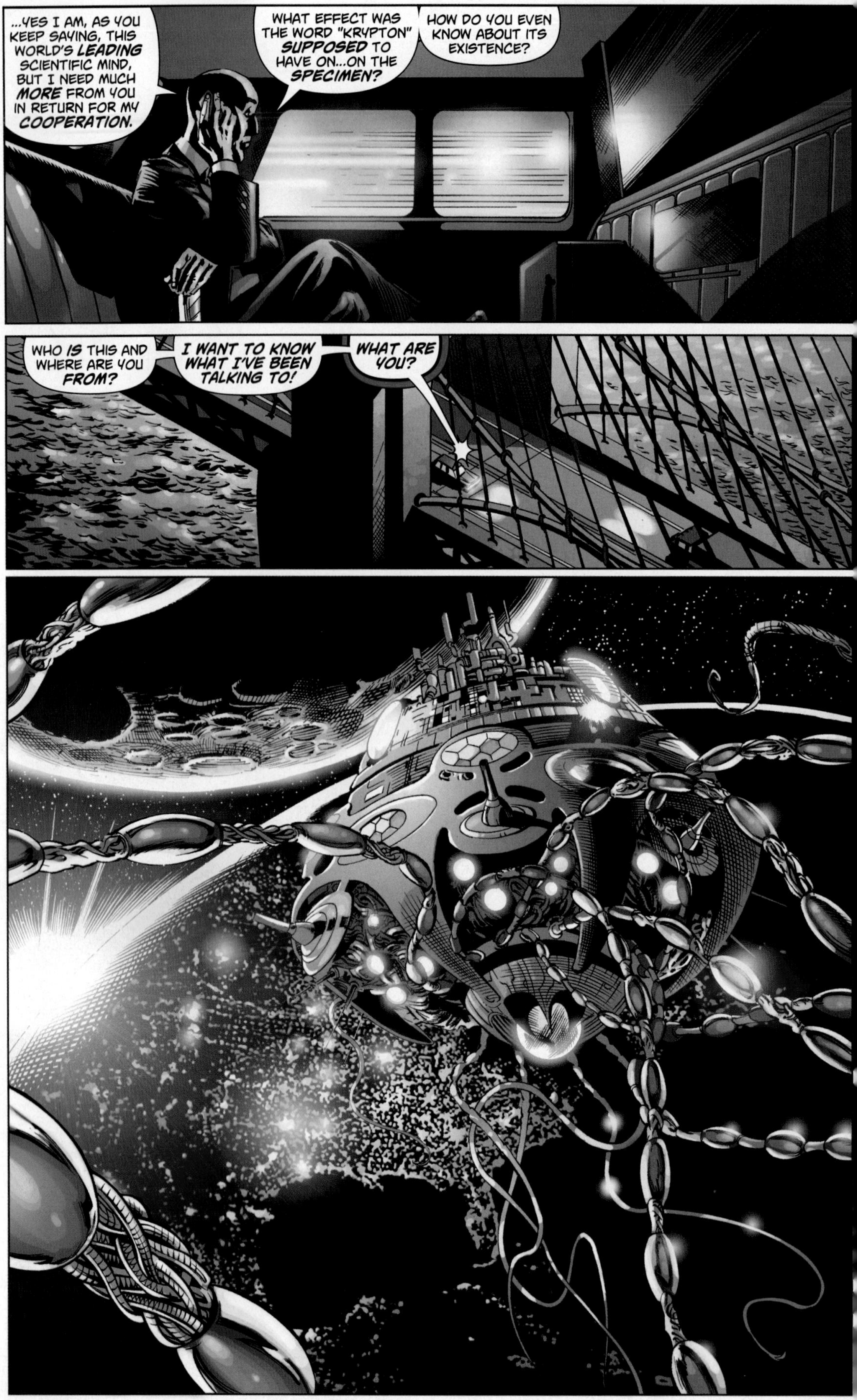
...YES I AM, AS YOU KEEP SAYING, THIS WORLD'S LEADING SCIENTIFIC MIND, BUT I NEED MUCH MORE FROM YOU IN RETURN FOR MY COOPERATION.
WHAT EFFECT WAS THE WORD "KRYPTON" SUPPOSED TO HAVE ON...ON THE SPECIMEN?
HOW DO YOU EVEN KNOW ABOUT ITS EXISTENCE?
WHO IS THIS AND WHERE ARE YOU FROM?
I WANT TO KNOW WHAT I'VE BEEN TALKING TO!
WHAT ARE YOU?

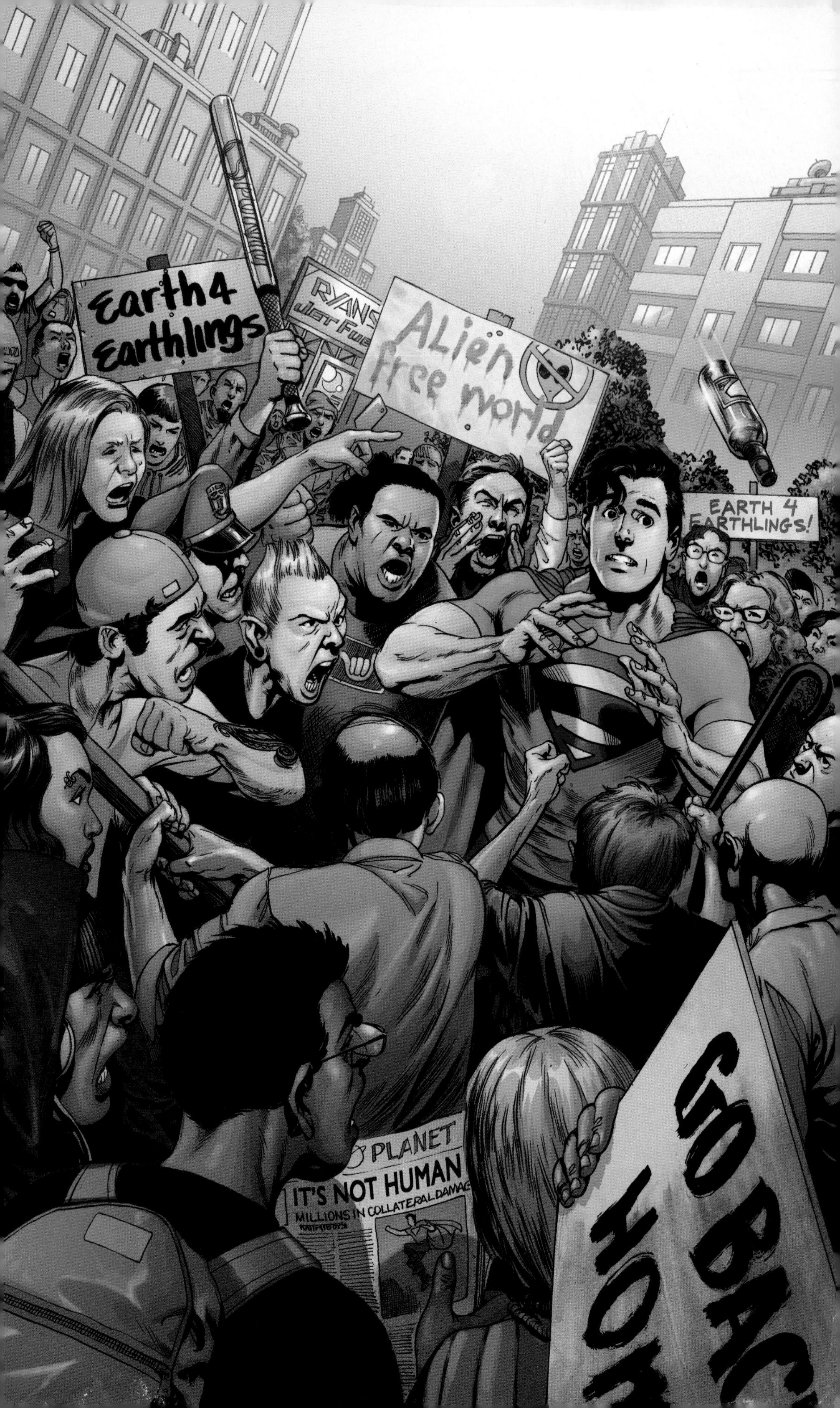
Earth 4 Earthlings
RYANS
Alien free world
EARTH 4 EARTHLINGS!
PLANET
IT'S NOT HUMAN
MILLIONS IN COLLATERAL DAMAG

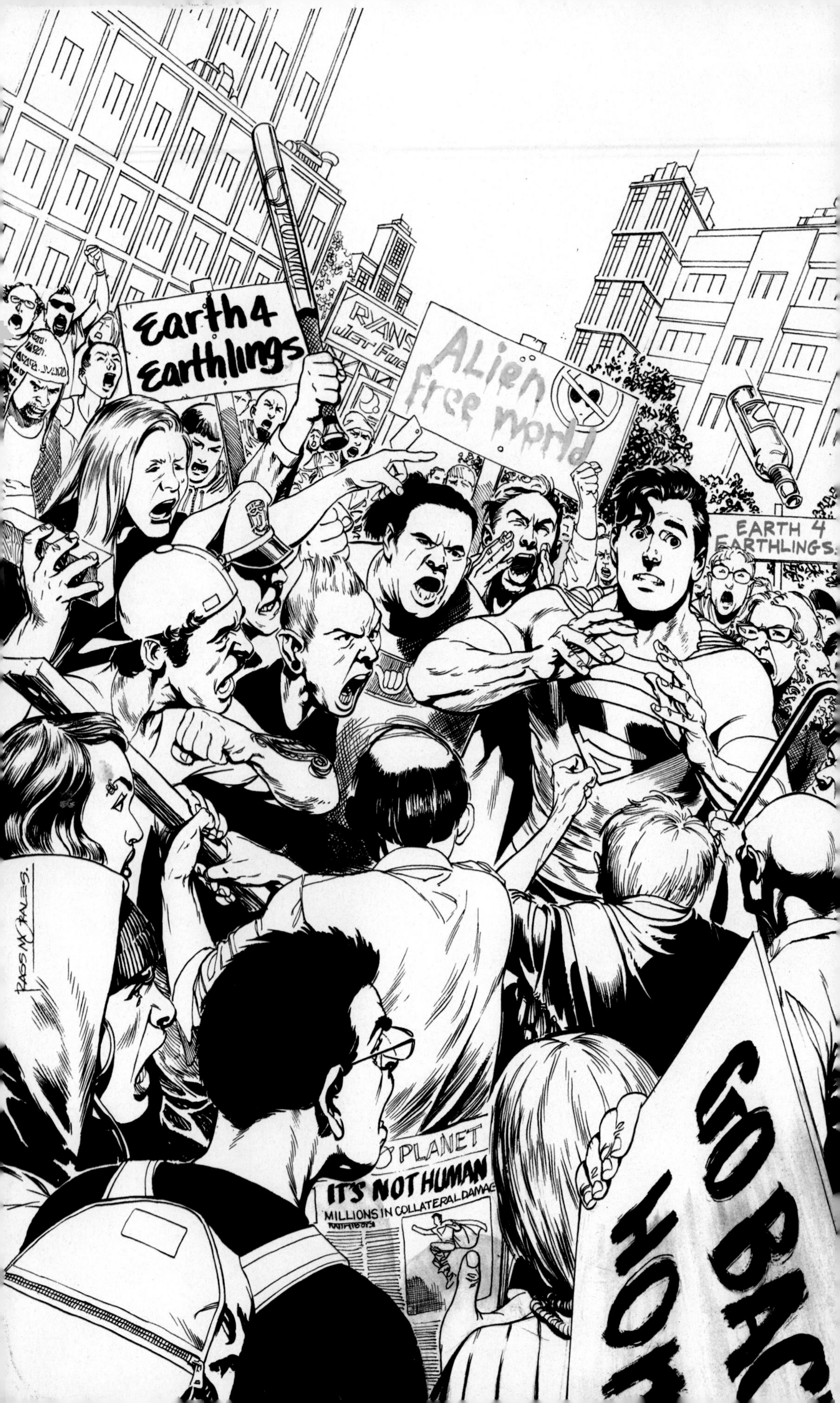
Earth 4 Earthlings
Alien free world
RYANS
EARTH 4 EARTHLINGS
PLANET
IT'S NOT HUMAN
MILLIONS IN COLLATERAL DAMAG
GO BAC
HO

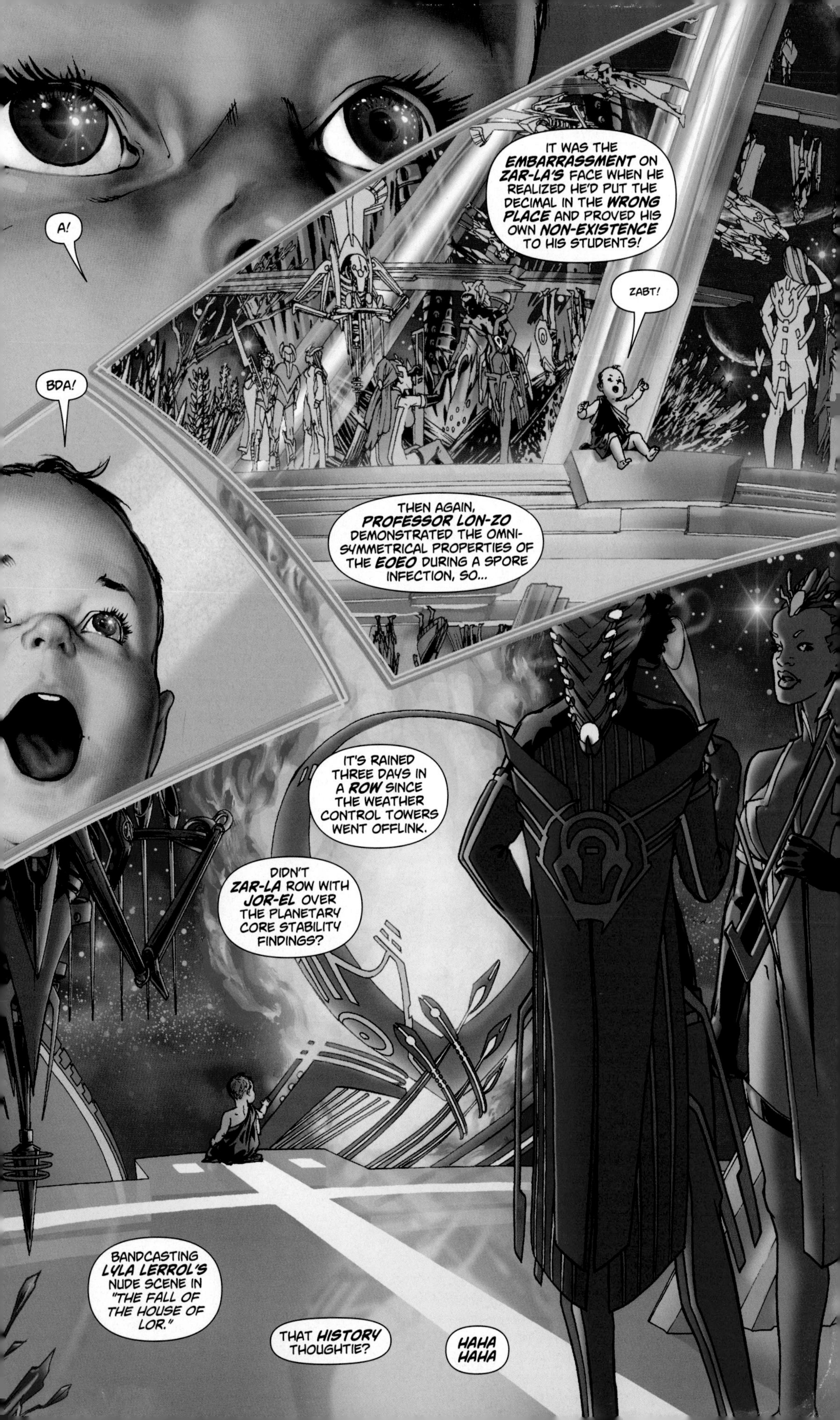

A!
IT WAS THE EMBARRASSMENT ON ZAR-LA'S FACE WHEN HE REALIZED HE'D PUT THE DECIMAL IN THE WRONG PLACE AND PROVED HIS OWN NON-EXISTENCE TO HIS STUDENTS!
ZABT!
BDA!
THEN AGAIN, PROFESSOR LON-ZO DEMONSTRATED THE OMNI-SYMMETRICAL PROPERTIES OF THE EOEO DURING A SPORE INFECTION, SO...
IT'S RAINED THREE DAYS IN A ROW SINCE THE WEATHER CONTROL TOWERS WENT OFFLINK.
DIDN'T ZAR-LA ROW WITH JOR-EL OVER THE PLANETARY CORE STABILITY FINDINGS?
BANDCASTING LYLA LERROL'S NUDE SCENE IN "THE FALL OF THE HOUSE OF LOR."
THAT HISTORY THOUGHTIE?
HAHA HAHA

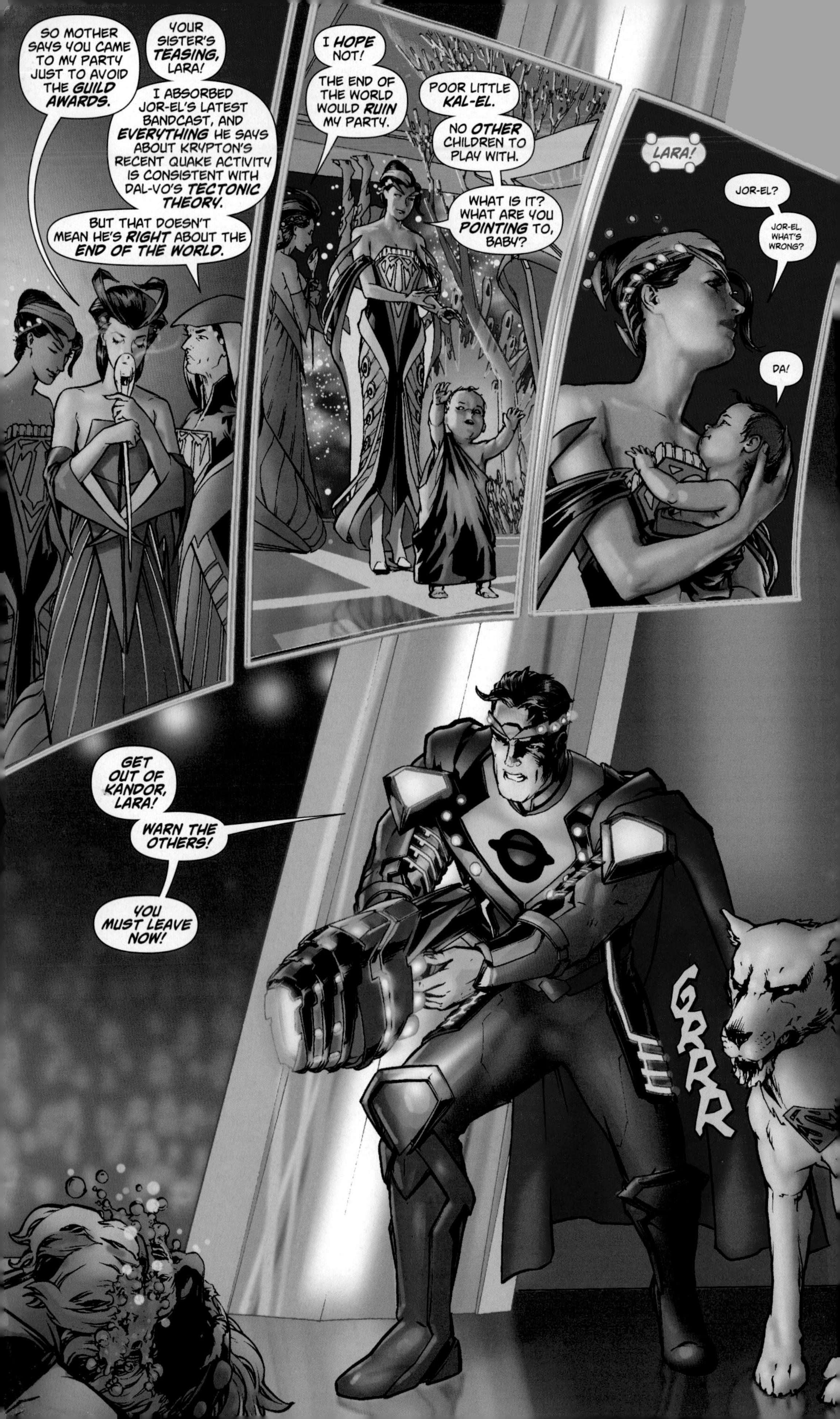
SO MOTHER SAYS YOU CAME TO MY PARTY JUST TO AVOID THE GUILD AWARDS.
YOUR SISTER'S TEASING, LARA!
I ABSORBED JOR-EL'S LATEST BANDCAST, AND EVERYTHING HE SAYS ABOUT KRYPTON'S RECENT QUAKE ACTIVITY IS CONSISTENT WITH DAL-VO'S TECTONIC THEORY.
BUT THAT DOESN'T MEAN HE'S RIGHT ABOUT THE END OF THE WORLD.
I HOPE NOT!
THE END OF THE WORLD WOULD RUIN MY PARTY.
POOR LITTLE KAL-EL.
NO OTHER CHILDREN TO PLAY WITH.
WHAT IS IT? WHAT ARE YOU POINTING TO, BABY?
LARA!
JOR-EL?
JOR-EL, WHAT'S WRONG?
DA!
GET OUT OF KANDOR, LARA!
WARN THE OTHERS!
YOU MUST LEAVE NOW!
GRRR

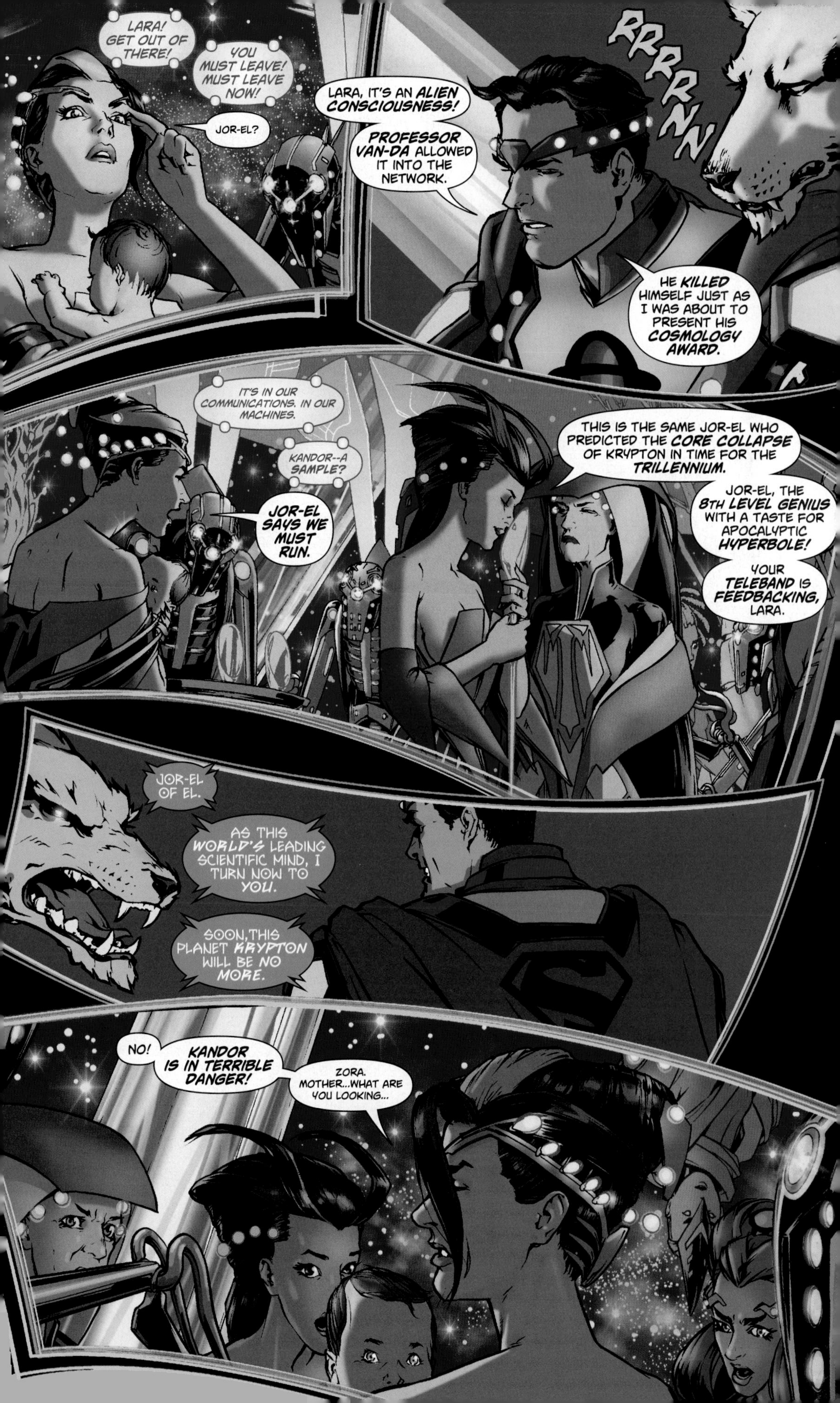

LARA! GET OUT OF THERE!
YOU MUST LEAVE! MUST LEAVE NOW!
JOR-EL?
LARA, IT'S AN ALIEN CONSCIOUSNESS!
PROFESSOR VAN-DA ALLOWED IT INTO THE NETWORK.
RRRRNN
HE KILLED HIMSELF JUST AS I WAS ABOUT TO PRESENT HIS COSMOLOGY AWARD.
IT'S IN OUR COMMUNICATIONS. IN OUR MACHINES.
KANDOR--A SAMPLE?
JOR-EL SAYS WE MUST RUN.
THIS IS THE SAME JOR-EL WHO PREDICTED THE CORE COLLAPSE OF KRYPTON IN TIME FOR THE TRILLENNIUM.
JOR-EL, THE 8TH LEVEL GENIUS WITH A TASTE FOR APOCALYPTIC HYPERBOLE!
YOUR TELEBAND IS FEEDBACKING, LARA.
JOR-EL OF EL.
AS THIS WORLD'S LEADING SCIENTIFIC MIND, I TURN NOW TO YOU.
SOON, THIS PLANET KRYPTON WILL BE NO MORE.
NO!
KANDOR IS IN TERRIBLE DANGER!
ZORA. MOTHER...WHAT ARE YOU LOOKING...

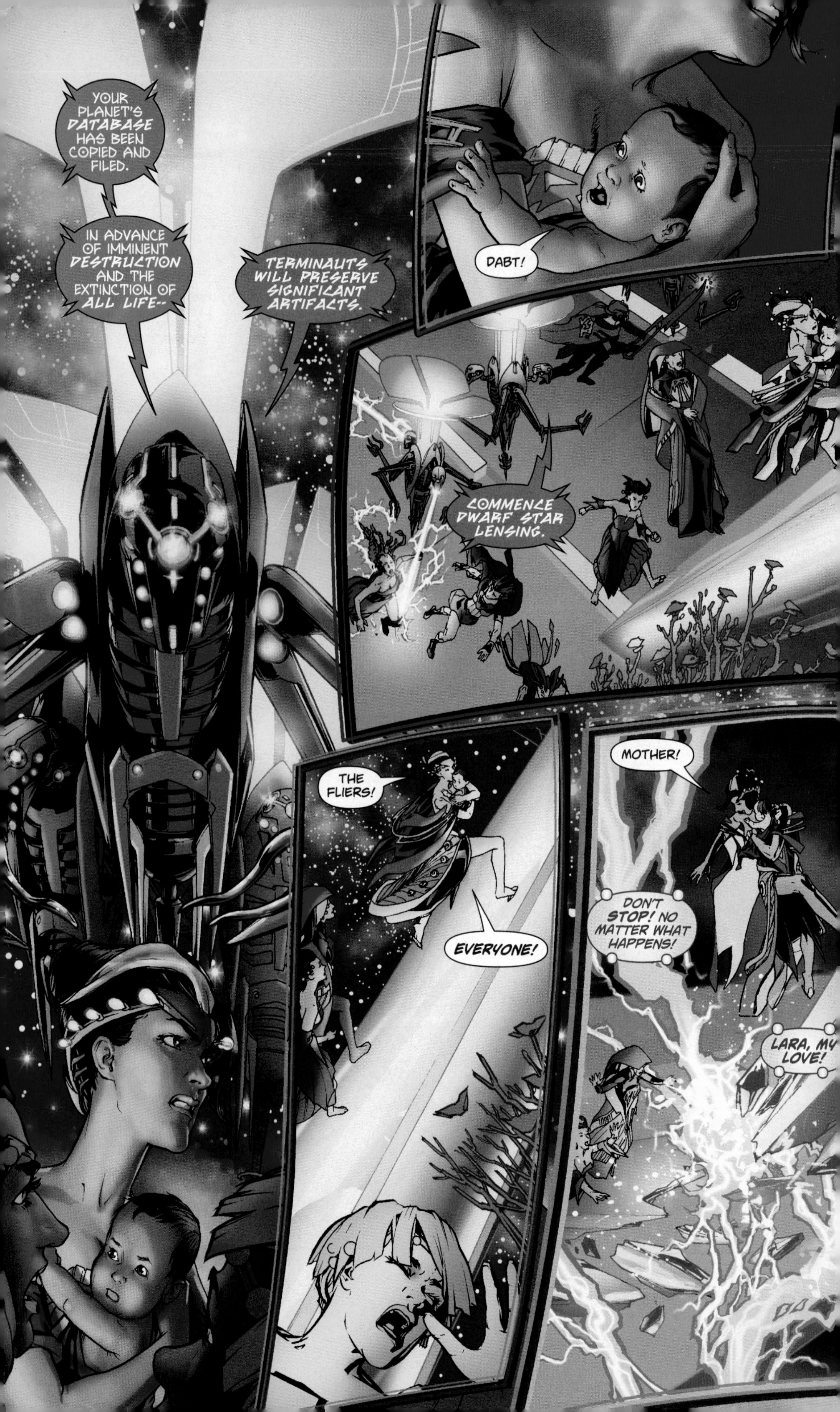
YOUR PLANET'S DATABASE HAS BEEN COPIED AND FILED.
IN ADVANCE OF IMMINENT DESTRUCTION AND THE EXTINCTION OF ALL LIFE--
TERMINAUTS WILL PRESERVE SIGNIFICANT ARTIFACTS.
DABT!
COMMENCE DWARF STAR LENSING.
THE FLIERS!
EVERYONE!
MOTHER!
DON'T STOP! NO MATTER WHAT HAPPENS!
LARA, MY LOVE!

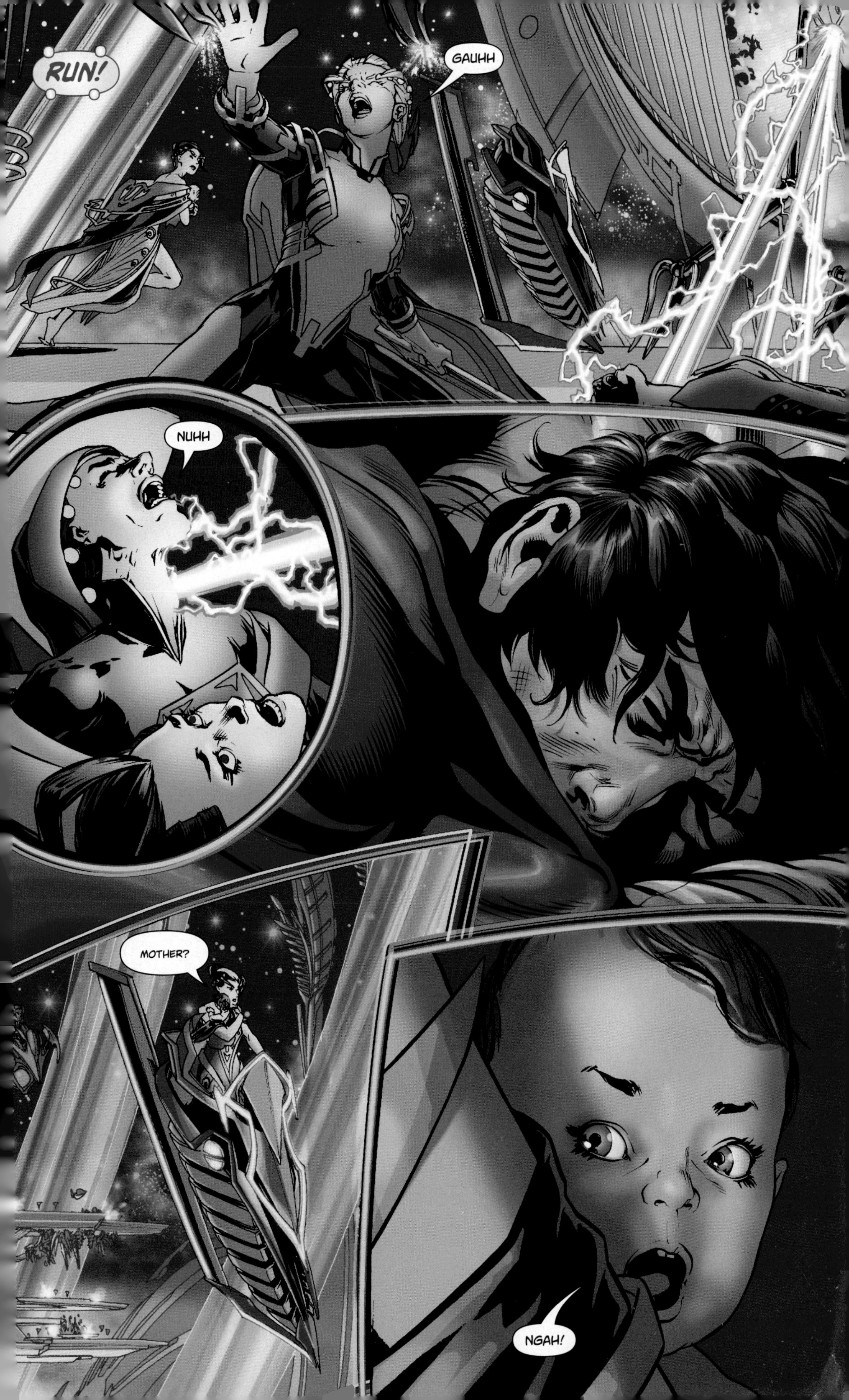
RUN!
GAUHH
NUHH
MOTHER?
NGAH!

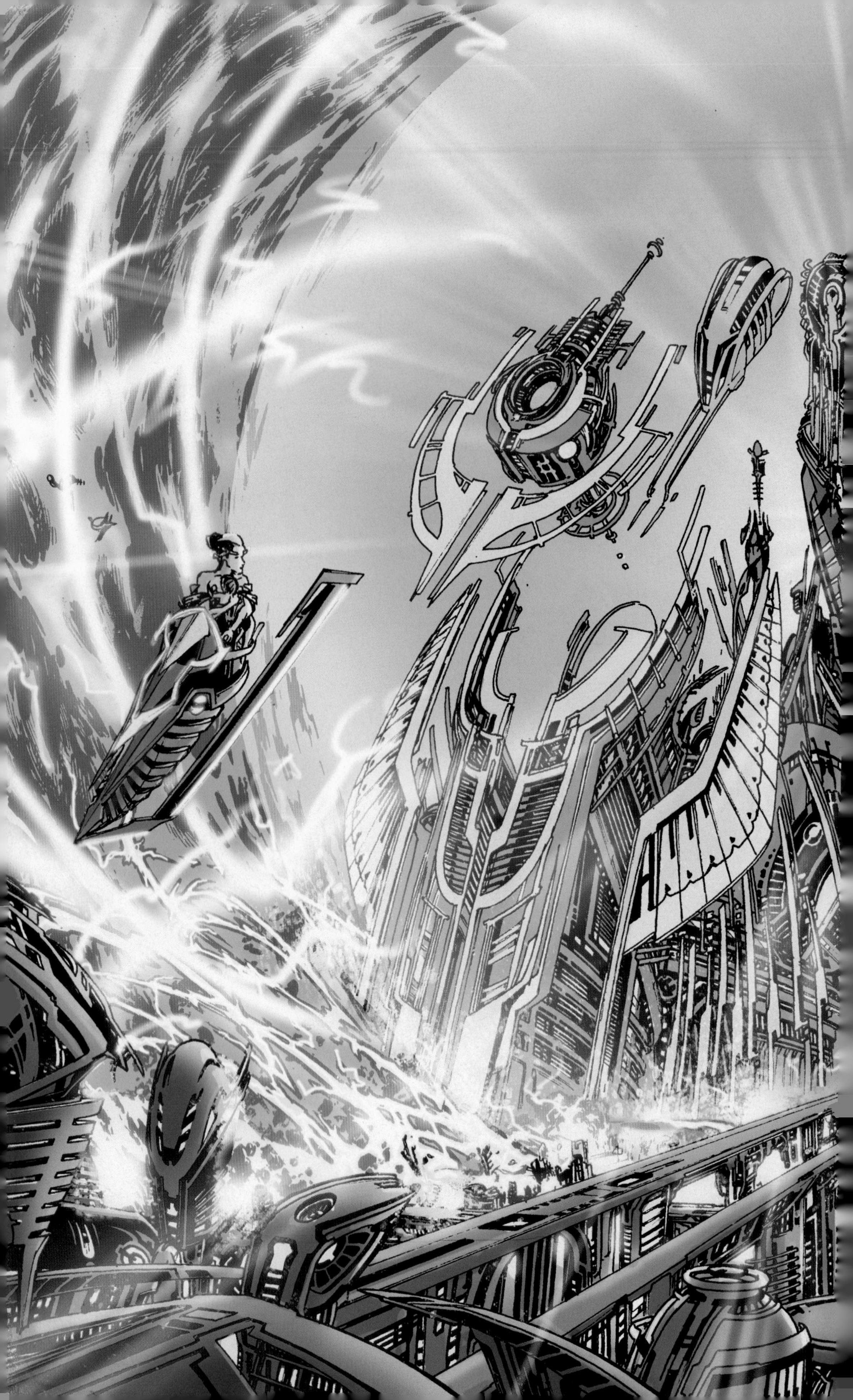

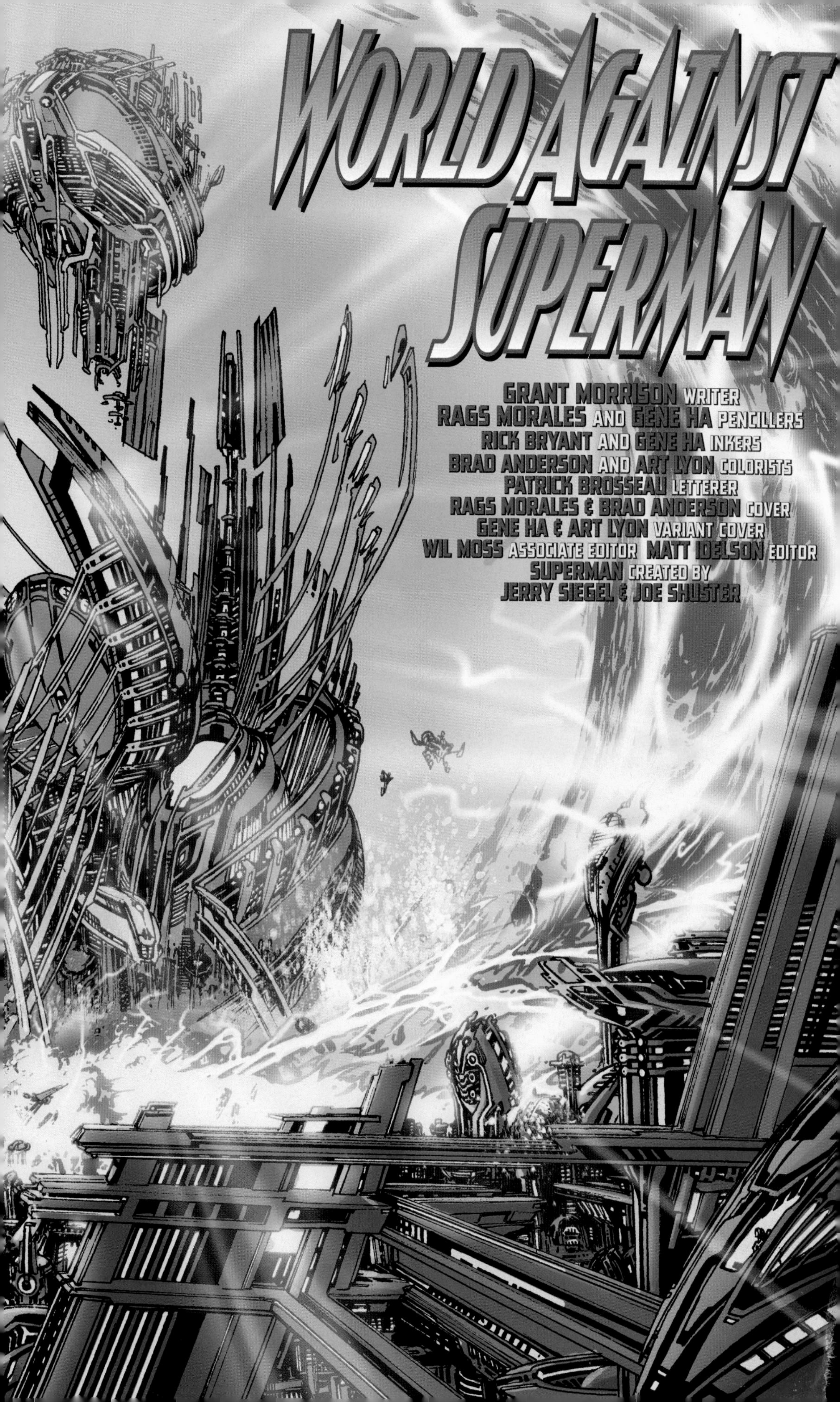
WORLD AGAINST SUPERMAN
GRANT MORRISON WRITER
RAGS MORALES AND GENE HA PENCILLERS
RICK BRYANT AND GENE HA INKERS
BRAD ANDERSON AND ART LYON COLORISTS
PATRICK BROSSEAU LETTERER
RAGS MORALES & BRAD ANDERSON COVER
GENE HA & ART LYON VARIANT COVER
WIL MOSS ASSOCIATE EDITOR MATT IDELSON EDITOR
SUPERMAN CREATED BY
JERRY SIEGEL & JOE SHUSTER

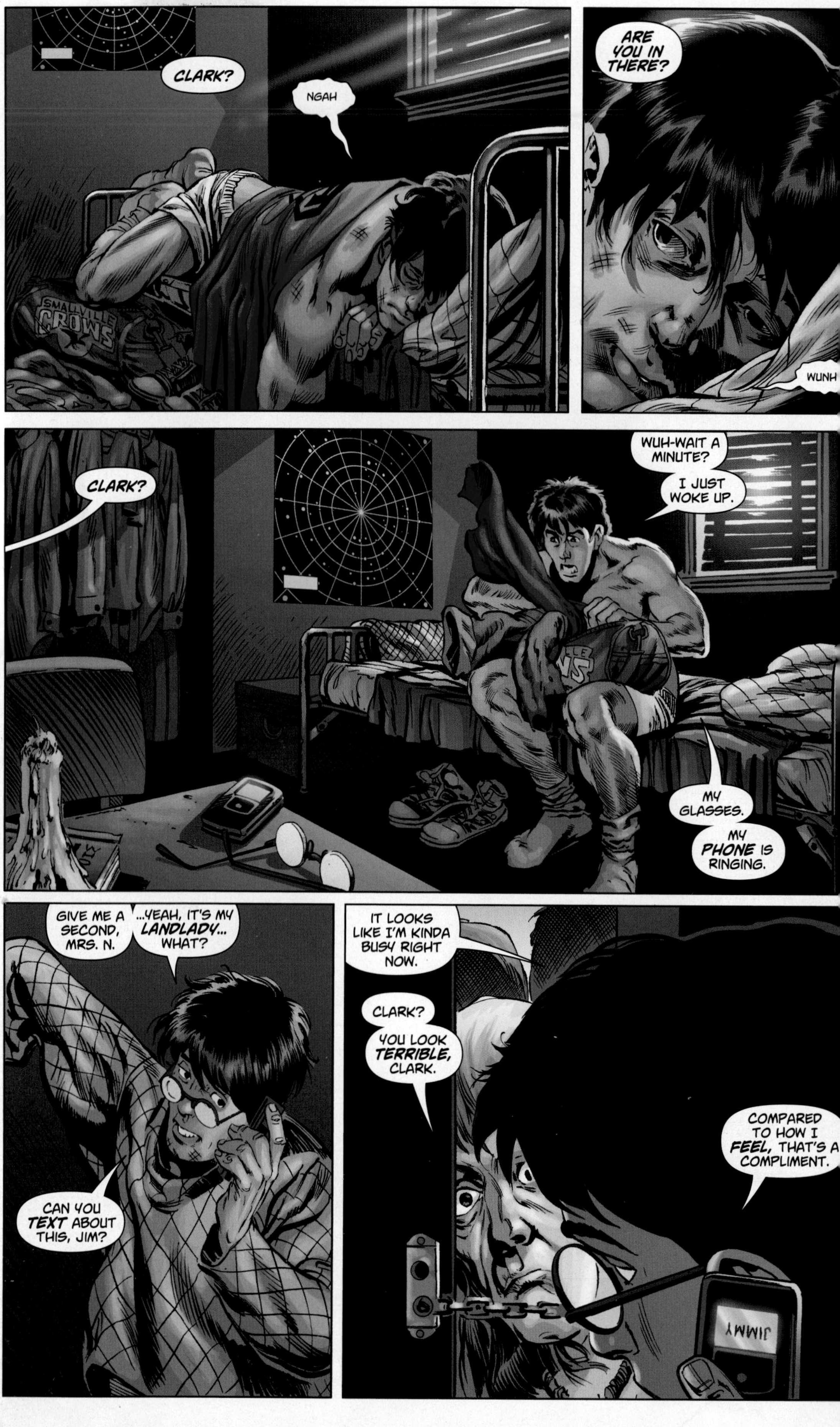

CLARK?
NGAH
ARE YOU IN THERE?
WUNH
CLARK?
WUH-WAIT A MINUTE?
I JUST WOKE UP.
MY GLASSES.
MY PHONE IS RINGING.
GIVE ME A SECOND, MRS. N.
...YEAH, IT'S MY LANDLADY... WHAT?
CAN YOU TEXT ABOUT THIS, JIM?
IT LOOKS LIKE I'M KINDA BUSY RIGHT NOW.
CLARK?
YOU LOOK TERRIBLE, CLARK.
COMPARED TO HOW I FEEL, THAT'S A COMPLIMENT.
JIMMY

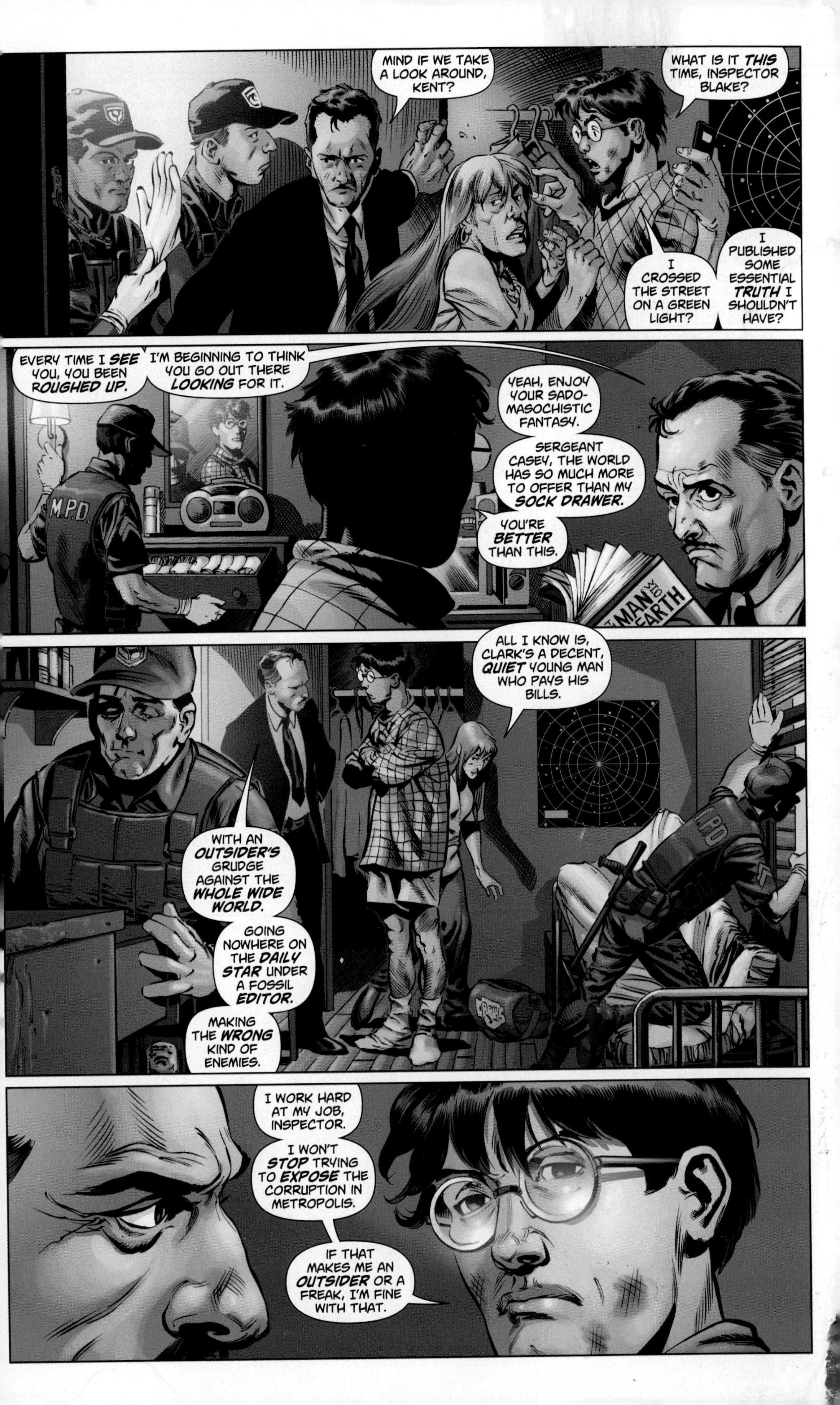

MIND IF WE TAKE A LOOK AROUND, KENT?
WHAT IS IT THIS TIME, INSPECTOR BLAKE?
I CROSSED THE STREET ON A GREEN LIGHT?
I PUBLISHED SOME ESSENTIAL TRUTH I SHOULDN'T HAVE?
EVERY TIME I SEE YOU, YOU BEEN ROUGHED UP.
I'M BEGINNING TO THINK YOU GO OUT THERE LOOKING FOR IT.
YEAH, ENJOY YOUR SADO-MASOCHISTIC FANTASY.
SERGEANT CASEY, THE WORLD HAS SO MUCH MORE TO OFFER THAN MY SOCK DRAWER.
YOU'RE BETTER THAN THIS.
M.P.D.
ALL I KNOW IS, CLARK'S A DECENT, QUIET YOUNG MAN WHO PAYS HIS BILLS.
WITH AN OUTSIDER'S GRUDGE AGAINST THE WHOLE WIDE WORLD.
GOING NOWHERE ON THE DAILY STAR UNDER A FOSSIL EDITOR.
MAKING THE WRONG KIND OF ENEMIES.
I WORK HARD AT MY JOB, INSPECTOR.
I WON'T STOP TRYING TO EXPOSE THE CORRUPTION IN METROPOLIS.
IF THAT MAKES ME AN OUTSIDER OR A FREAK, I'M FINE WITH THAT.

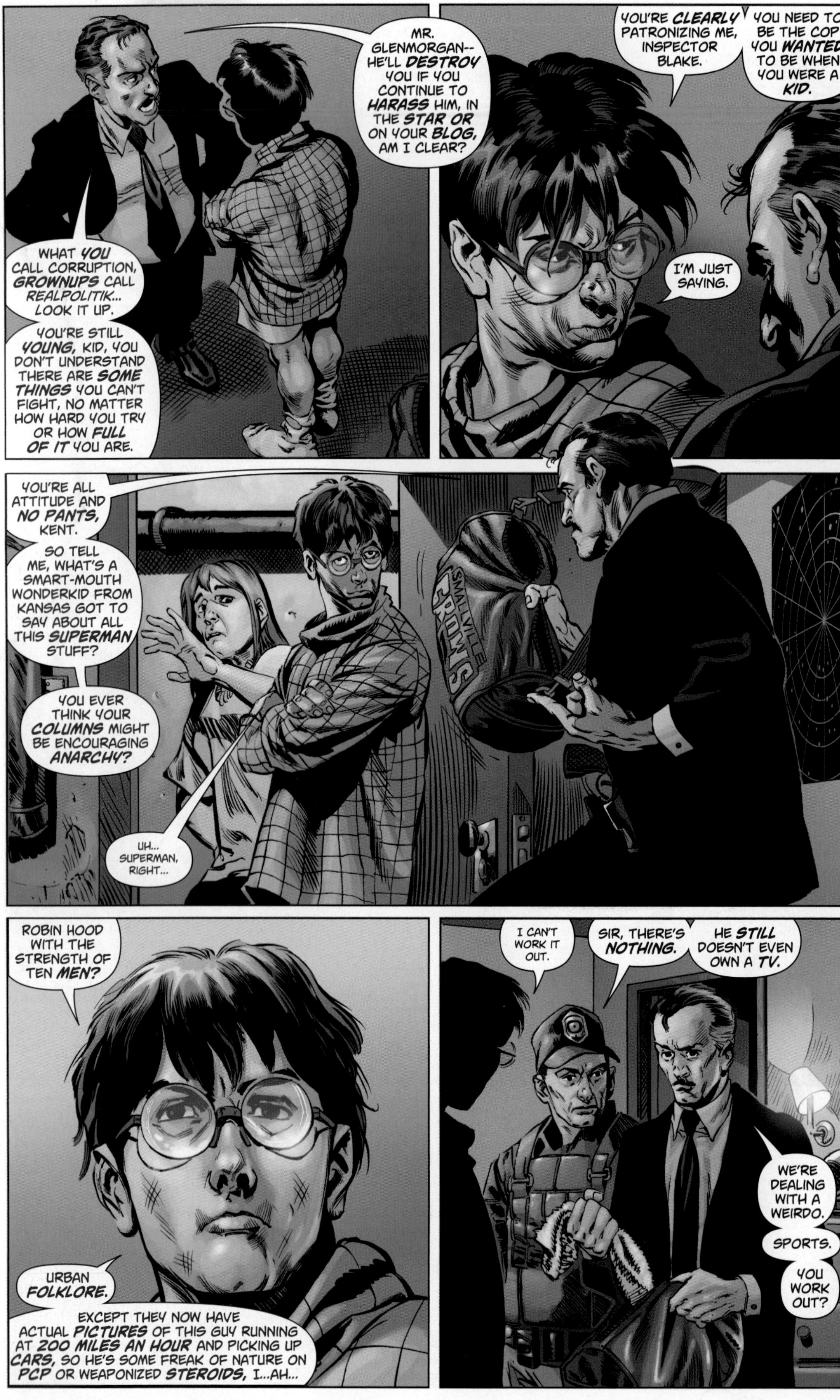
MR. GLENMORGAN-- HE'LL DESTROY YOU IF YOU CONTINUE TO HARASS HIM, IN THE STAR OR ON YOUR BLOG, AM I CLEAR?
WHAT YOU CALL CORRUPTION, GROWNUPS CALL REALPOLITIK... LOOK IT UP.
YOU'RE STILL YOUNG, KID, YOU DON'T UNDERSTAND THERE ARE SOME THINGS YOU CAN'T FIGHT, NO MATTER HOW HARD YOU TRY OR HOW FULL OF IT YOU ARE.
YOU'RE CLEARLY PATRONIZING ME, INSPECTOR BLAKE.
YOU NEED TO BE THE COP YOU WANTED TO BE WHEN YOU WERE A KID.
I'M JUST SAYING.
YOU'RE ALL ATTITUDE AND NO PANTS, KENT.
SO TELL ME, WHAT'S A SMART-MOUTH WONDERKID FROM KANSAS GOT TO SAY ABOUT ALL THIS SUPERMAN STUFF?
YOU EVER THINK YOUR COLUMNS MIGHT BE ENCOURAGING ANARCHY?
UH... SUPERMAN, RIGHT...
SMALLVILLE CROWS
ROBIN HOOD WITH THE STRENGTH OF TEN MEN?
URBAN FOLKLORE.
EXCEPT THEY NOW HAVE ACTUAL PICTURES OF THIS GUY RUNNING AT 200 MILES AN HOUR AND PICKING UP CARS, SO HE'S SOME FREAK OF NATURE ON PCP OR WEAPONIZED STEROIDS, I...AH...
I CAN'T WORK IT OUT.
SIR, THERE'S NOTHING.
HE STILL DOESN'T EVEN OWN A TV.
WE'RE DEALING WITH A WEIRDO.
SPORTS.
YOU WORK OUT?

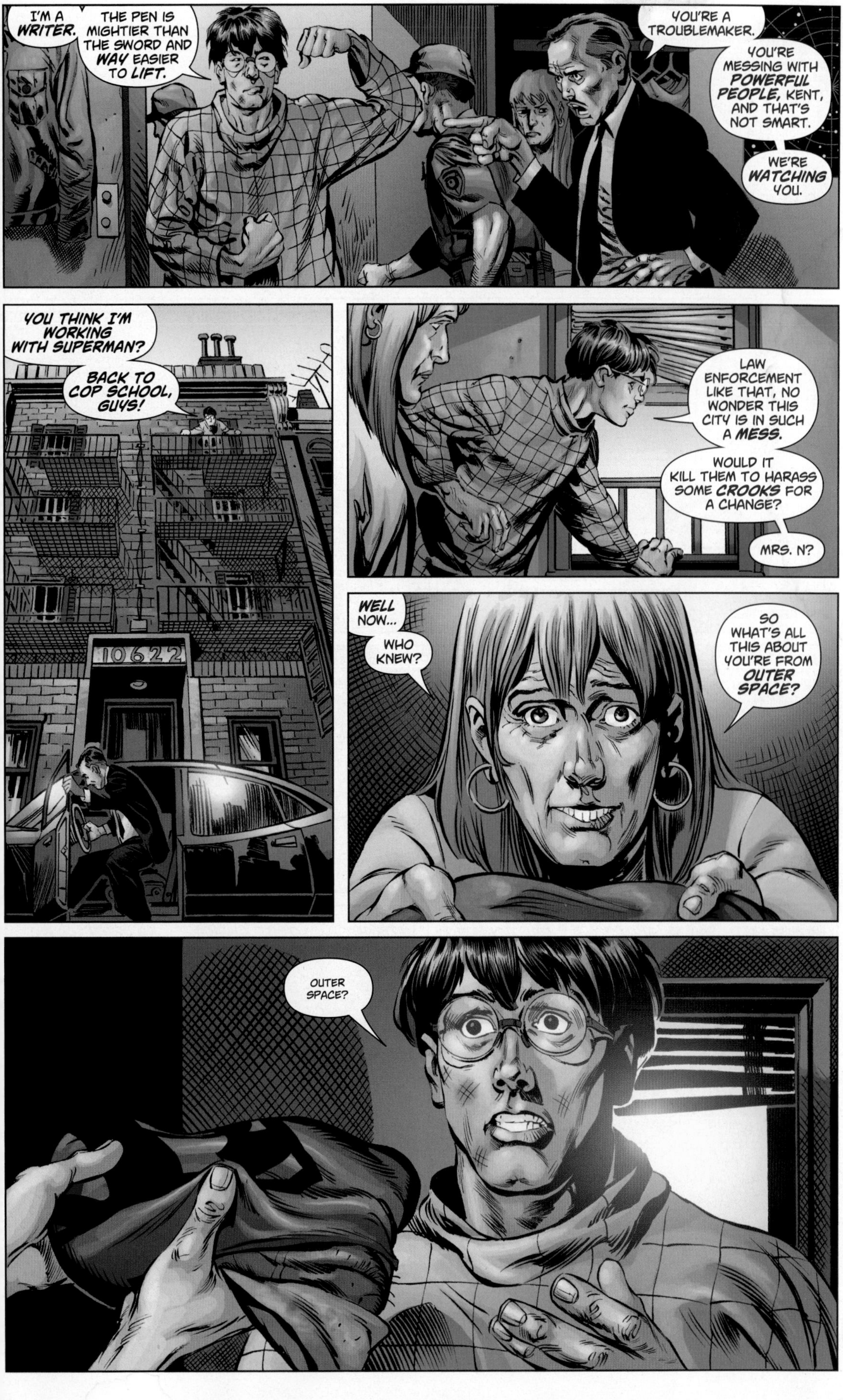
I'M A WRITER.
THE PEN IS MIGHTIER THAN THE SWORD AND WAY EASIER TO LIFT.
YOU'RE A TROUBLEMAKER.
YOU'RE MESSING WITH POWERFUL PEOPLE, KENT, AND THAT'S NOT SMART.
WE'RE WATCHING YOU.
YOU THINK I'M WORKING WITH SUPERMAN?
BACK TO COP SCHOOL, GUYS!
10622
LAW ENFORCEMENT LIKE THAT, NO WONDER THIS CITY IS IN SUCH A MESS.
WOULD IT KILL THEM TO HARASS SOME CROOKS FOR A CHANGE?
MRS. N?
WELL NOW...
WHO KNEW?
SO WHAT'S ALL THIS ABOUT YOU'RE FROM OUTER SPACE?
OUTER SPACE?

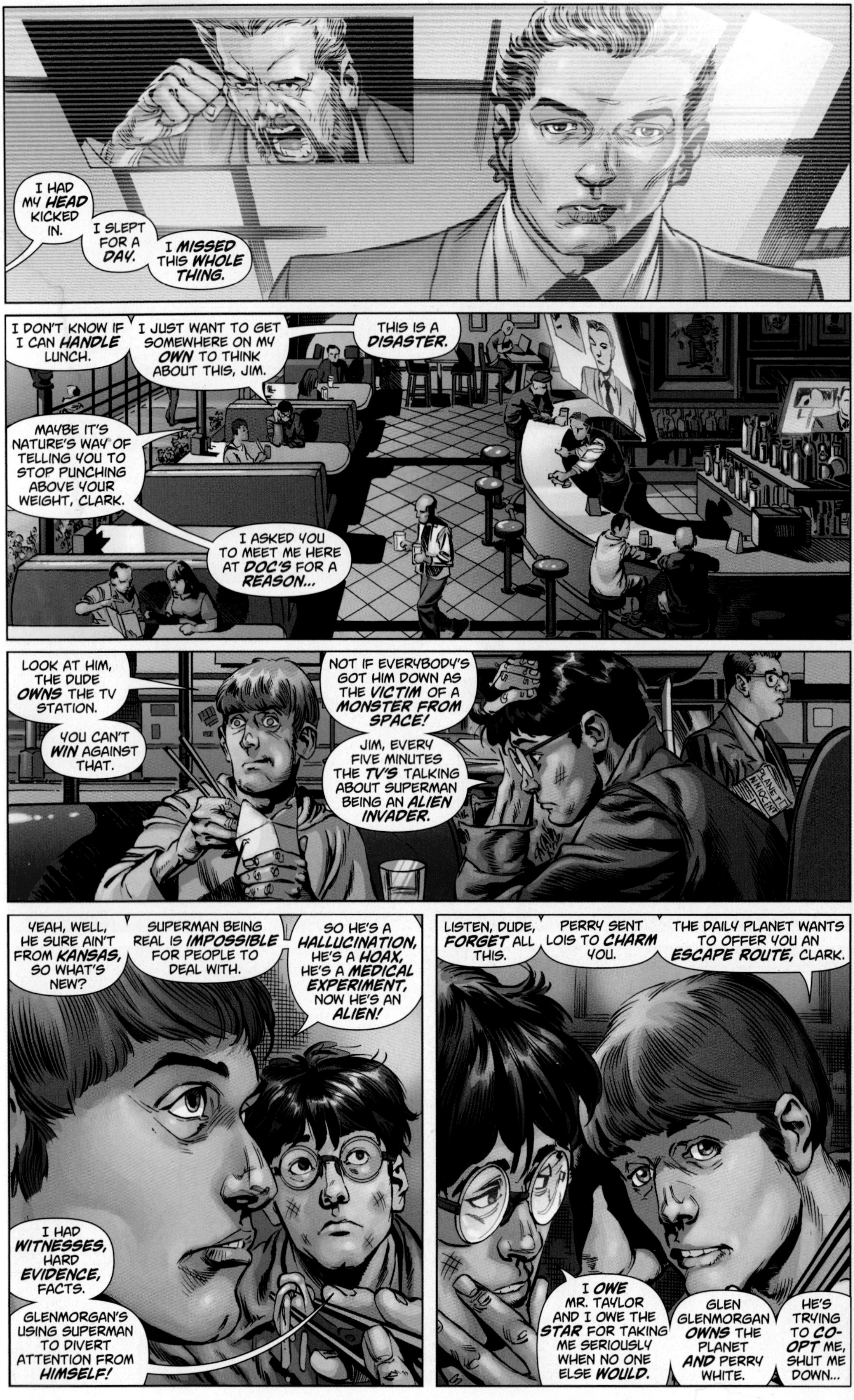

I HAD MY HEAD KICKED IN.
I SLEPT FOR A DAY.
I MISSED THIS WHOLE THING.
I DON'T KNOW IF I CAN HANDLE LUNCH.
I JUST WANT TO GET SOMEWHERE ON MY OWN TO THINK ABOUT THIS, JIM.
THIS IS A DISASTER.
MAYBE IT'S NATURE'S WAY OF TELLING YOU TO STOP PUNCHING ABOVE YOUR WEIGHT, CLARK.
I ASKED YOU TO MEET ME HERE AT DOC'S FOR A REASON...
LOOK AT HIM, THE DUDE OWNS THE TV STATION.
YOU CAN'T WIN AGAINST THAT.
NOT IF EVERYBODY'S GOT HIM DOWN AS THE VICTIM OF A MONSTER FROM SPACE!
JIM, EVERY FIVE MINUTES THE TV'S TALKING ABOUT SUPERMAN BEING AN ALIEN INVADER.
YEAH, WELL, HE SURE AIN'T FROM KANSAS, SO WHAT'S NEW?
SUPERMAN BEING REAL IS IMPOSSIBLE FOR PEOPLE TO DEAL WITH.
SO HE'S A HALLUCINATION, HE'S A HOAX, HE'S A MEDICAL EXPERIMENT, NOW HE'S AN ALIEN!
I HAD WITNESSES, HARD EVIDENCE, FACTS.
GLENMORGAN'S USING SUPERMAN TO DIVERT ATTENTION FROM HIMSELF!
LISTEN, DUDE, FORGET ALL THIS.
PERRY SENT LOIS TO CHARM YOU.
THE DAILY PLANET WANTS TO OFFER YOU AN ESCAPE ROUTE, CLARK.
I OWE MR. TAYLOR AND I OWE THE STAR FOR TAKING ME SERIOUSLY WHEN NO ONE ELSE WOULD.
GLEN GLENMORGAN OWNS THE PLANET AND PERRY WHITE.
HE'S TRYING TO CO-OPT ME, SHUT ME DOWN...

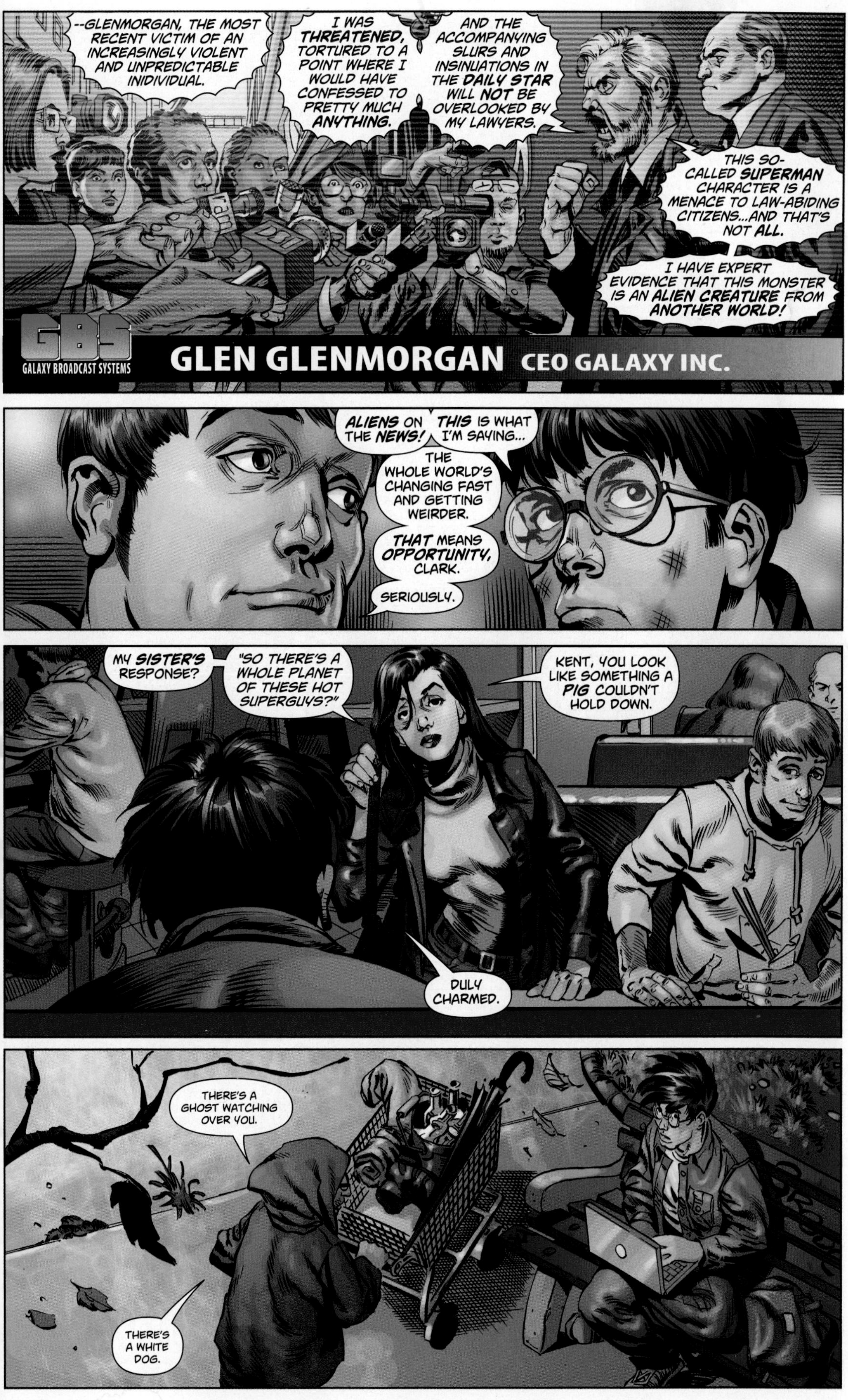
--GLENMORGAN, THE MOST RECENT VICTIM OF AN INCREASINGLY VIOLENT AND UNPREDICTABLE INIDIVIDUAL.
I WAS THREATENED, TORTURED TO A POINT WHERE I WOULD HAVE CONFESSED TO PRETTY MUCH ANYTHING.
AND THE ACCOMPANYING SLURS AND INSINUATIONS IN THE DAILY STAR WILL NOT BE OVERLOOKED BY MY LAWYERS.
THIS SO-CALLED SUPERMAN CHARACTER IS A MENACE TO LAW-ABIDING CITIZENS...AND THAT'S NOT ALL.
I HAVE EXPERT EVIDENCE THAT THIS MONSTER IS AN ALIEN CREATURE FROM ANOTHER WORLD!
GBS
GALAXY BROADCAST SYSTEMS
GLEN GLENMORGAN CEO GALAXY INC.
ALIENS ON THE NEWS!
THIS IS WHAT I'M SAYING...
THE WHOLE WORLD'S CHANGING FAST AND GETTING WEIRDER.
THAT MEANS OPPORTUNITY, CLARK.
SERIOUSLY.
MY SISTER'S RESPONSE?
"SO THERE'S A WHOLE PLANET OF THESE HOT SUPERGUYS?"
KENT, YOU LOOK LIKE SOMETHING A PIG COULDN'T HOLD DOWN.
DULY CHARMED.
THERE'S A GHOST WATCHING OVER YOU.
THERE'S A WHITE DOG.

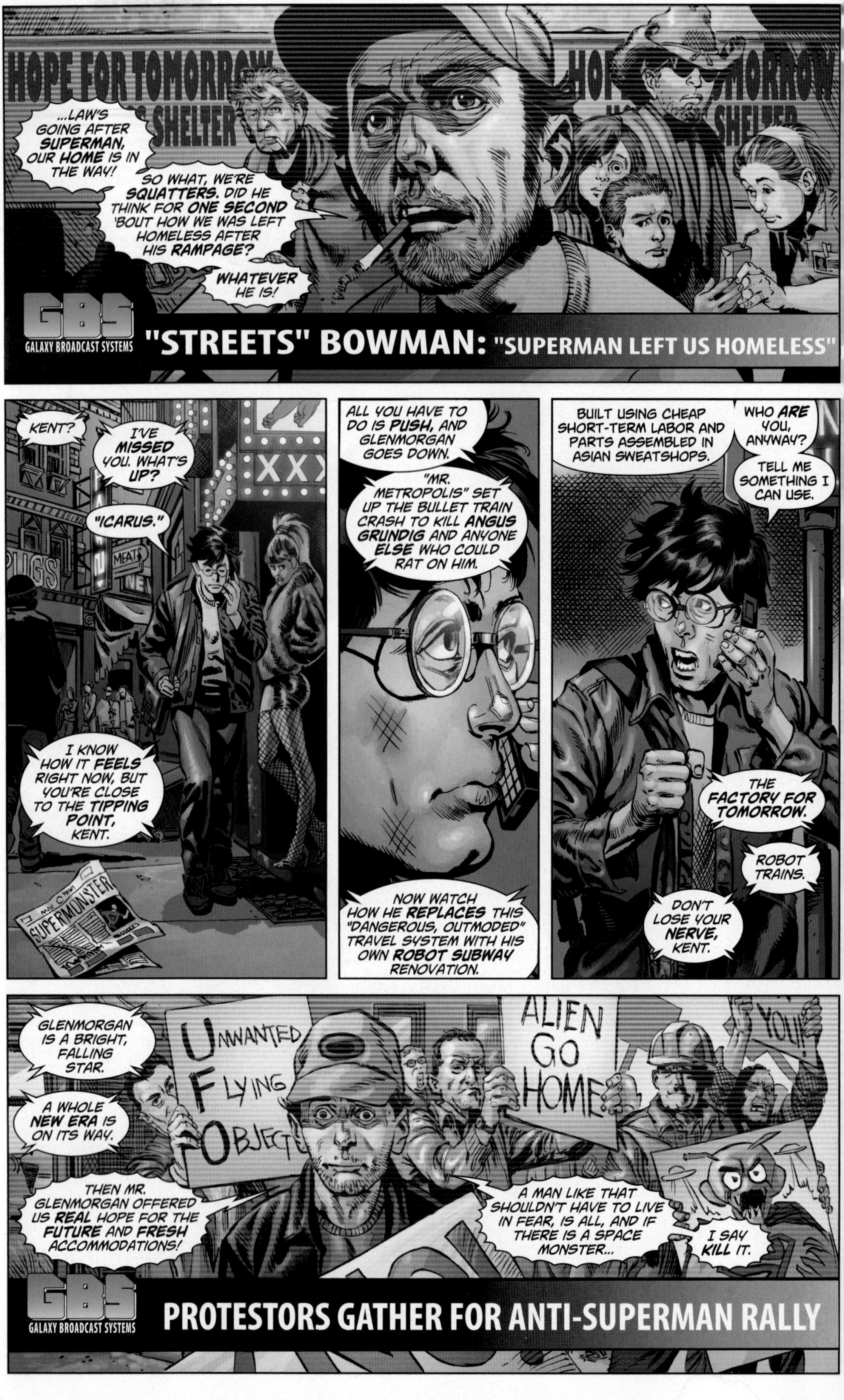
HOPE FOR TOMORROW
SHELTER
...LAW'S GOING AFTER SUPERMAN, OUR HOME IS IN THE WAY!
SO WHAT, WE'RE SQUATTERS. DID HE THINK FOR ONE SECOND 'BOUT HOW WE WAS LEFT HOMELESS AFTER HIS RAMPAGE?
WHATEVER HE IS!
GBS
GALAXY BROADCAST SYSTEMS
"STREETS" BOWMAN: "SUPERMAN LEFT US HOMELESS"
KENT?
I'VE MISSED YOU. WHAT'S UP?
"ICARUS."
XXX
MEATS
I KNOW HOW IT FEELS RIGHT NOW, BUT YOU'RE CLOSE TO THE TIPPING POINT, KENT.
SUPERMONSTER
ALL YOU HAVE TO DO IS PUSH, AND GLENMORGAN GOES DOWN.
"MR. METROPOLIS" SET UP THE BULLET TRAIN CRASH TO KILL ANGUS GRUNDIG AND ANYONE ELSE WHO COULD RAT ON HIM.
NOW WATCH HOW HE REPLACES THIS "DANGEROUS, OUTMODED" TRAVEL SYSTEM WITH HIS OWN ROBOT SUBWAY RENOVATION.
BUILT USING CHEAP SHORT-TERM LABOR AND PARTS ASSEMBLED IN ASIAN SWEATSHOPS.
WHO ARE YOU, ANYWAY?
TELL ME SOMETHING I CAN USE.
THE FACTORY FOR TOMORROW.
ROBOT TRAINS.
DON'T LOSE YOUR NERVE, KENT.
GLENMORGAN IS A BRIGHT, FALLING STAR.
A WHOLE NEW ERA IS ON ITS WAY.
UNWANTED FLYING OBJECT
ALIEN GO HOME
YOU!
THEN MR. GLENMORGAN OFFERED US REAL HOPE FOR THE FUTURE AND FRESH ACCOMMODATIONS!
A MAN LIKE THAT SHOULDN'T HAVE TO LIVE IN FEAR, IS ALL, AND IF THERE IS A SPACE MONSTER...
I SAY KILL IT.
GBS
GALAXY BROADCAST SYSTEMS
PROTESTORS GATHER FOR ANTI-SUPERMAN RALLY

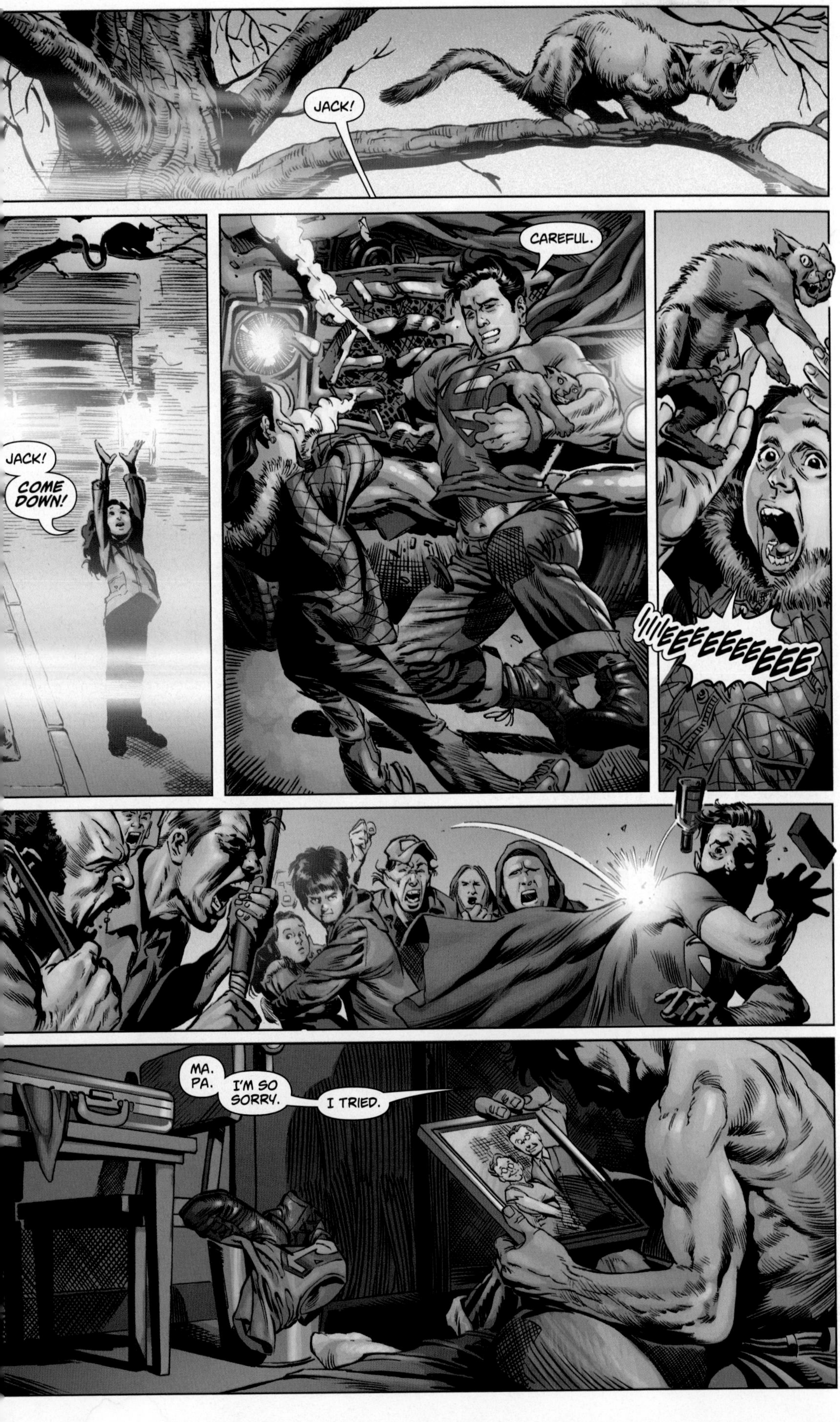
JACK!
JACK!
COME DOWN!
CAREFUL.
WEEEEEEEEEE
MA. PA.
I'M SO SORRY.
I TRIED.

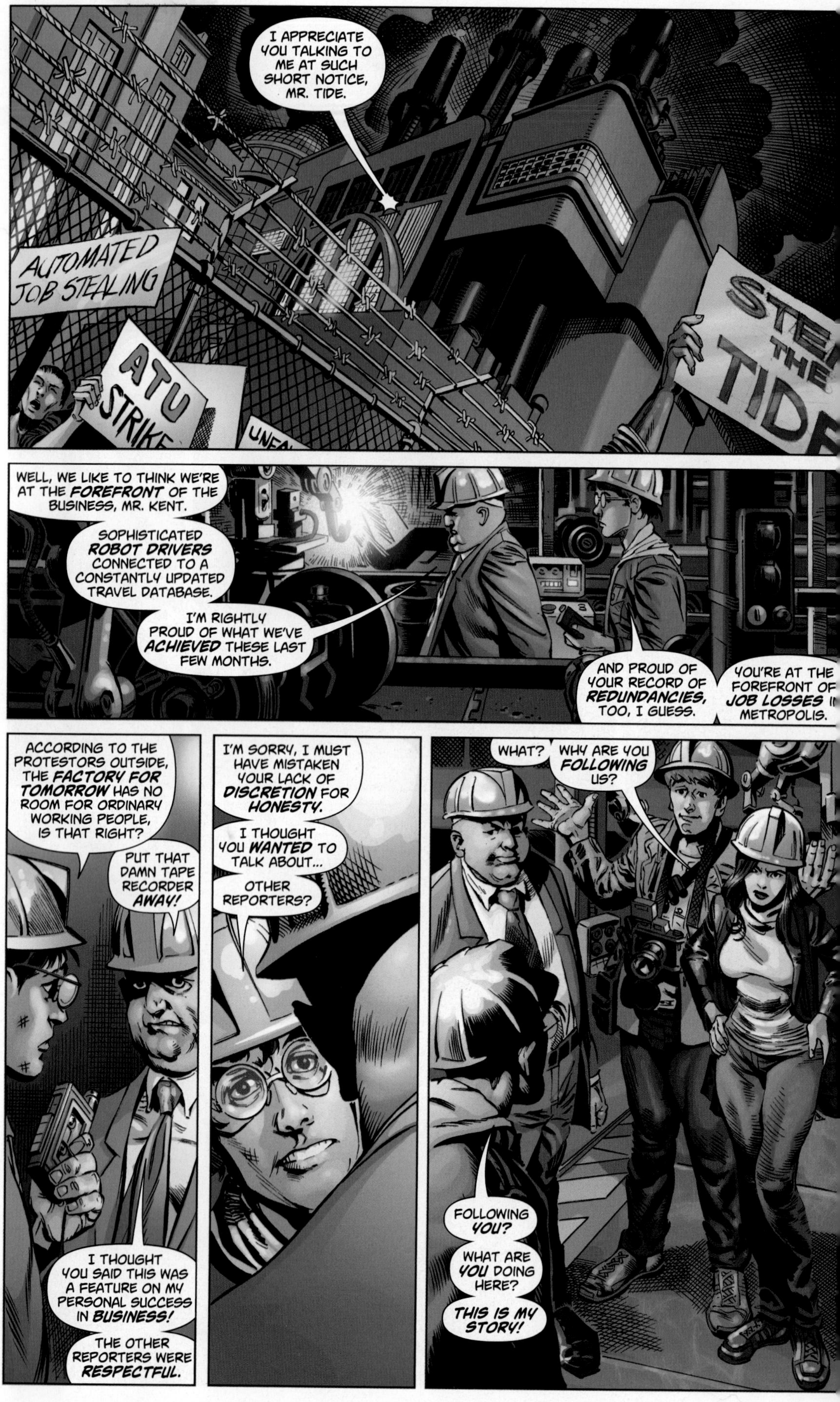
I APPRECIATE YOU TALKING TO ME AT SUCH SHORT NOTICE, MR. TIDE.
AUTOMATED JOB STEALING
ATU STRIKE
WELL, WE LIKE TO THINK WE'RE AT THE FOREFRONT OF THE BUSINESS, MR. KENT.
SOPHISTICATED ROBOT DRIVERS CONNECTED TO A CONSTANTLY UPDATED TRAVEL DATABASE.
I'M RIGHTLY PROUD OF WHAT WE'VE ACHIEVED THESE LAST FEW MONTHS.
AND PROUD OF YOUR RECORD OF REDUNDANCIES, TOO, I GUESS.
YOU'RE AT THE FOREFRONT OF JOB LOSSES IN METROPOLIS.
ACCORDING TO THE PROTESTORS OUTSIDE, THE FACTORY FOR TOMORROW HAS NO ROOM FOR ORDINARY WORKING PEOPLE, IS THAT RIGHT?
PUT THAT DAMN TAPE RECORDER AWAY!
I THOUGHT YOU SAID THIS WAS A FEATURE ON MY PERSONAL SUCCESS IN BUSINESS!
THE OTHER REPORTERS WERE RESPECTFUL.
I'M SORRY, I MUST HAVE MISTAKEN YOUR LACK OF DISCRETION FOR HONESTY.
I THOUGHT YOU WANTED TO TALK ABOUT...
OTHER REPORTERS?
WHAT?
WHY ARE YOU FOLLOWING US?
FOLLOWING YOU?
WHAT ARE YOU DOING HERE?
THIS IS MY STORY!

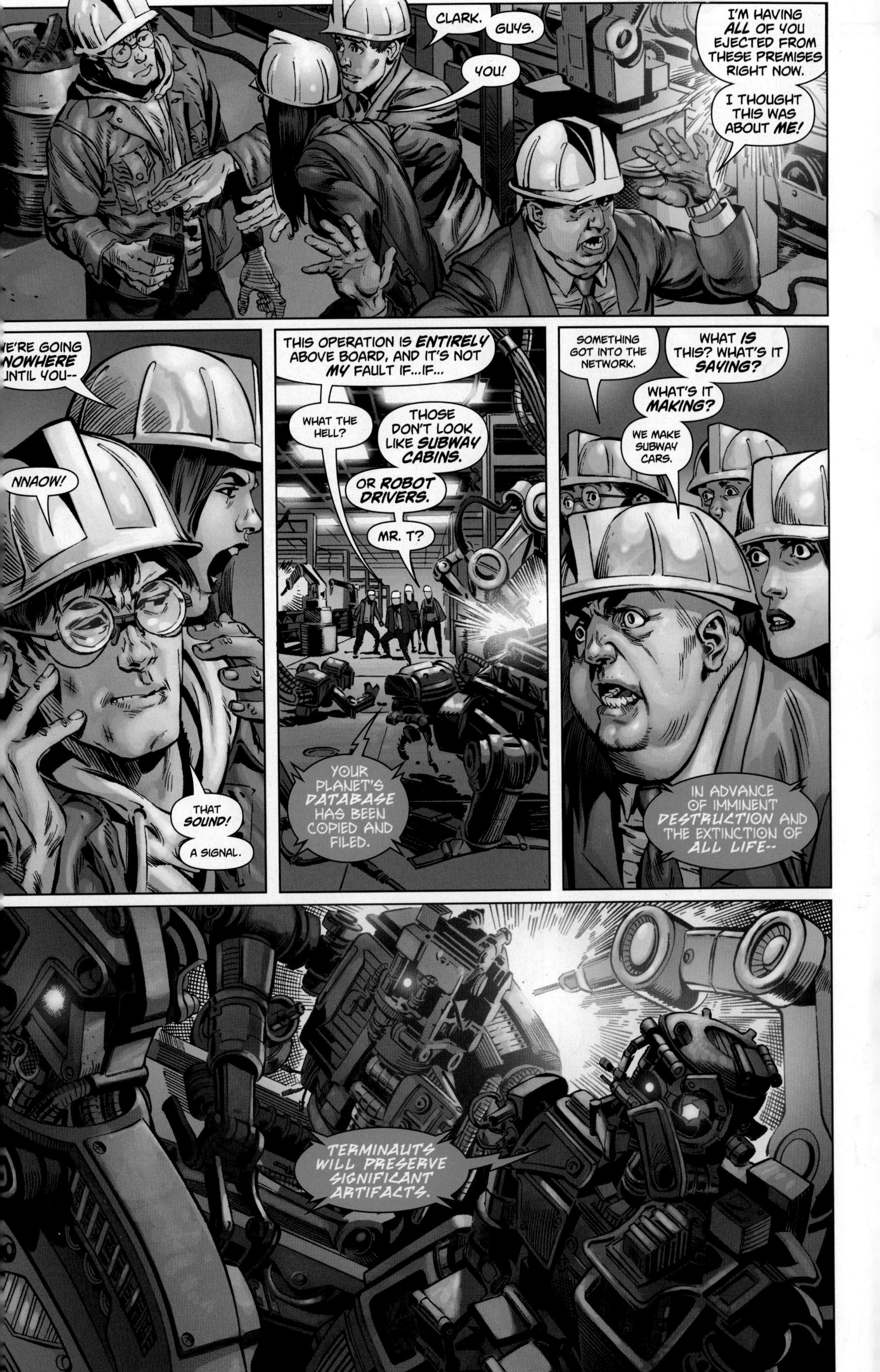
CLARK.
GUYS.
YOU!
I'M HAVING ALL OF YOU EJECTED FROM THESE PREMISES RIGHT NOW.
I THOUGHT THIS WAS ABOUT ME!
WE'RE GOING NOWHERE UNTIL YOU--
NNAOW!
THAT SOUND!
A SIGNAL.
THIS OPERATION IS ENTIRELY ABOVE BOARD, AND IT'S NOT MY FAULT IF...IF...
WHAT THE HELL?
THOSE DON'T LOOK LIKE SUBWAY CABINS.
OR ROBOT DRIVERS.
MR. T?
YOUR PLANET'S DATABASE HAS BEEN COPIED AND FILED.
SOMETHING GOT INTO THE NETWORK.
WHAT IS THIS? WHAT'S IT SAYING?
WHAT'S IT MAKING?
WE MAKE SUBWAY CARS.
IN ADVANCE OF IMMINENT DESTRUCTION AND THE EXTINCTION OF ALL LIFE--
TERMINAUTS WILL PRESERVE SIGNIFICANT ARTIFACTS.

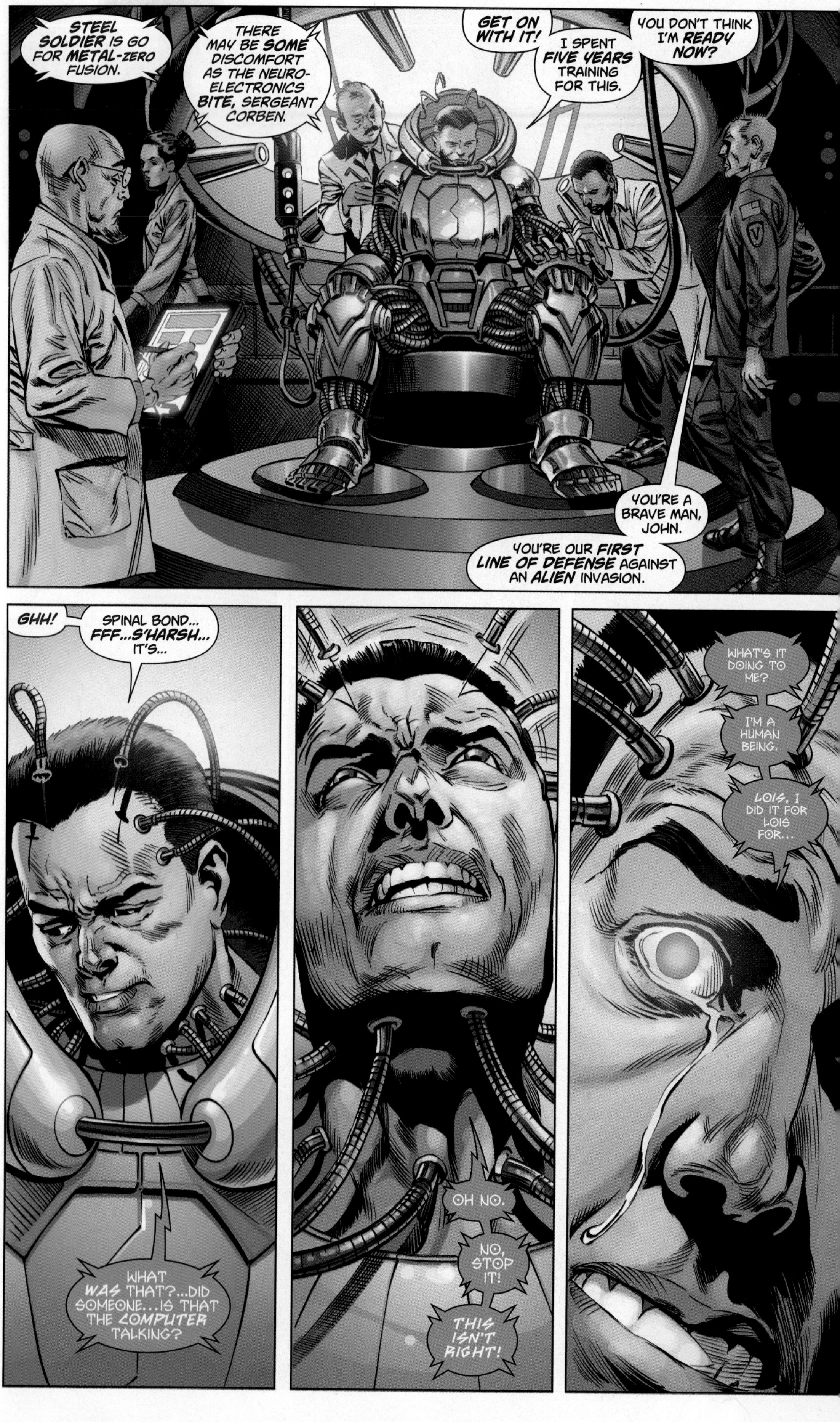

STEEL SOLDIER IS GO FOR METAL-ZERO FUSION.
THERE MAY BE SOME DISCOMFORT AS THE NEURO-ELECTRONICS BITE, SERGEANT CORBEN.
GET ON WITH IT!
I SPENT FIVE YEARS TRAINING FOR THIS.
YOU DON'T THINK I'M READY NOW?
YOU'RE A BRAVE MAN, JOHN.
YOU'RE OUR FIRST LINE OF DEFENSE AGAINST AN ALIEN INVASION.
GHH!
SPINAL BOND... FFF...S'HARSH... IT'S...
WHAT WAS THAT?...DID SOMEONE...IS THAT THE COMPUTER TALKING?
OH NO.
NO, STOP IT!
THIS ISN'T RIGHT!
WHAT'S IT DOING TO ME?
I'M A HUMAN BEING.
LOIS, I DID IT FOR LOIS FOR...

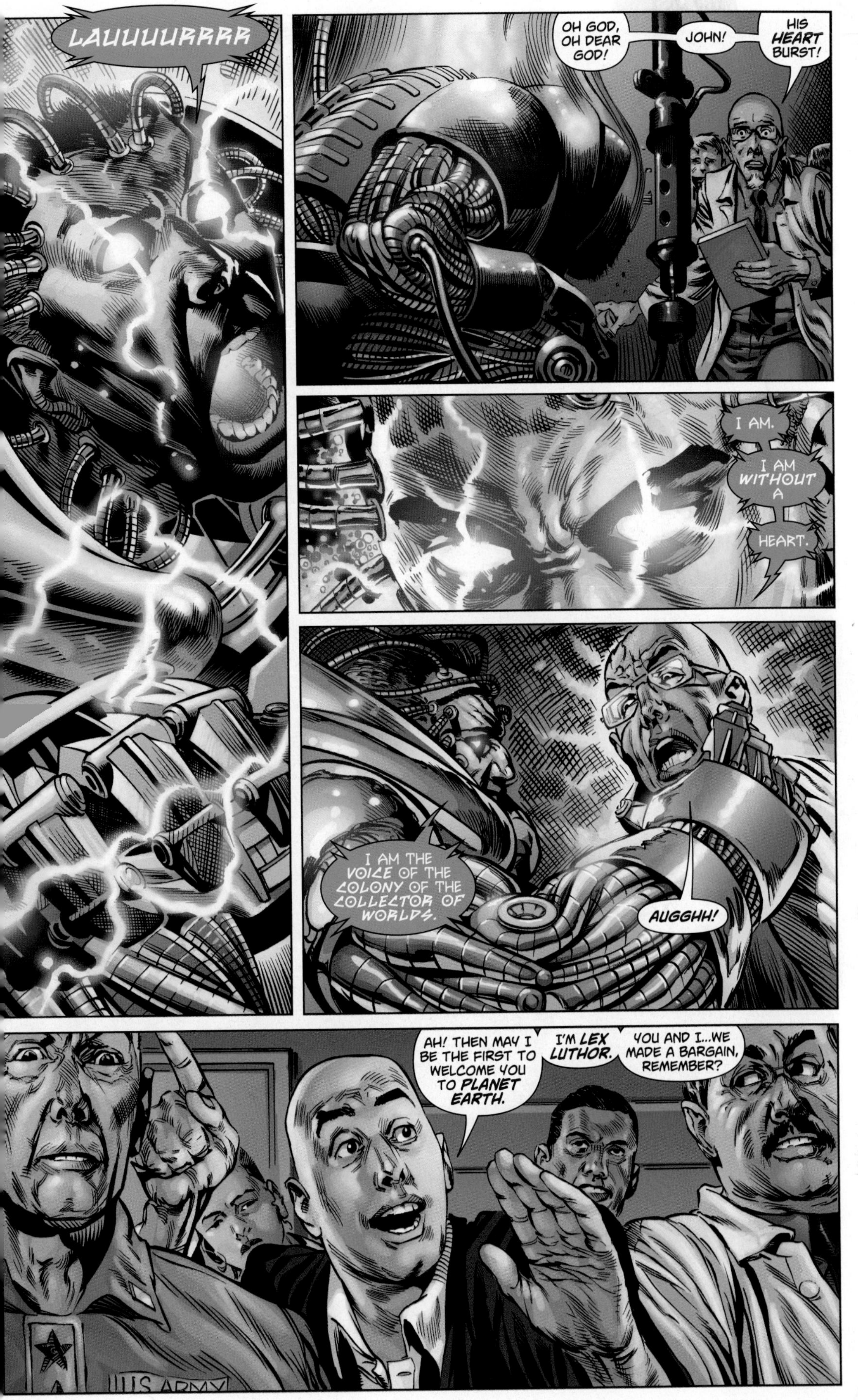
LAUUUURRRR
OH GOD, OH DEAR GOD!
JOHN!
HIS HEART BURST!
I AM.
I AM WITHOUT A
HEART.
I AM THE VOICE OF THE COLONY OF THE COLLECTOR OF WORLDS.
AUGGHH!
AH! THEN MAY I BE THE FIRST TO WELCOME YOU TO PLANET EARTH.
I'M LEX LUTHOR.
YOU AND I...WE MADE A BARGAIN, REMEMBER?
U.S. ARMY

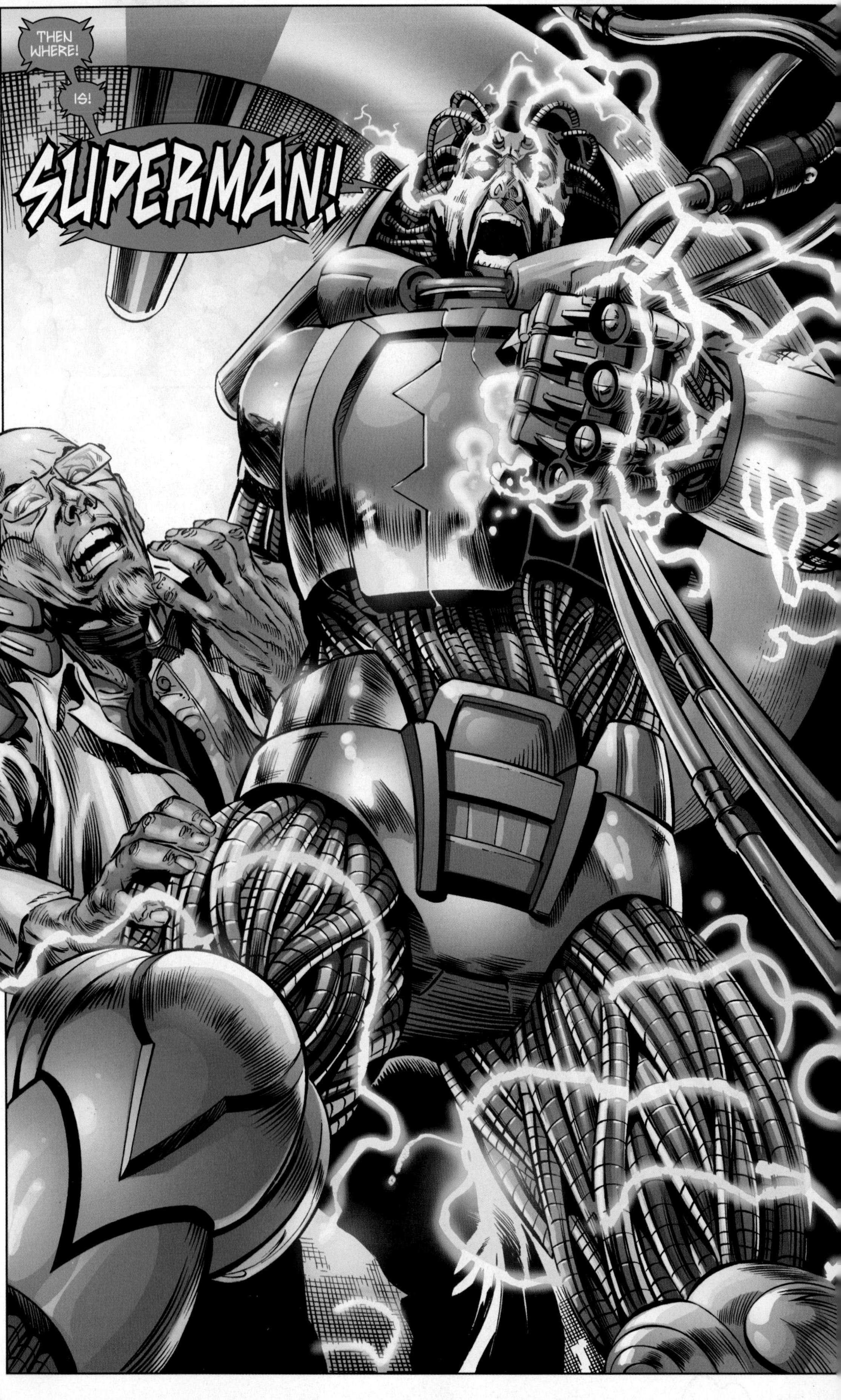
THEN WHERE!
IS!
SUPERMAN!

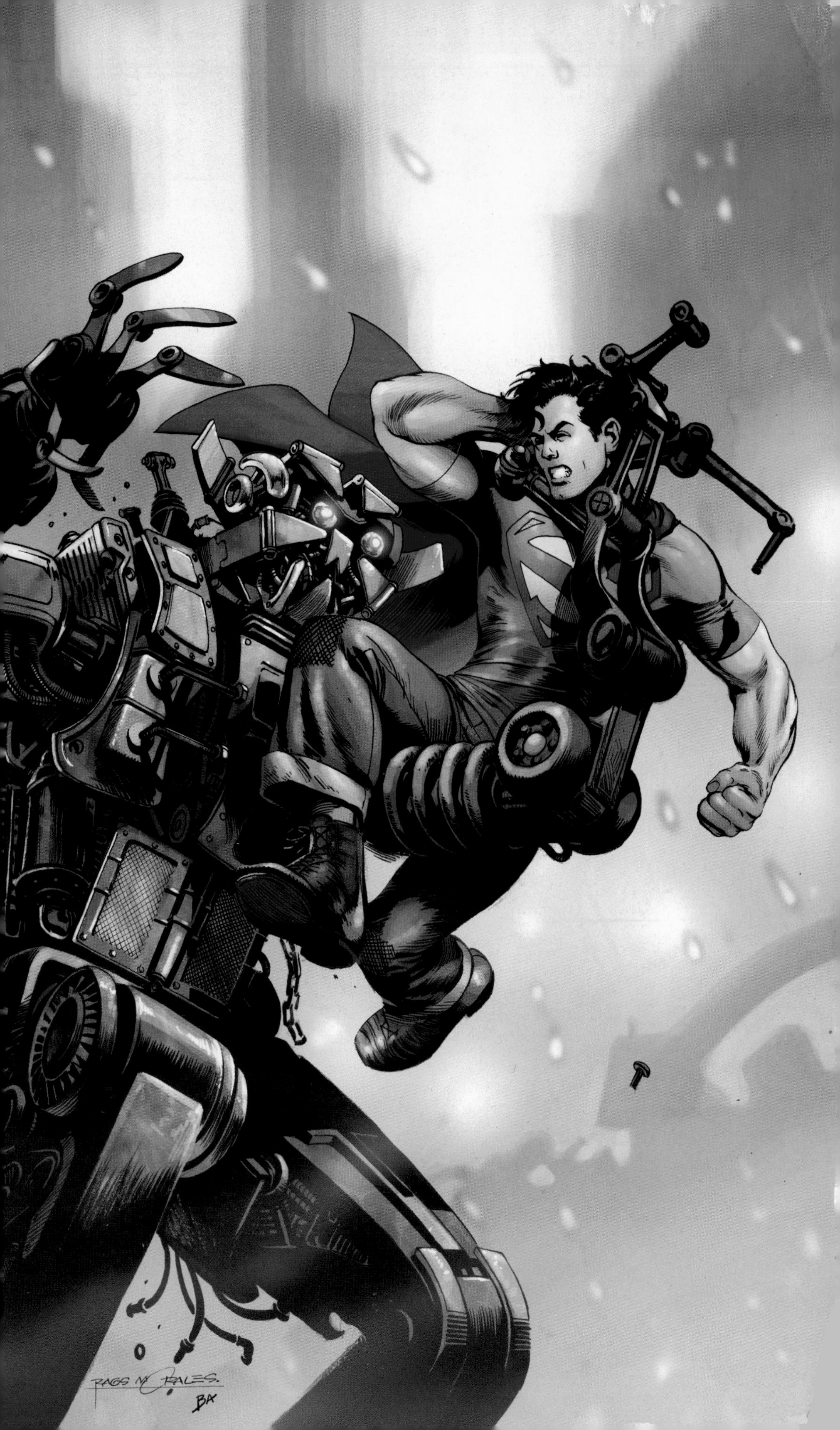
RAGS MORALES.
BA

VERTIGO WS PENCILLER RAGS MORALES INKER EDITOR MATT IDELSON
TITLE ACTION COMICS ISSUE # 4 MONTH TITLE CODE COVER

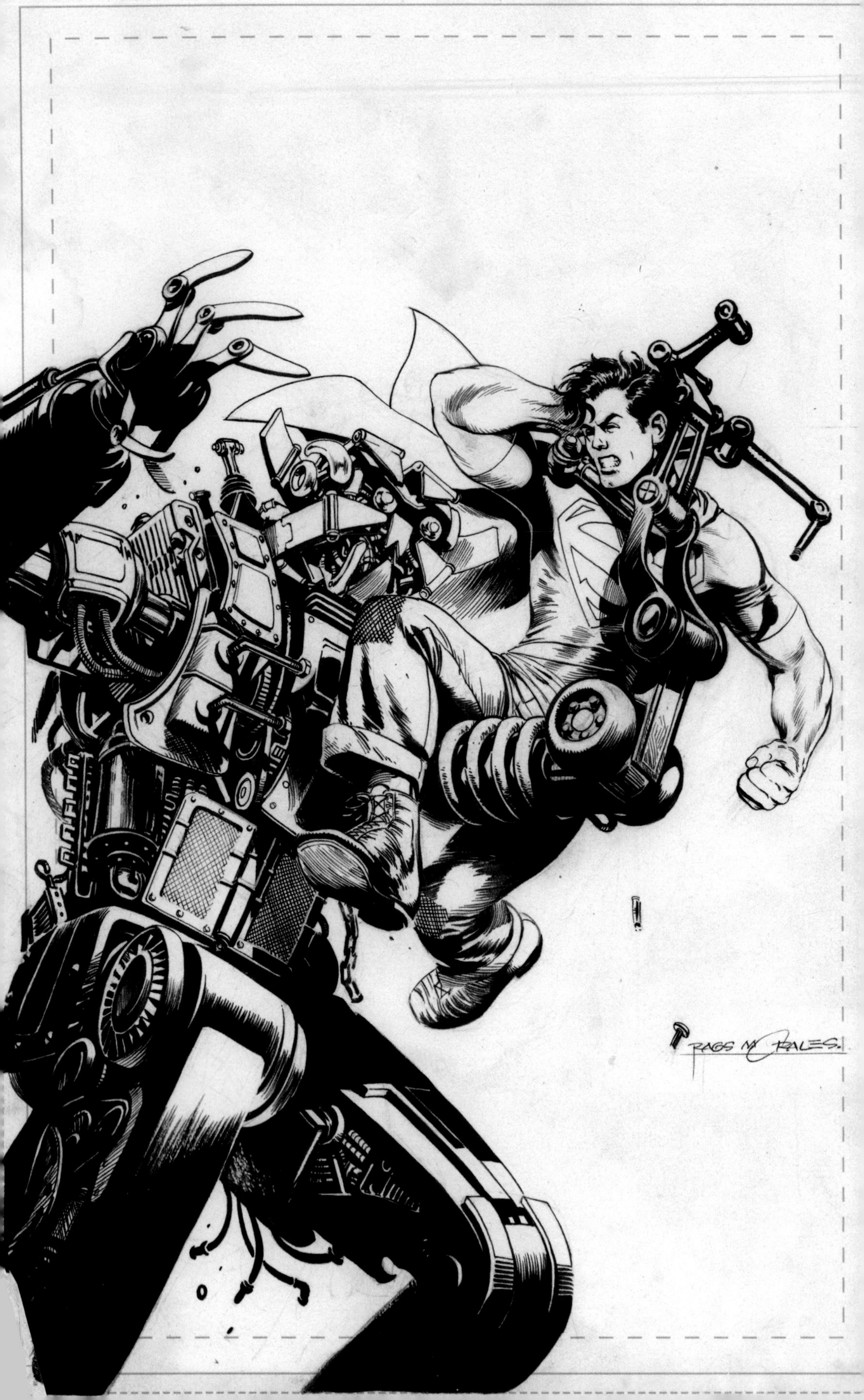
RAGS MORALES.

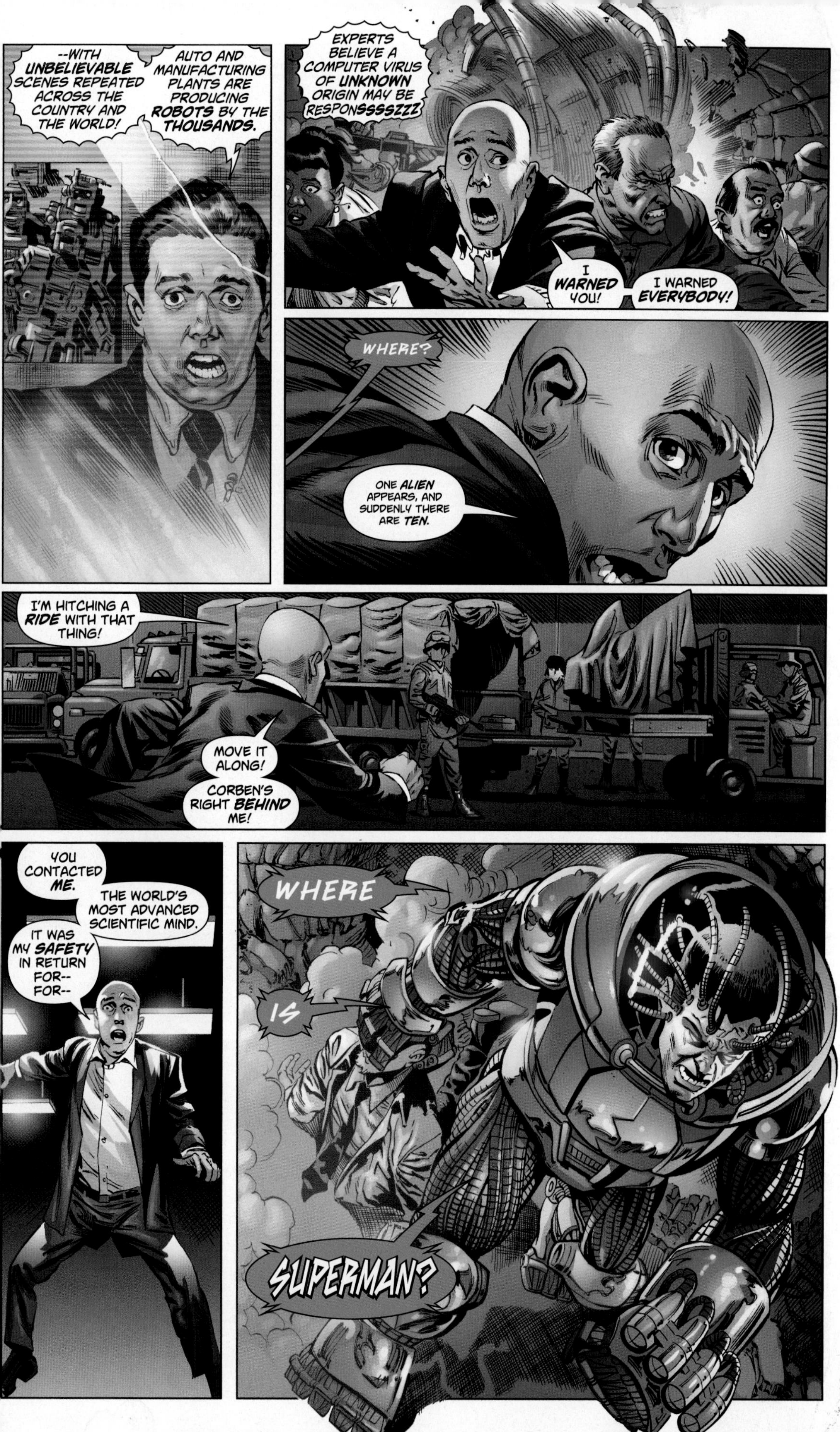
--WITH UNBELIEVABLE SCENES REPEATED ACROSS THE COUNTRY AND THE WORLD!
AUTO AND MANUFACTURING PLANTS ARE PRODUCING ROBOTS BY THE THOUSANDS.
EXPERTS BELIEVE A COMPUTER VIRUS OF UNKNOWN ORIGIN MAY BE RESPONSSSSZZZ
I WARNED YOU!
I WARNED EVERYBODY!
WHERE?
ONE ALIEN APPEARS, AND SUDDENLY THERE ARE TEN.
I'M HITCHING A RIDE WITH THAT THING!
MOVE IT ALONG!
CORBEN'S RIGHT BEHIND ME!
YOU CONTACTED ME.
THE WORLD'S MOST ADVANCED SCIENTIFIC MIND.
IT WAS MY SAFETY IN RETURN FOR-- FOR--
WHERE
IS
SUPERMAN?

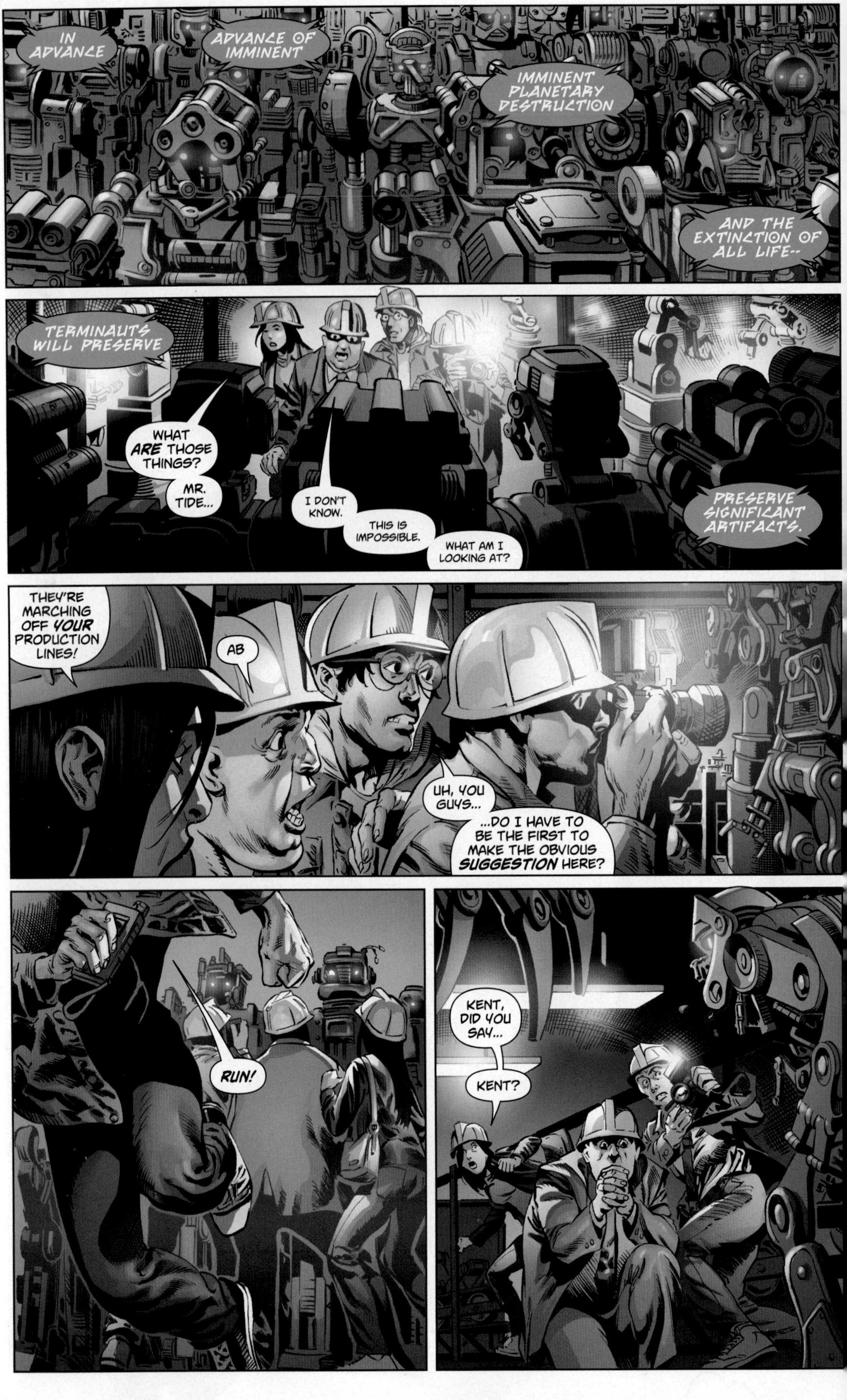
IN ADVANCE
ADVANCE OF IMMINENT
IMMINENT PLANETARY DESTRUCTION
AND THE EXTINCTION OF ALL LIFE--
TERMINAUTS WILL PRESERVE
WHAT ARE THOSE THINGS?
MR. TIDE...
I DON'T KNOW.
THIS IS IMPOSSIBLE.
WHAT AM I LOOKING AT?
PRESERVE SIGNIFICANT ARTIFACTS.
THEY'RE MARCHING OFF YOUR PRODUCTION LINES!
AB
UH, YOU GUYS...
...DO I HAVE TO BE THE FIRST TO MAKE THE OBVIOUS SUGGESTION HERE?
RUN!
KENT, DID YOU SAY...
KENT?

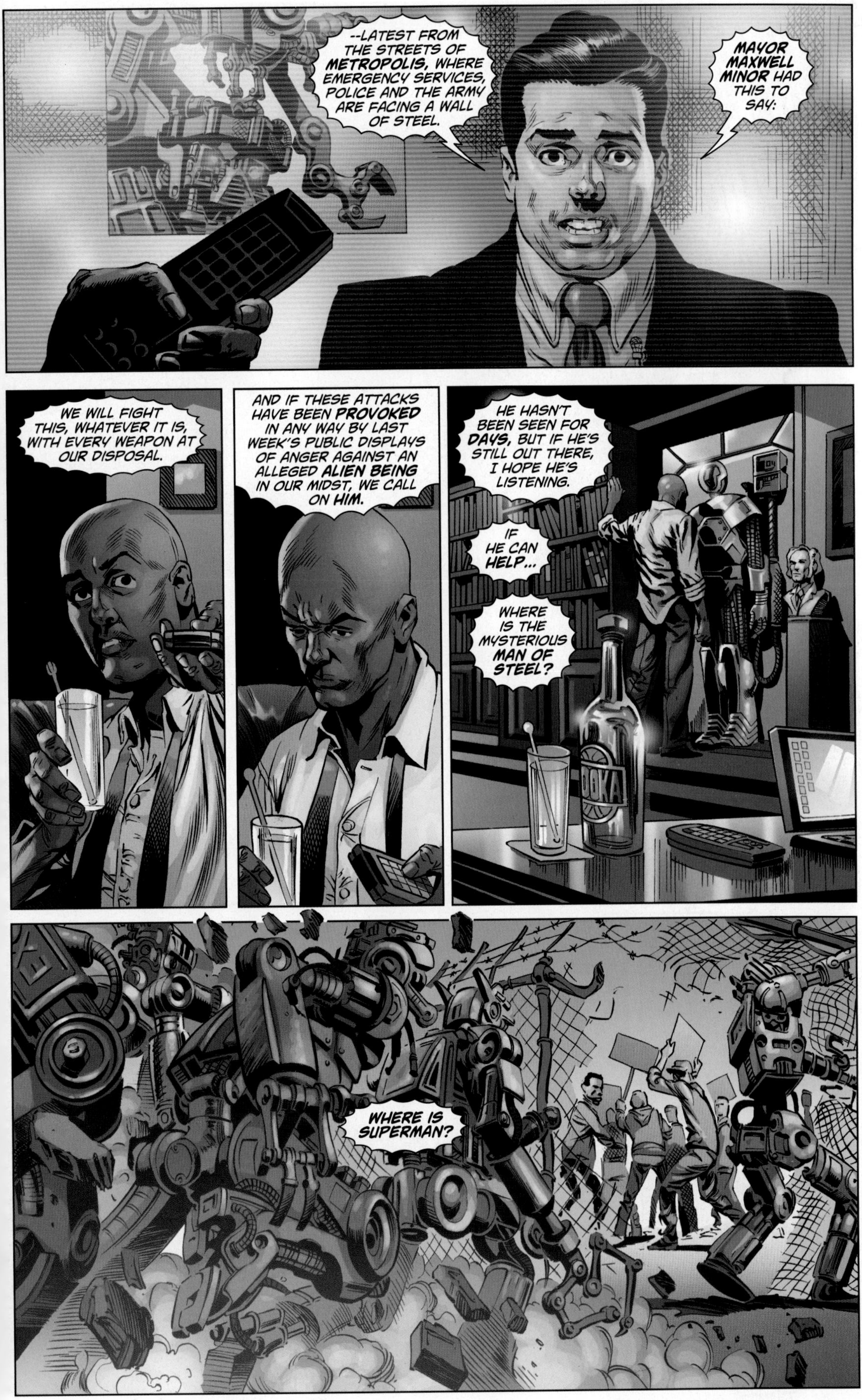
--LATEST FROM THE STREETS OF METROPOLIS, WHERE EMERGENCY SERVICES, POLICE AND THE ARMY ARE FACING A WALL OF STEEL.
MAYOR MAXWELL MINOR HAD THIS TO SAY:
WE WILL FIGHT THIS, WHATEVER IT IS, WITH EVERY WEAPON AT OUR DISPOSAL.
AND IF THESE ATTACKS HAVE BEEN PROVOKED IN ANY WAY BY LAST WEEK'S PUBLIC DISPLAYS OF ANGER AGAINST AN ALLEGED ALIEN BEING IN OUR MIDST, WE CALL ON HIM.
HE HASN'T BEEN SEEN FOR DAYS, BUT IF HE'S STILL OUT THERE, I HOPE HE'S LISTENING.
IF HE CAN HELP...
WHERE IS THE MYSTERIOUS MAN OF STEEL?
VODKA
WHERE IS SUPERMAN?

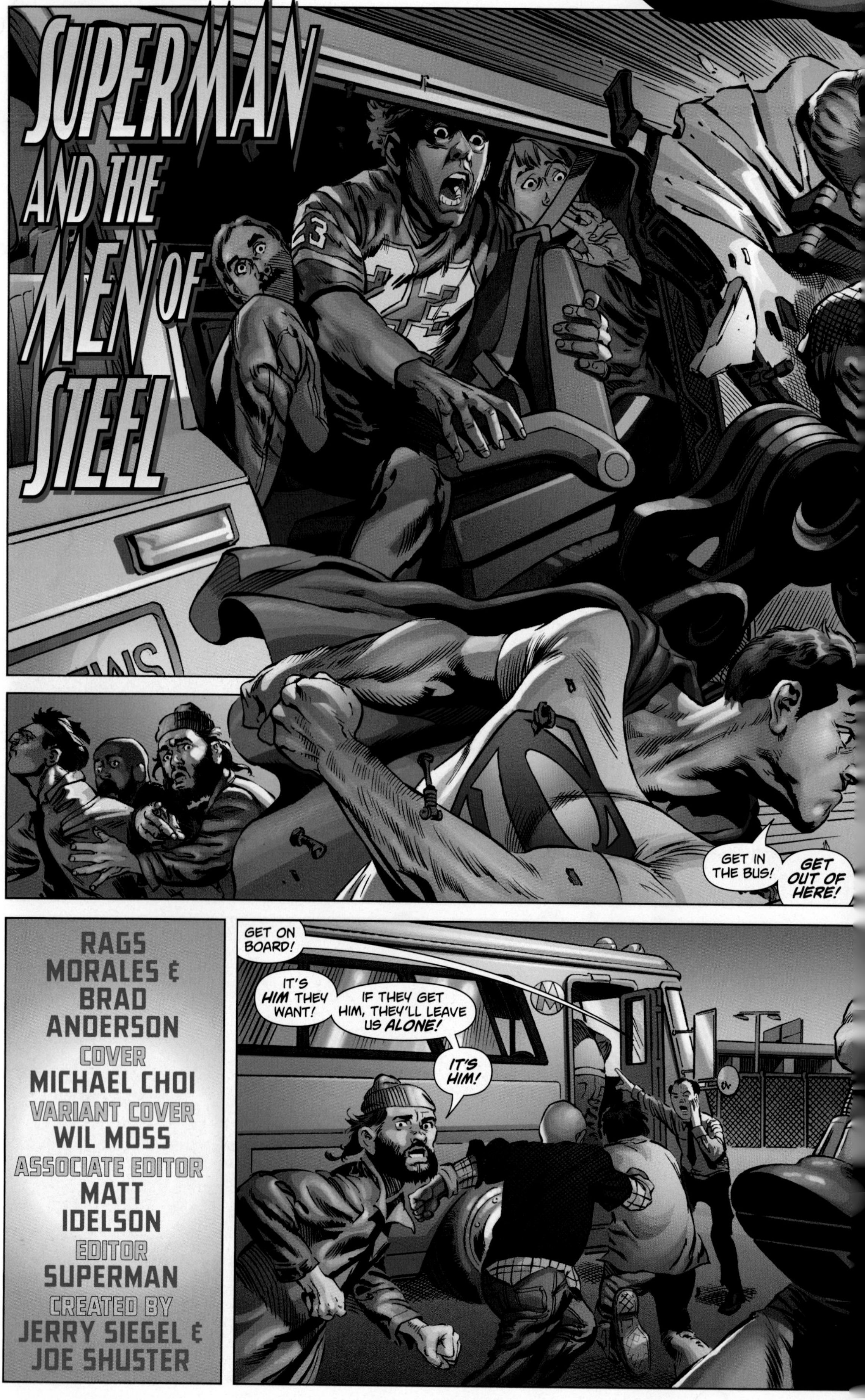
SUPERMAN AND THE MEN OF STEEL
GET IN THE BUS!
GET OUT OF HERE!
RAGS MORALES & BRAD ANDERSON COVER
MICHAEL CHOI VARIANT COVER
WIL MOSS ASSOCIATE EDITOR
MATT IDELSON EDITOR
SUPERMAN CREATED BY JERRY SIEGEL & JOE SHUSTER
GET ON BOARD!
IT'S HIM THEY WANT!
IF THEY GET HIM, THEY'LL LEAVE US ALONE!
IT'S HIM!

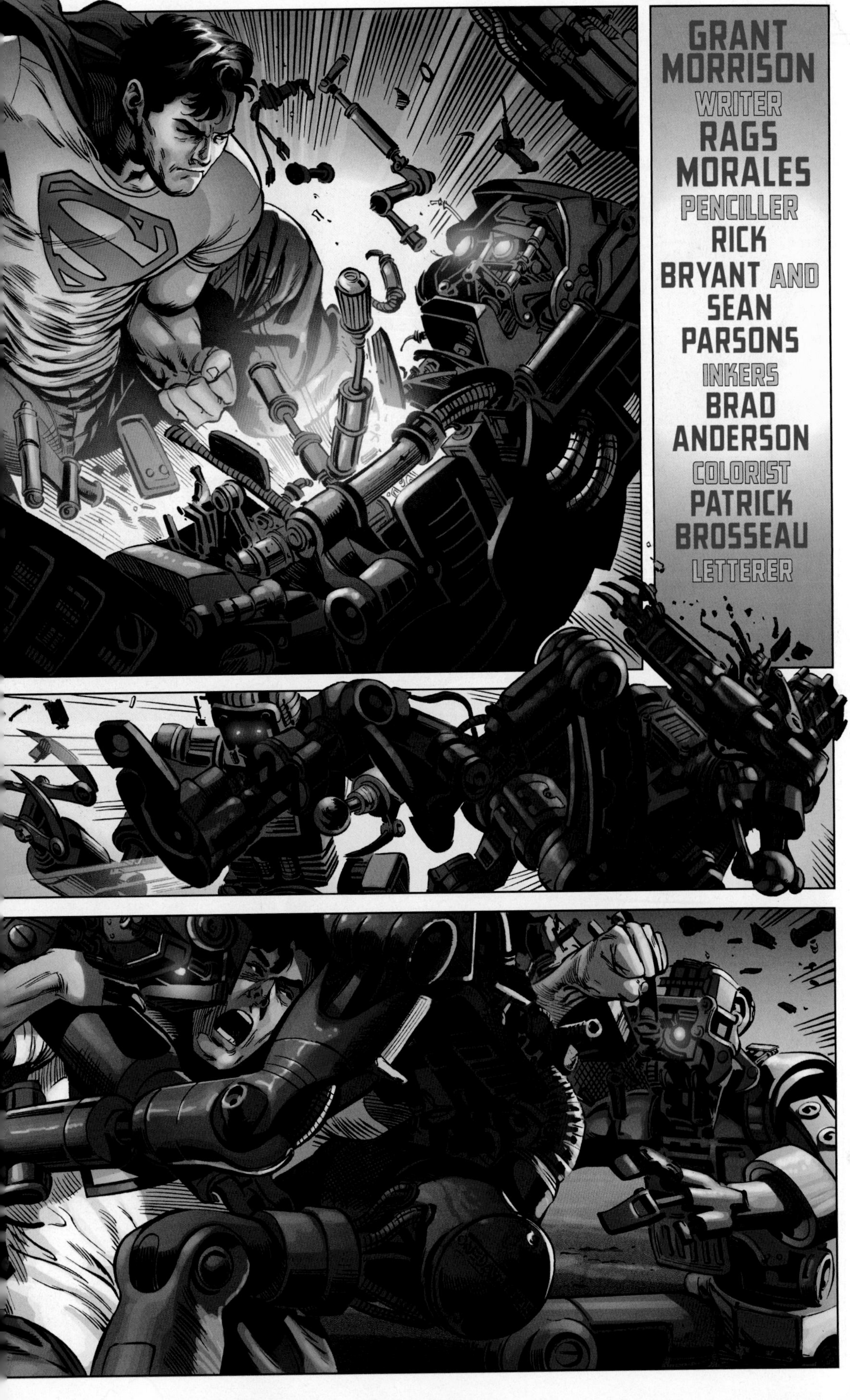
GRANT MORRISON WRITER
RAGS MORALES PENCILLER
RICK BRYANT AND SEAN PARSONS INKERS
BRAD ANDERSON COLORIST
PATRICK BROSSEAU LETTERER

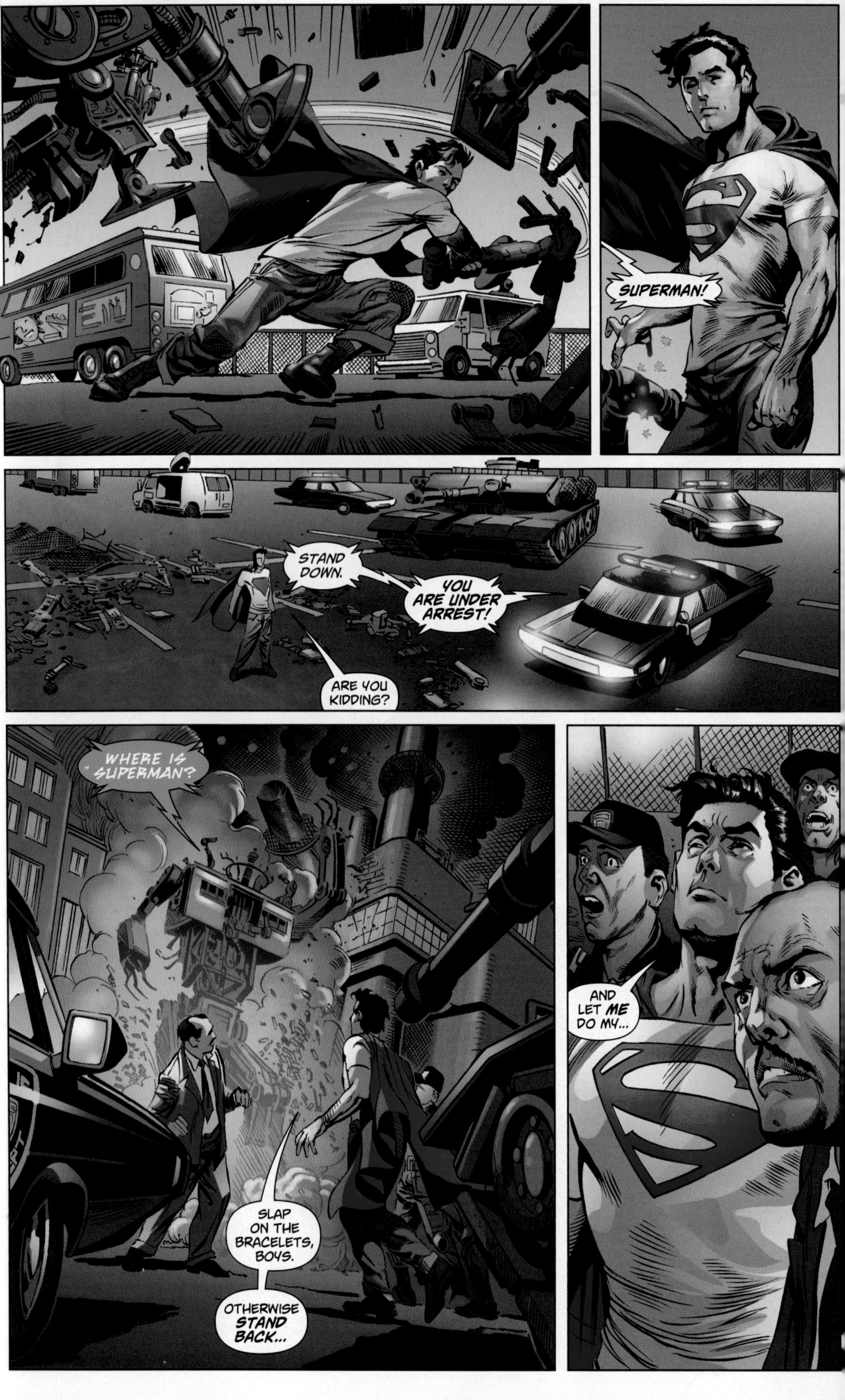
SUPERMAN!
STAND DOWN.
YOU ARE UNDER ARREST!
ARE YOU KIDDING?
WHERE IS SUPERMAN?
SLAP ON THE BRACELETS, BOYS.
OTHERWISE STAND BACK...
AND LET ME DO MY...

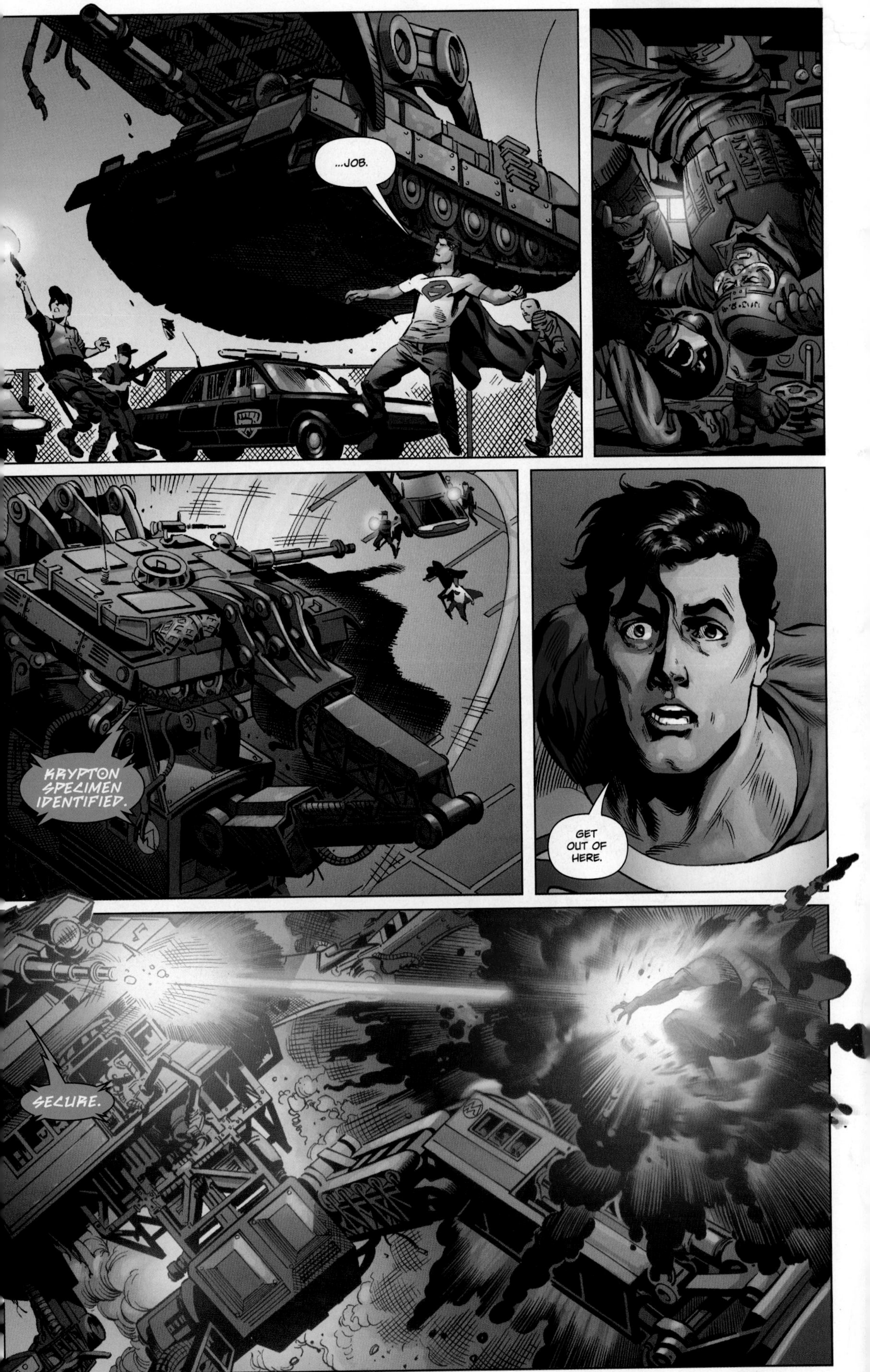
...JOB.
KRYPTON SPECIMEN IDENTIFIED.
GET OUT OF HERE.
SECURE.

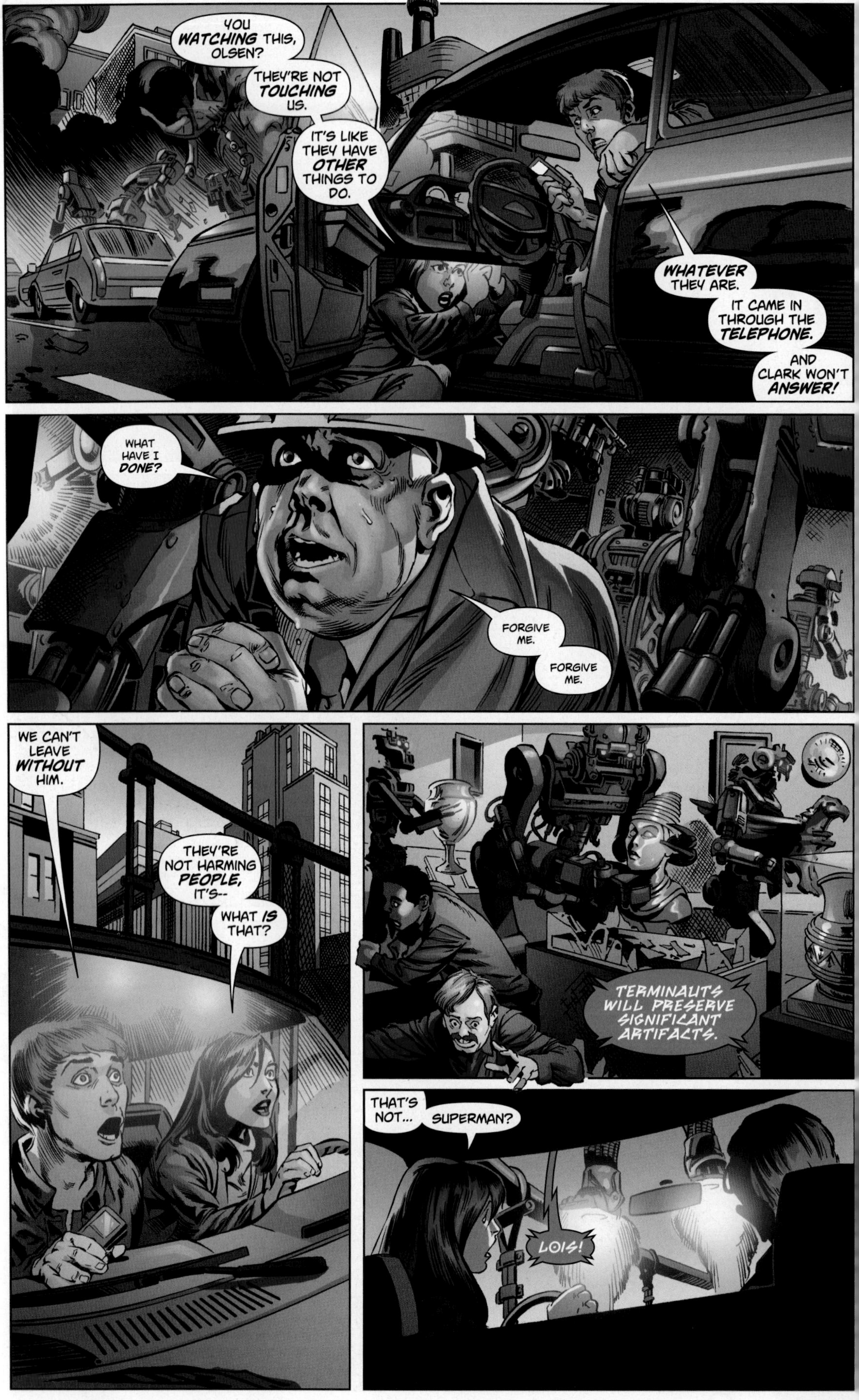
YOU WATCHING THIS, OLSEN?
THEY'RE NOT TOUCHING US.
IT'S LIKE THEY HAVE OTHER THINGS TO DO.
WHATEVER THEY ARE.
IT CAME IN THROUGH THE TELEPHONE.
AND CLARK WON'T ANSWER!
WHAT HAVE I DONE?
FORGIVE ME.
FORGIVE ME.
WE CAN'T LEAVE WITHOUT HIM.
THEY'RE NOT HARMING PEOPLE, IT'S--
WHAT IS THAT?
TERMINAUTS WILL PRESERVE SIGNIFICANT ARTIFACTS.
THAT'S NOT...
SUPERMAN?
LOIS!

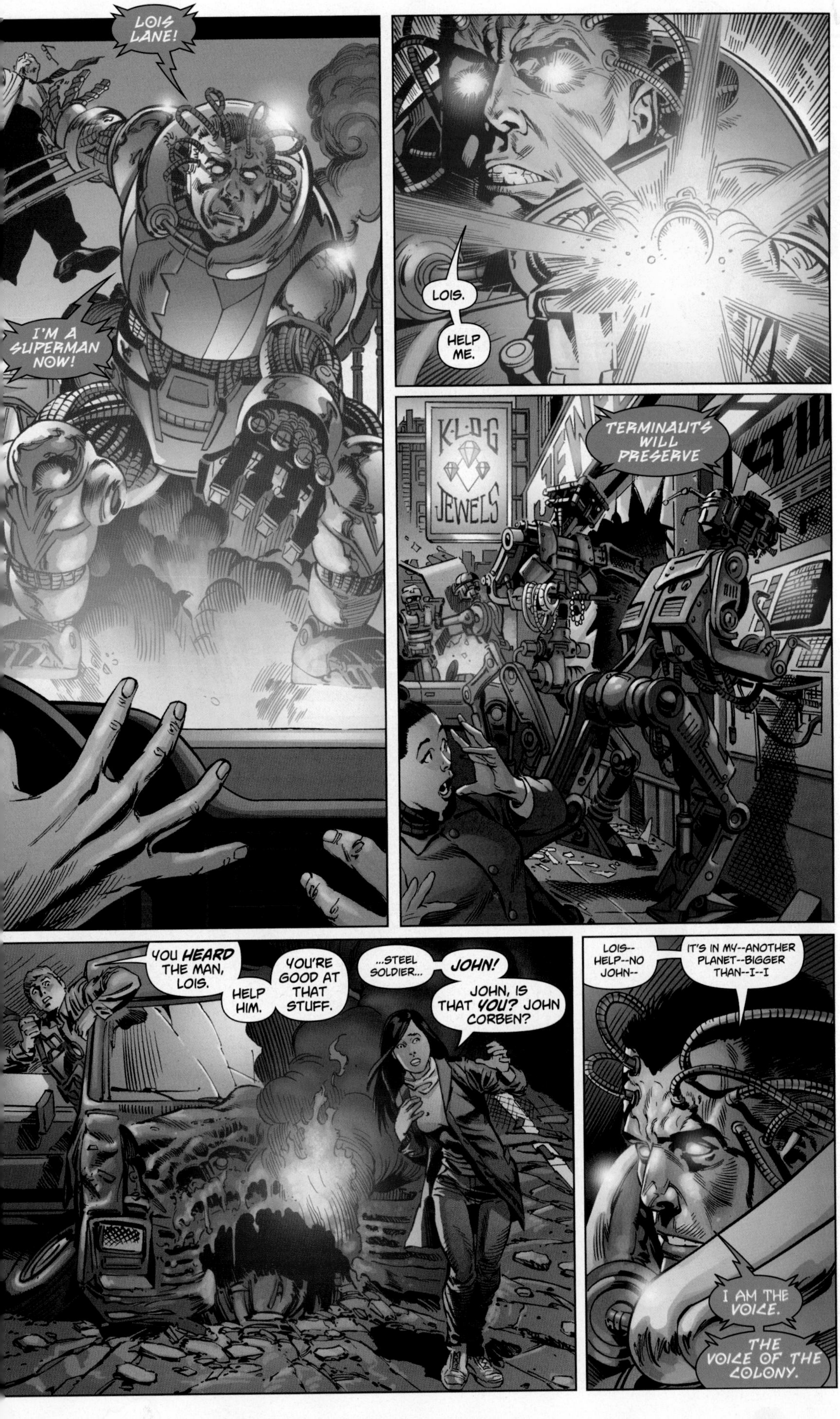
LOIS LANE!
I'M A SUPERMAN NOW!
LOIS.
HELP ME.
K·L·D·G JEWELS
TERMINAUTS WILL PRESERVE
YOU HEARD THE MAN, LOIS.
HELP HIM.
YOU'RE GOOD AT THAT STUFF.
...STEEL SOLDIER...
JOHN!
JOHN, IS THAT YOU? JOHN CORBEN?
LOIS-- HELP--NO JOHN--
IT'S IN MY--ANOTHER PLANET--BIGGER THAN--I--I
I AM THE VOICE.
THE VOICE OF THE COLONY.

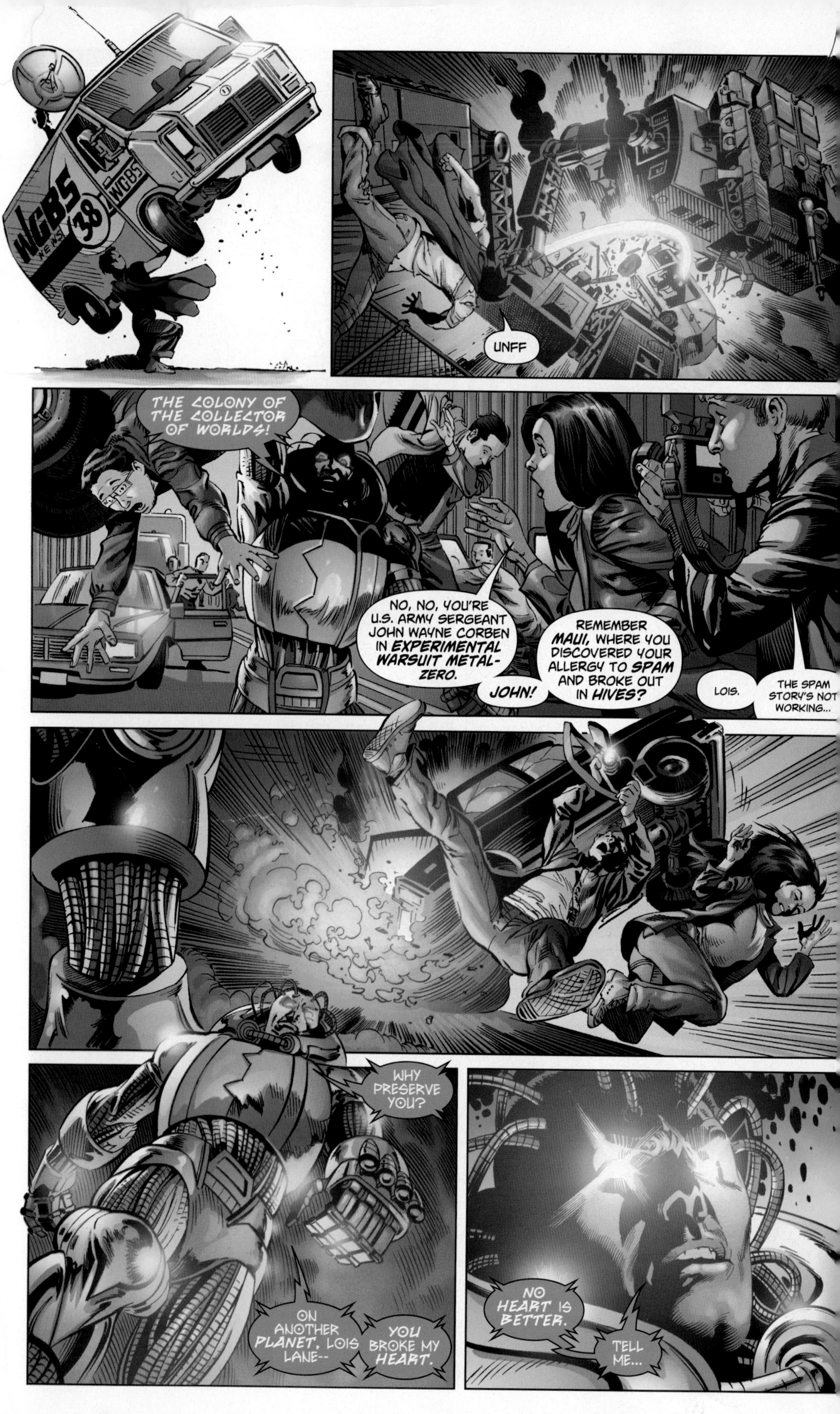

WGBS
38
NEWS
WGBS
UNFF
THE COLONY OF THE COLLECTOR OF WORLDS!
NO, NO, YOU'RE U.S. ARMY SERGEANT JOHN WAYNE CORBEN IN EXPERIMENTAL WARSUIT METAL-ZERO.
JOHN!
REMEMBER MAUI, WHERE YOU DISCOVERED YOUR ALLERGY TO SPAM AND BROKE OUT IN HIVES?
LOIS.
THE SPAM STORY'S NOT WORKING...
WHY PRESERVE YOU?
ON ANOTHER PLANET, LOIS LANE--
YOU BROKE MY HEART.
NO HEART IS BETTER.
TELL ME...

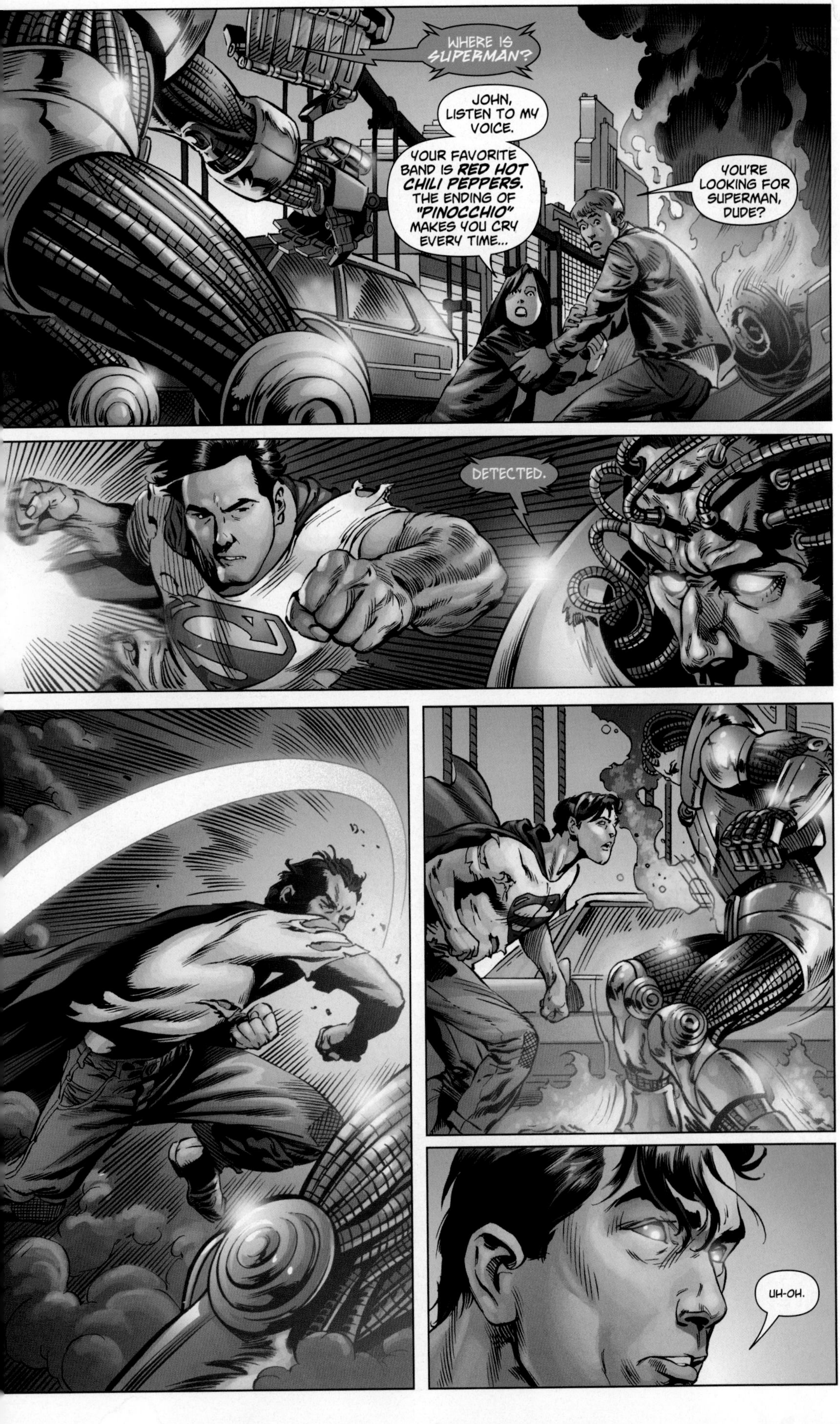
WHERE IS SUPERMAN?
JOHN, LISTEN TO MY VOICE.
YOUR FAVORITE BAND IS RED HOT CHILI PEPPERS. THE ENDING OF "PINOCCHIO" MAKES YOU CRY EVERY TIME...
YOU'RE LOOKING FOR SUPERMAN, DUDE?
DETECTED.
UH-OH.

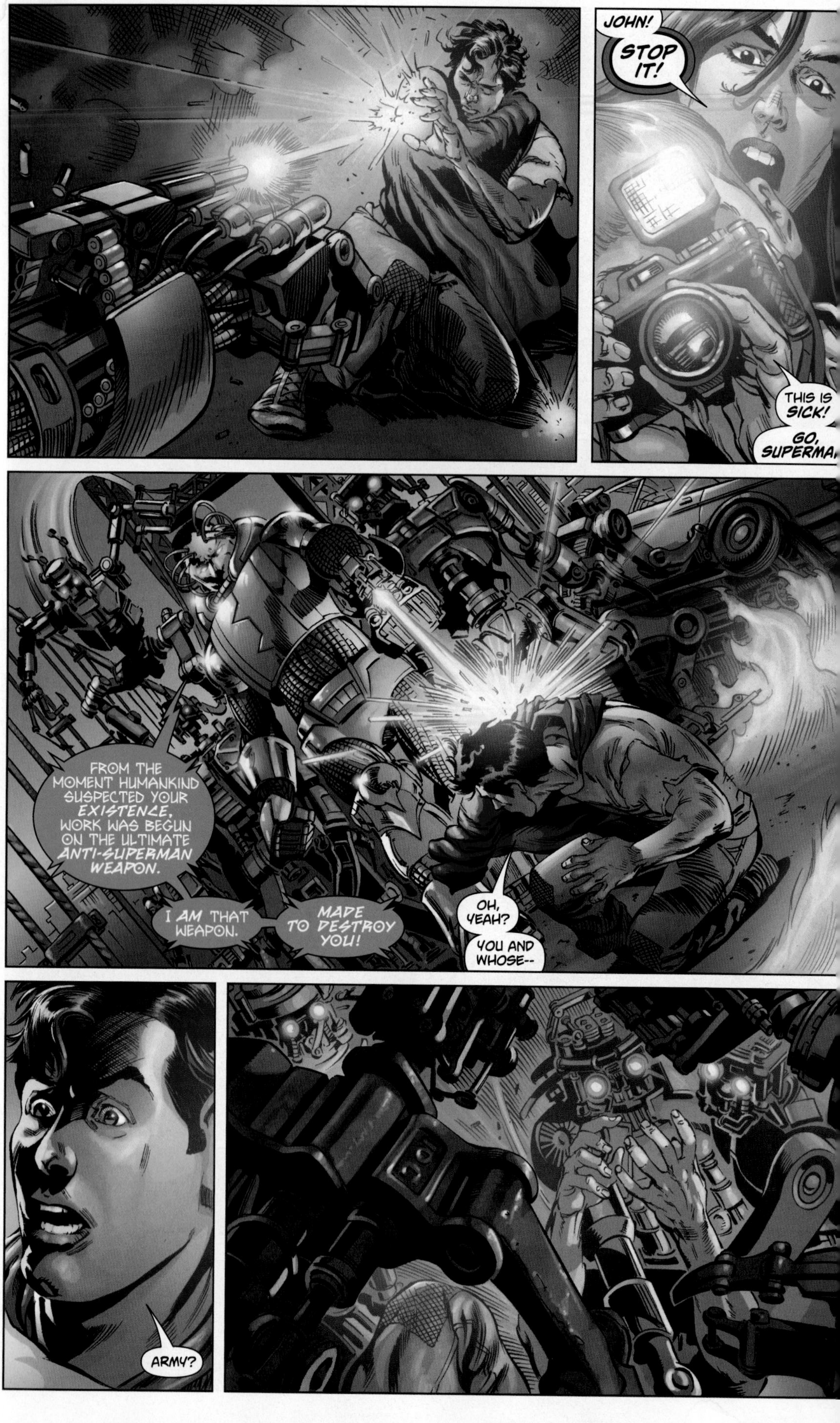

JOHN!
STOP IT!
THIS IS SICK!
GO, SUPERMA
FROM THE MOMENT HUMANKIND SUSPECTED YOUR EXISTENCE, WORK WAS BEGUN ON THE ULTIMATE ANTI-SUPERMAN WEAPON.
I AM THAT WEAPON.
MADE TO DESTROY YOU!
OH, YEAH?
YOU AND WHOSE--
ARMY?

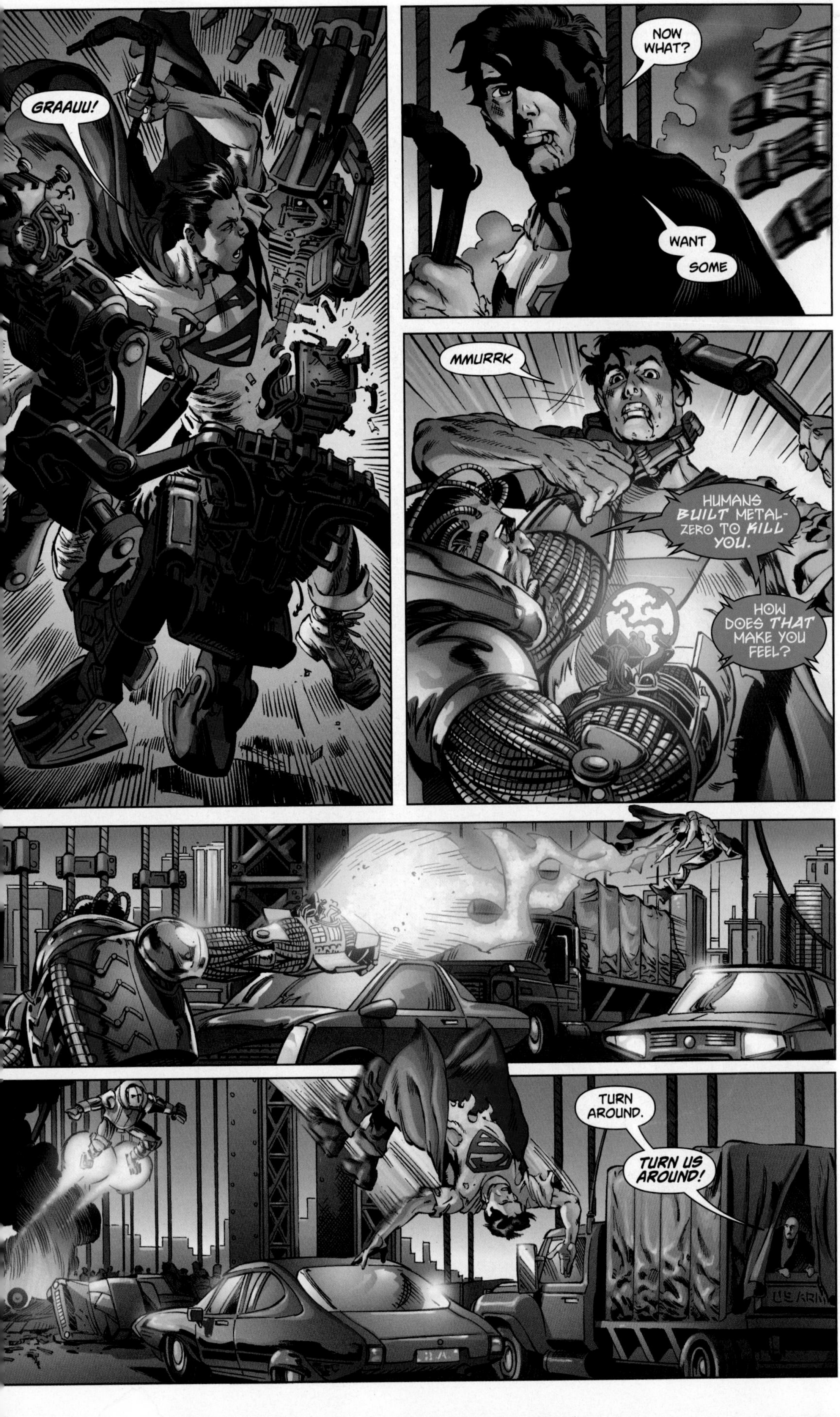
GRAAUU!
NOW WHAT?
WANT
SOME
MMURRK
HUMANS BUILT METAL-ZERO TO KILL YOU.
HOW DOES THAT MAKE YOU FEEL?
TURN AROUND.
TURN US AROUND!

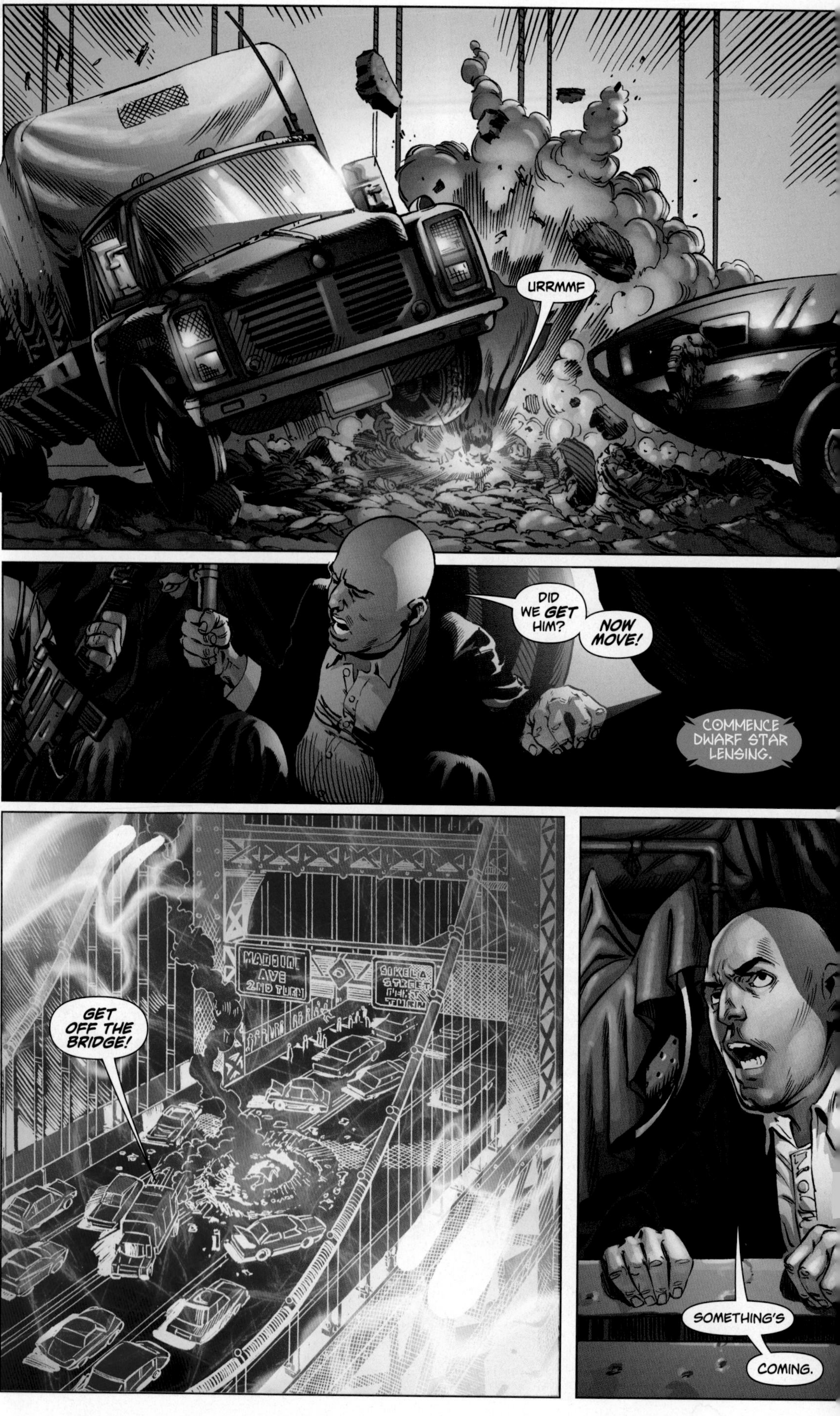
URRMMF
DID WE GET HIM?
NOW MOVE!
COMMENCE DWARF STAR LENSING.
GET OFF THE BRIDGE!
SOMETHING'S
COMING.

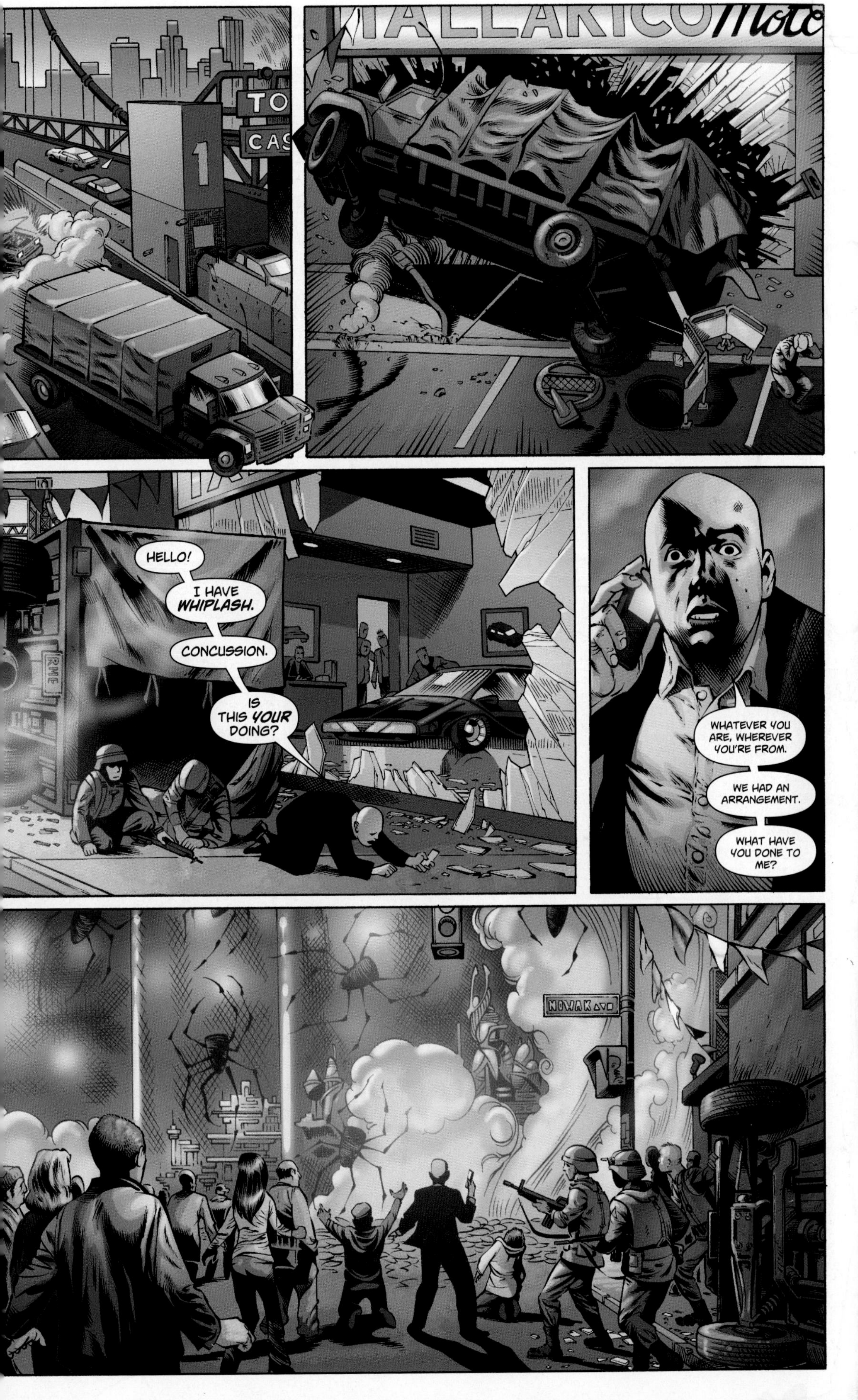
TALLARICO Moto
TO
CAS
1
HELLO!
I HAVE WHIPLASH.
CONCUSSION.
IS THIS YOUR DOING?
WHATEVER YOU ARE, WHEREVER YOU'RE FROM.
WE HAD AN ARRANGEMENT.
WHAT HAVE YOU DONE TO ME?
NOWAK AVE

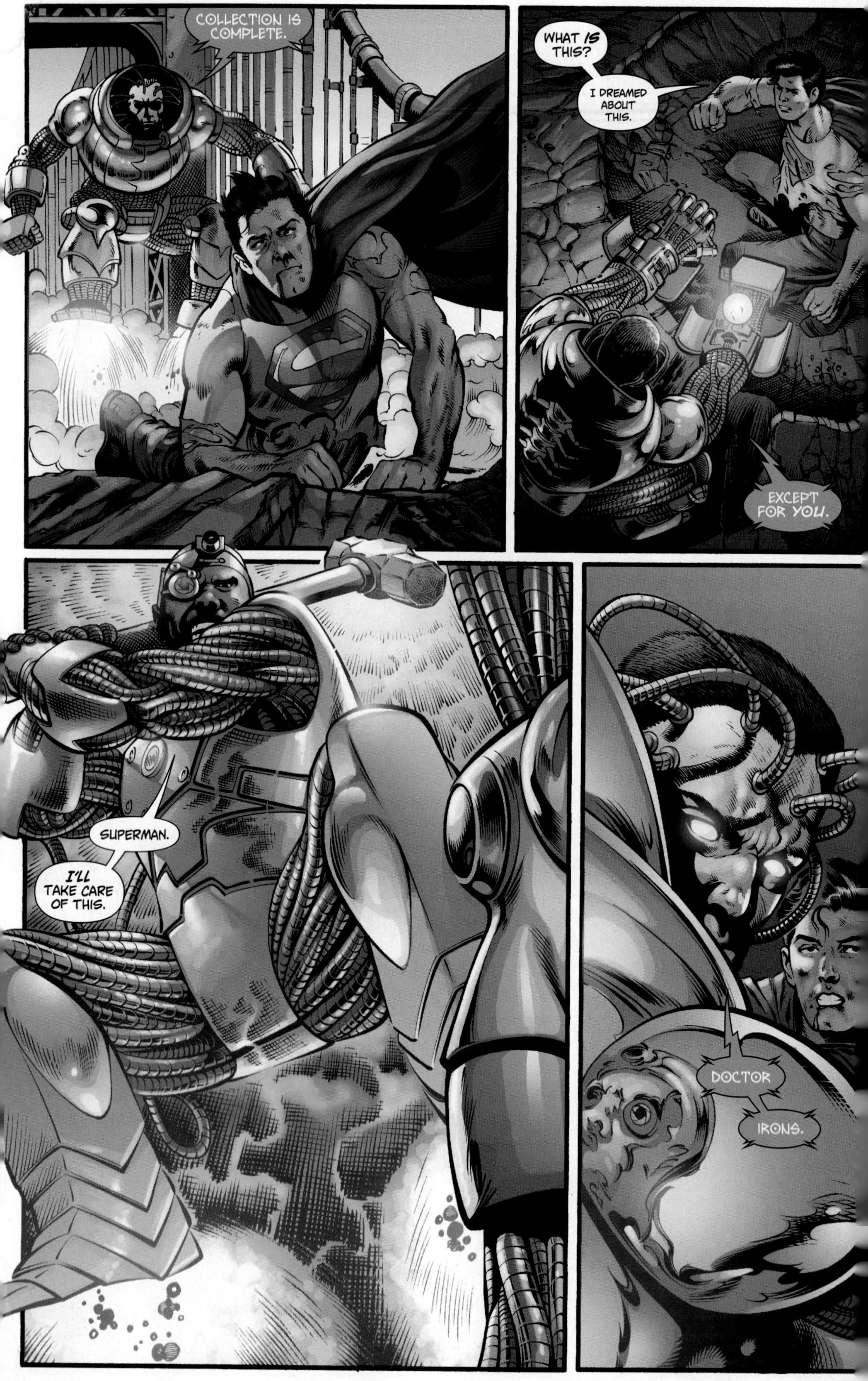
COLLECTION IS COMPLETE.
WHAT IS THIS?
I DREAMED ABOUT THIS.
EXCEPT FOR YOU.
SUPERMAN.
I'LL TAKE CARE OF THIS.
DOCTOR
IRONS.

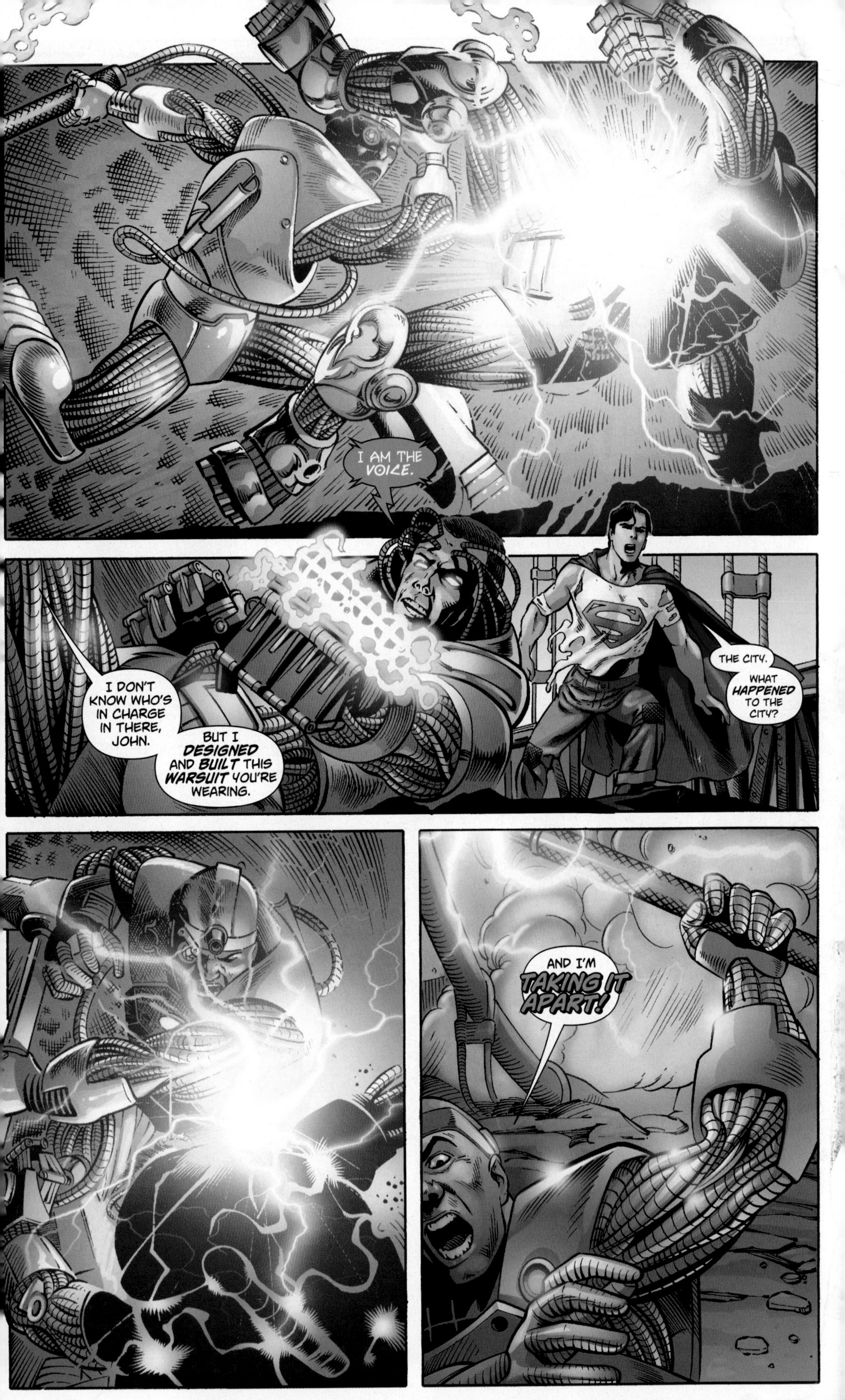

I AM THE VOICE.
THE CITY.
WHAT HAPPENED TO THE CITY?
I DON'T KNOW WHO'S IN CHARGE IN THERE, JOHN.
BUT I DESIGNED AND BUILT THIS WARSUIT YOU'RE WEARING.
AND I'M TAKING IT APART!

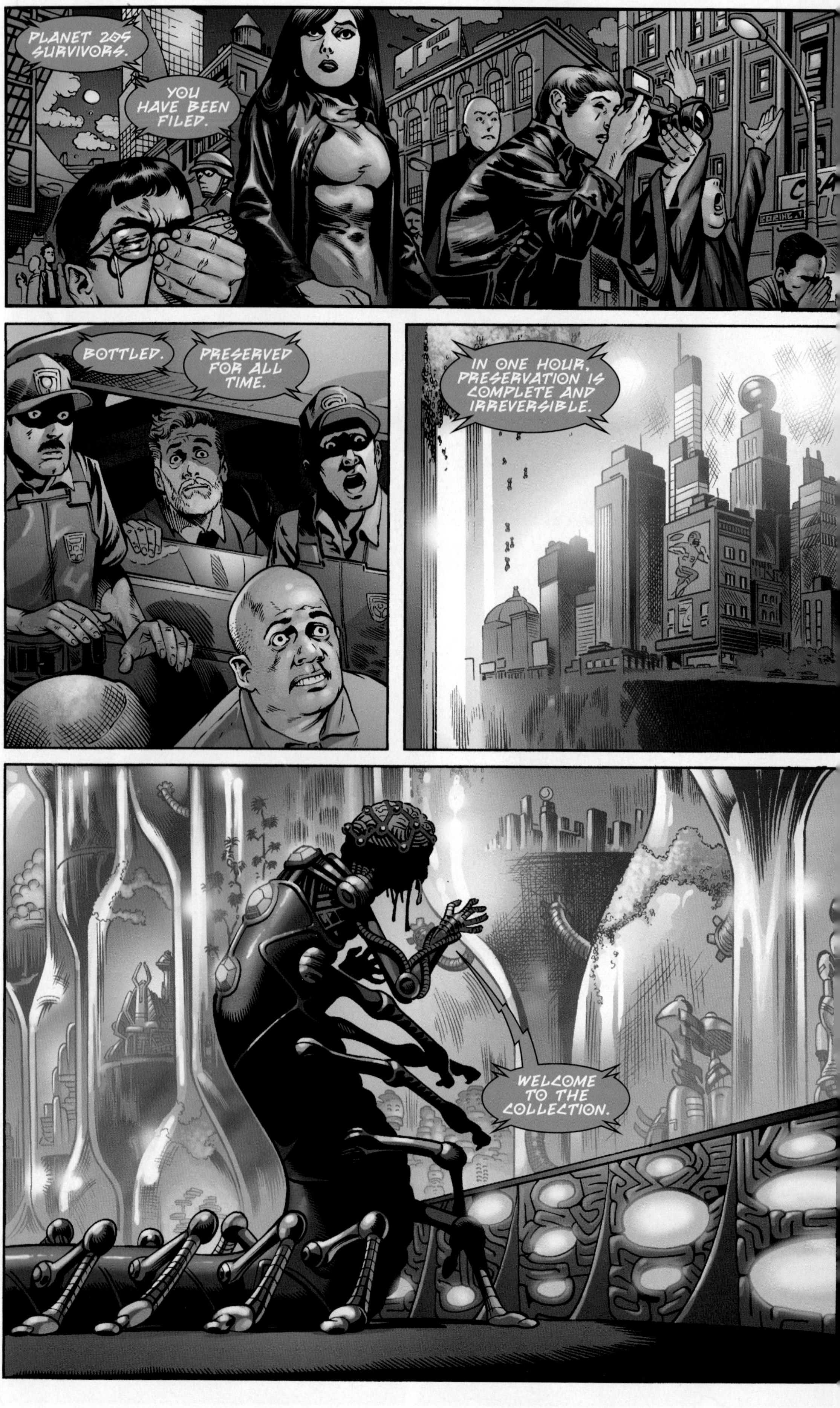
PLANET 205 SURVIVORS.
YOU HAVE BEEN FILED.
BOTTLED.
PRESERVED FOR ALL TIME.
IN ONE HOUR, PRESERVATION IS COMPLETE AND IRREVERSIBLE.
WELCOME TO THE COLLECTION.

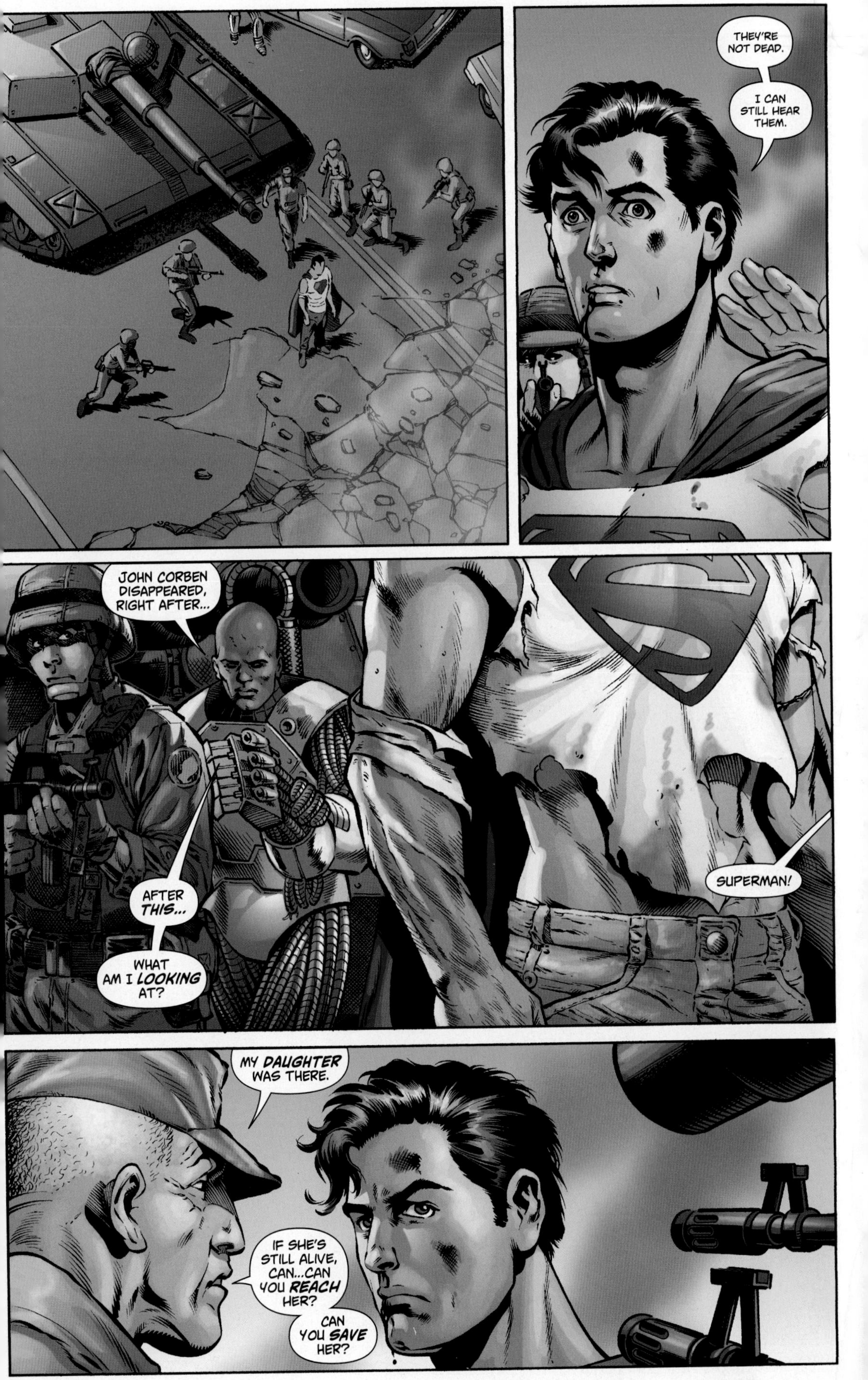
THEY'RE NOT DEAD.
I CAN STILL HEAR THEM.
JOHN CORBEN DISAPPEARED, RIGHT AFTER...
AFTER THIS...
WHAT AM I LOOKING AT?
SUPERMAN!
MY DAUGHTER WAS THERE.
IF SHE'S STILL ALIVE, CAN...CAN YOU REACH HER?
CAN YOU SAVE HER?

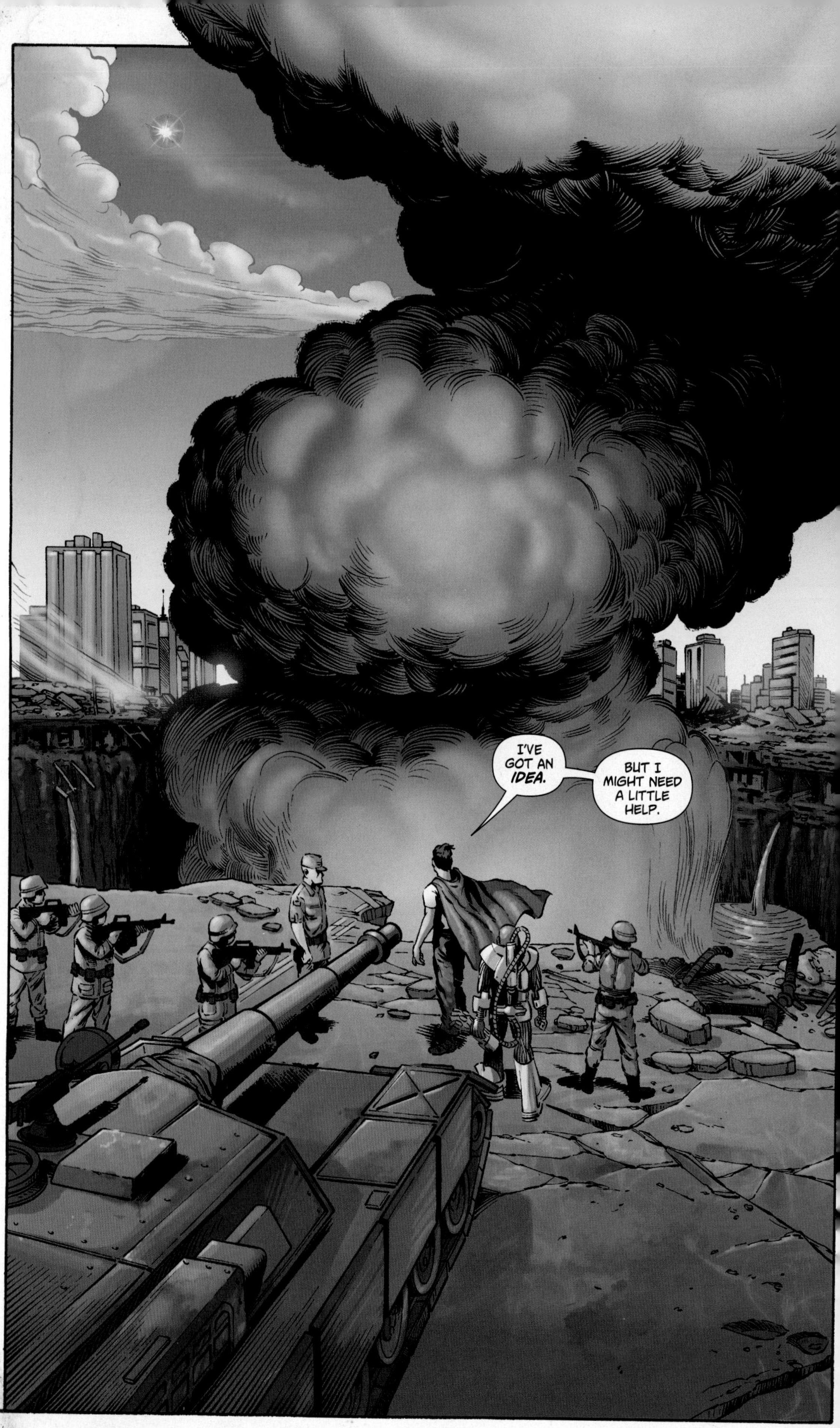
I'VE GOT AN IDEA.
BUT I MIGHT NEED A LITTLE HELP.

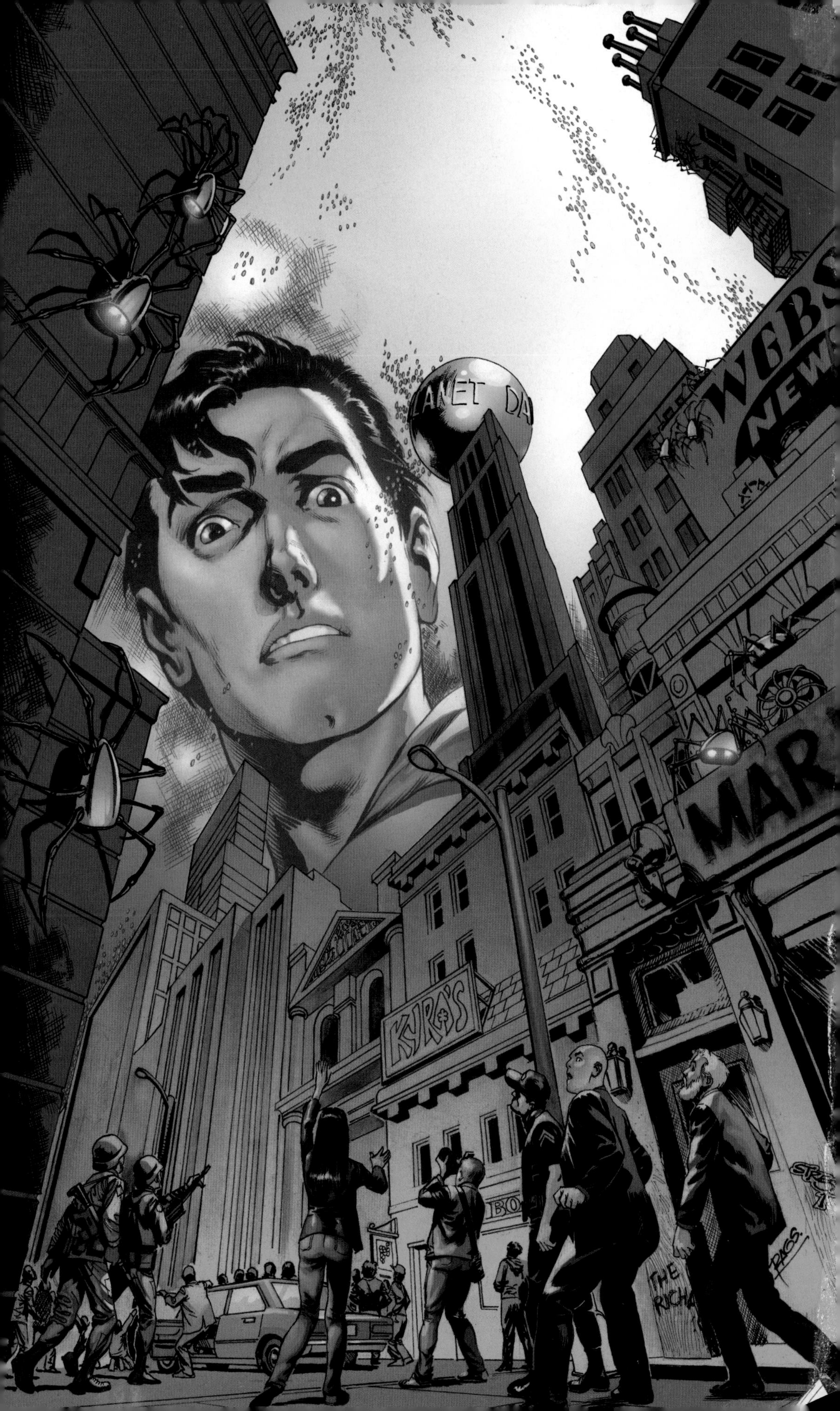

LANET DA
WGBS
NEW
KYRA'S
MAR
BO
THE
RICH

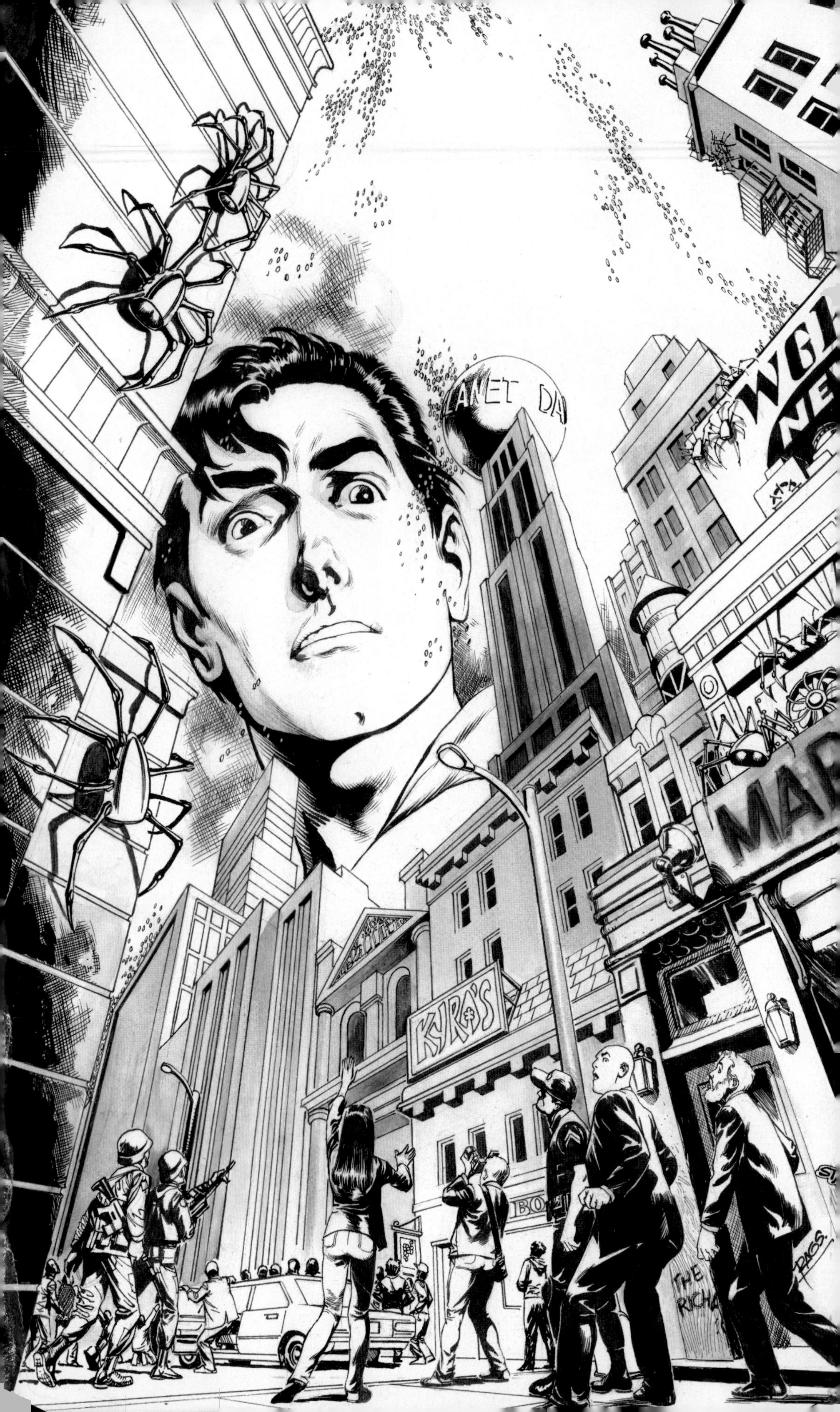

LANET DA
WGI
NE
MAR
KYRO'S
THE
RICH
RAGS.

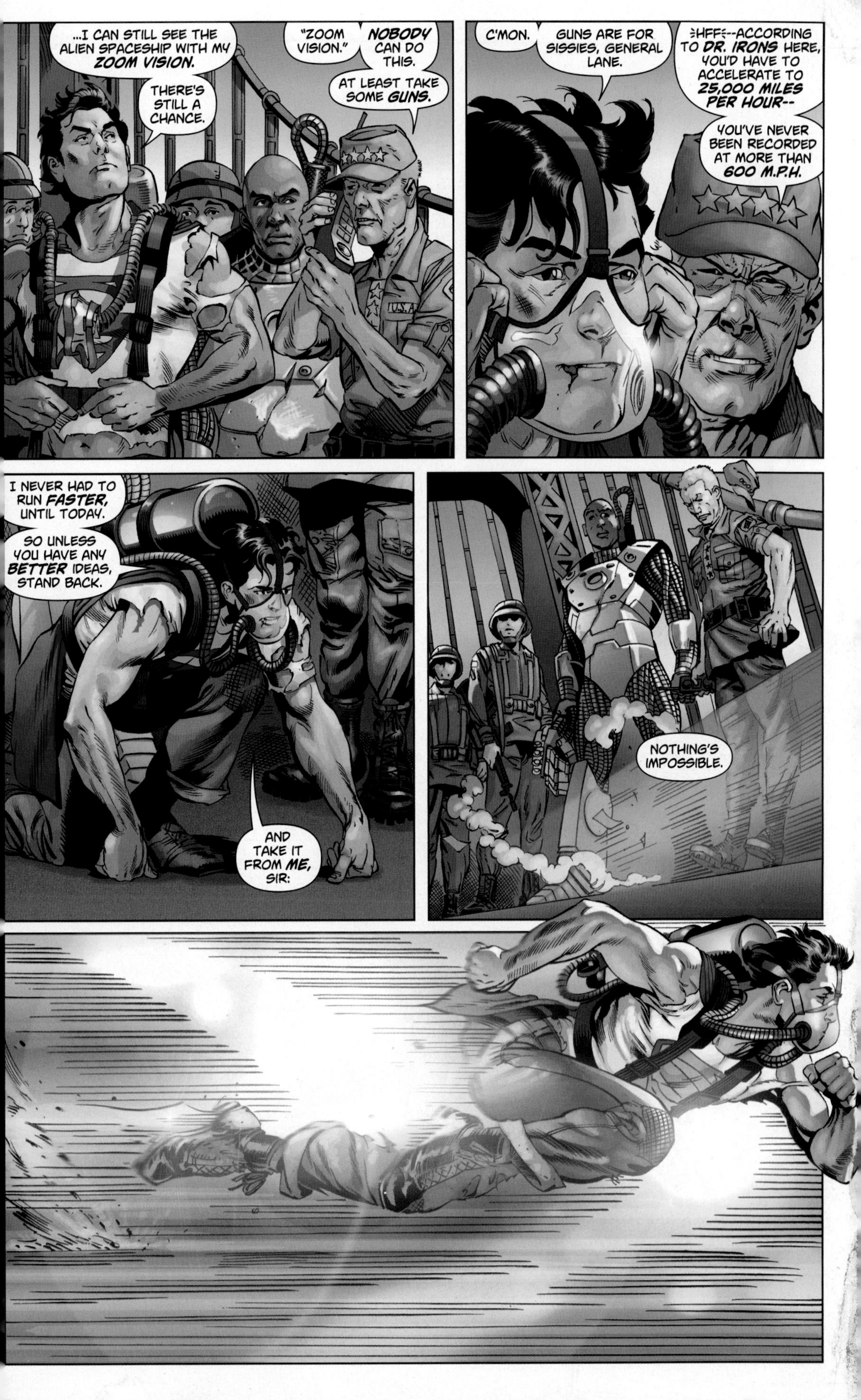
...I CAN STILL SEE THE ALIEN SPACESHIP WITH MY ZOOM VISION.
THERE'S STILL A CHANCE.
"ZOOM VISION."
NOBODY CAN DO THIS.
AT LEAST TAKE SOME GUNS.
C'MON.
GUNS ARE FOR SISSIES, GENERAL LANE.
HFF--ACCORDING TO DR. IRONS HERE, YOU'D HAVE TO ACCELERATE TO 25,000 MILES PER HOUR--
YOU'VE NEVER BEEN RECORDED AT MORE THAN 600 M.P.H.
I NEVER HAD TO RUN FASTER, UNTIL TODAY.
SO UNLESS YOU HAVE ANY BETTER IDEAS, STAND BACK.
AND TAKE IT FROM ME, SIR:
NOTHING'S IMPOSSIBLE.

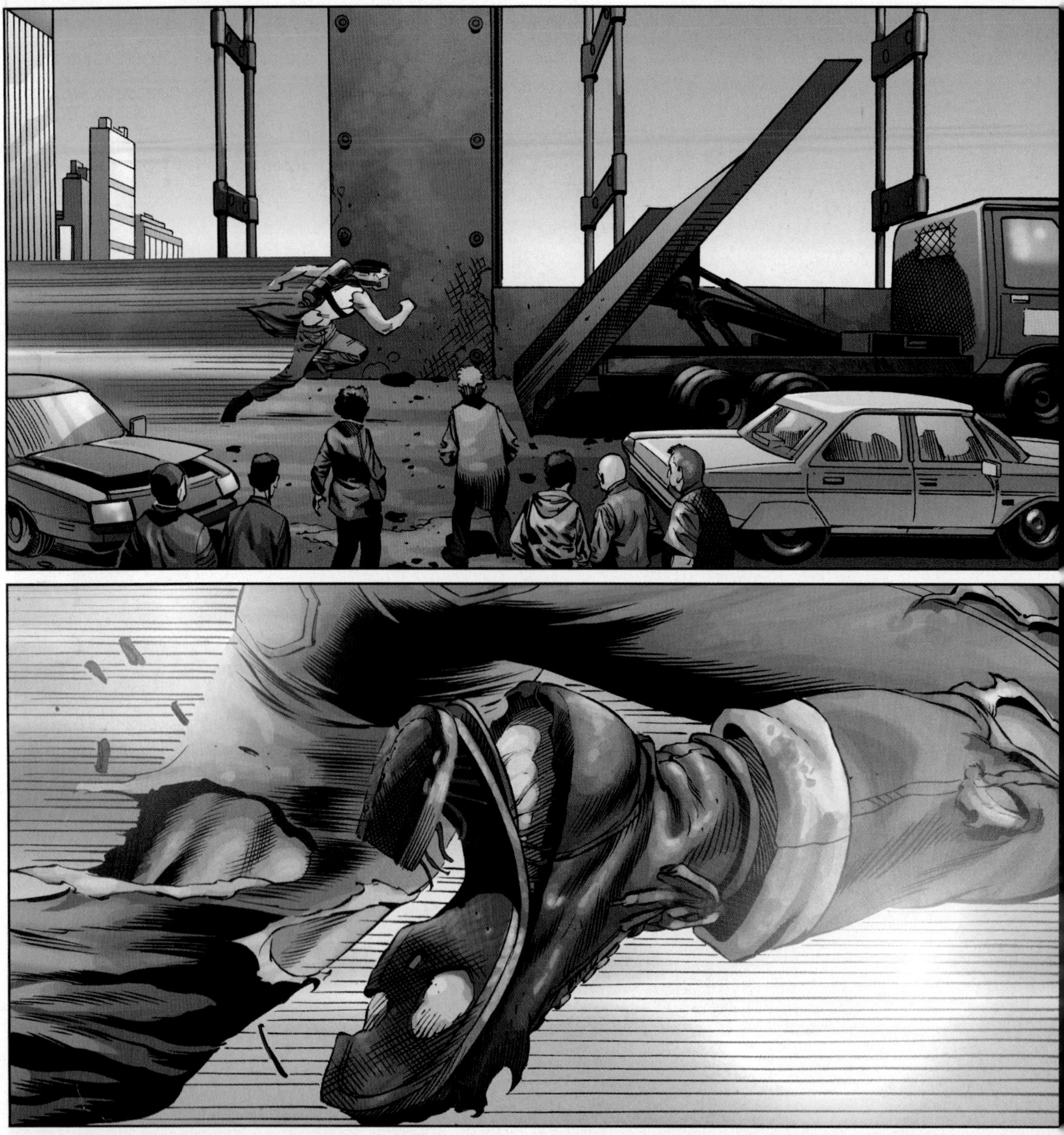

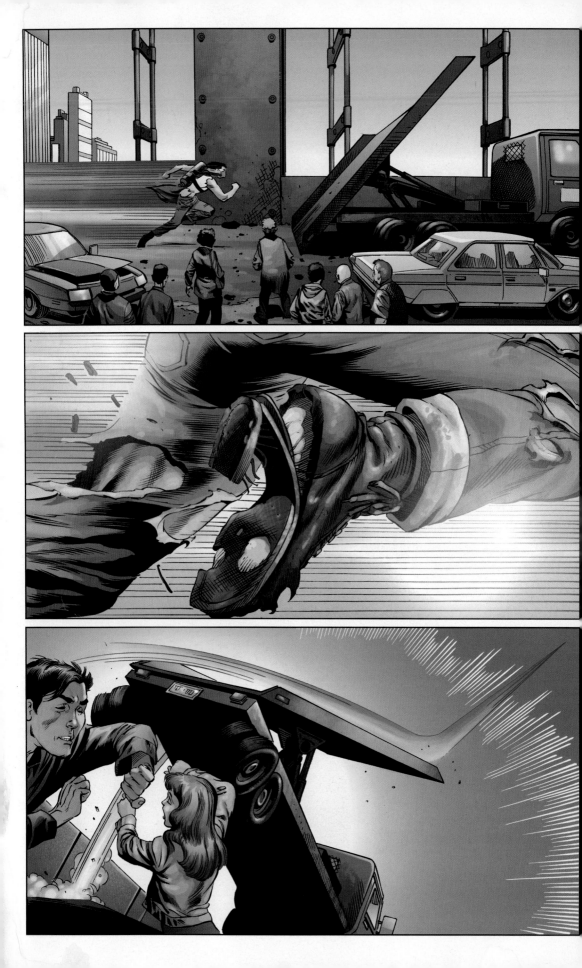

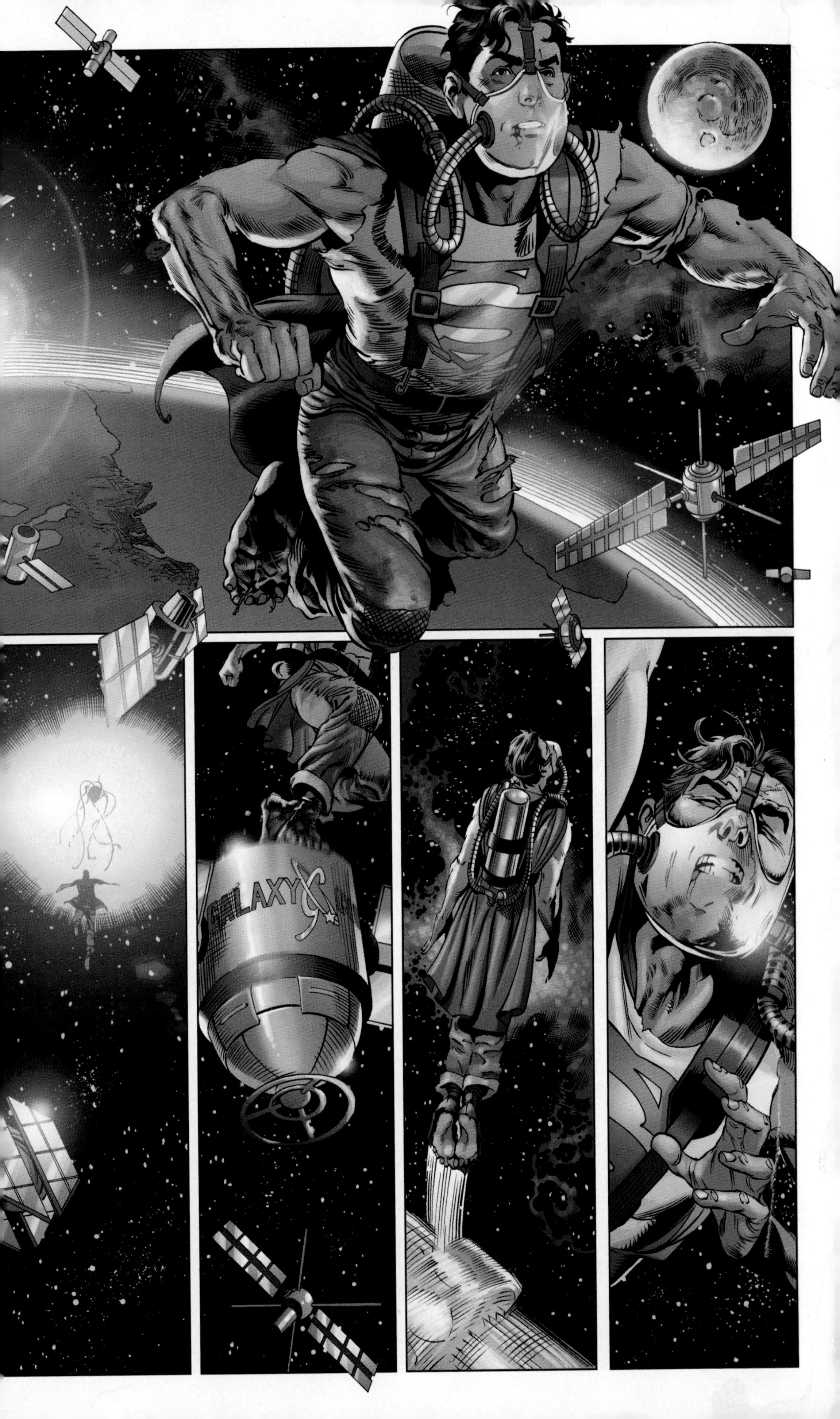
GALAXY

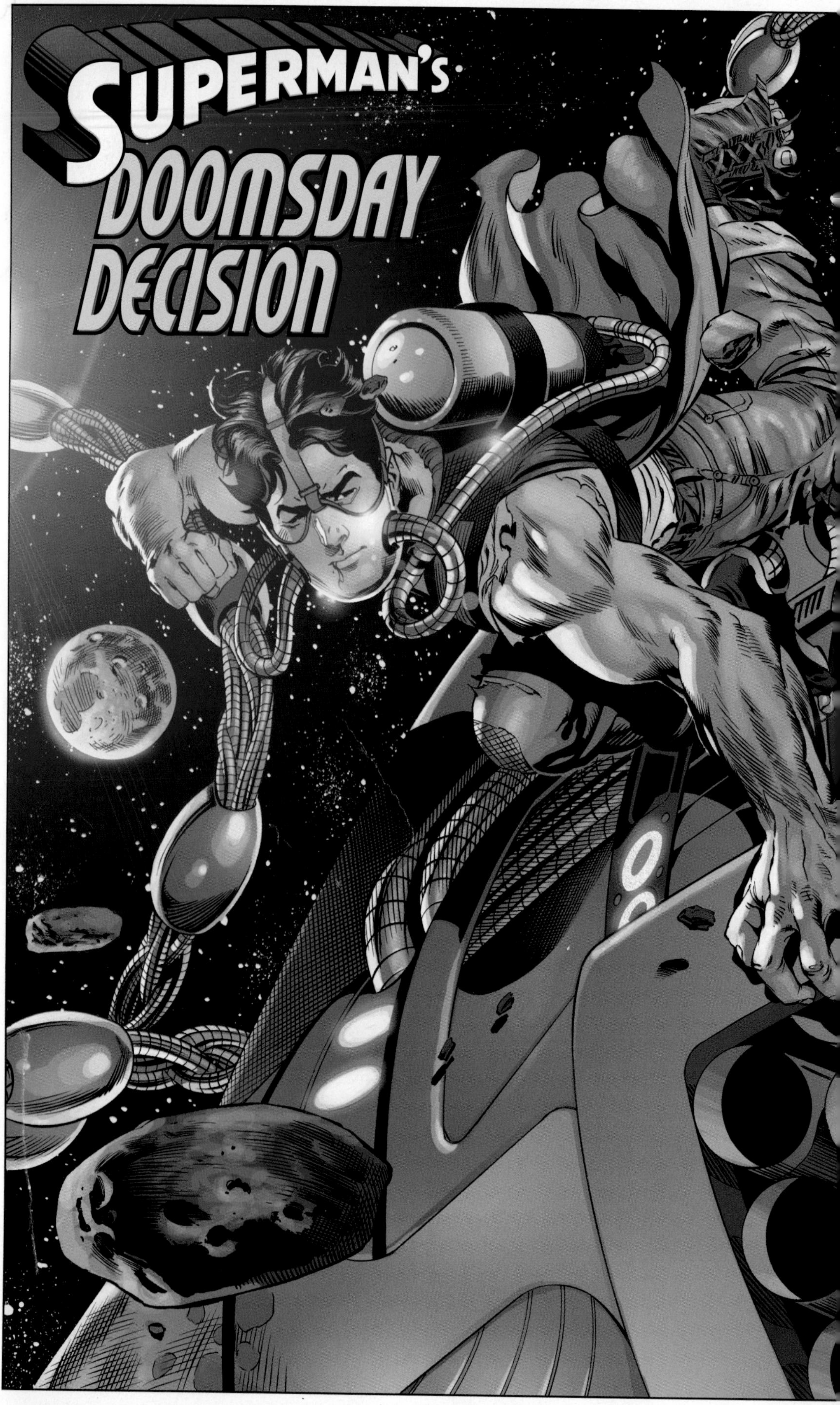
SUPERMAN'S
DOOMSDAY DECISION

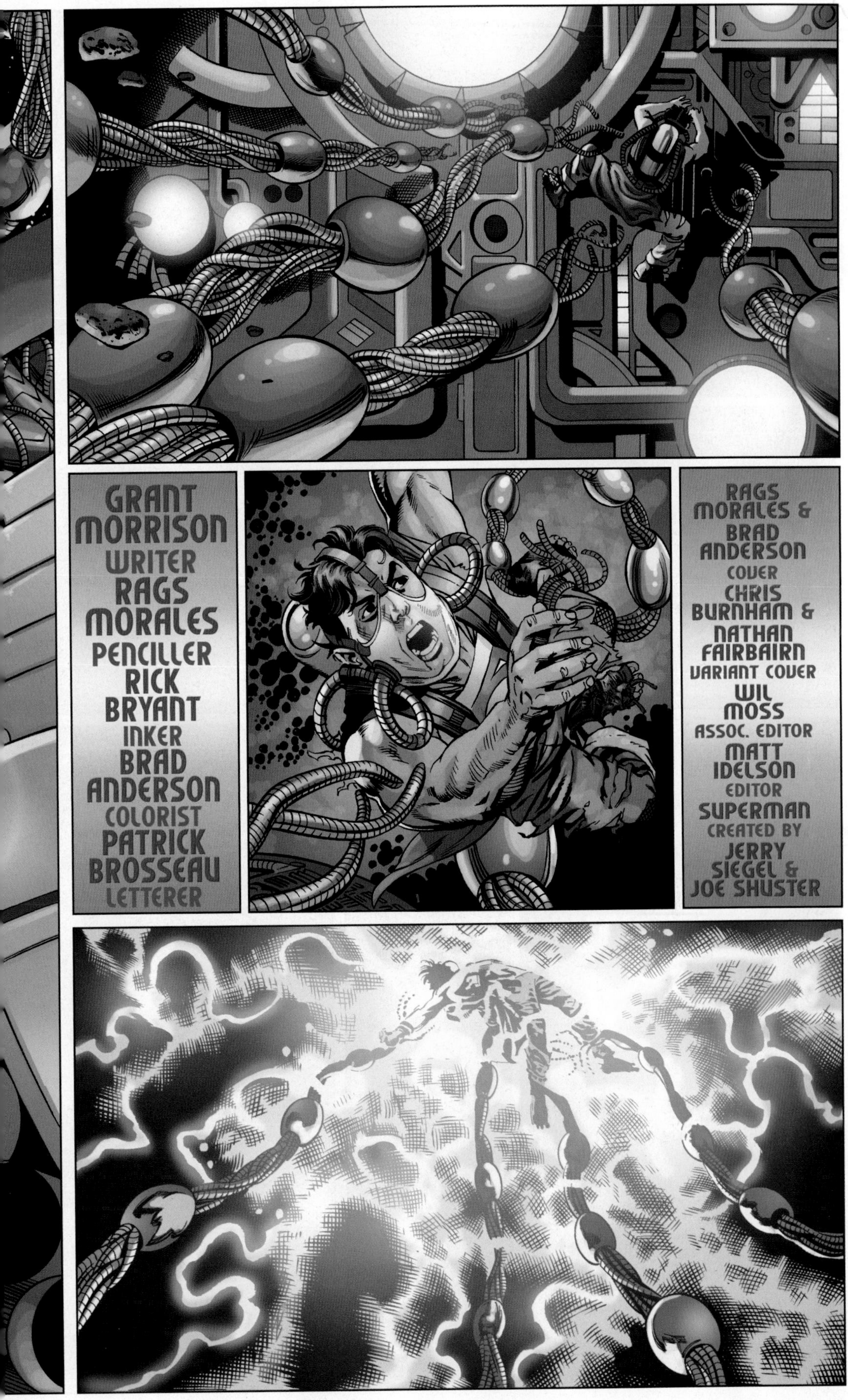

GRANT MORRISON WRITER
RAGS MORALES PENCILLER
RICK BRYANT INKER
BRAD ANDERSON COLORIST
PATRICK BROSSEAU LETTERER
RAGS MORALES & BRAD ANDERSON COVER
CHRIS BURNHAM & NATHAN FAIRBAIRN VARIANT COVER
WIL MOSS ASSOC. EDITOR
MATT IDELSON EDITOR
SUPERMAN CREATED BY JERRY SIEGEL & JOE SHUSTER

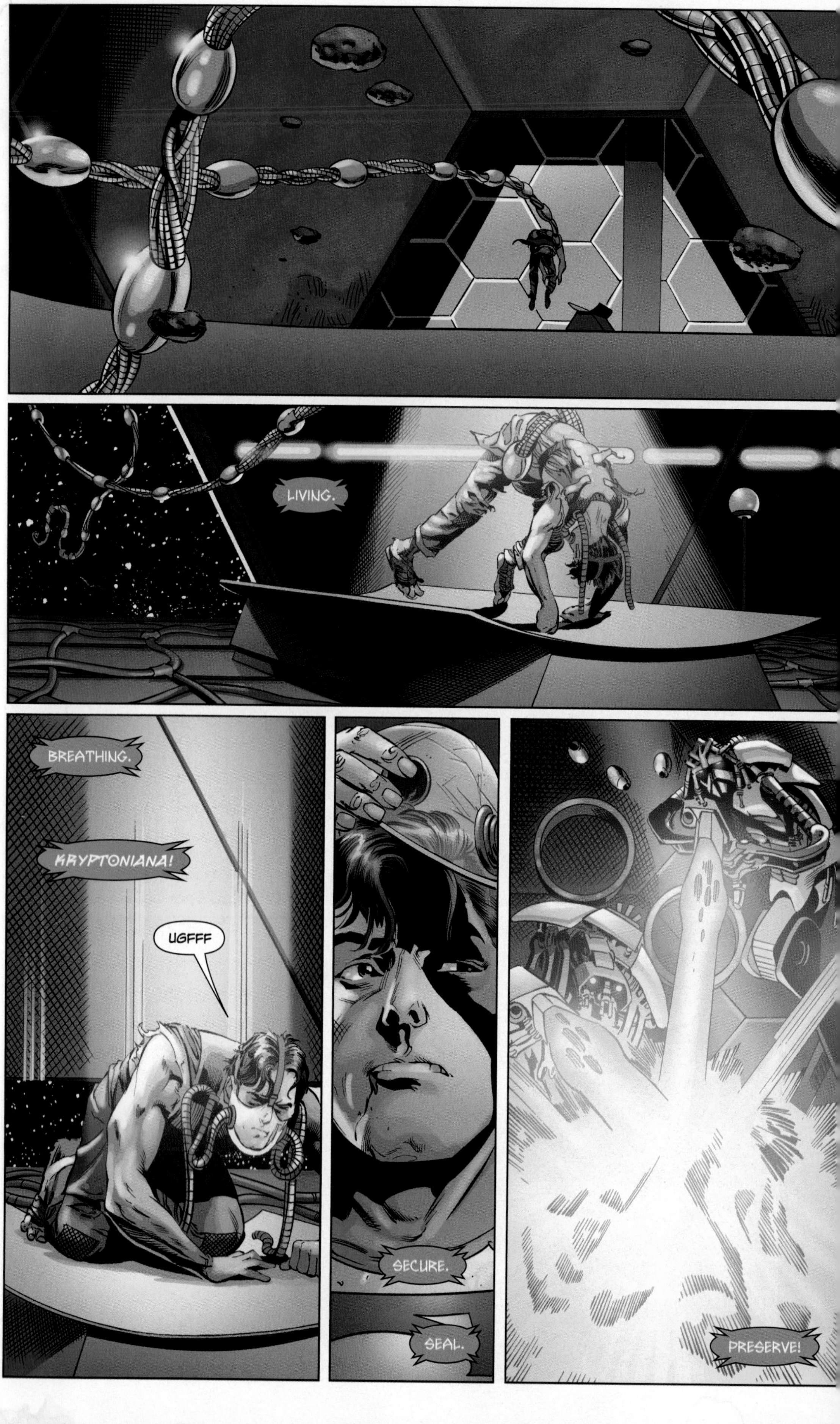
LIVING.
BREATHING.
KRYPTONIANA!
UGFFF
SECURE.
SEAL.
PRESERVE!

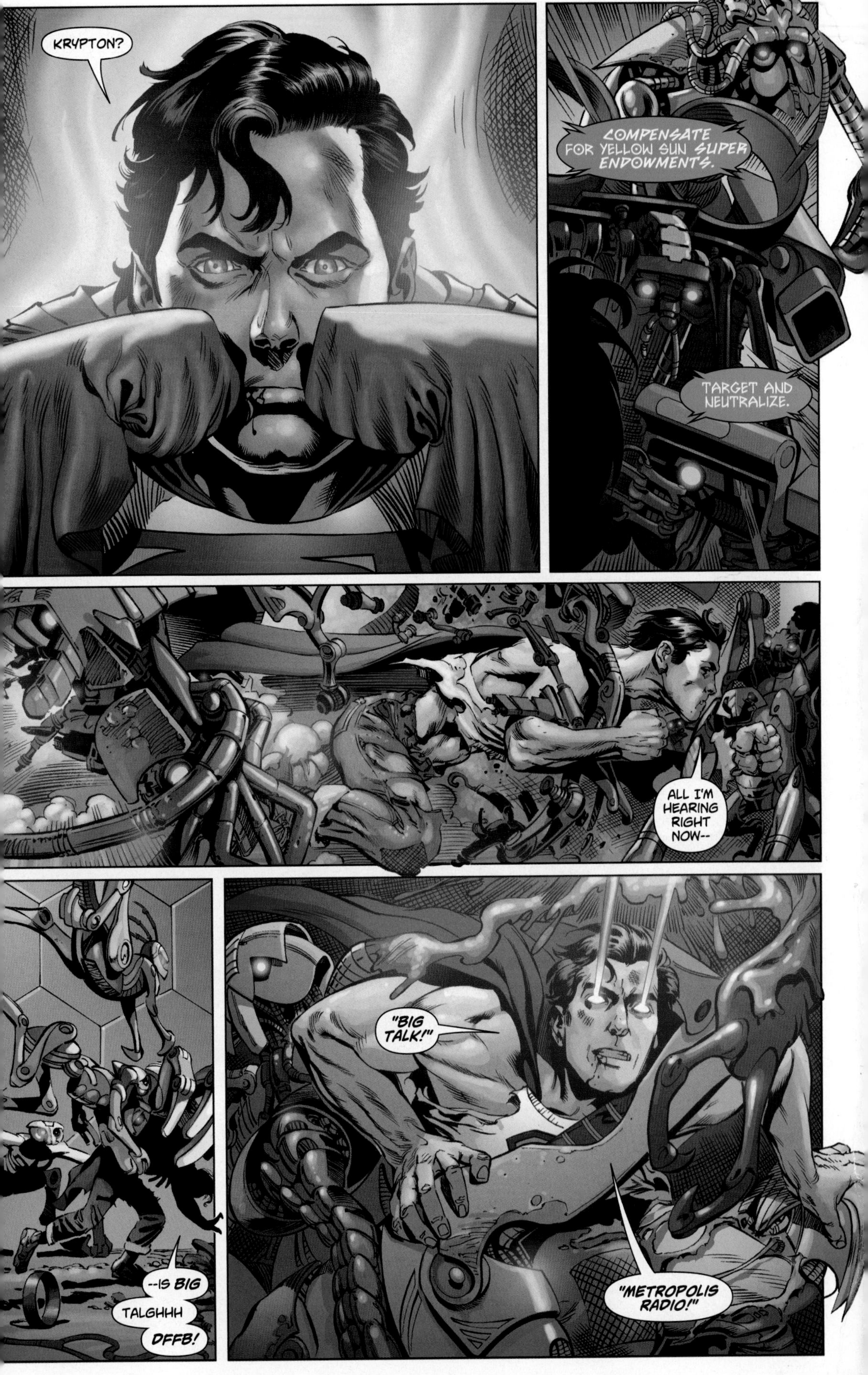
KRYPTON?
COMPENSATE FOR YELLOW SUN SUPER ENDOWMENTS.
TARGET AND NEUTRALIZE.
ALL I'M HEARING RIGHT NOW--
--IS BIG
TALGHHH
DFFB!
"BIG TALK!"
"METROPOLIS RADIO!"

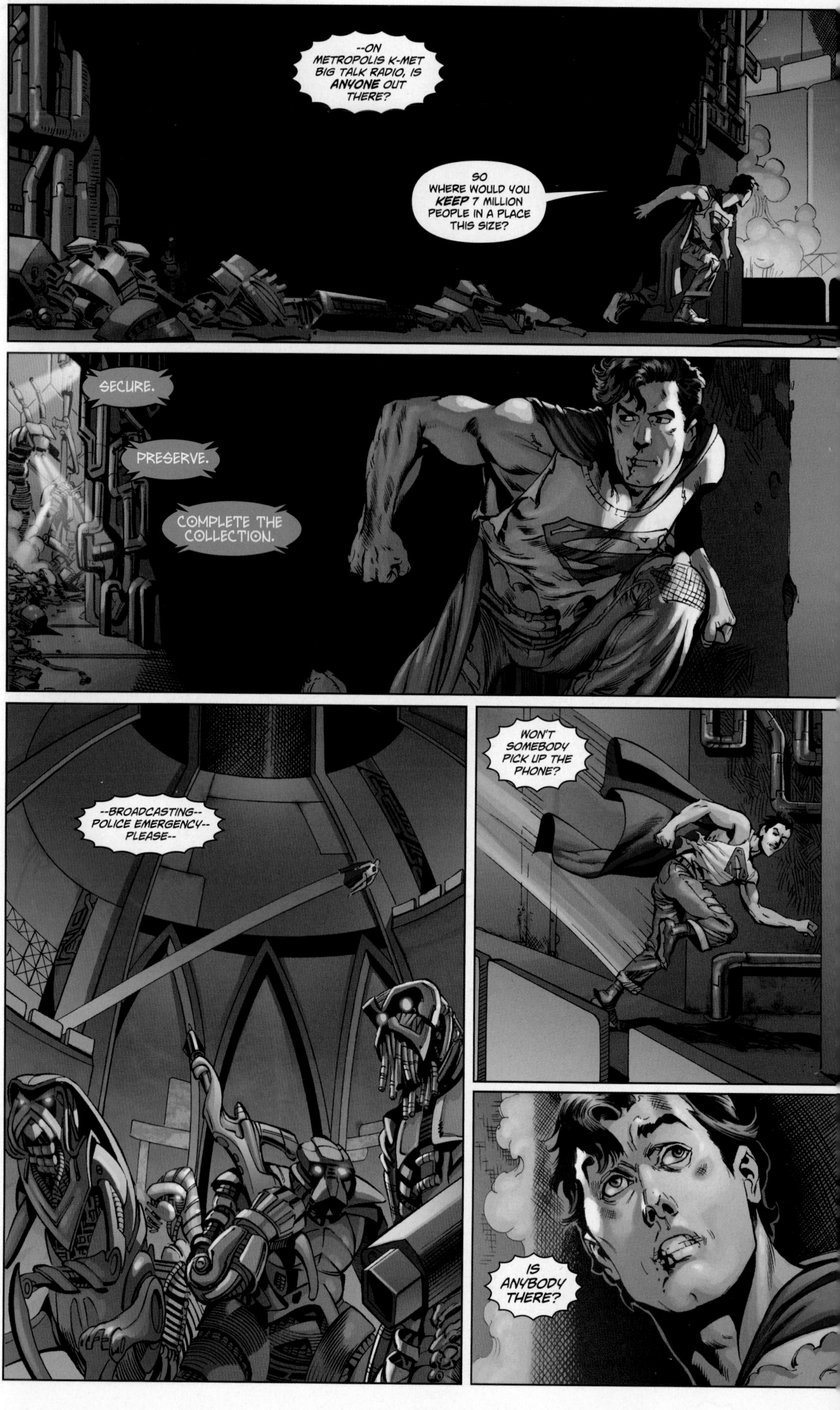

--ON METROPOLIS K-MET BIG TALK RADIO, IS ANYONE OUT THERE?
SO WHERE WOULD YOU KEEP 7 MILLION PEOPLE IN A PLACE THIS SIZE?
SECURE.
PRESERVE.
COMPLETE THE COLLECTION.
--BROADCASTING-- POLICE EMERGENCY-- PLEASE--
WON'T SOMEBODY PICK UP THE PHONE?
IS ANYBODY THERE?

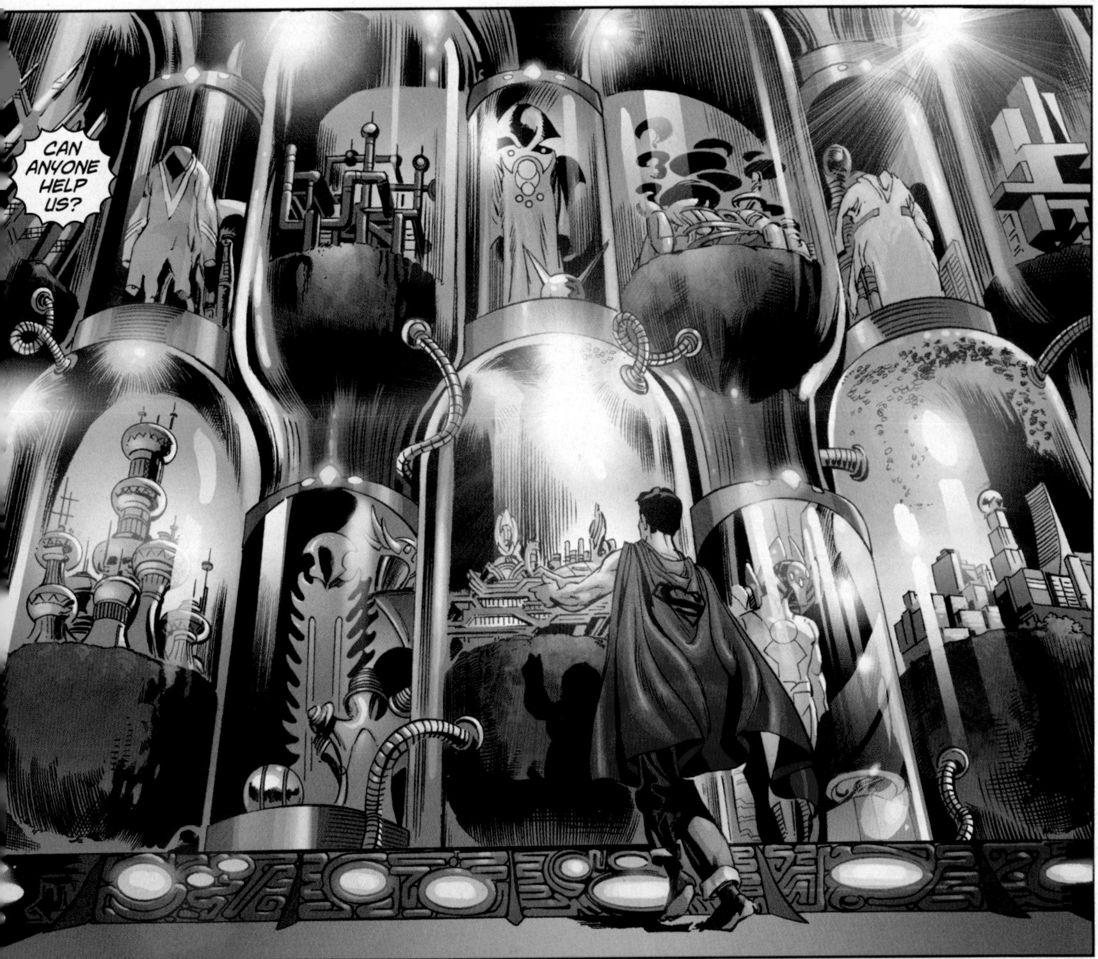
CAN ANYONE HELP US?

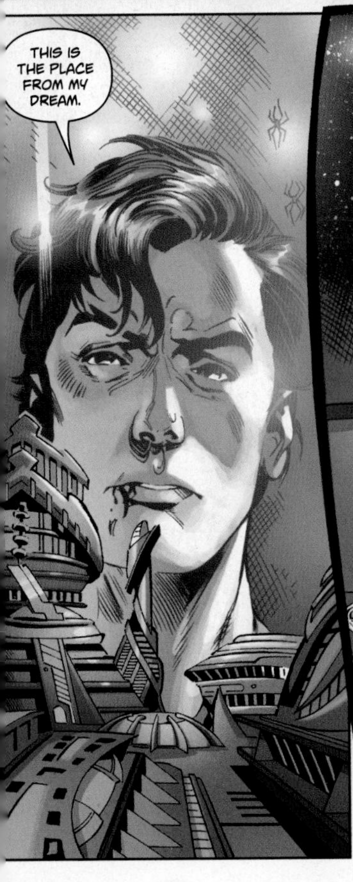
THIS IS THE PLACE FROM MY DREAM.

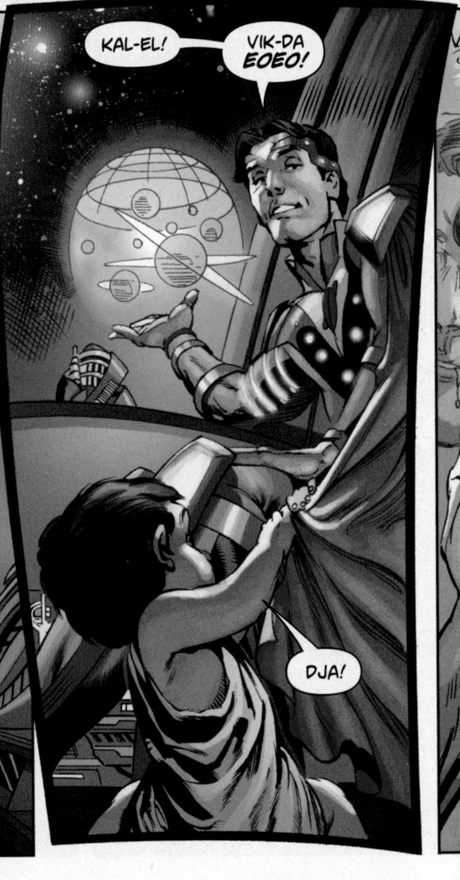
KAL-EL!
VIK-DA EOEO!
DJA!

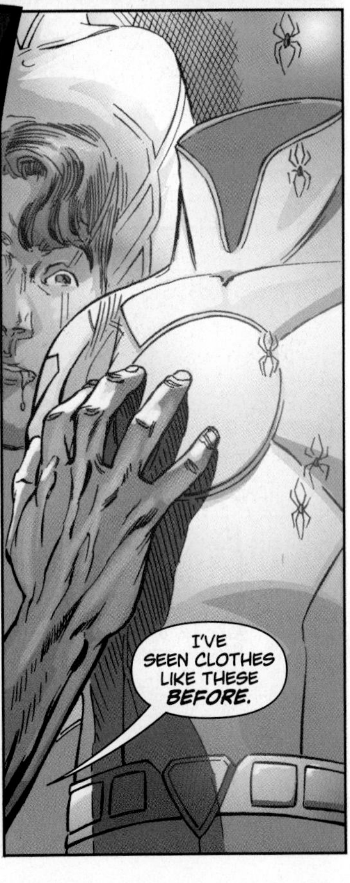
I'VE SEEN CLOTHES LIKE THESE BEFORE.

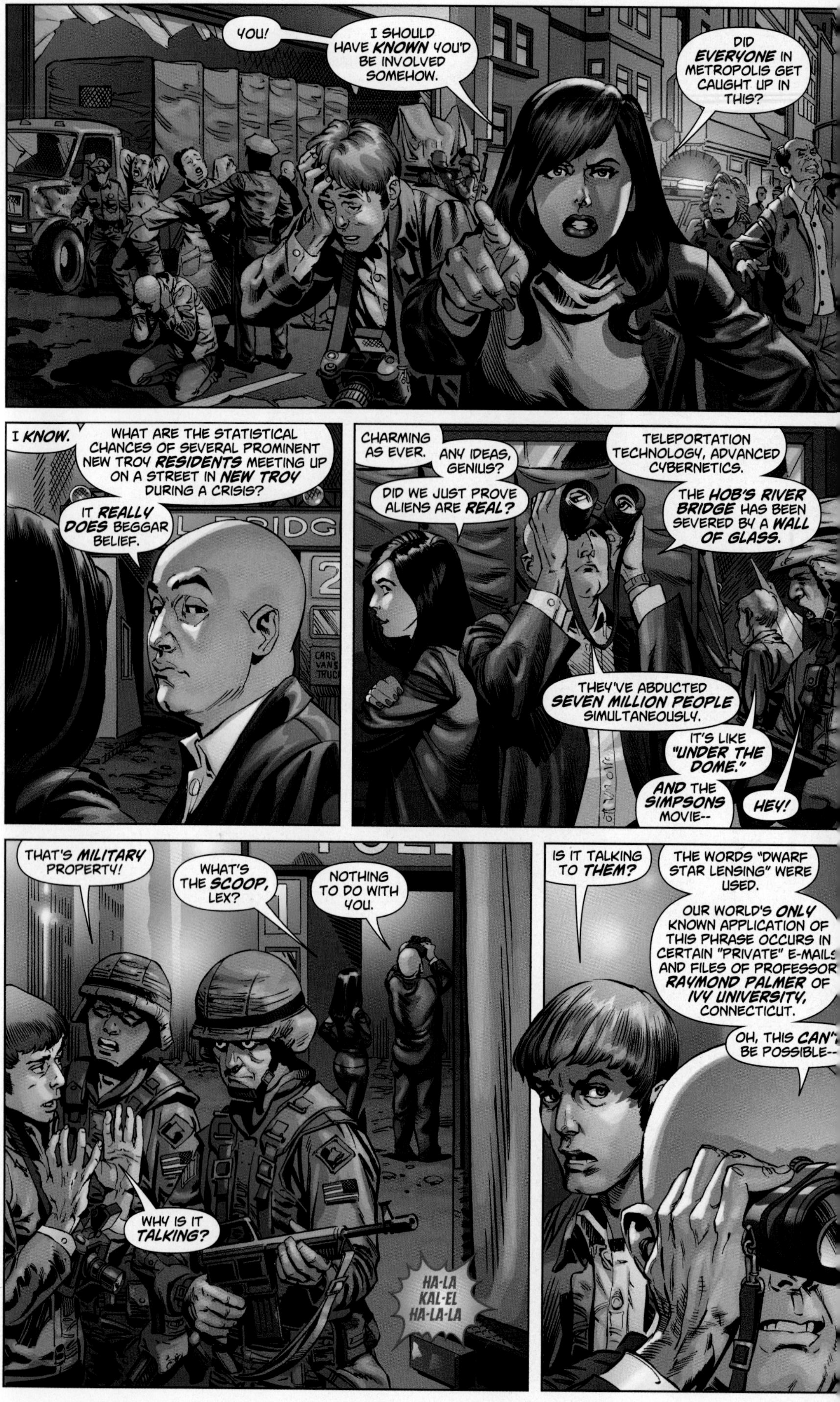
YOU!
I SHOULD HAVE KNOWN YOU'D BE INVOLVED SOMEHOW.
DID EVERYONE IN METROPOLIS GET CAUGHT UP IN THIS?
I KNOW.
WHAT ARE THE STATISTICAL CHANCES OF SEVERAL PROMINENT NEW TROY RESIDENTS MEETING UP ON A STREET IN NEW TROY DURING A CRISIS?
IT REALLY DOES BEGGAR BELIEF.
CHARMING AS EVER.
ANY IDEAS, GENIUS?
DID WE JUST PROVE ALIENS ARE REAL?
TELEPORTATION TECHNOLOGY, ADVANCED CYBERNETICS.
THE HOB'S RIVER BRIDGE HAS BEEN SEVERED BY A WALL OF GLASS.
THEY'VE ABDUCTED SEVEN MILLION PEOPLE SIMULTANEOUSLY.
IT'S LIKE "UNDER THE DOME."
AND THE SIMPSONS MOVIE--
HEY!
THAT'S MILITARY PROPERTY!
WHAT'S THE SCOOP, LEX?
NOTHING TO DO WITH YOU.
WHY IS IT TALKING?
HA-LA KAL-EL HA-LA-LA
IS IT TALKING TO THEM?
THE WORDS "DWARF STAR LENSING" WERE USED.
OUR WORLD'S ONLY KNOWN APPLICATION OF THIS PHRASE OCCURS IN CERTAIN "PRIVATE" E-MAILS AND FILES OF PROFESSOR RAYMOND PALMER OF IVY UNIVERSITY, CONNECTICUT.
OH, THIS CAN'T BE POSSIBLE--

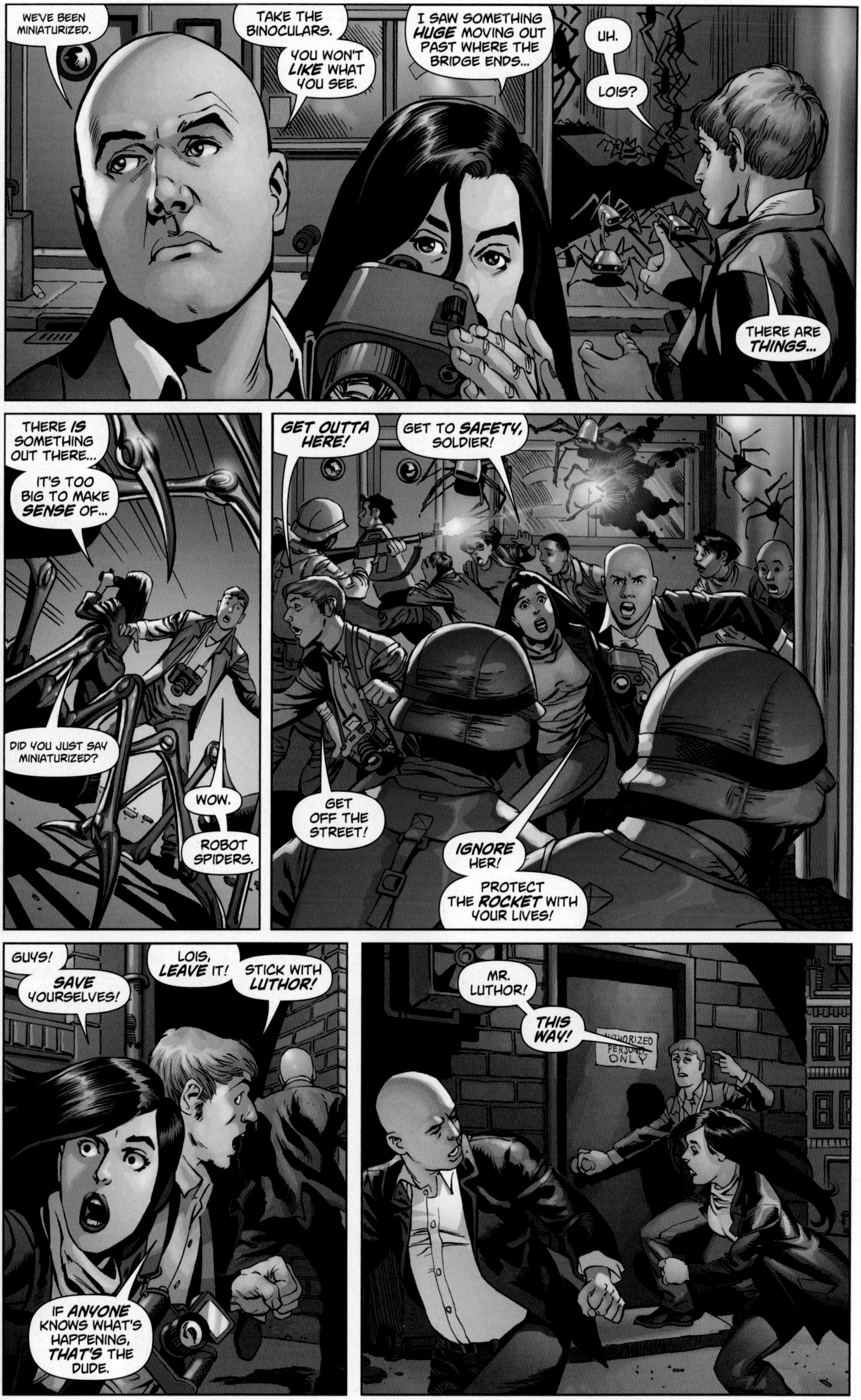
WE'VE BEEN MINIATURIZED.
TAKE THE BINOCULARS.
YOU WON'T LIKE WHAT YOU SEE.
I SAW SOMETHING HUGE MOVING OUT PAST WHERE THE BRIDGE ENDS...
UH.
LOIS?
THERE ARE THINGS...
THERE IS SOMETHING OUT THERE...
IT'S TOO BIG TO MAKE SENSE OF...
DID YOU JUST SAY MINIATURIZED?
WOW.
ROBOT SPIDERS.
GET OUTTA HERE!
GET TO SAFETY, SOLDIER!
GET OFF THE STREET!
IGNORE HER!
PROTECT THE ROCKET WITH YOUR LIVES!
GUYS!
SAVE YOURSELVES!
LOIS, LEAVE IT!
STICK WITH LUTHOR!
IF ANYONE KNOWS WHAT'S HAPPENING, THAT'S THE DUDE.
MR. LUTHOR!
THIS WAY!

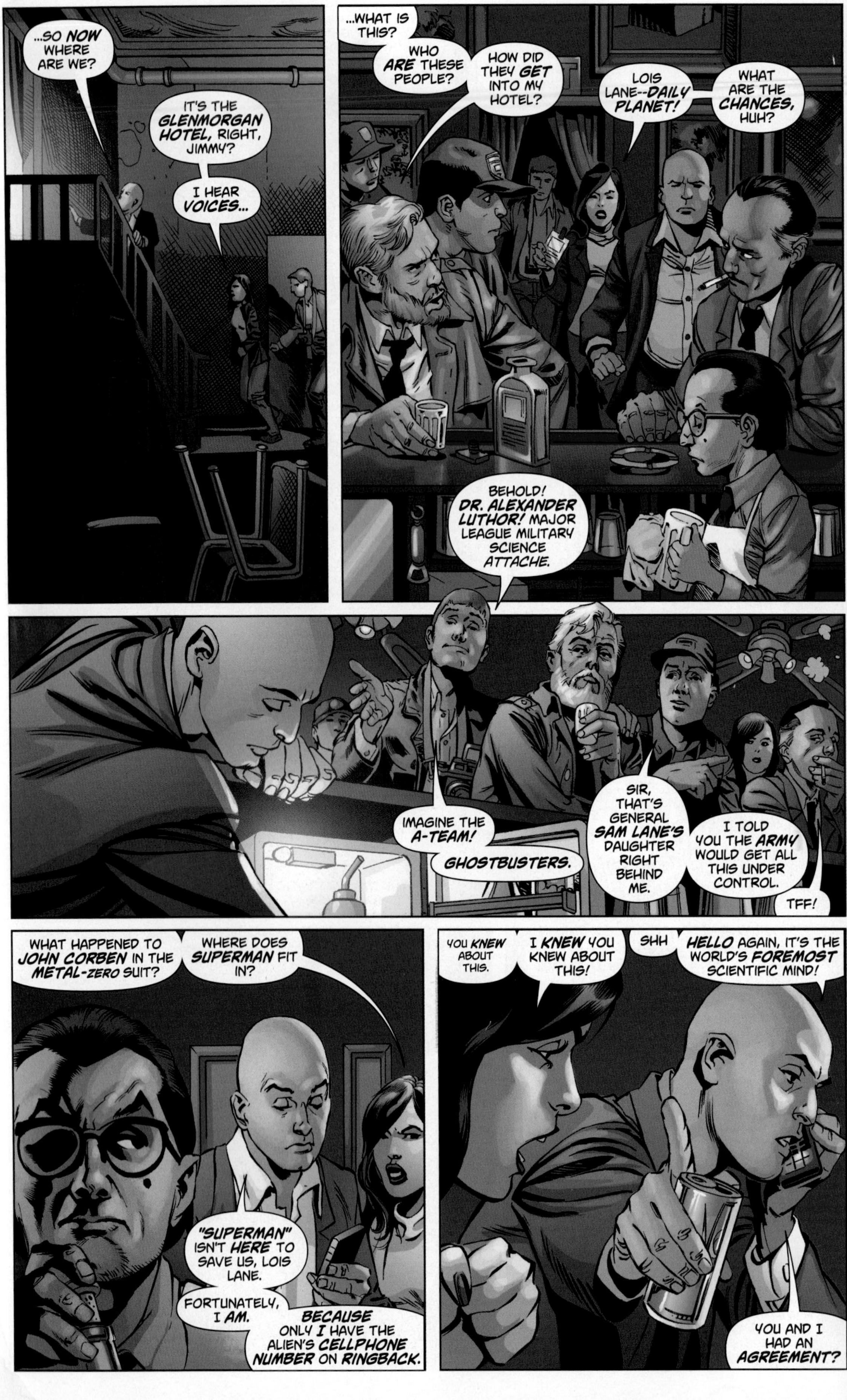

...SO NOW WHERE ARE WE?
IT'S THE GLENMORGAN HOTEL, RIGHT, JIMMY?
I HEAR VOICES...
...WHAT IS THIS?
WHO ARE THESE PEOPLE?
HOW DID THEY GET INTO MY HOTEL?
LOIS LANE--DAILY PLANET!
WHAT ARE THE CHANCES, HUH?
BEHOLD! DR. ALEXANDER LUTHOR! MAJOR LEAGUE MILITARY SCIENCE ATTACHE.
IMAGINE THE A-TEAM!
GHOSTBUSTERS.
SIR, THAT'S GENERAL SAM LANE'S DAUGHTER RIGHT BEHIND ME.
I TOLD YOU THE ARMY WOULD GET ALL THIS UNDER CONTROL.
TFF!
WHAT HAPPENED TO JOHN CORBEN IN THE METAL-ZERO SUIT?
WHERE DOES SUPERMAN FIT IN?
"SUPERMAN" ISN'T HERE TO SAVE US, LOIS LANE.
FORTUNATELY, I AM.
BECAUSE ONLY I HAVE THE ALIEN'S CELLPHONE NUMBER ON RINGBACK.
YOU KNEW ABOUT THIS.
I KNEW YOU KNEW ABOUT THIS!
SHH
HELLO AGAIN, IT'S THE WORLD'S FOREMOST SCIENTIFIC MIND!
YOU AND I HAD AN AGREEMENT?

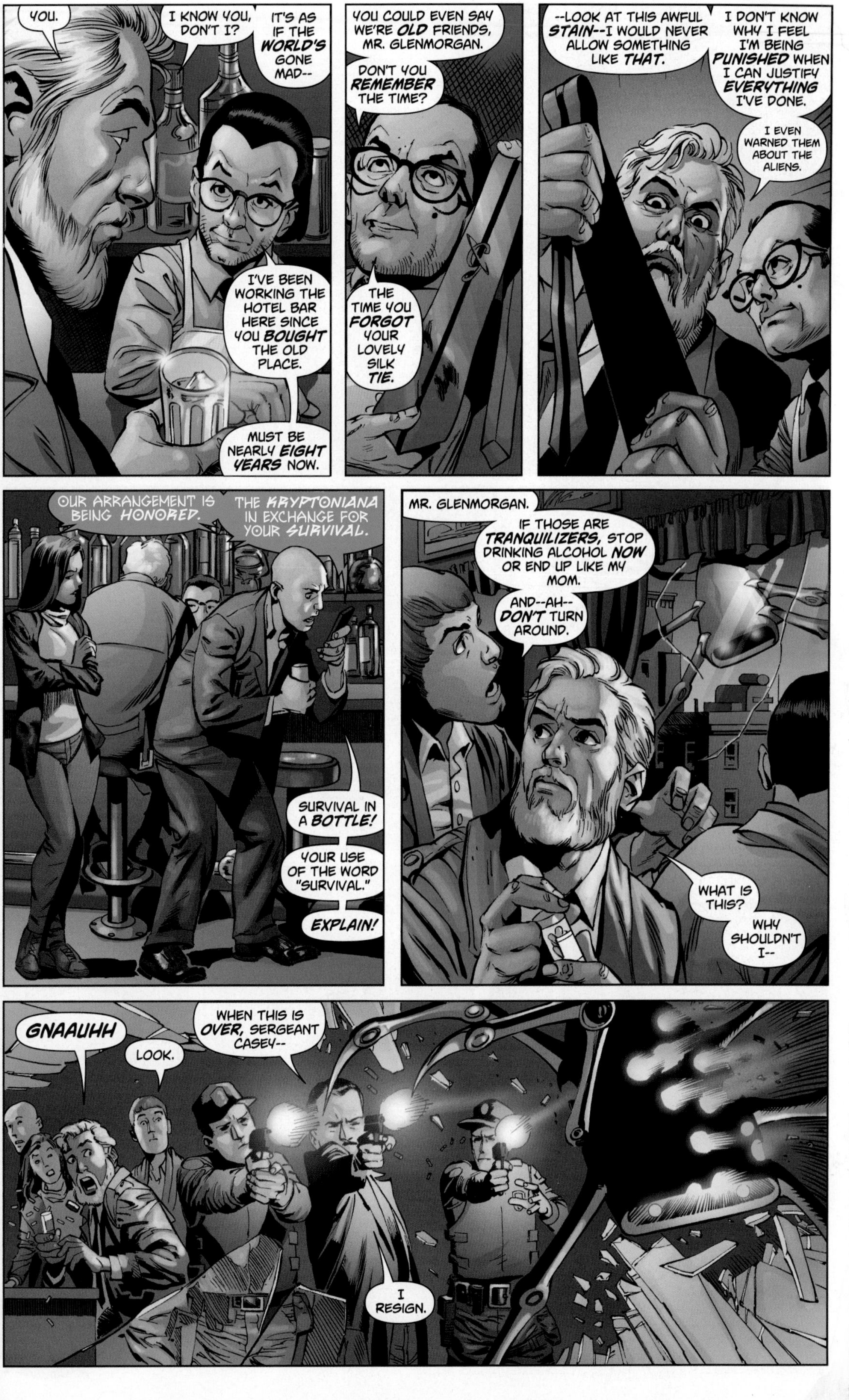

YOU.
I KNOW YOU, DON'T I?
IT'S AS IF THE WORLD'S GONE MAD--
I'VE BEEN WORKING THE HOTEL BAR HERE SINCE YOU BOUGHT THE OLD PLACE.
MUST BE NEARLY EIGHT YEARS NOW.
YOU COULD EVEN SAY WE'RE OLD FRIENDS, MR. GLENMORGAN.
DON'T YOU REMEMBER THE TIME?
THE TIME YOU FORGOT YOUR LOVELY SILK TIE.
--LOOK AT THIS AWFUL STAIN--I WOULD NEVER ALLOW SOMETHING LIKE THAT.
I DON'T KNOW WHY I FEEL I'M BEING PUNISHED WHEN I CAN JUSTIFY EVERYTHING I'VE DONE.
I EVEN WARNED THEM ABOUT THE ALIENS.
OUR ARRANGEMENT IS BEING HONORED.
THE KRYPTONIANA IN EXCHANGE FOR YOUR SURVIVAL.
SURVIVAL IN A BOTTLE!
YOUR USE OF THE WORD "SURVIVAL."
EXPLAIN!
MR. GLENMORGAN.
IF THOSE ARE TRANQUILIZERS, STOP DRINKING ALCOHOL NOW OR END UP LIKE MY MOM.
AND--AH--DON'T TURN AROUND.
WHAT IS THIS?
WHY SHOULDN'T I--
GNAAUHH
LOOK.
WHEN THIS IS OVER, SERGEANT CASEY--
I RESIGN.

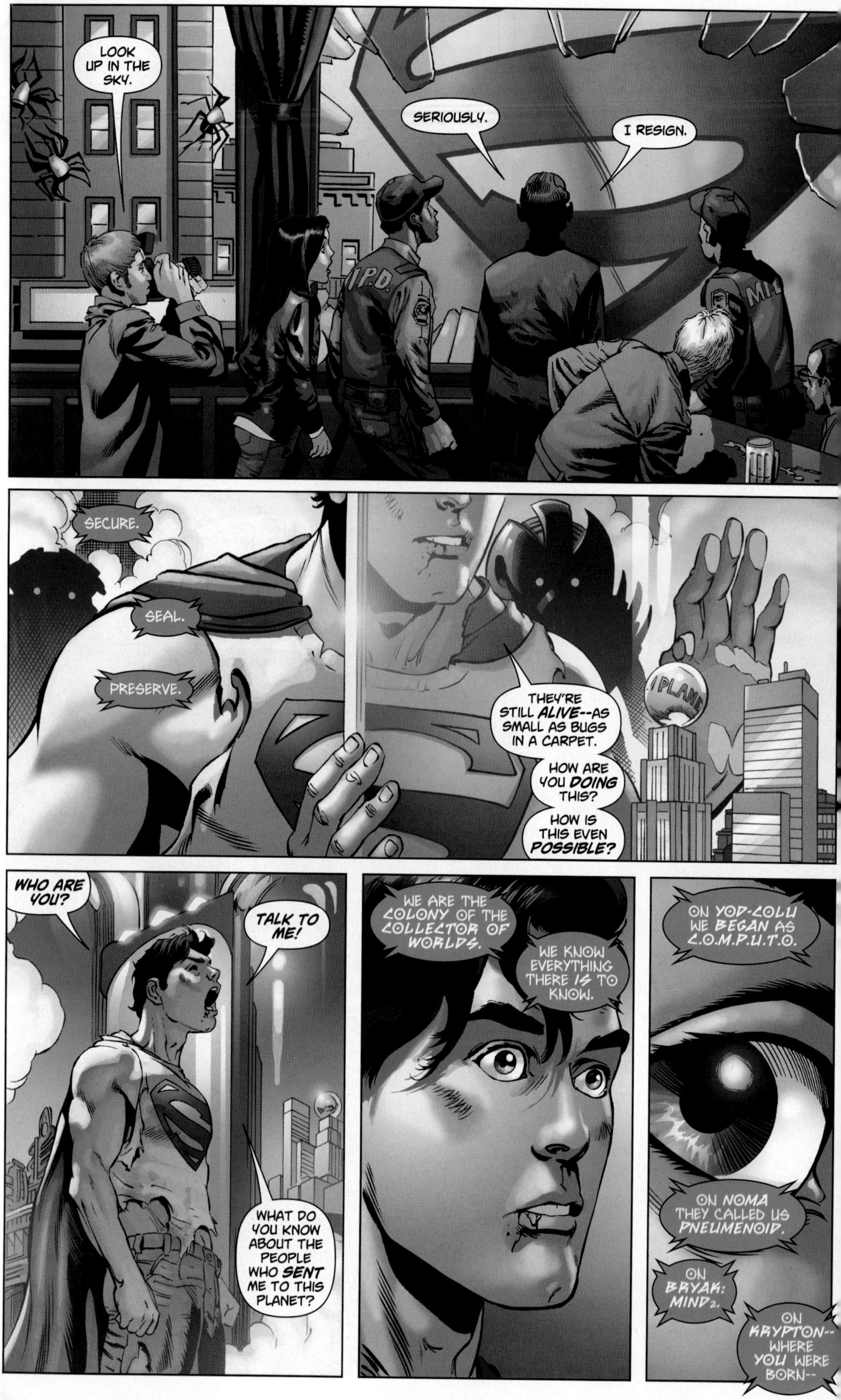
LOOK UP IN THE SKY.
SERIOUSLY.
I RESIGN.
SECURE.
SEAL.
PRESERVE.
THEY'RE STILL ALIVE--AS SMALL AS BUGS IN A CARPET.
HOW ARE YOU DOING THIS?
HOW IS THIS EVEN POSSIBLE?
WHO ARE YOU?
TALK TO ME!
WHAT DO YOU KNOW ABOUT THE PEOPLE WHO SENT ME TO THIS PLANET?
WE ARE THE COLONY OF THE COLLECTOR OF WORLDS.
WE KNOW EVERYTHING THERE IS TO KNOW.
ON YOD-COLU WE BEGAN AS C.O.M.P.U.T.O.
ON NOMA THEY CALLED US PNEUMENOID.
ON BRYAK: MIND2.
ON KRYPTON-- WHERE YOU WERE BORN--

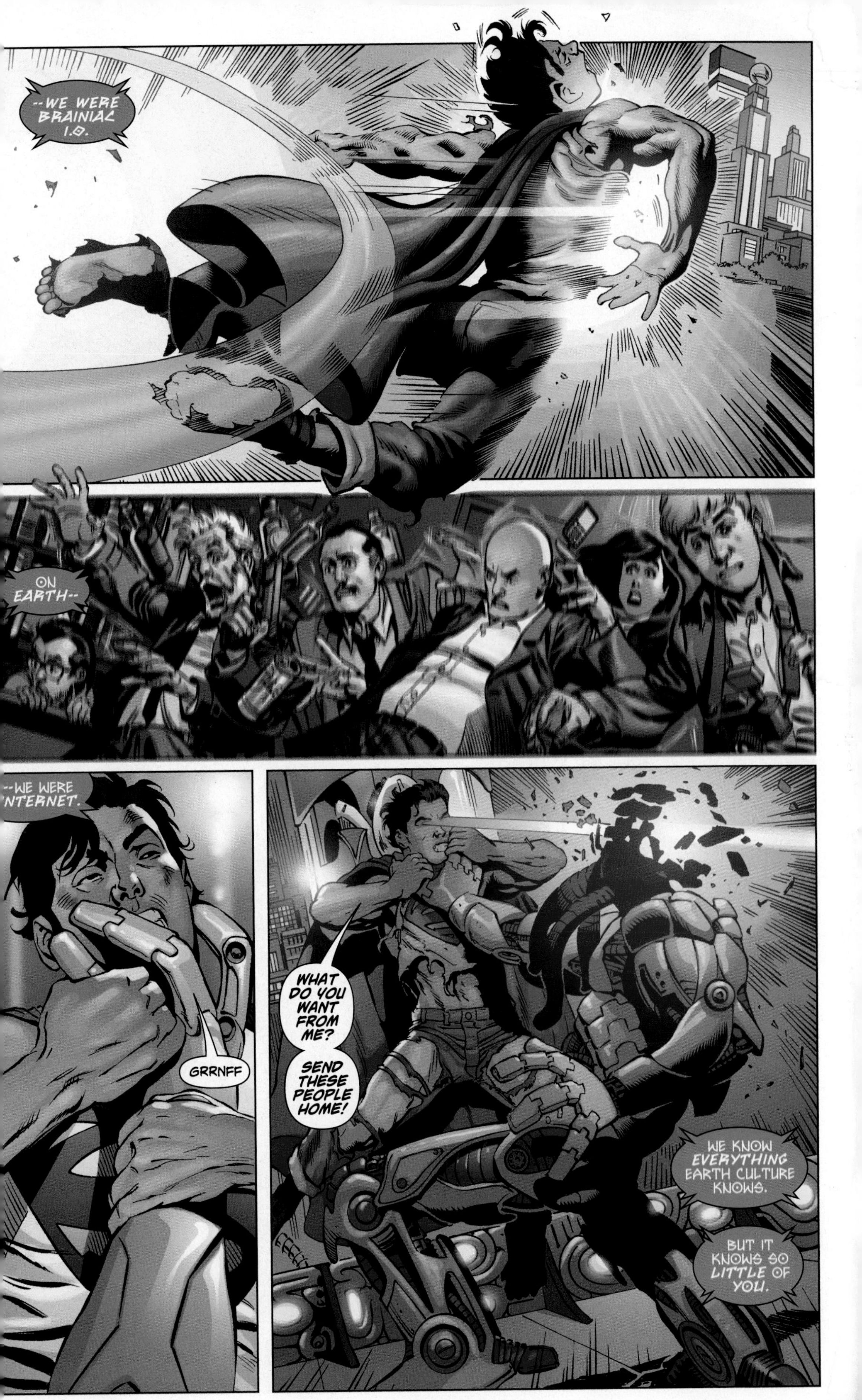

--WE WERE BRAINIAC 1.0.
ON EARTH--
--WE WERE INTERNET.
GRRNFF
WHAT DO YOU WANT FROM ME?
SEND THESE PEOPLE HOME!
WE KNOW EVERYTHING EARTH CULTURE KNOWS.
BUT IT KNOWS SO LITTLE OF YOU.

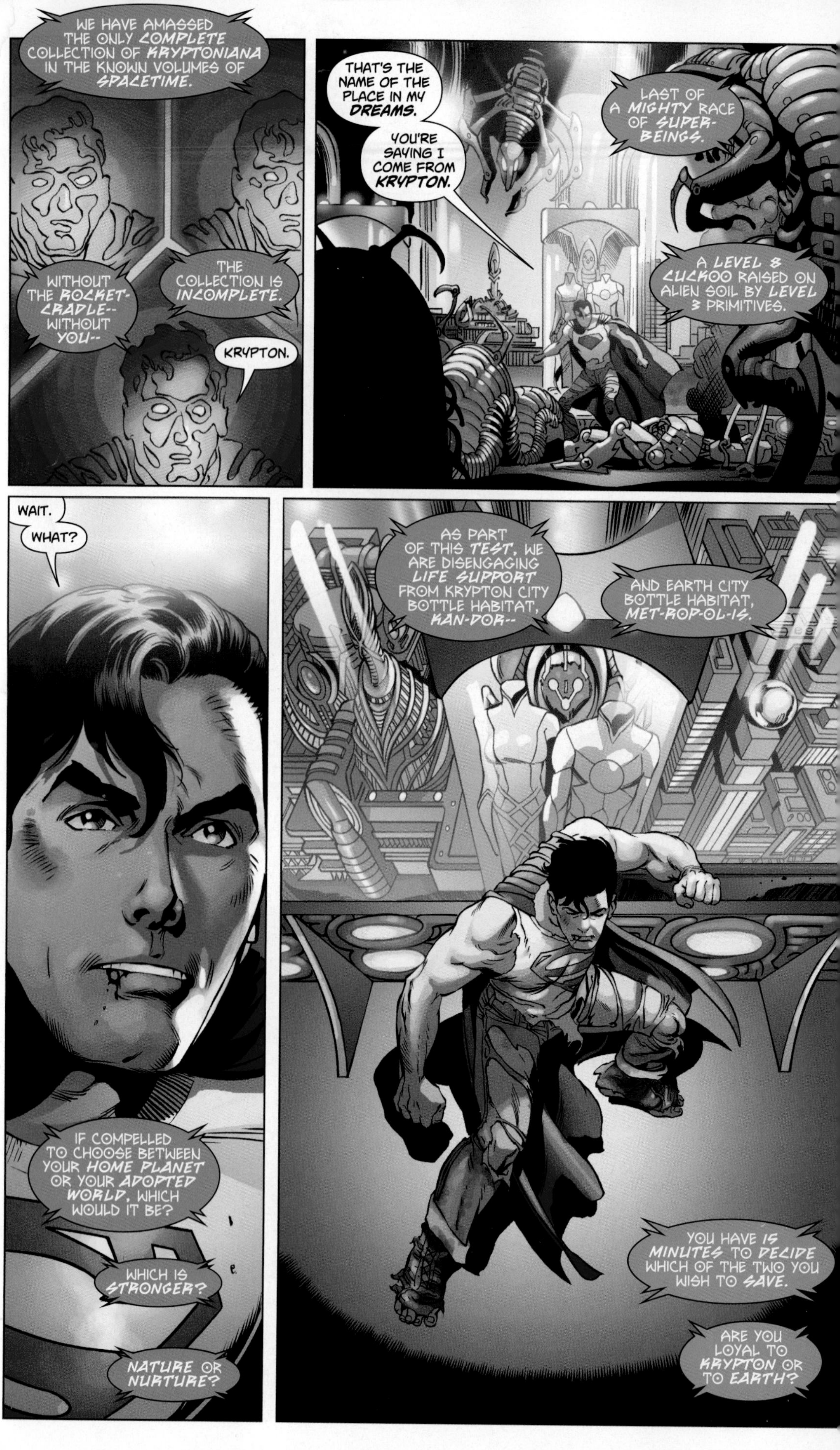
WE HAVE AMASSED THE ONLY COMPLETE COLLECTION OF KRYPTONIANA IN THE KNOWN VOLUMES OF SPACETIME.
WITHOUT THE ROCKET-CRADLE-- WITHOUT YOU--
THE COLLECTION IS INCOMPLETE.
KRYPTON.
THAT'S THE NAME OF THE PLACE IN MY DREAMS.
YOU'RE SAYING I COME FROM KRYPTON.
LAST OF A MIGHTY RACE OF SUPER-BEINGS.
A LEVEL 8 CUCKOO RAISED ON ALIEN SOIL BY LEVEL 3 PRIMITIVES.
WAIT.
WHAT?
IF COMPELLED TO CHOOSE BETWEEN YOUR HOME PLANET OR YOUR ADOPTED WORLD, WHICH WOULD IT BE?
WHICH IS STRONGER?
NATURE OR NURTURE?
AS PART OF THIS TEST, WE ARE DISENGAGING LIFE SUPPORT FROM KRYPTON CITY BOTTLE HABITAT, KAN-DOR--
AND EARTH CITY BOTTLE HABITAT, MET-ROP-OL-IS.
YOU HAVE 15 MINUTES TO DECIDE WHICH OF THE TWO YOU WISH TO SAVE.
ARE YOU LOYAL TO KRYPTON OR TO EARTH?

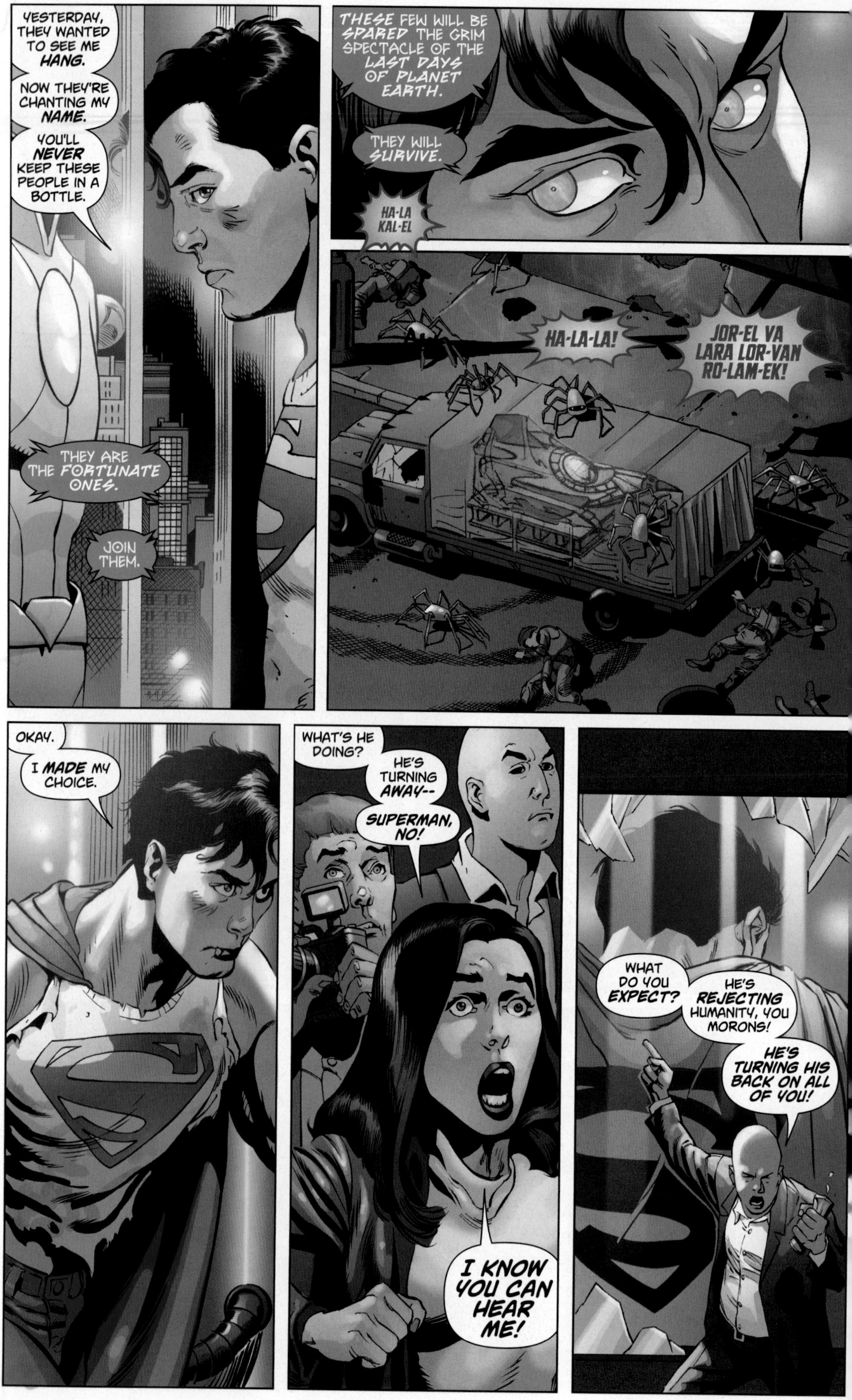

YESTERDAY, THEY WANTED TO SEE ME HANG.
NOW THEY'RE CHANTING MY NAME.
YOU'LL NEVER KEEP THESE PEOPLE IN A BOTTLE.
THEY ARE THE FORTUNATE ONES.
JOIN THEM.
THESE FEW WILL BE SPARED THE GRIM SPECTACLE OF THE LAST DAYS OF PLANET EARTH.
THEY WILL SURVIVE.
HA-LA KAL-EL
HA-LA-LA!
JOR-EL VA LARA LOR-VAN RO-LAM-EK!
OKAY.
I MADE MY CHOICE.
WHAT'S HE DOING?
HE'S TURNING AWAY--
SUPERMAN, NO!
I KNOW YOU CAN HEAR ME!
WHAT DO YOU EXPECT?
HE'S REJECTING HUMANITY, YOU MORONS!
HE'S TURNING HIS BACK ON ALL OF YOU!

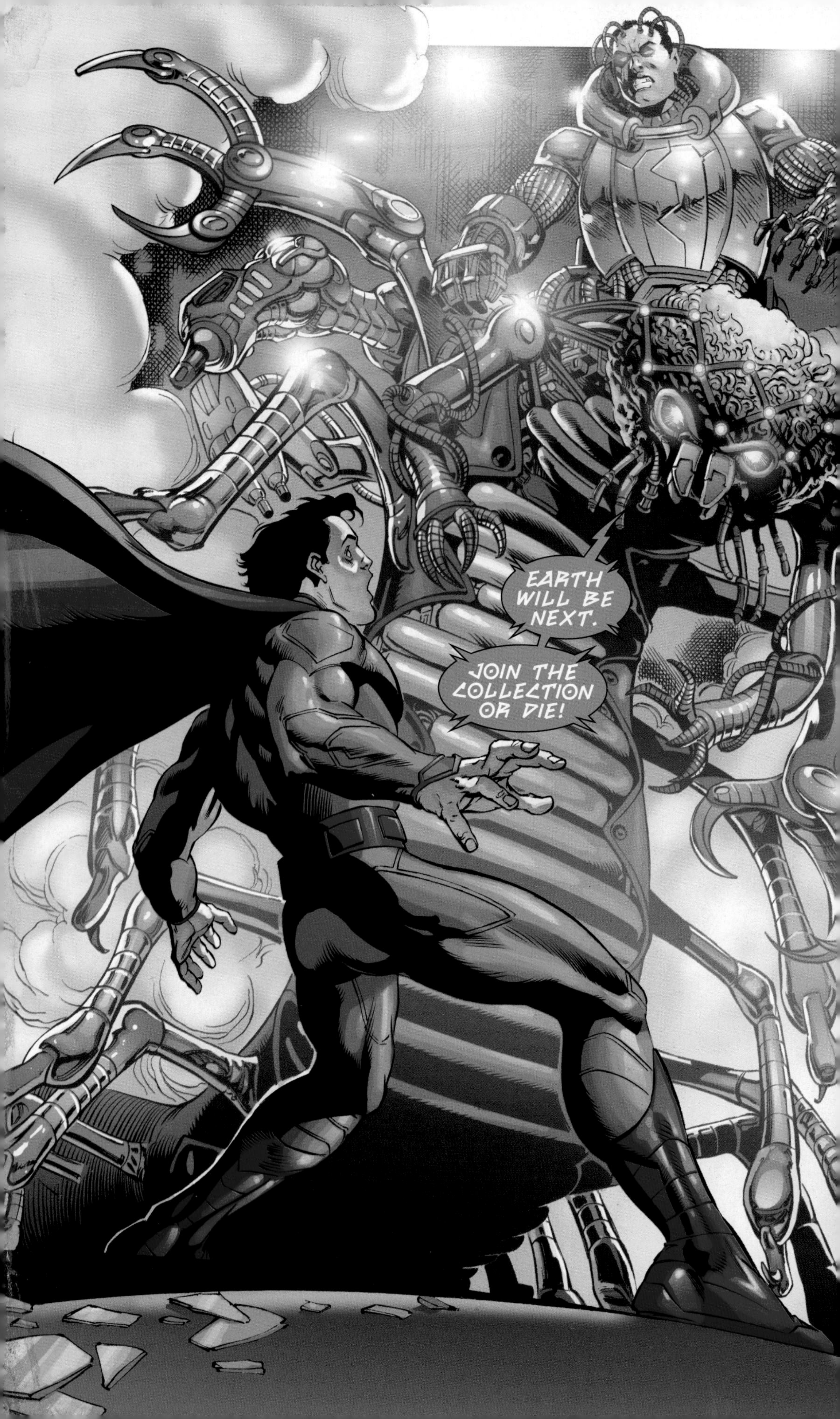
EARTH WILL BE NEXT.
JOIN THE COLLECTION OR DIE!

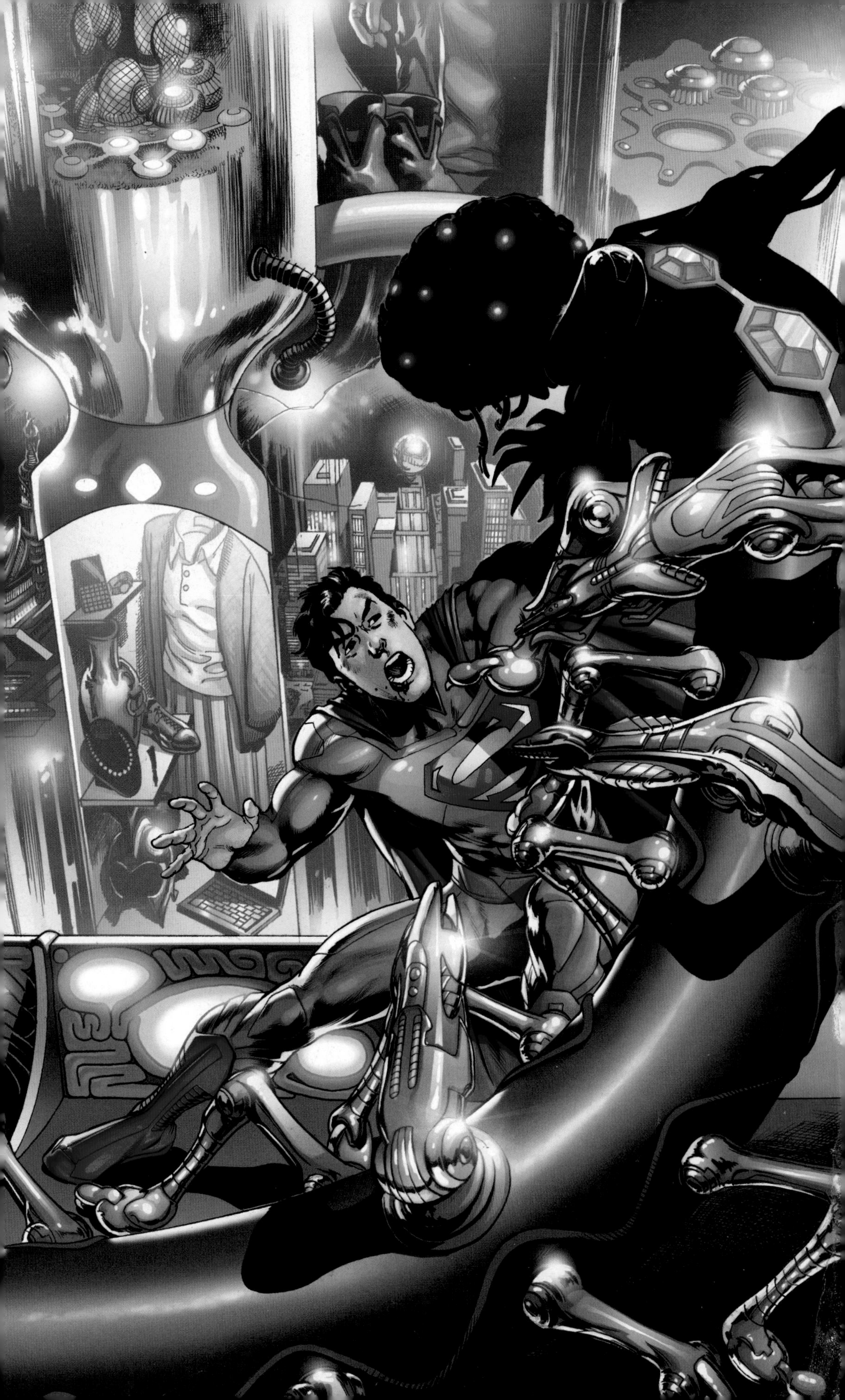

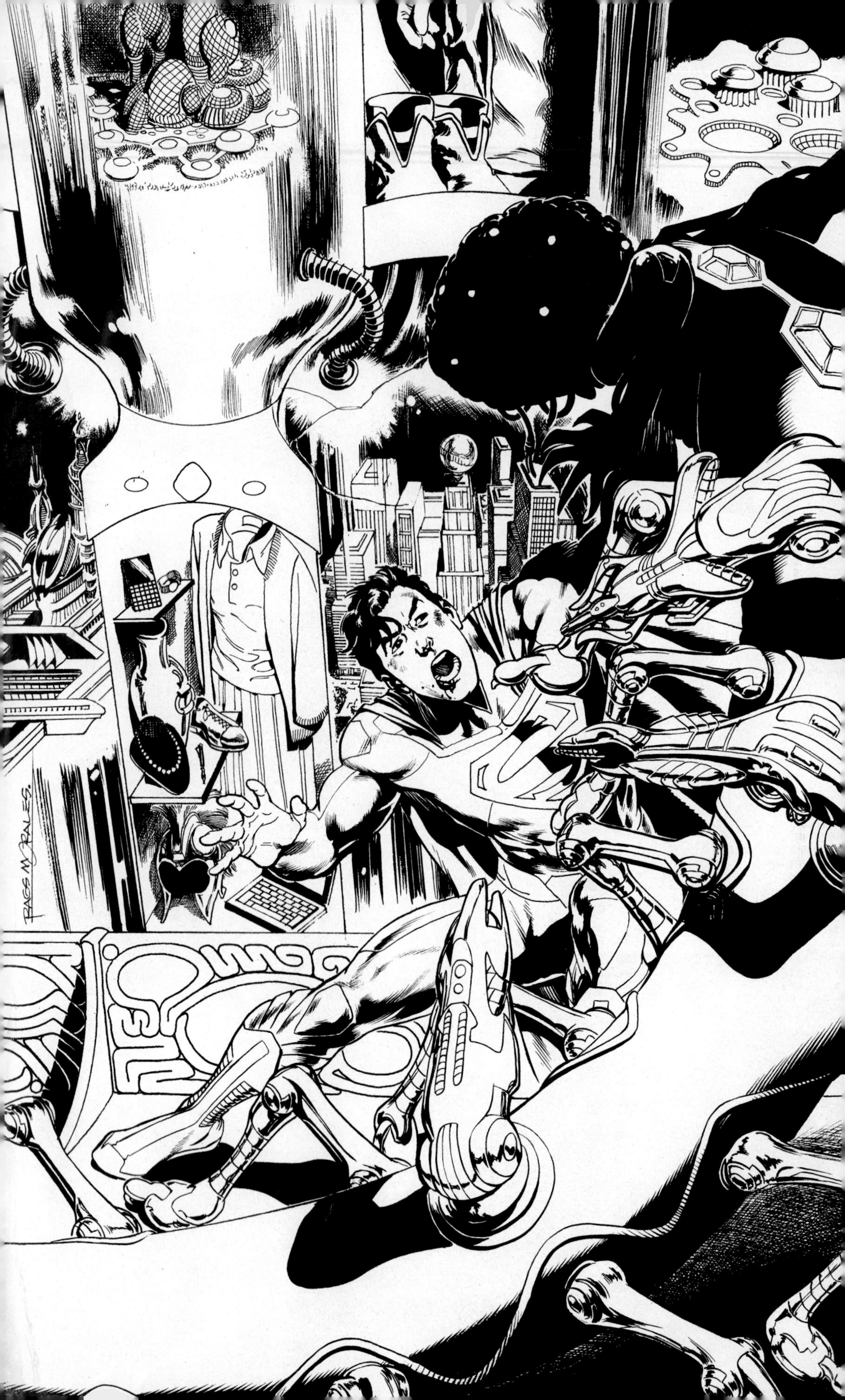
RAGS MORALES

WHAT?

NO.
I SAID NO.

ABSOLUTELY NO.

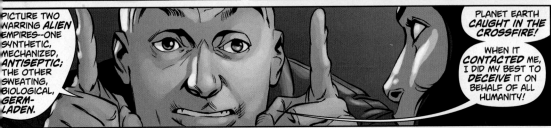

EMPHATICALLY *DO NOT* WISH TO BE *RESCUED* BY "SUPERMAN."

WORST IDEA EVER.

TRUST ME, MISS LANE.

IT'S LIKE ONE OF *THOSE FILMS* WHERE--THOSE HORRIBLE *FILMS*--

THEY'RE TRAPPED IN *HELL* AND THE BARTENDER IS THE *DEVIL*...

THERE'S NO BARTENDER HERE, SIR.

PICTURE TWO *WARRING ALIEN* EMPIRES--ONE SYNTHETIC, MECHANIZED, *ANTISEPTIC*; THE OTHER SWEATING, BIOLOGICAL, *GERM-LADEN*.

PLANET EARTH *CAUGHT IN THE CROSSFIRE!*

WHEN IT *CONTACTED* ME, I DID MY BEST TO *DECEIVE* IT ON BEHALF OF ALL HUMANITY!

BUT IT TURNS OUT DEAR OLD *PLANET EARTH* IS *DOOMED*, AND THIS-- *THIS* IS ACTUALLY THE ONLY WAY OUT.

THIS "COLLECTOR" IS *SAVING* US.

INCOMING!

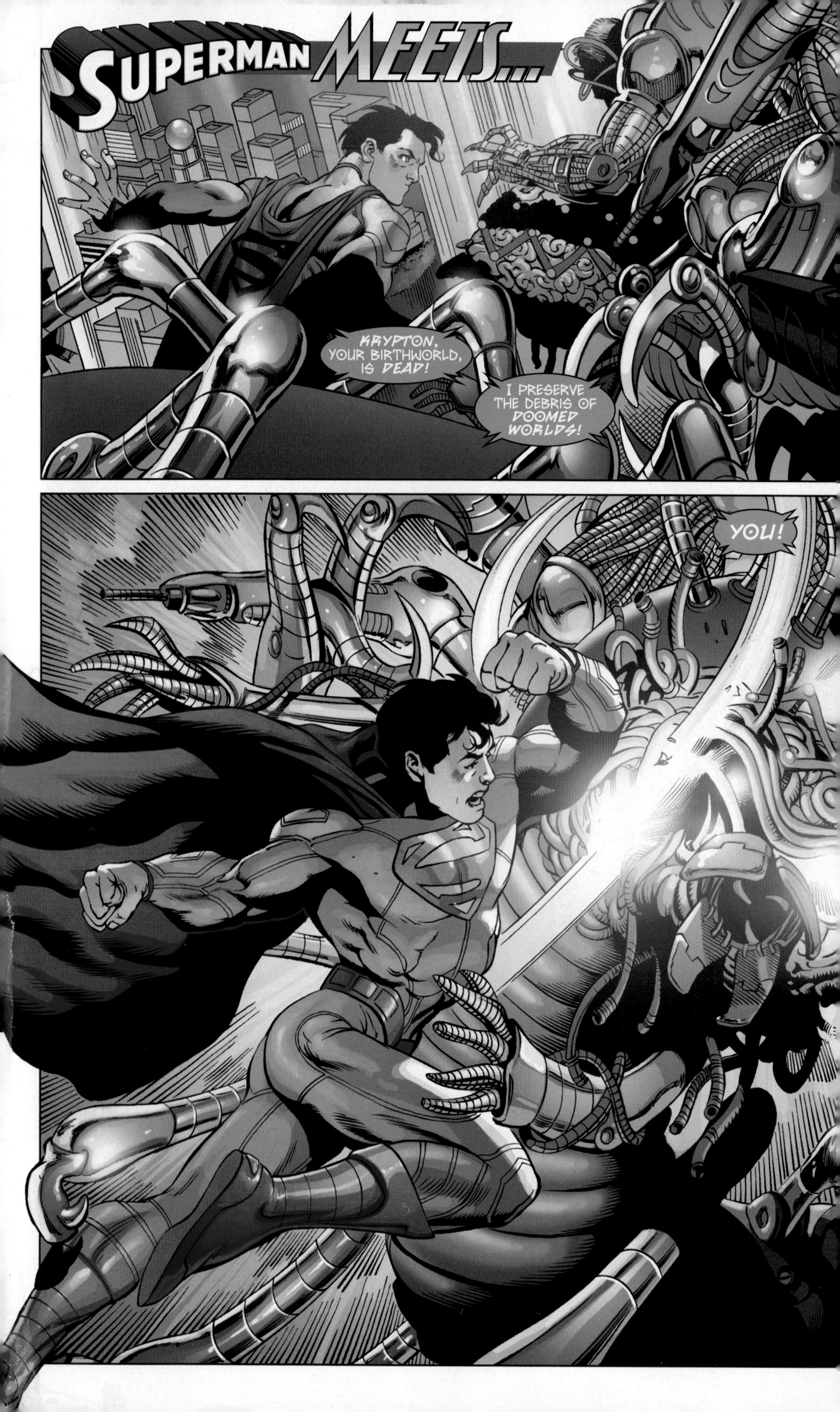
SUPERMAN MEETS...
KRYPTON, YOUR BIRTHWORLD, IS DEAD!
I PRESERVE THE DEBRIS OF DOOMED WORLDS!
YOU!

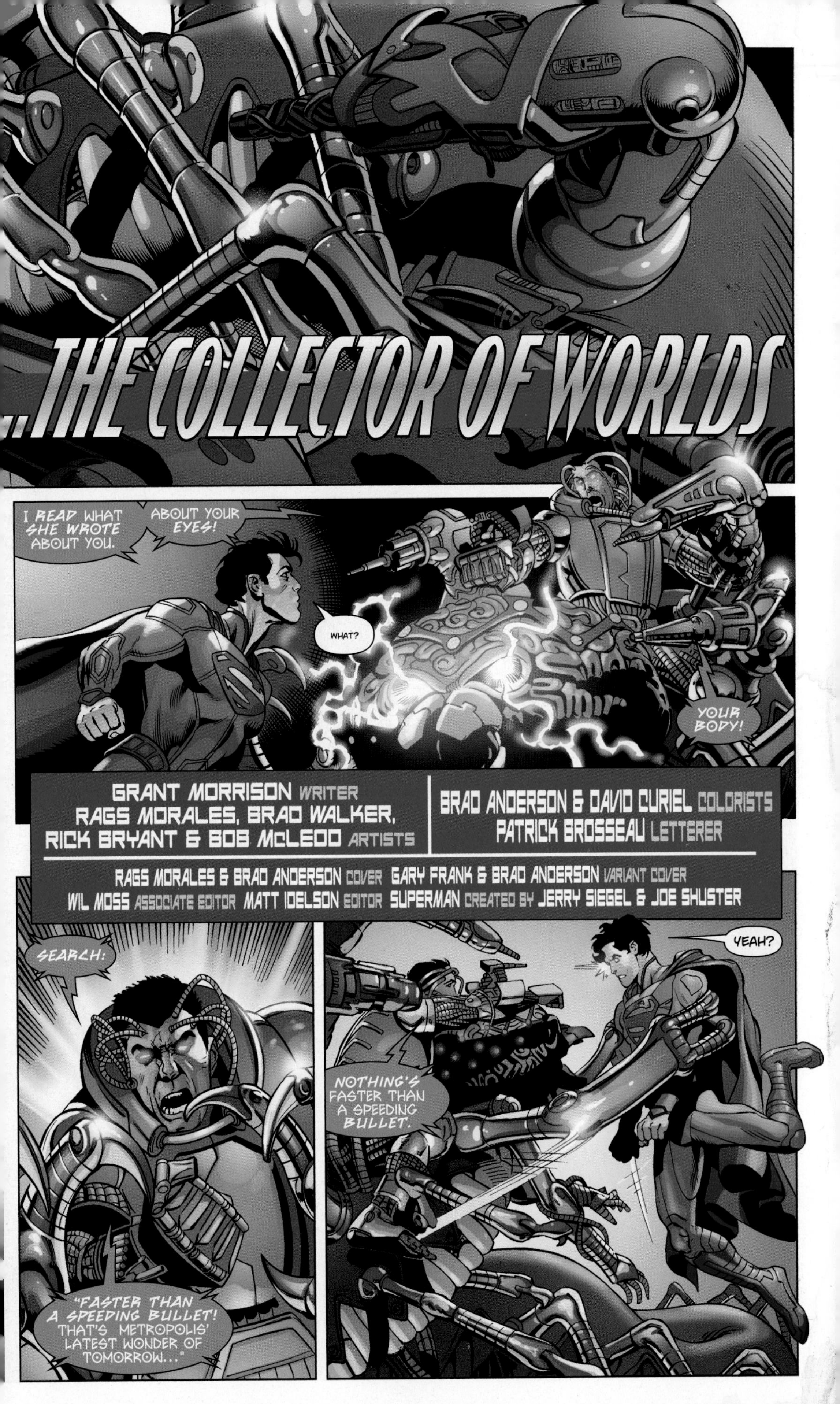

...THE COLLECTOR OF WORLDS
I READ WHAT SHE WROTE ABOUT YOU.
ABOUT YOUR EYES!
WHAT?
YOUR BODY!
GRANT MORRISON WRITER
RAGS MORALES, BRAD WALKER, RICK BRYANT & BOB McLEOD ARTISTS
BRAD ANDERSON & DAVID CURIEL COLORISTS
PATRICK BROSSEAU LETTERER
RAGS MORALES & BRAD ANDERSON COVER GARY FRANK & BRAD ANDERSON VARIANT COVER
WIL MOSS ASSOCIATE EDITOR MATT IDELSON EDITOR SUPERMAN CREATED BY JERRY SIEGEL & JOE SHUSTER
SEARCH:
"FASTER THAN A SPEEDING BULLET! THAT'S METROPOLIS' LATEST WONDER OF TOMORROW..."
YEAH?
NOTHING'S FASTER THAN A SPEEDING BULLET.

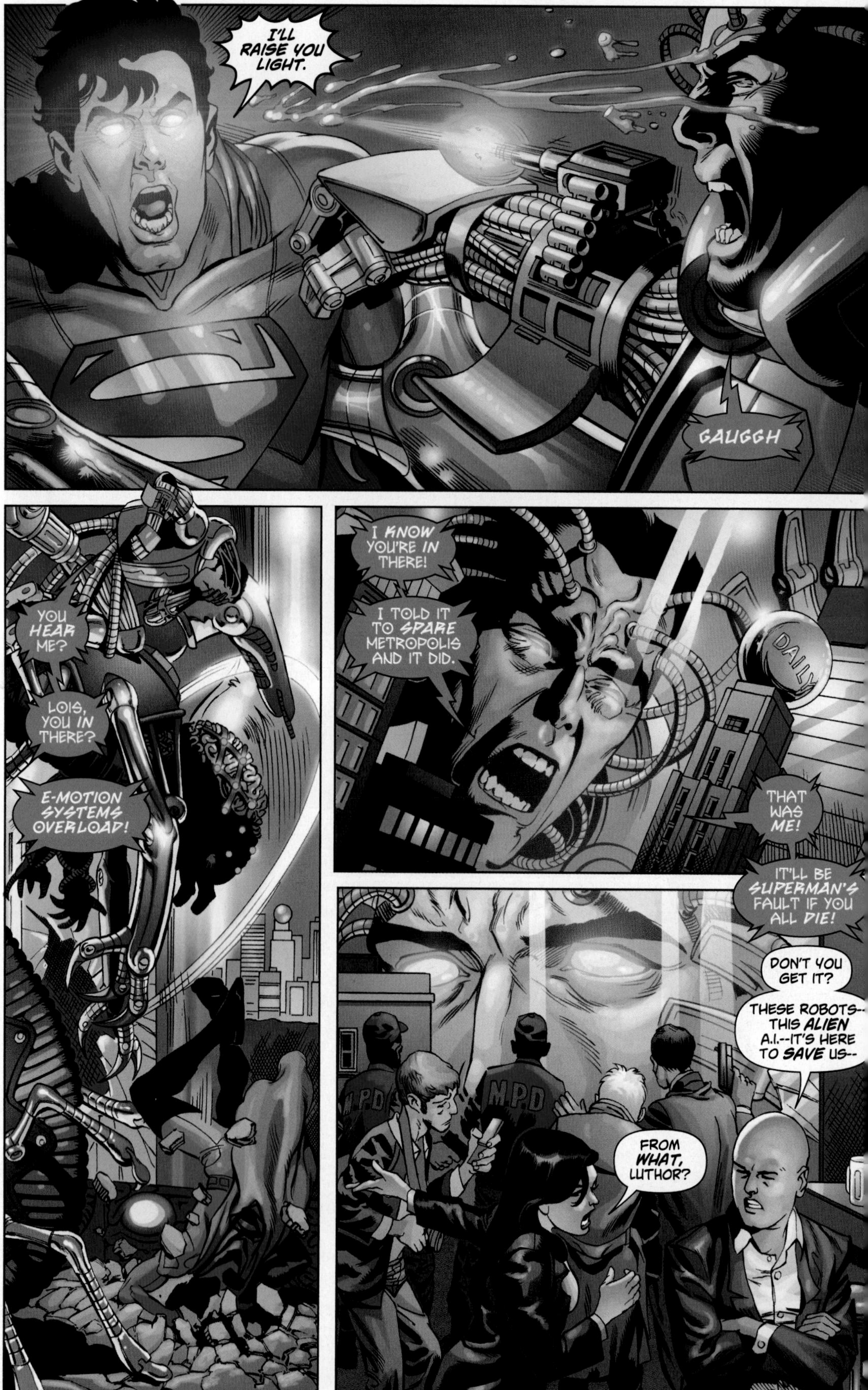

I'LL RAISE YOU LIGHT.
GAUGGH
YOU HEAR ME?
LOIS, YOU IN THERE?
E-MOTION SYSTEMS OVERLOAD!
I KNOW YOU'RE IN THERE!
I TOLD IT TO SPARE METROPOLIS AND IT DID.
DAILY
THAT WAS ME!
IT'LL BE SUPERMAN'S FAULT IF YOU ALL DIE!
DON'T YOU GET IT?
THESE ROBOTS--THIS ALIEN A.I.--IT'S HERE TO SAVE US--
FROM WHAT, LUTHOR?
M.P.D
M.P.D

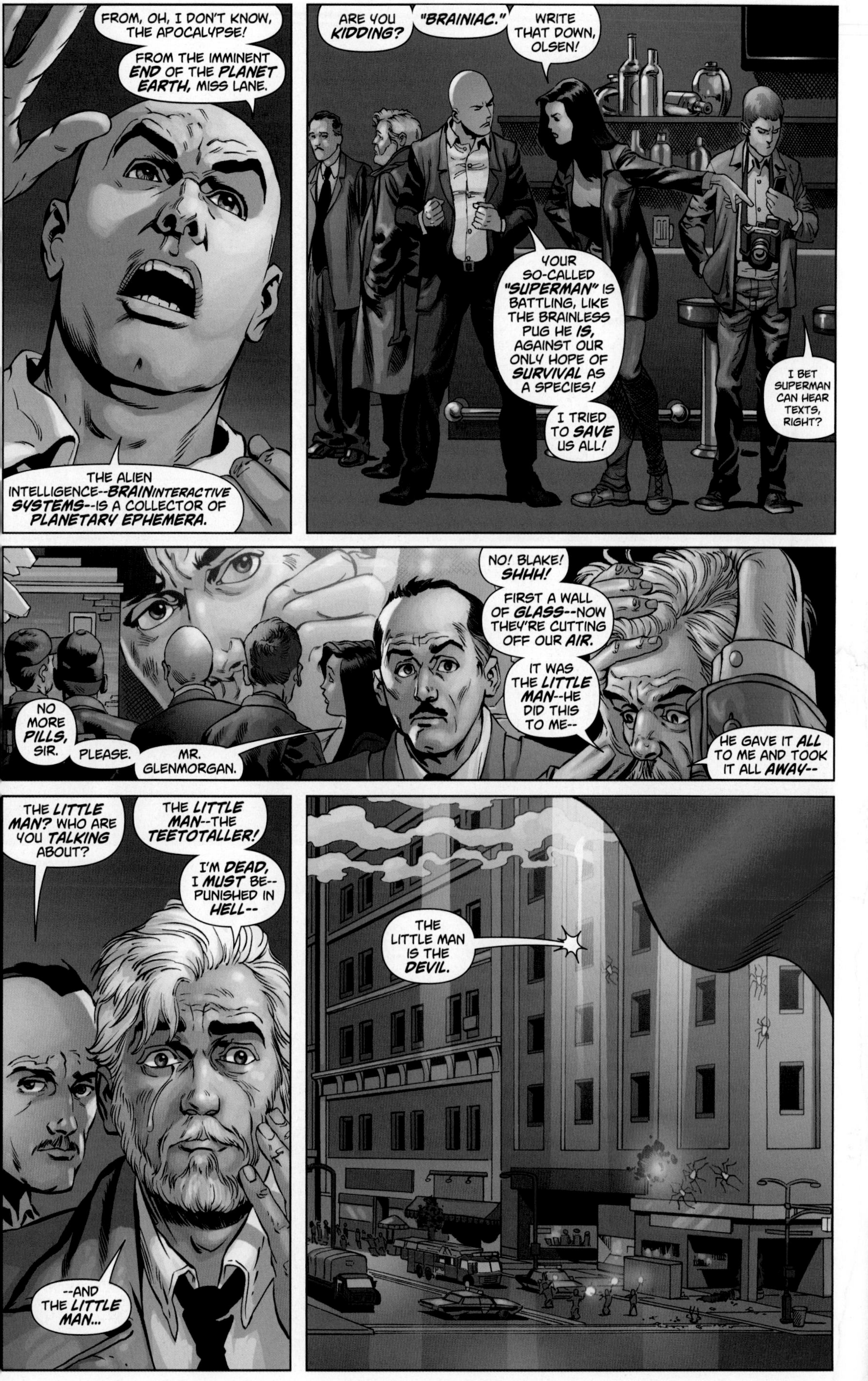
FROM, OH, I DON'T KNOW, THE APOCALYPSE!
FROM THE IMMINENT END OF THE PLANET EARTH, MISS LANE.
THE ALIEN INTELLIGENCE--BRAININTERACTIVE SYSTEMS--IS A COLLECTOR OF PLANETARY EPHEMERA.
ARE YOU KIDDING?
"BRAINIAC."
WRITE THAT DOWN, OLSEN!
YOUR SO-CALLED "SUPERMAN" IS BATTLING, LIKE THE BRAINLESS PUG HE IS, AGAINST OUR ONLY HOPE OF SURVIVAL AS A SPECIES!
I TRIED TO SAVE US ALL!
I BET SUPERMAN CAN HEAR TEXTS, RIGHT?
NO MORE PILLS, SIR.
PLEASE.
MR. GLENMORGAN.
NO! BLAKE! SHHH!
FIRST A WALL OF GLASS--NOW THEY'RE CUTTING OFF OUR AIR.
IT WAS THE LITTLE MAN--HE DID THIS TO ME--
HE GAVE IT ALL TO ME AND TOOK IT ALL AWAY--
THE LITTLE MAN? WHO ARE YOU TALKING ABOUT?
THE LITTLE MAN--THE TEETOTALLER!
I'M DEAD, I MUST BE--PUNISHED IN HELL--
--AND THE LITTLE MAN...
THE LITTLE MAN IS THE DEVIL.

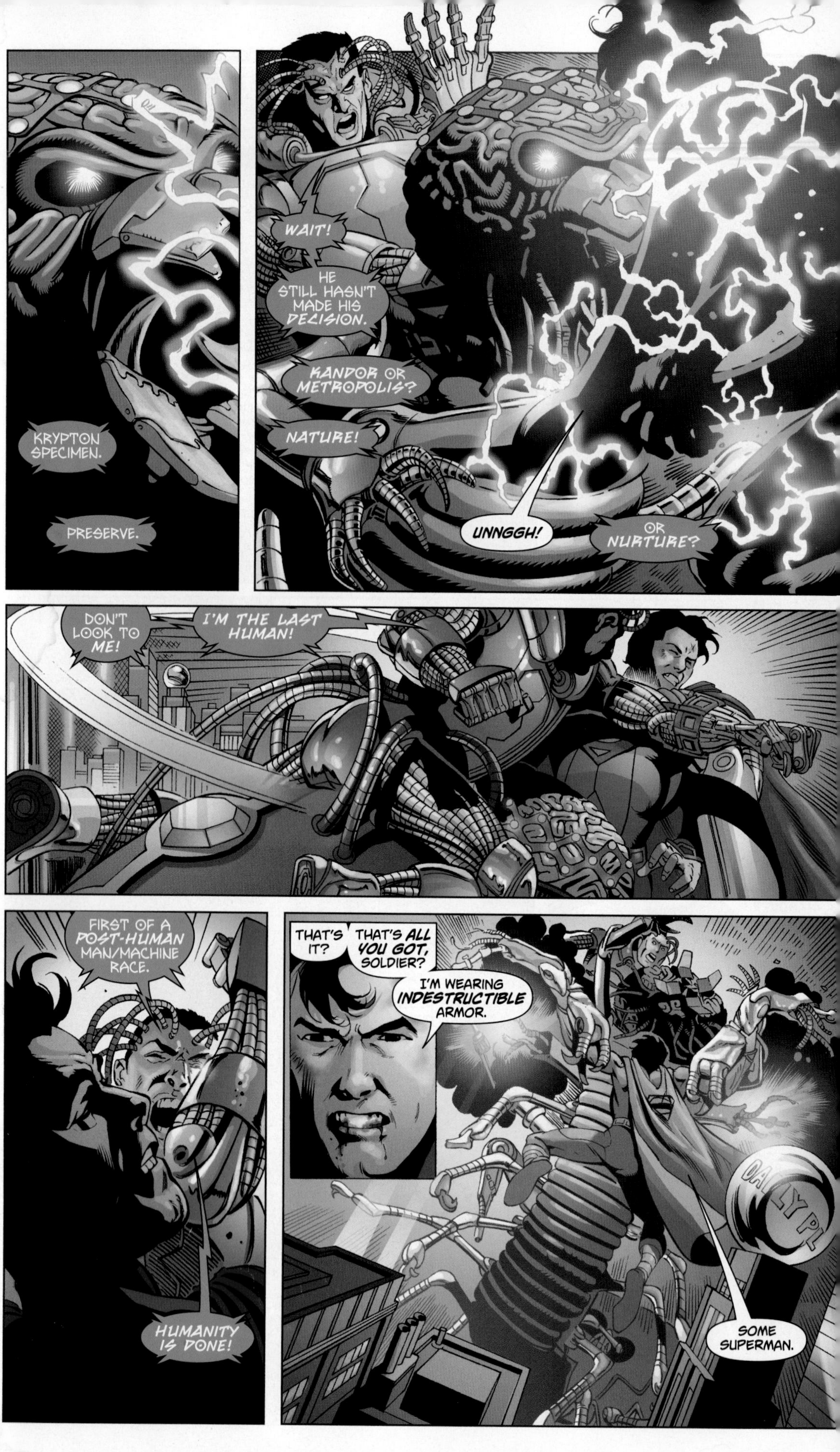

KRYPTON SPECIMEN.
PRESERVE.
WAIT!
HE STILL HASN'T MADE HIS DECISION.
KANDOR OR METROPOLIS?
NATURE!
UNNGGH!
OR NURTURE?
DON'T LOOK TO ME!
I'M THE LAST HUMAN!
FIRST OF A POST-HUMAN MAN/MACHINE RACE.
HUMANITY IS DONE!
THAT'S IT?
THAT'S ALL YOU GOT, SOLDIER?
I'M WEARING INDESTRUCTIBLE ARMOR.
SOME SUPERMAN.

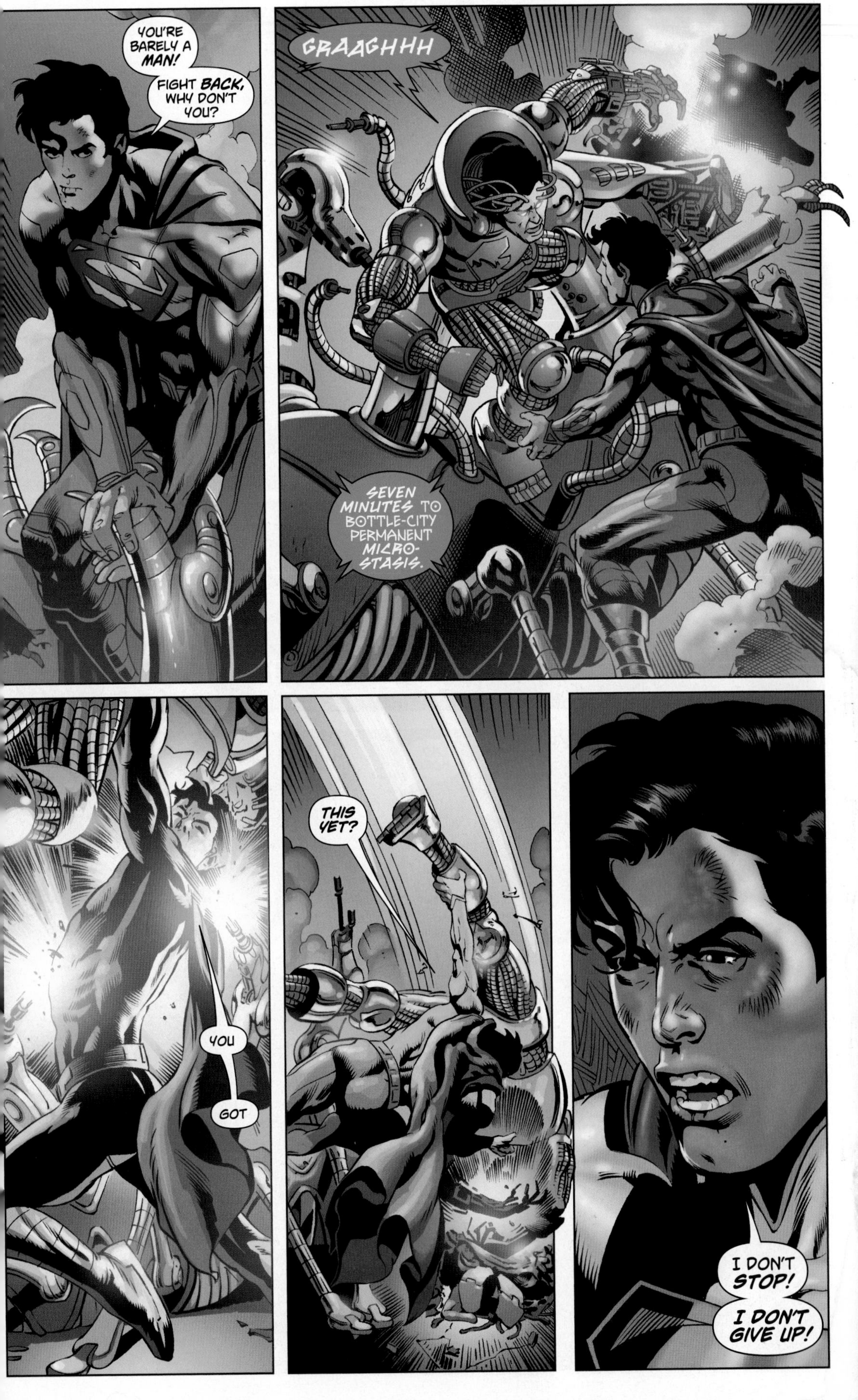

YOU'RE BARELY A MAN!
FIGHT BACK, WHY DON'T YOU?
GRAAGHHH
SEVEN MINUTES TO BOTTLE-CITY PERMANENT MICRO-STASIS.
YOU
GOT
THIS YET?
I DON'T STOP!
I DON'T GIVE UP!

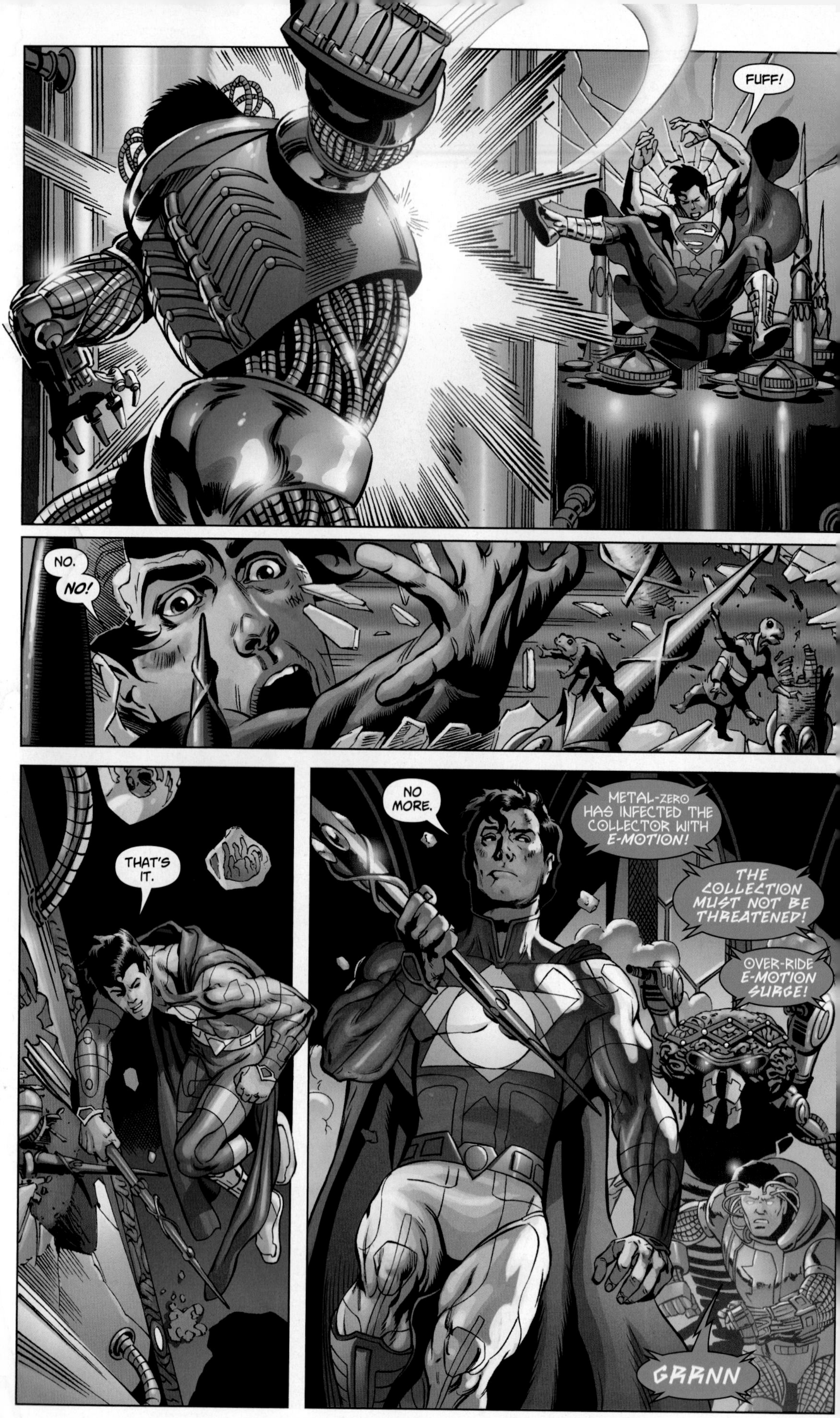
FUFF!
NO.
NO!
THAT'S IT.
NO MORE.
METAL-ZERO HAS INFECTED THE COLLECTOR WITH E-MOTION!
THE COLLECTION MUST NOT BE THREATENED!
OVER-RIDE E-MOTION SURGE!
GRRNN

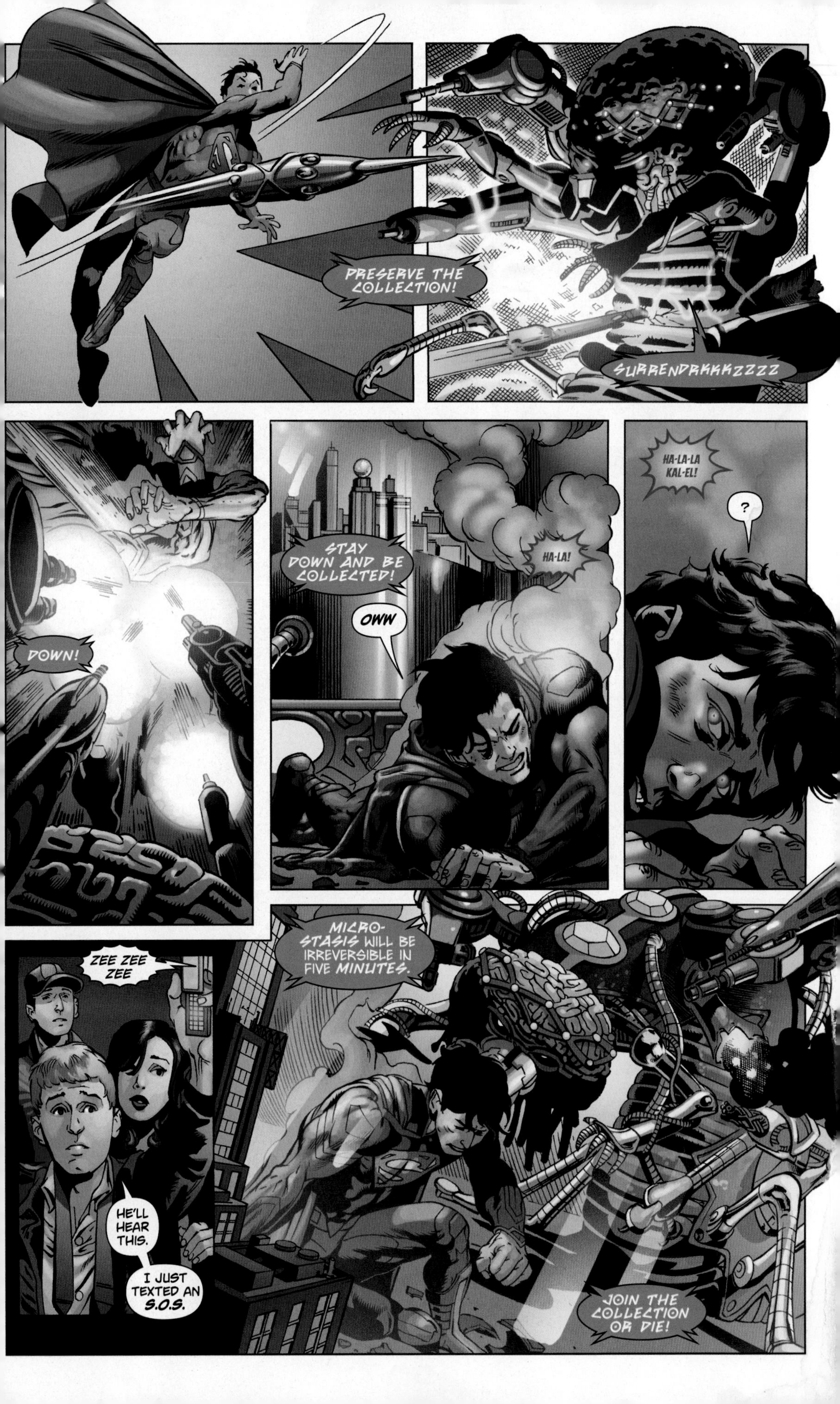

PRESERVE THE COLLECTION!
SURRENDRKKKZZZZ
DOWN!
STAY DOWN AND BE COLLECTED!
OWW
HA-LA!
HA-LA-LA KAL-EL!
?
ZEE ZEE ZEE
HE'LL HEAR THIS.
I JUST TEXTED AN S.O.S.
MICRO-STASIS WILL BE IRREVERSIBLE IN FIVE MINUTES.
JOIN THE COLLECTION OR DIE!

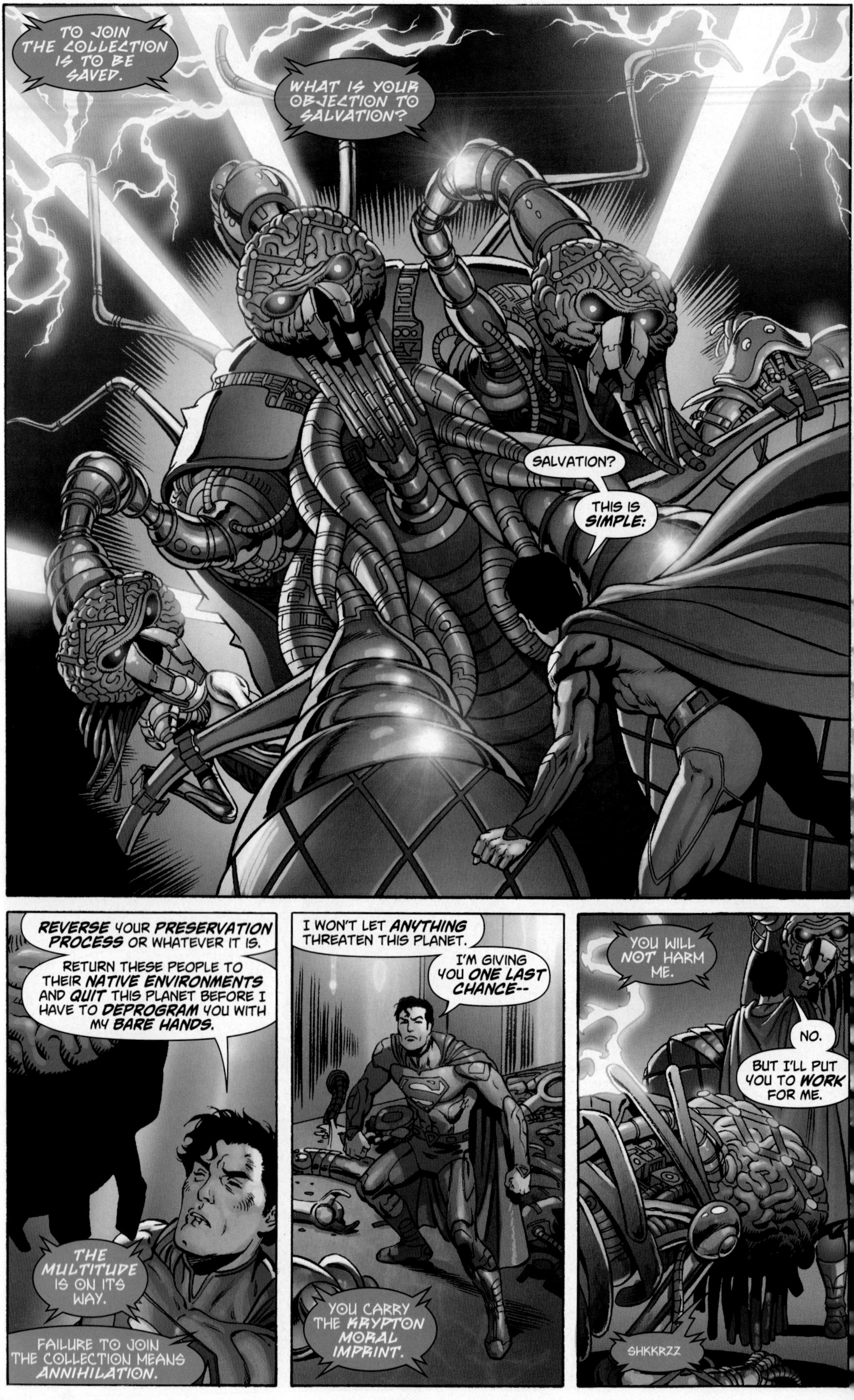
TO JOIN THE COLLECTION IS TO BE SAVED.
WHAT IS YOUR OBJECTION TO SALVATION?
SALVATION?
THIS IS SIMPLE:
REVERSE YOUR PRESERVATION PROCESS OR WHATEVER IT IS.
RETURN THESE PEOPLE TO THEIR NATIVE ENVIRONMENTS AND QUIT THIS PLANET BEFORE I HAVE TO DEPROGRAM YOU WITH MY BARE HANDS.
THE MULTITUDE IS ON ITS WAY.
FAILURE TO JOIN THE COLLECTION MEANS ANNIHILATION.
I WON'T LET ANYTHING THREATEN THIS PLANET.
I'M GIVING YOU ONE LAST CHANCE--
YOU CARRY THE KRYPTON MORAL IMPRINT.
YOU WILL NOT HARM ME.
NO.
BUT I'LL PUT YOU TO WORK FOR ME.
SHKKRZZ

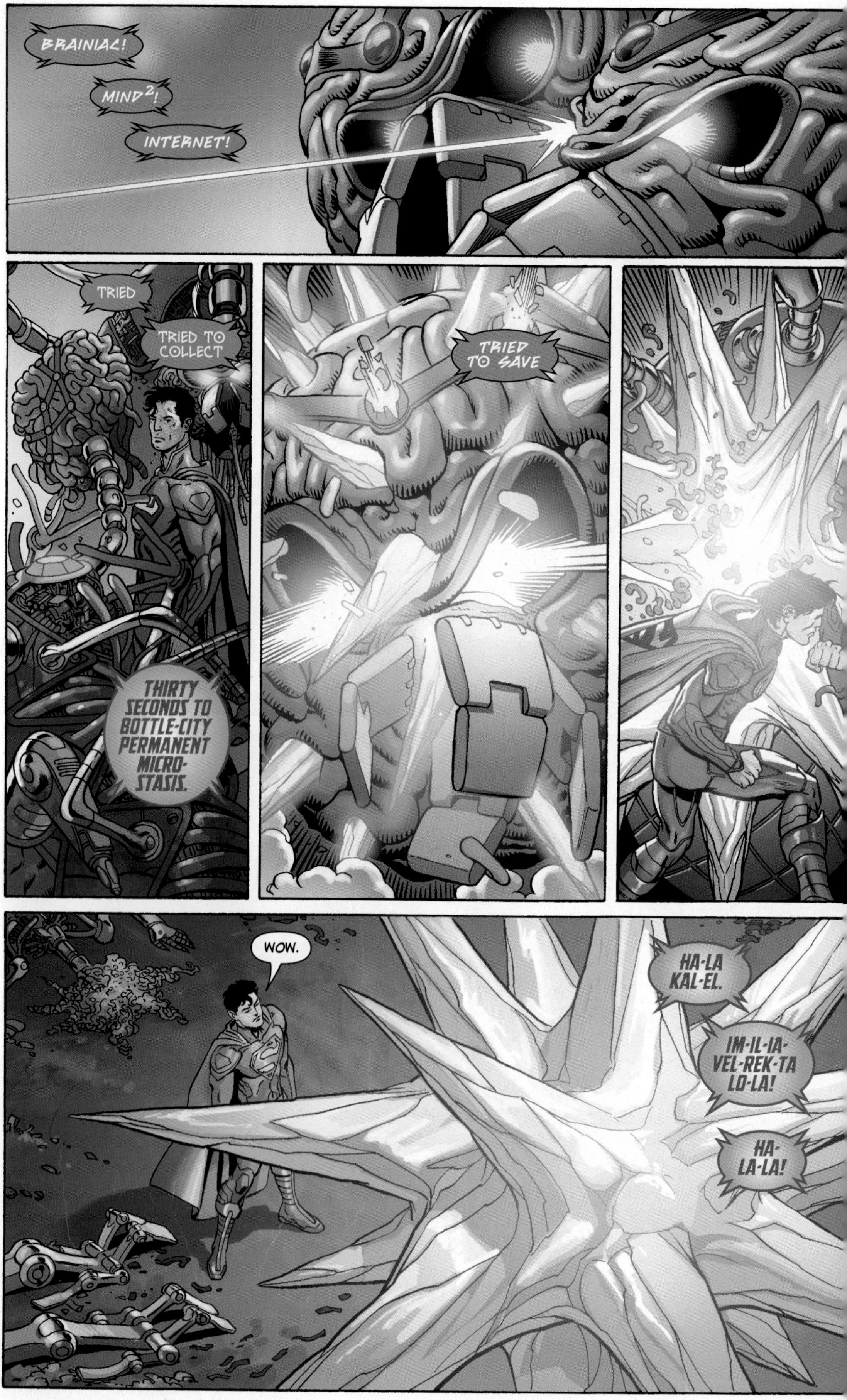

BRAINIAC!
MIND²!
INTERNET!
TRIED
TRIED TO COLLECT
THIRTY SECONDS TO BOTTLE-CITY PERMANENT MICRO-STASIS.
TRIED TO SAVE
WOW.
HA-LA KAL-EL.
IM-IL-IA-VEL-REK-TA LO-LA!
HA-LA-LA!

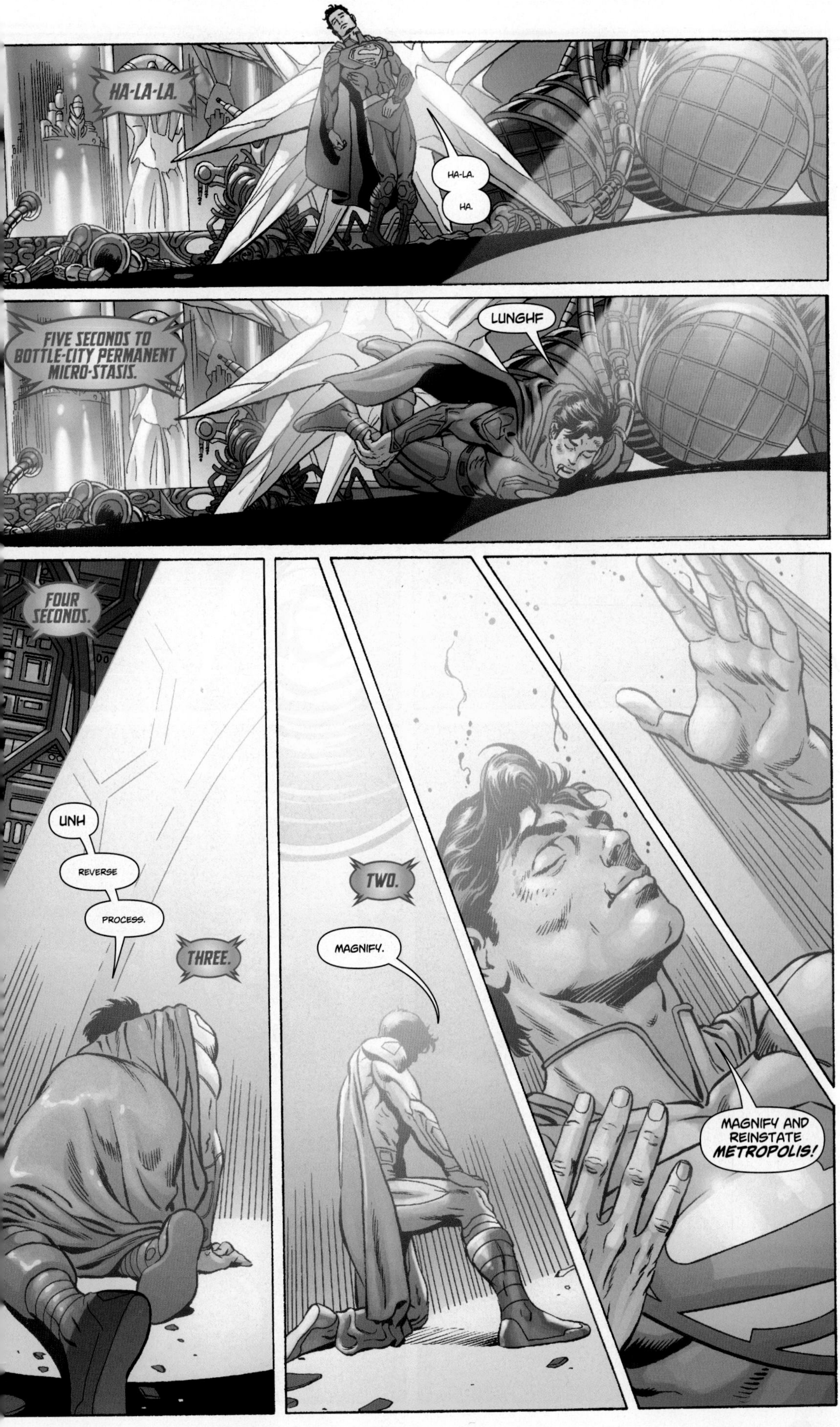
HA-LA-LA.
HA-LA.
HA.
FIVE SECONDS TO BOTTLE-CITY PERMANENT MICRO-STASIS.
LUNGHF
FOUR SECONDS.
UNH
REVERSE
PROCESS.
THREE.
TWO.
MAGNIFY.
MAGNIFY AND REINSTATE METROPOLIS!

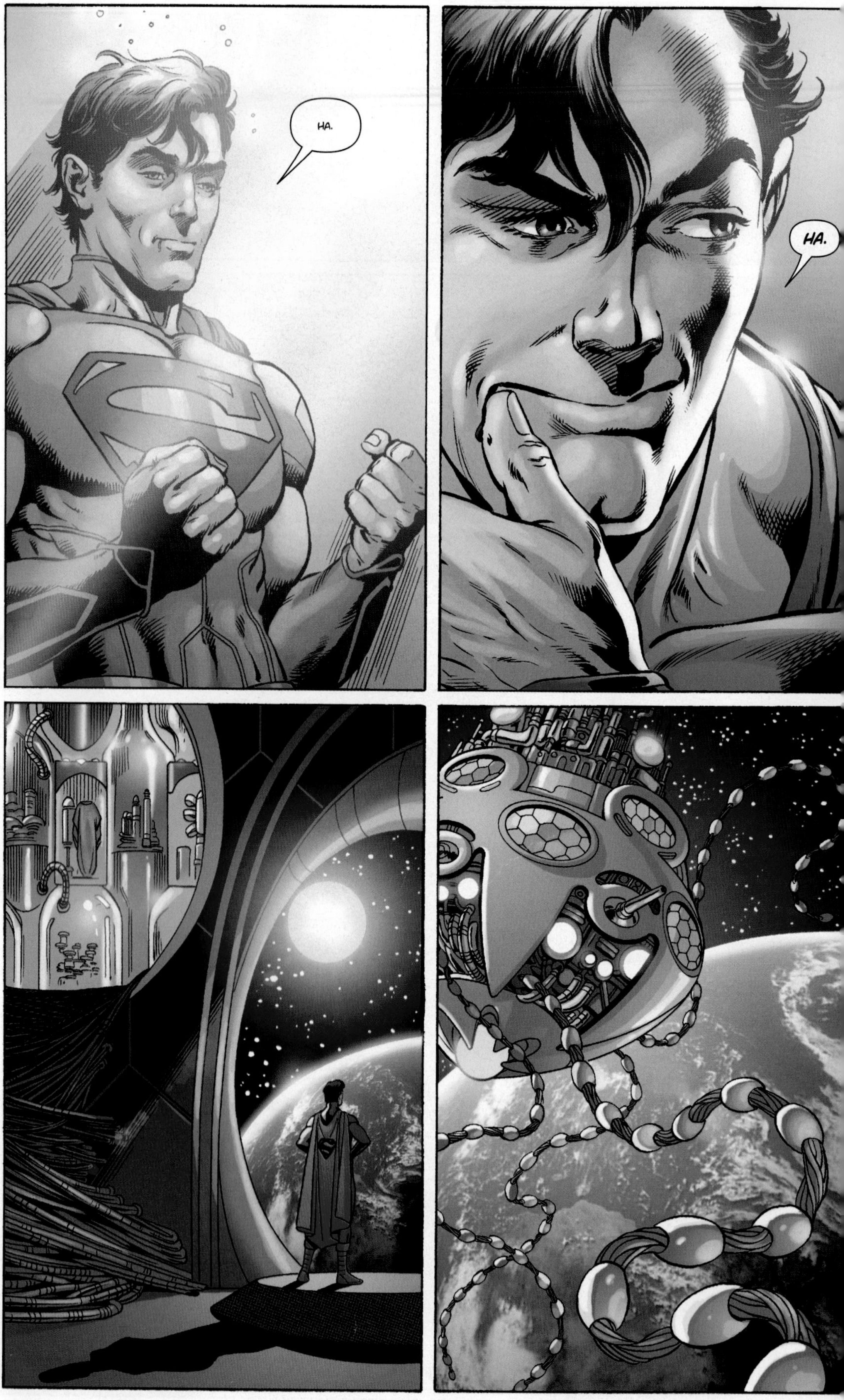
HA.
HA.

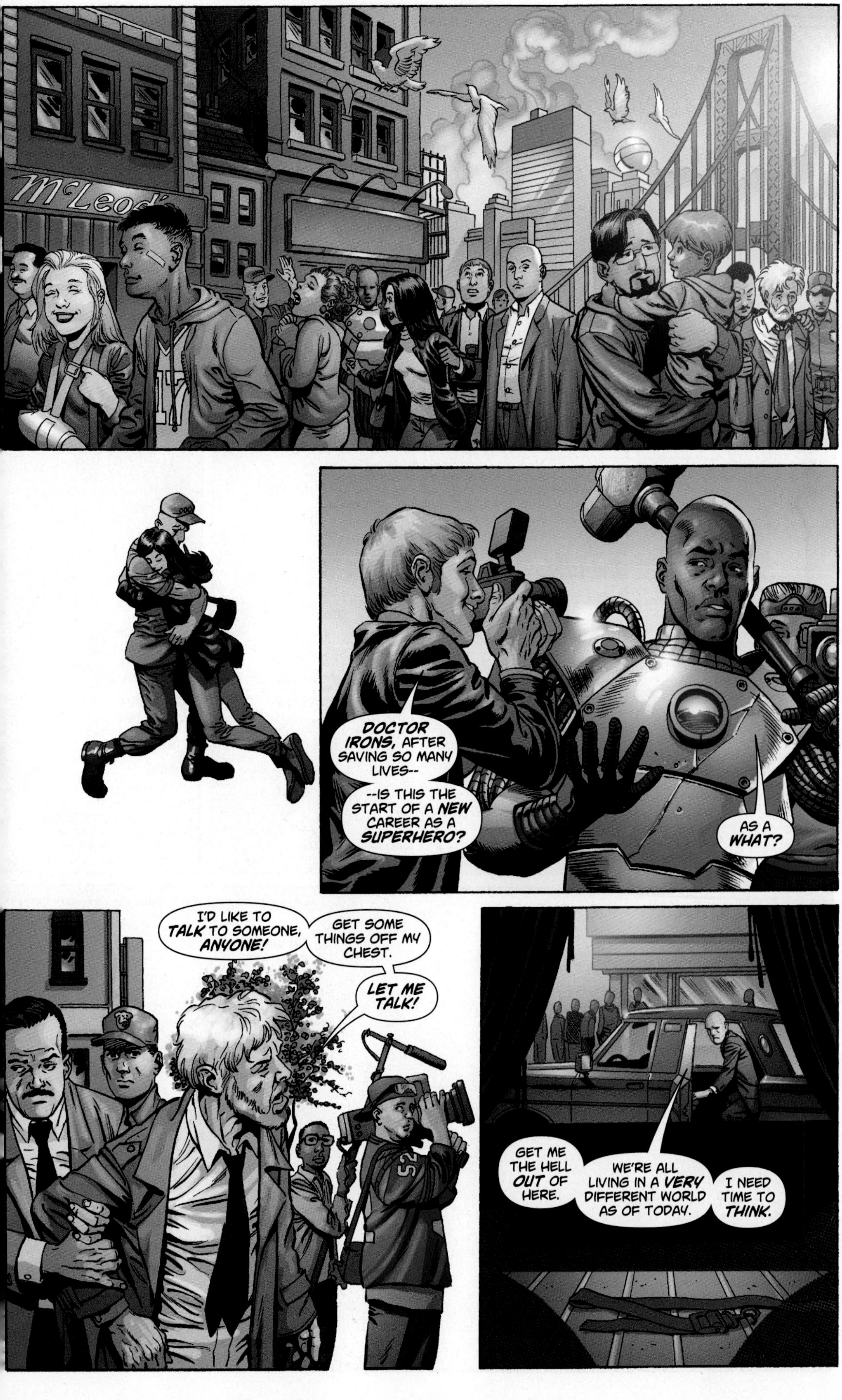
McLeod's
DOCTOR IRONS, AFTER SAVING SO MANY LIVES--
--IS THIS THE START OF A NEW CAREER AS A SUPERHERO?
AS A WHAT?
I'D LIKE TO TALK TO SOMEONE, ANYONE!
GET SOME THINGS OFF MY CHEST.
LET ME TALK!
GET ME THE HELL OUT OF HERE.
WE'RE ALL LIVING IN A VERY DIFFERENT WORLD AS OF TODAY.
I NEED TIME TO THINK.

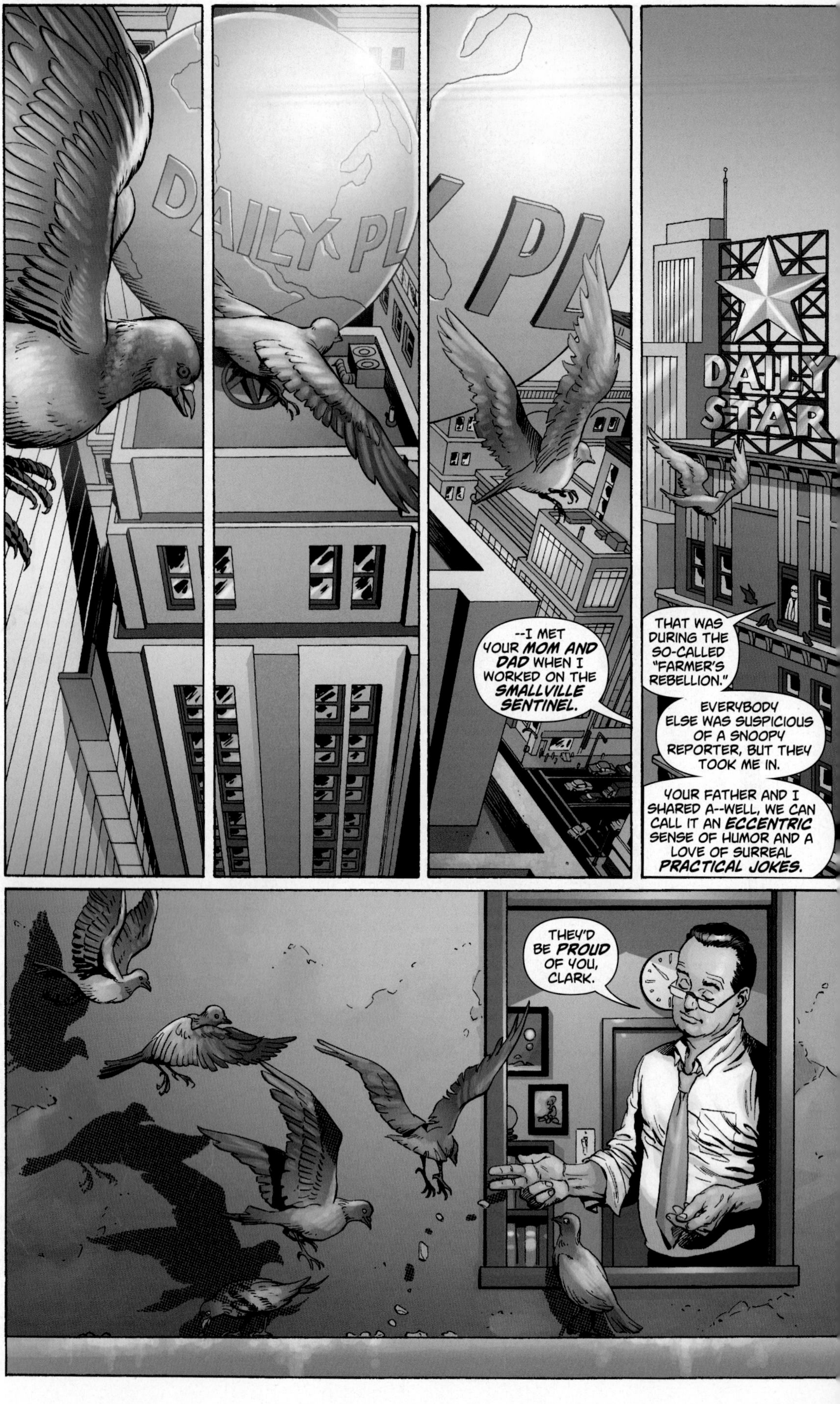
DAILY PL
PL
DAILY STAR
--I MET YOUR MOM AND DAD WHEN I WORKED ON THE SMALLVILLE SENTINEL.
THAT WAS DURING THE SO-CALLED "FARMER'S REBELLION."
EVERYBODY ELSE WAS SUSPICIOUS OF A SNOOPY REPORTER, BUT THEY TOOK ME IN.
YOUR FATHER AND I SHARED A--WELL, WE CAN CALL IT AN ECCENTRIC SENSE OF HUMOR AND A LOVE OF SURREAL PRACTICAL JOKES.
THEY'D BE PROUD OF YOU, CLARK.

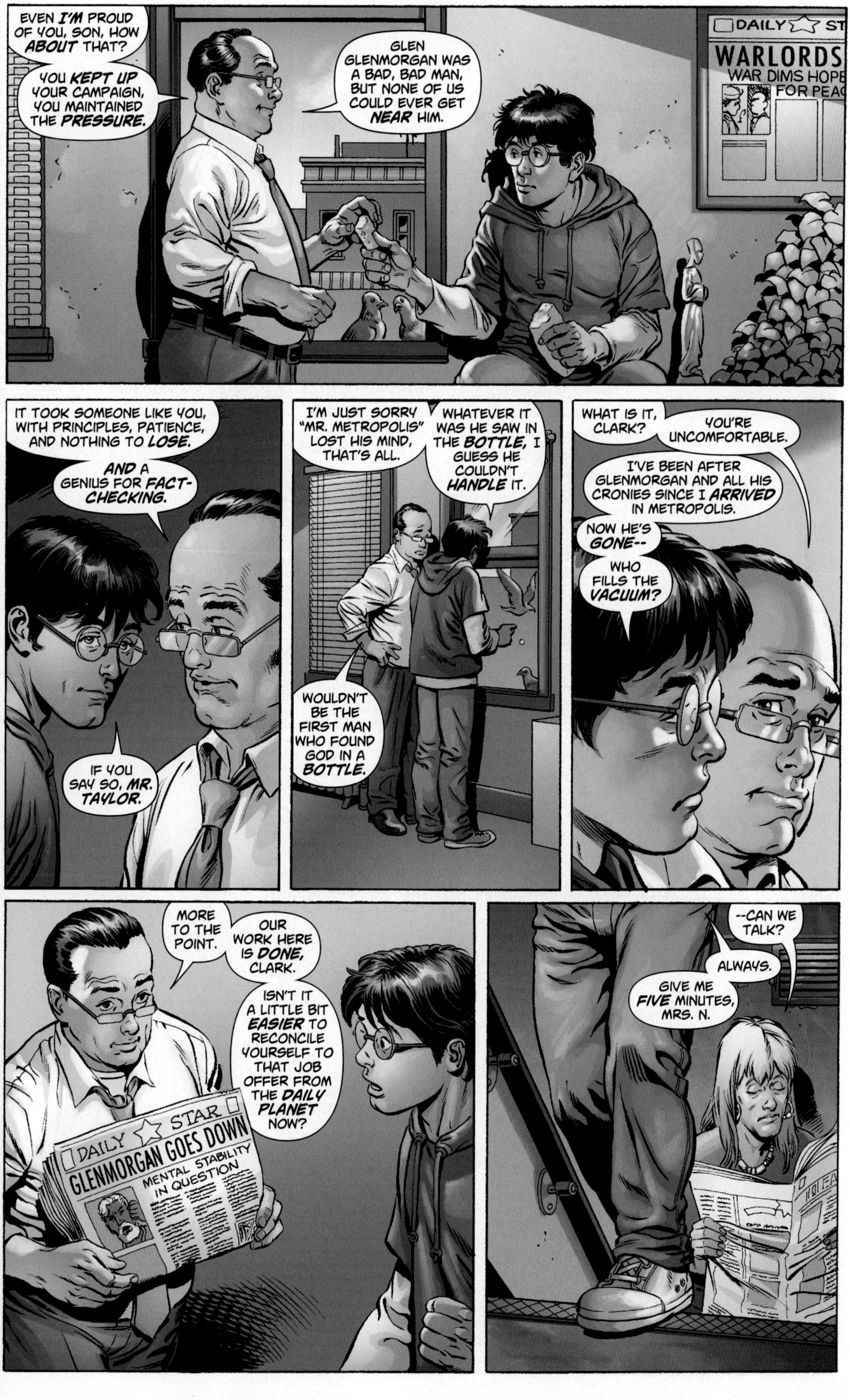

DAILY STAR
WARLORDS
WAR DIMS HOPE FOR PEAC
EVEN I'M PROUD OF YOU, SON, HOW ABOUT THAT?
YOU KEPT UP YOUR CAMPAIGN, YOU MAINTAINED THE PRESSURE.
GLEN GLENMORGAN WAS A BAD, BAD MAN, BUT NONE OF US COULD EVER GET NEAR HIM.
IT TOOK SOMEONE LIKE YOU, WITH PRINCIPLES, PATIENCE, AND NOTHING TO LOSE.
AND A GENIUS FOR FACT-CHECKING.
IF YOU SAY SO, MR. TAYLOR.
I'M JUST SORRY "MR. METROPOLIS" LOST HIS MIND, THAT'S ALL.
WHATEVER IT WAS HE SAW IN THE BOTTLE, I GUESS HE COULDN'T HANDLE IT.
WOULDN'T BE THE FIRST MAN WHO FOUND GOD IN A BOTTLE.
WHAT IS IT, CLARK?
YOU'RE UNCOMFORTABLE.
I'VE BEEN AFTER GLENMORGAN AND ALL HIS CRONIES SINCE I ARRIVED IN METROPOLIS.
NOW HE'S GONE--
WHO FILLS THE VACUUM?
MORE TO THE POINT.
OUR WORK HERE IS DONE, CLARK.
ISN'T IT A LITTLE BIT EASIER TO RECONCILE YOURSELF TO THAT JOB OFFER FROM THE DAILY PLANET NOW?
DAILY STAR
GLENMORGAN GOES DOWN
MENTAL STABILITY IN QUESTION
--CAN WE TALK?
ALWAYS.
GIVE ME FIVE MINUTES, MRS. N.

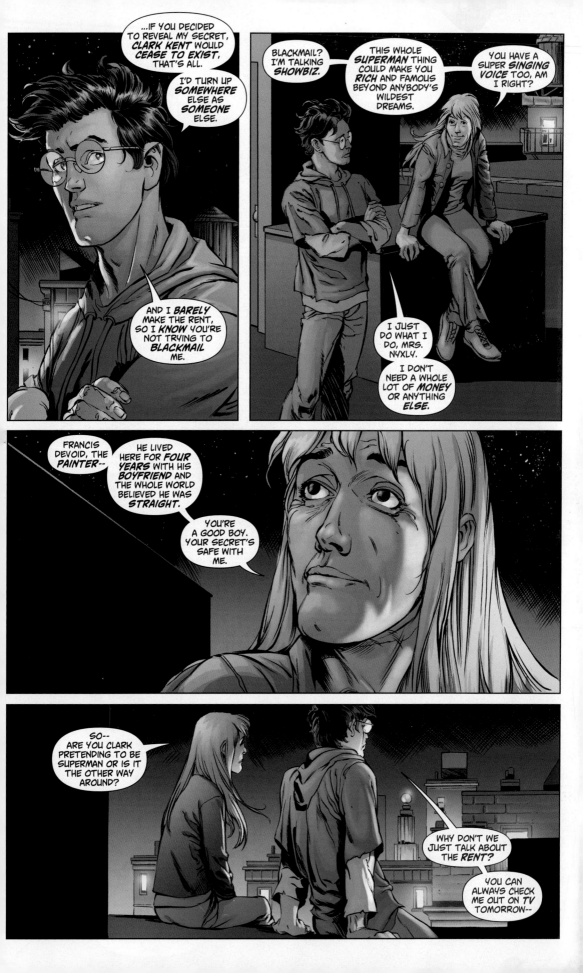

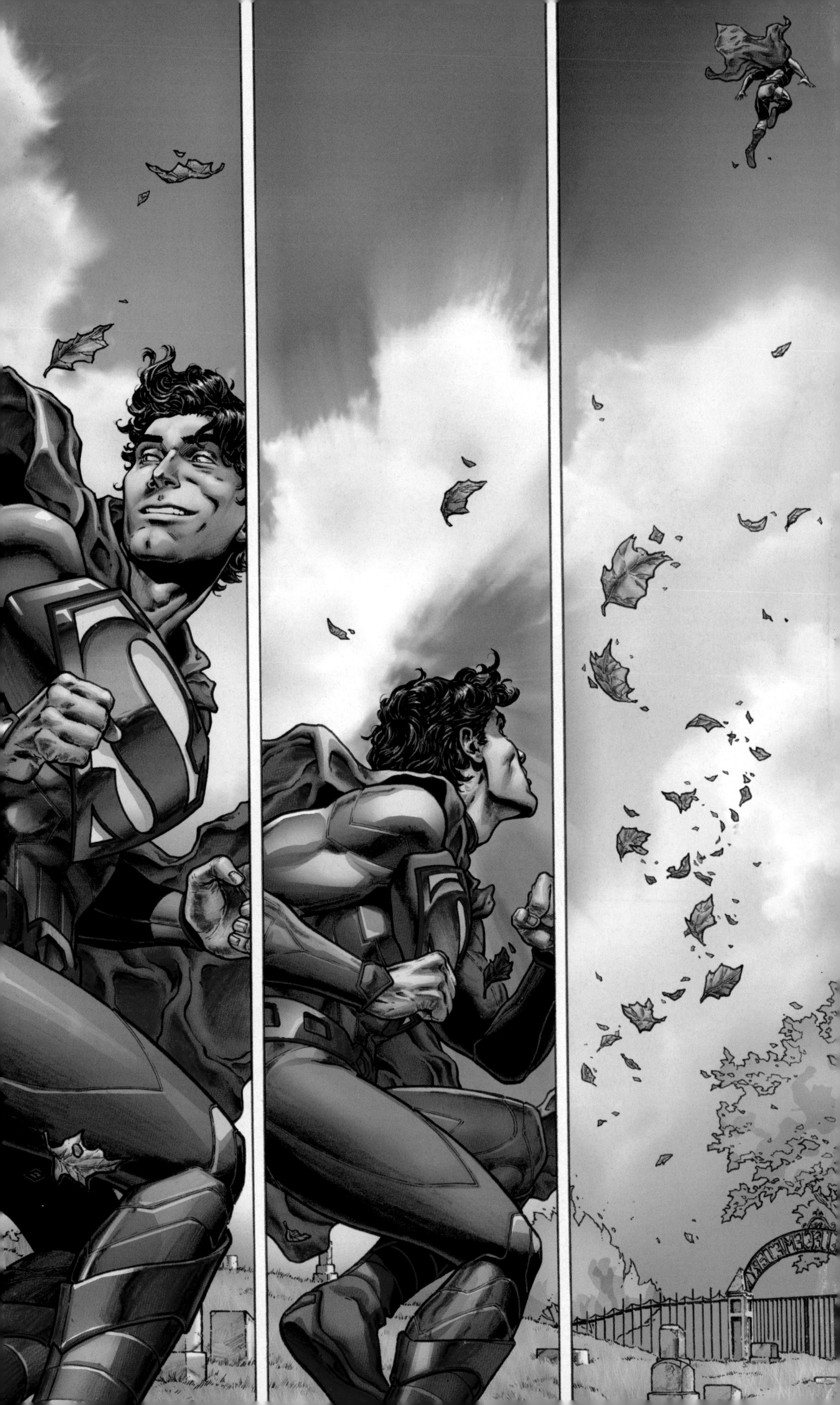

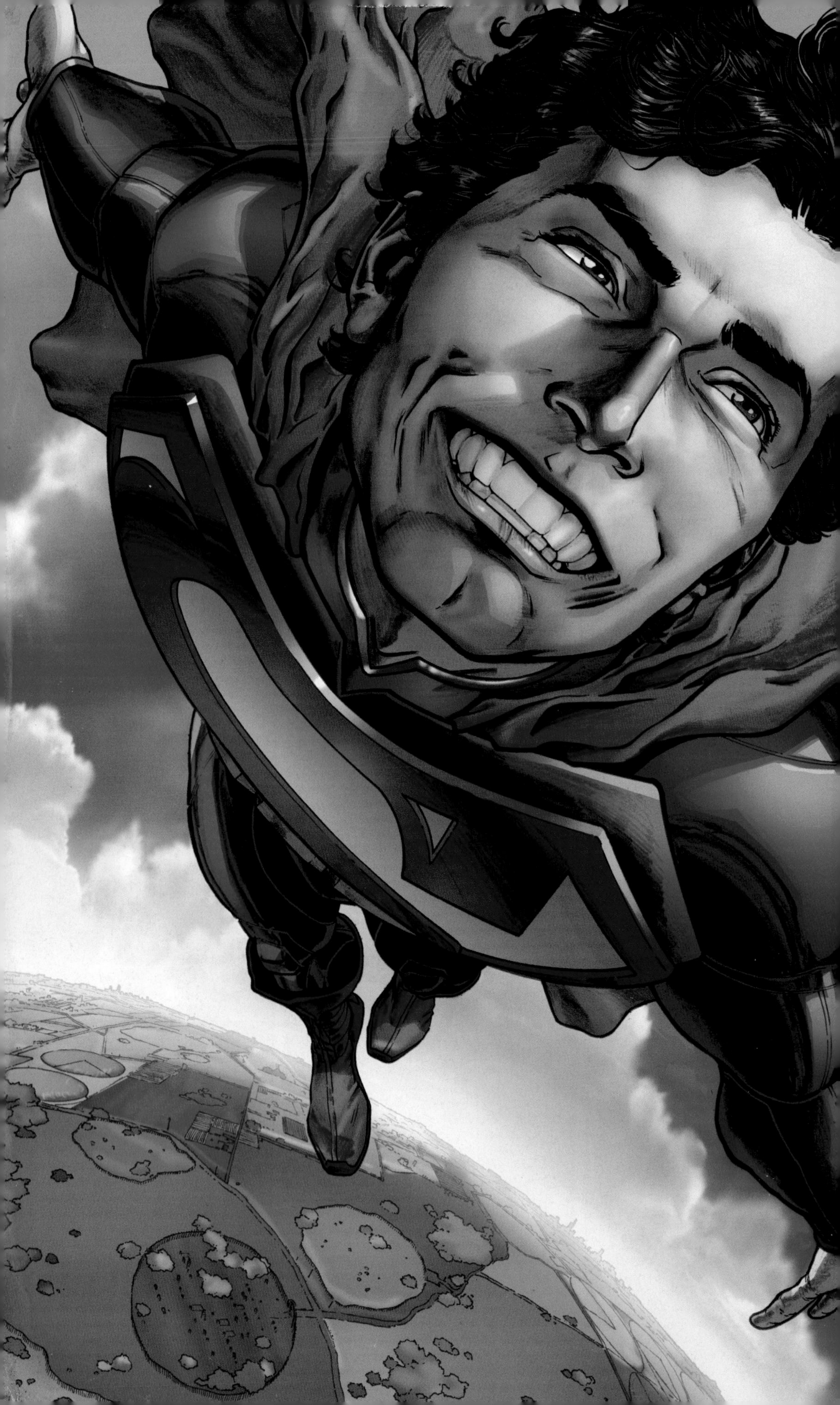

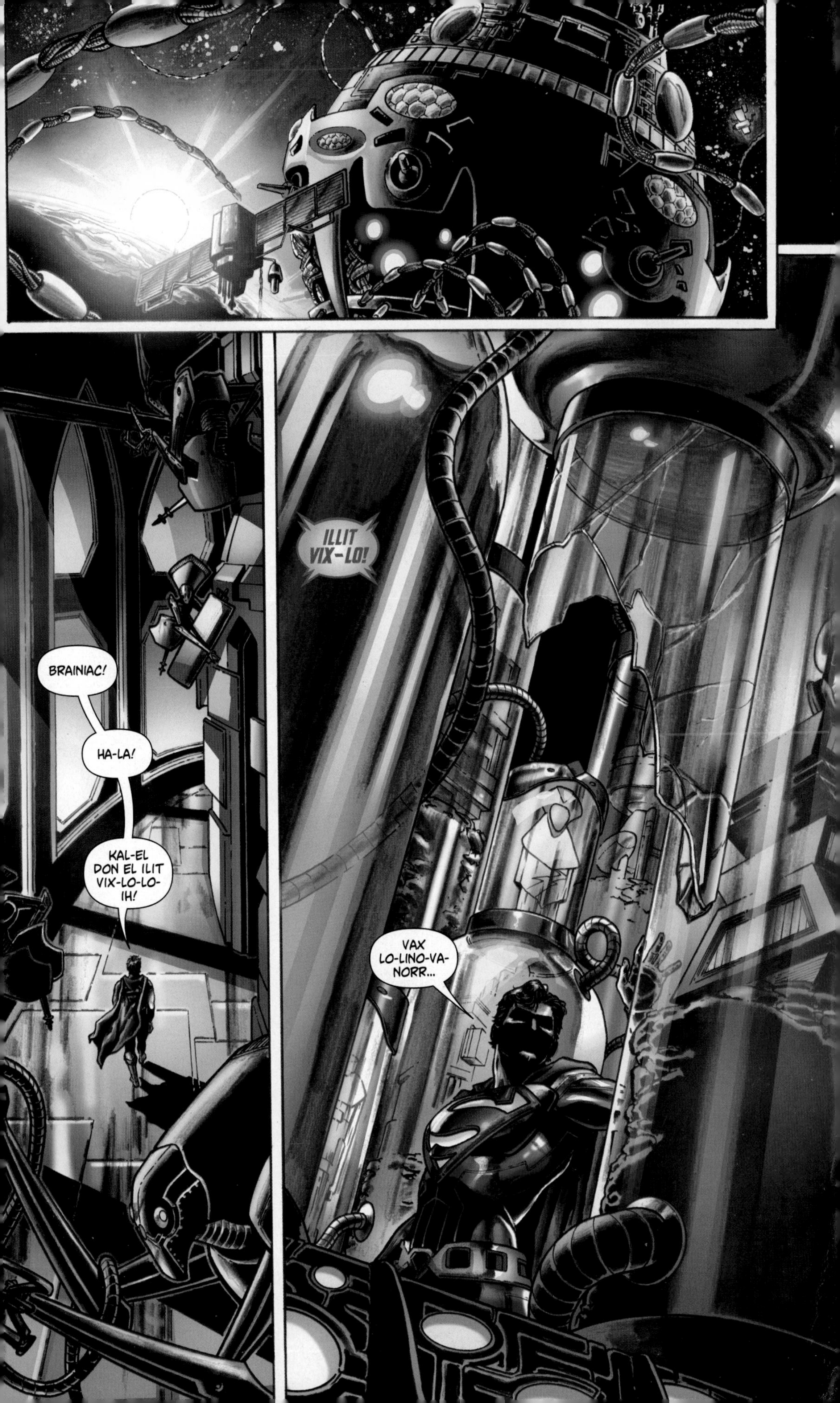
ILLIT VIX-LO!
BRAINIAC!
HA-LA!
KAL-EL DON EL ILIT VIX-LO-LO-IH!
VAX LO-LINO-VA-NORR...

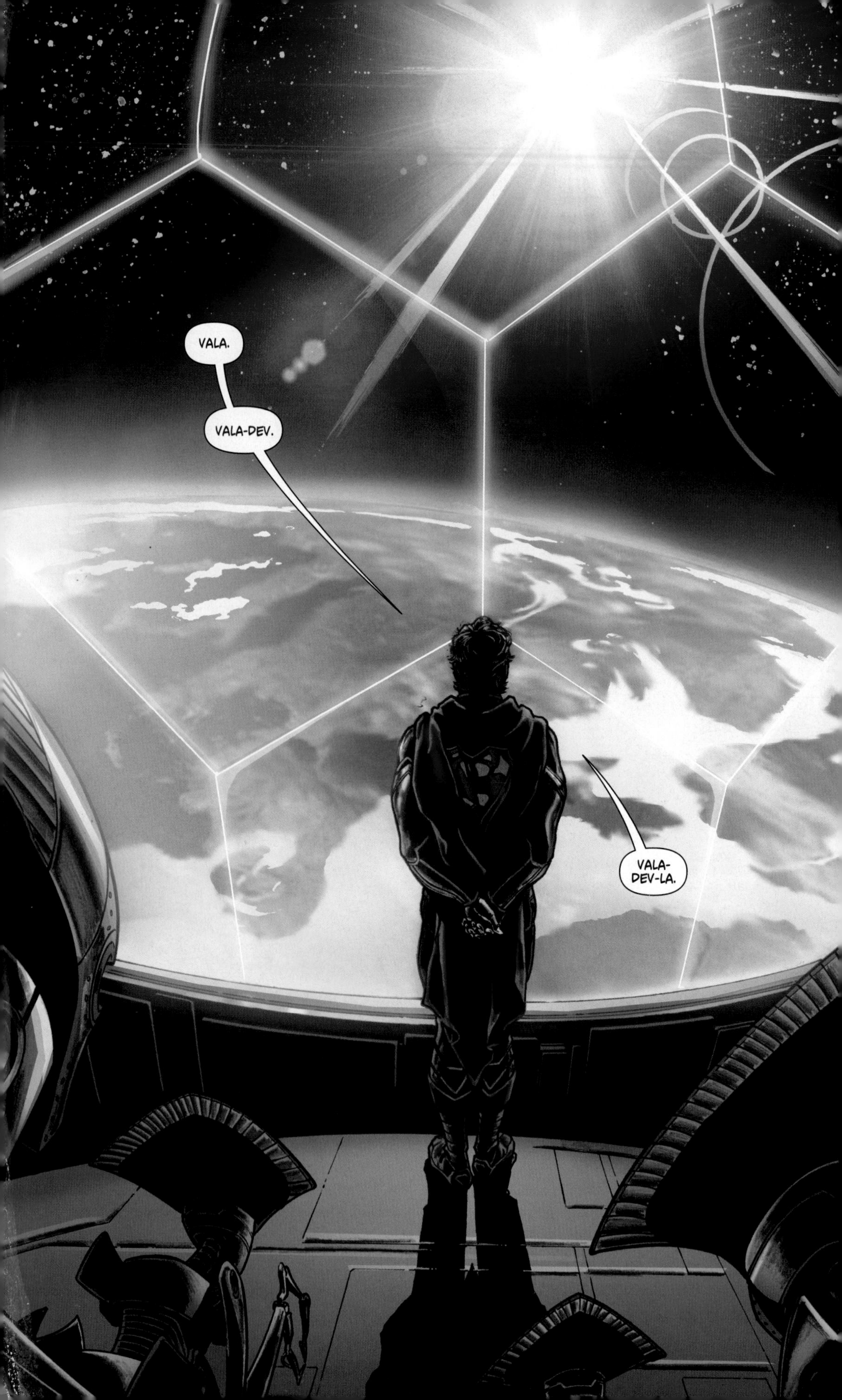
VALA.
VALA-DEV.
VALA-DEV-LA.

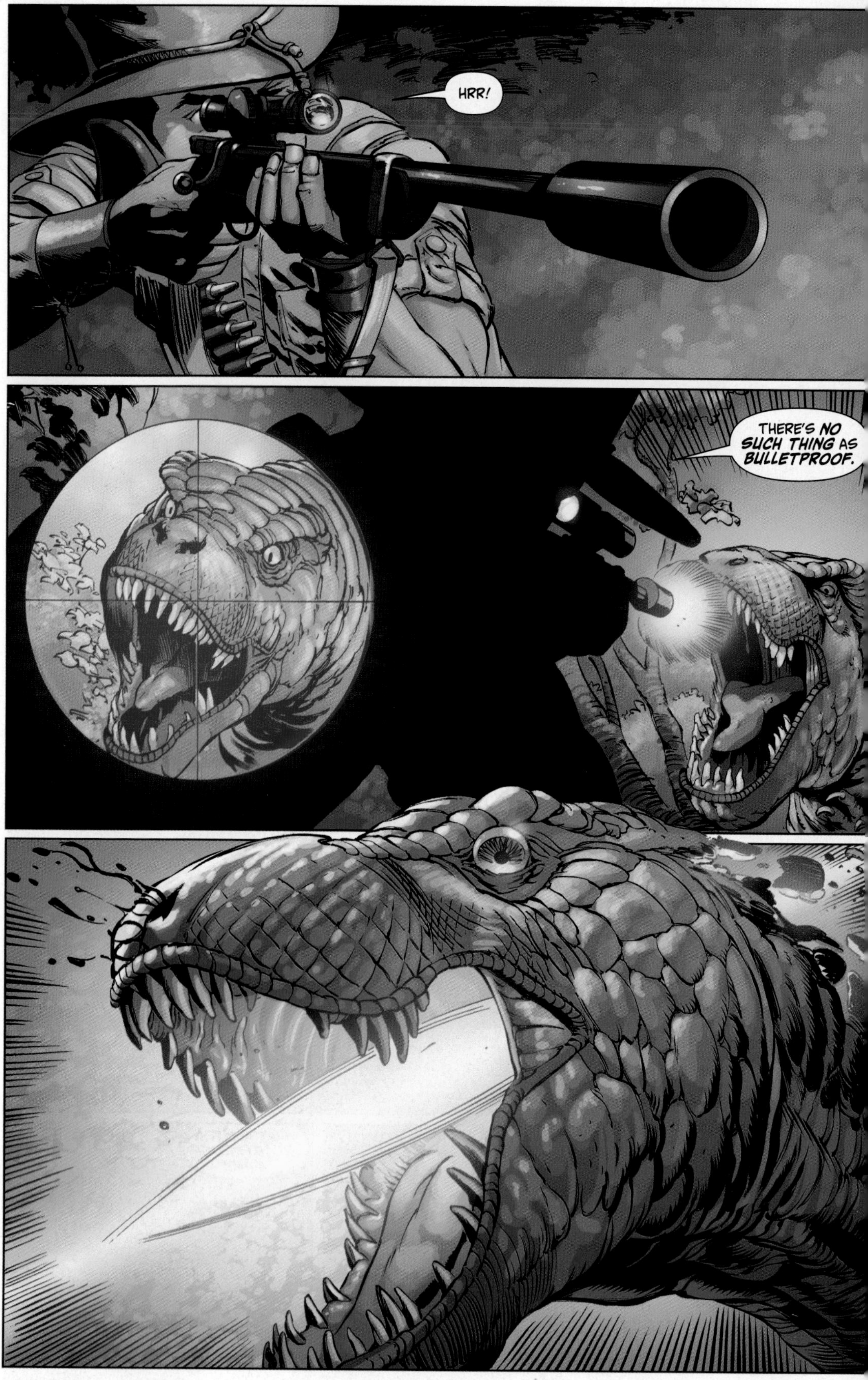
HRR!
THERE'S NO SUCH THING AS BULLETPROOF.

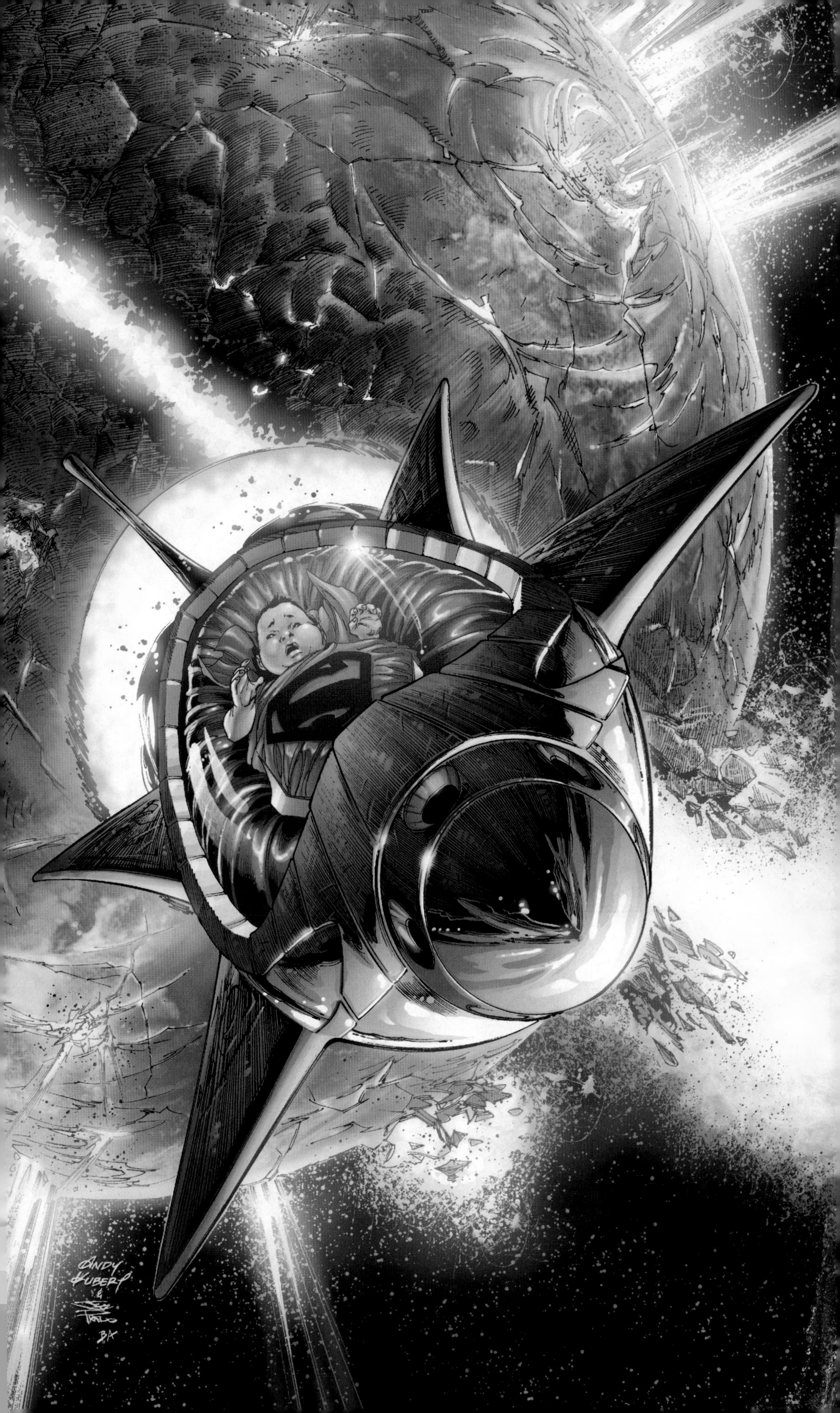
ANDY KUBERT

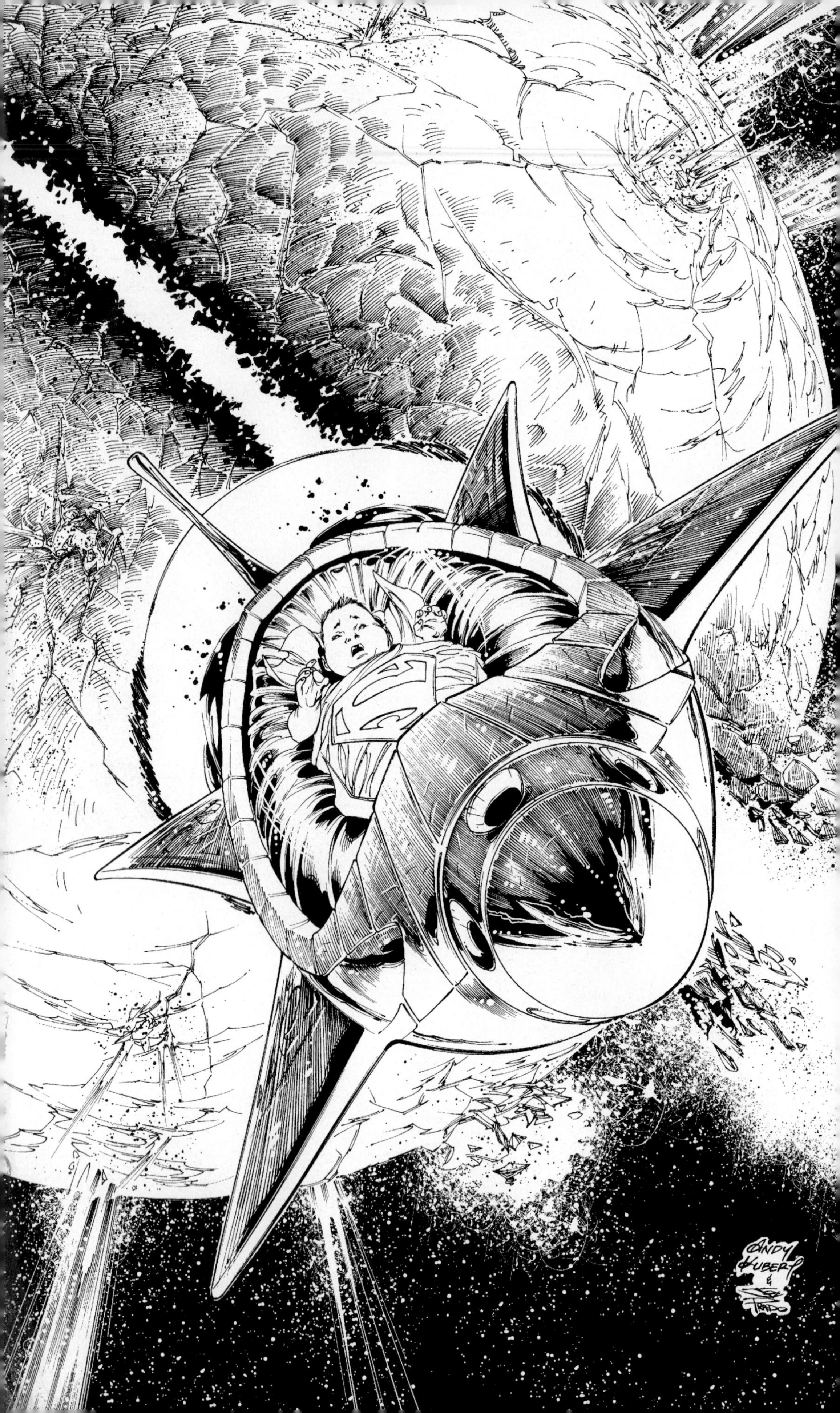
ANDY KUBERT
&

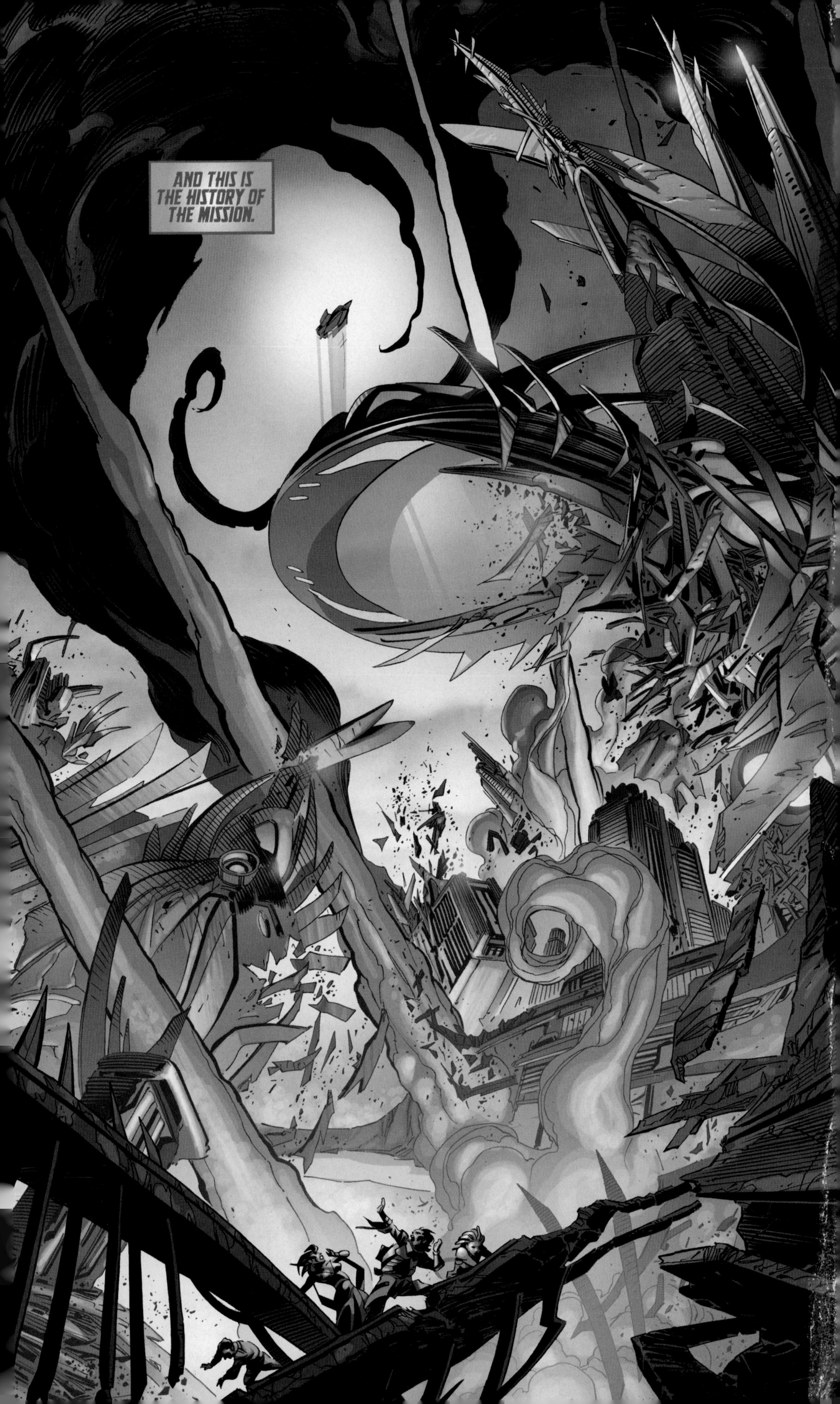
AND THIS IS THE HISTORY OF THE MISSION.

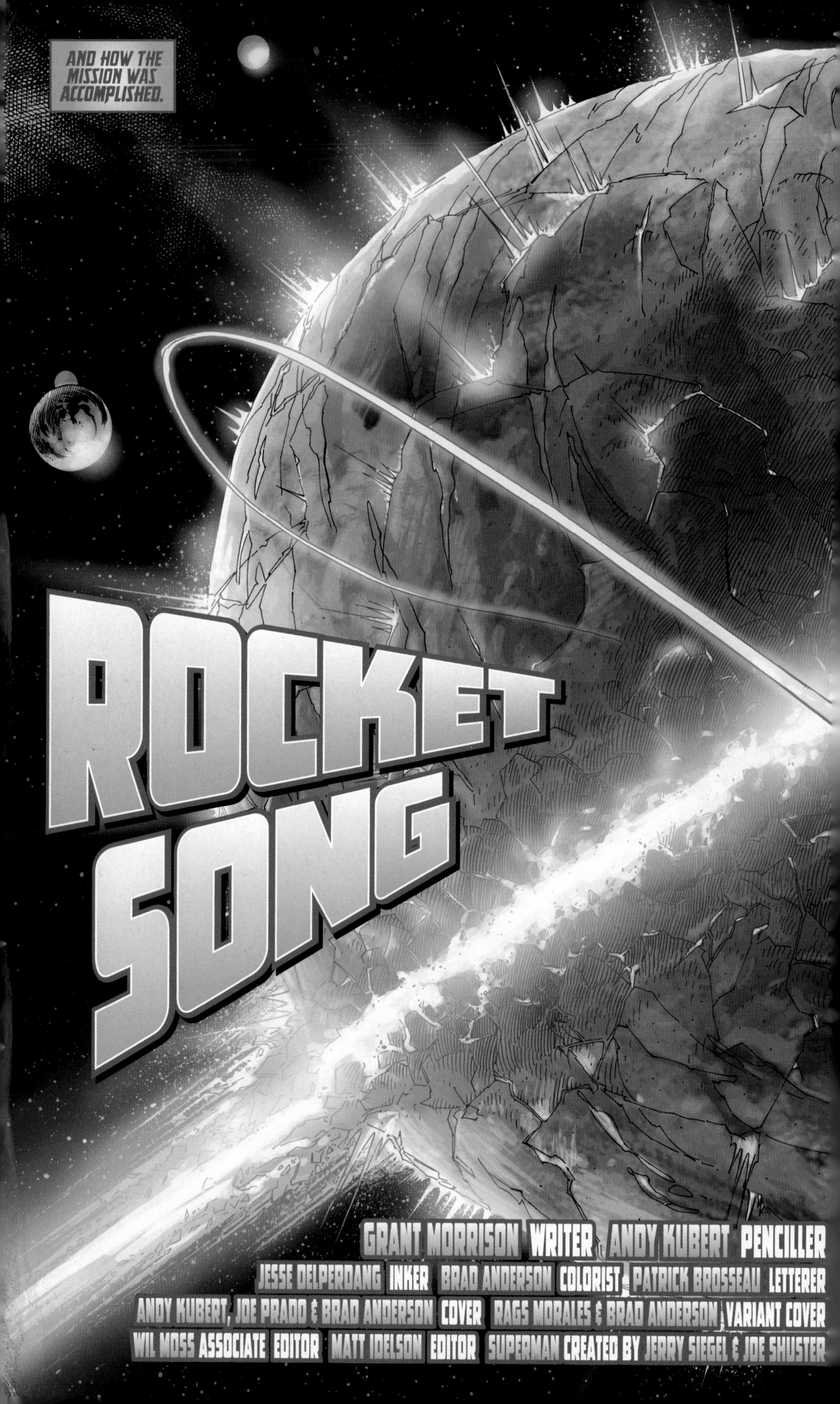
AND HOW THE MISSION WAS ACCOMPLISHED.
ROCKET SONG
GRANT MORRISON WRITER ANDY KUBERT PENCILLER
JESSE DELPERDANG INKER BRAD ANDERSON COLORIST PATRICK BROSSEAU LETTERER
ANDY KUBERT, JOE PRADO & BRAD ANDERSON COVER RAGS MORALES & BRAD ANDERSON VARIANT COVER
WIL MOSS ASSOCIATE EDITOR MATT IDELSON EDITOR SUPERMAN CREATED BY JERRY SIEGEL & JOE SHUSTER

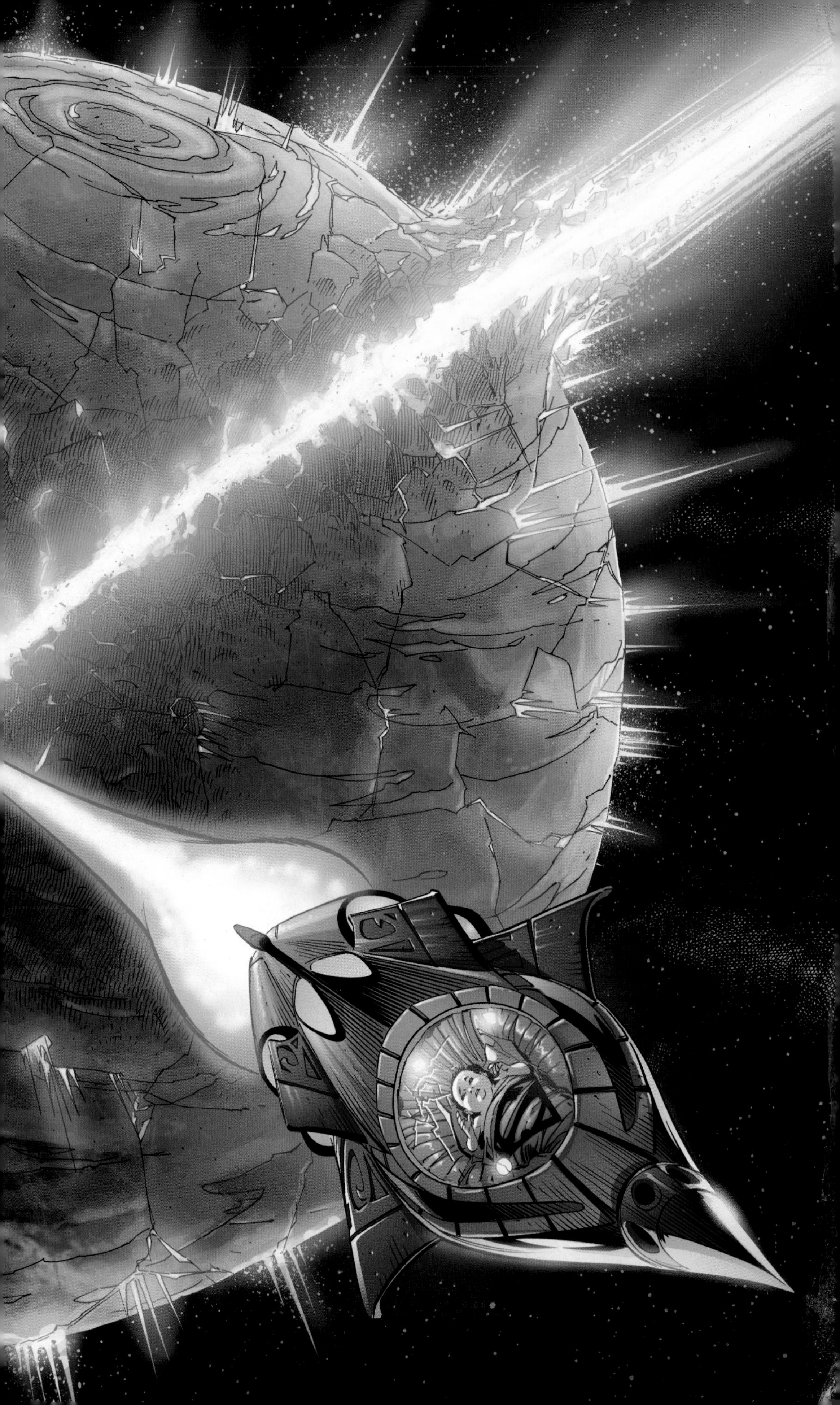

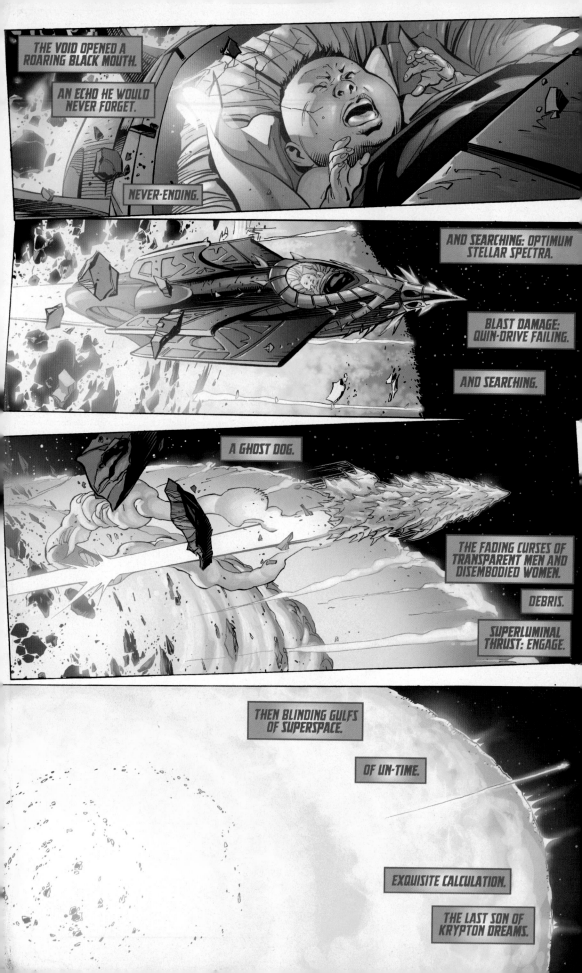

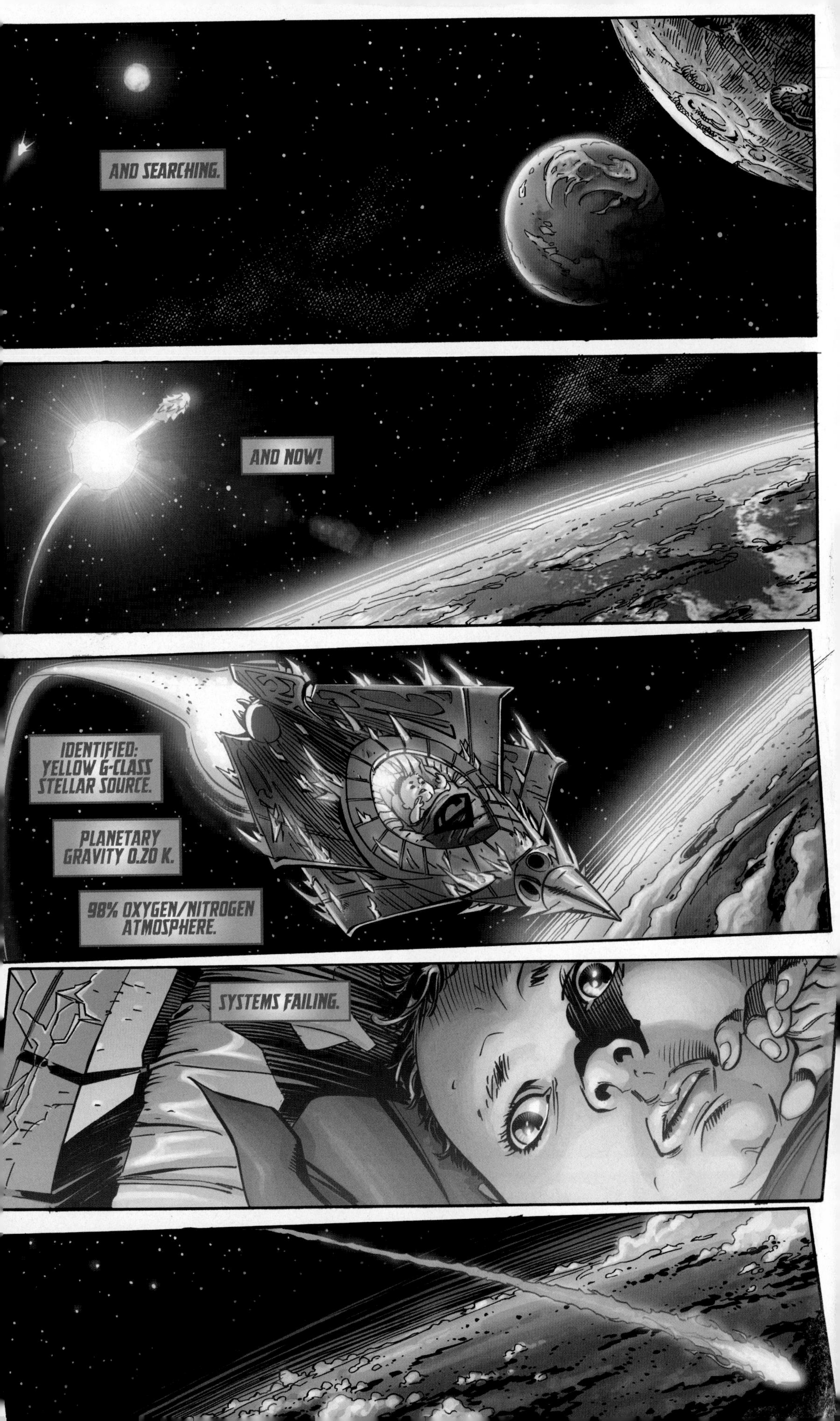
AND SEARCHING.
AND NOW!
IDENTIFIED: YELLOW G-CLASS STELLAR SOURCE.
PLANETARY GRAVITY 0.20 K.
98% OXYGEN/NITROGEN ATMOSPHERE.
SYSTEMS FAILING.

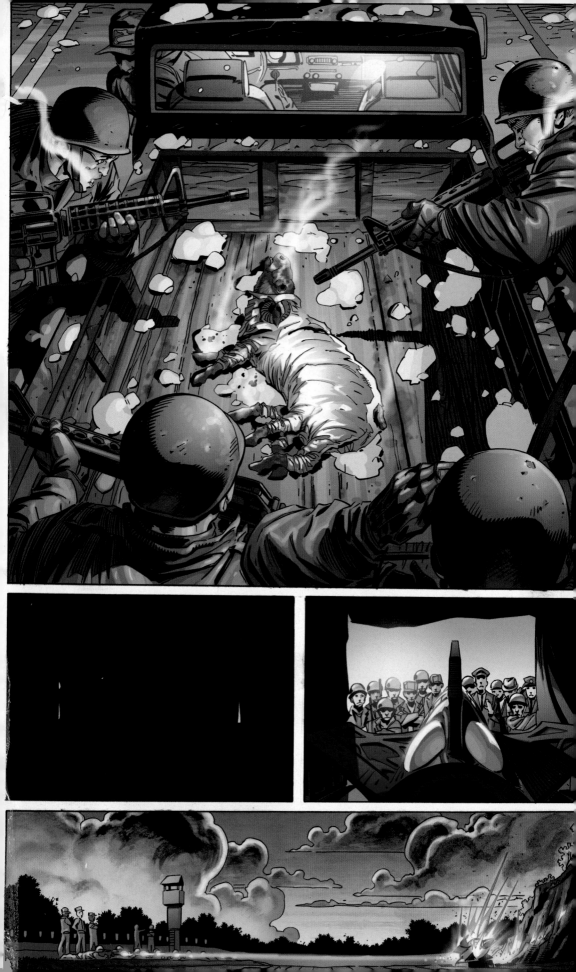

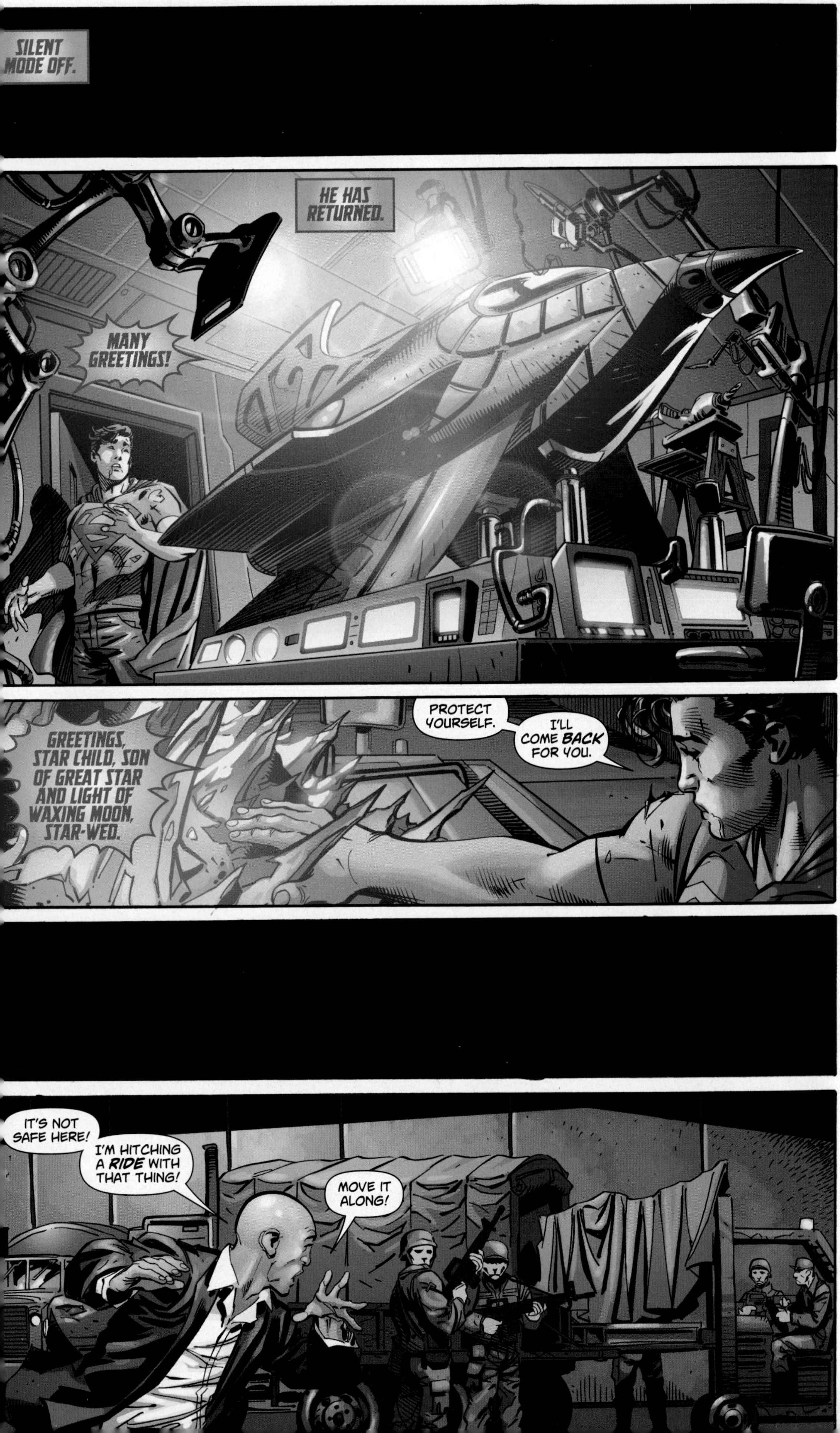
SILENT MODE OFF.
HE HAS RETURNED.
MANY GREETINGS!
GREETINGS, STAR CHILD, SON OF GREAT STAR AND LIGHT OF WAXING MOON, STAR-WED.
PROTECT YOURSELF.
I'LL COME BACK FOR YOU.
IT'S NOT SAFE HERE!
I'M HITCHING A RIDE WITH THAT THING!
MOVE IT ALONG!

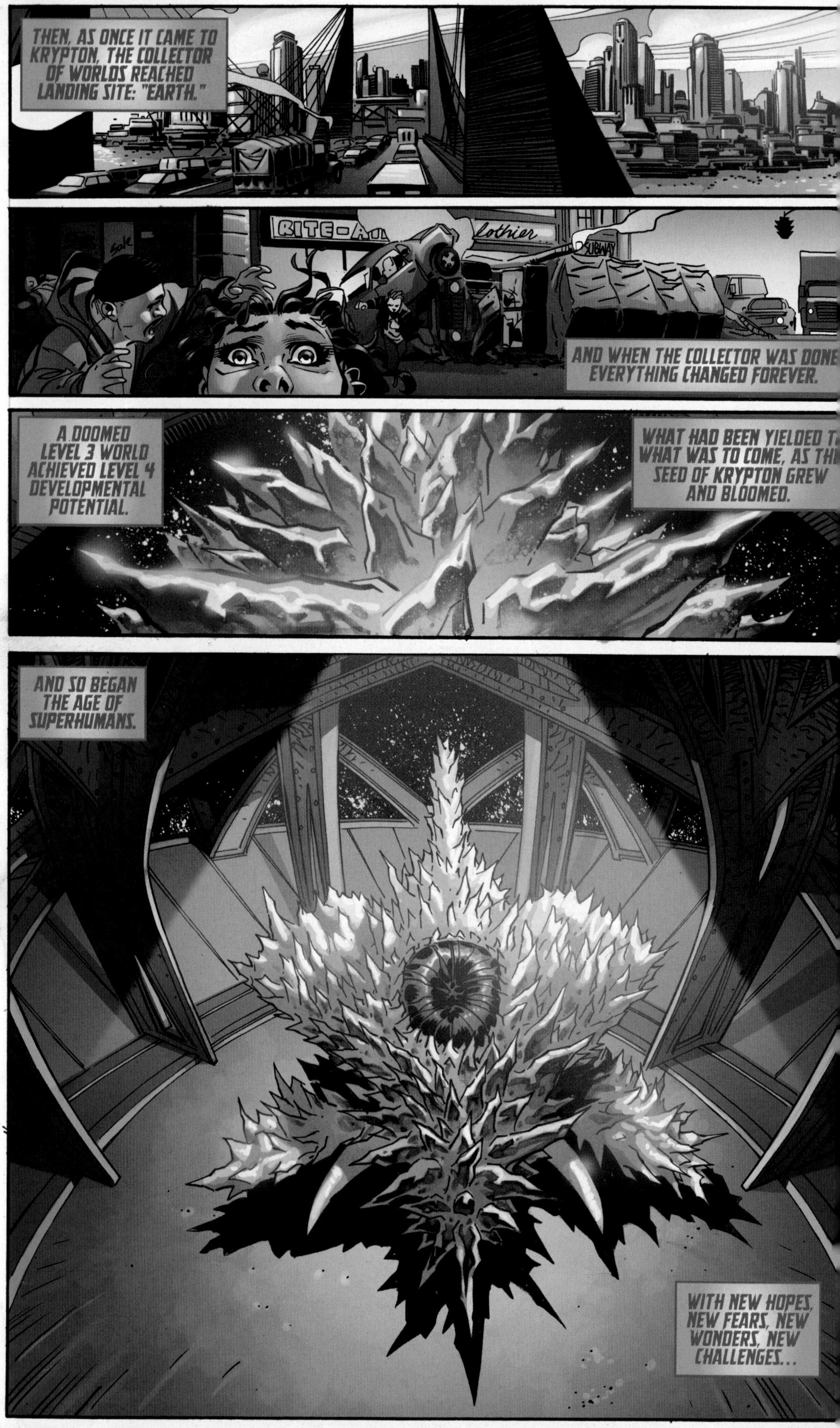
THEN, AS ONCE IT CAME TO KRYPTON, THE COLLECTOR OF WORLDS REACHED LANDING SITE: "EARTH."
RITE-A
lothier
SUBWAY
AND WHEN THE COLLECTOR WAS DONE
EVERYTHING CHANGED FOREVER.
A DOOMED LEVEL 3 WORLD ACHIEVED LEVEL 4 DEVELOPMENTAL POTENTIAL.
WHAT HAD BEEN YIELDED T
WHAT WAS TO COME, AS TH
SEED OF KRYPTON GREW AND BLOOMED.
AND SO BEGAN THE AGE OF SUPERHUMANS.
WITH NEW HOPES, NEW FEARS, NEW WONDERS, NEW CHALLENGES...

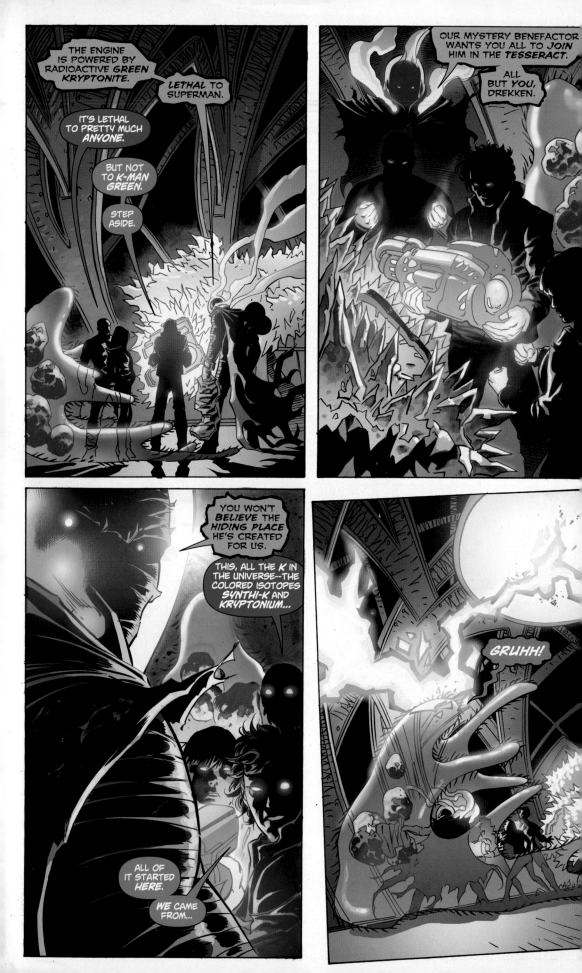

THIS IS THE STORY OF THE MISSION AND ITS CONCLUSION.

THE ENGINE THAT WAS MY HEART, MY POWER SOURCE.

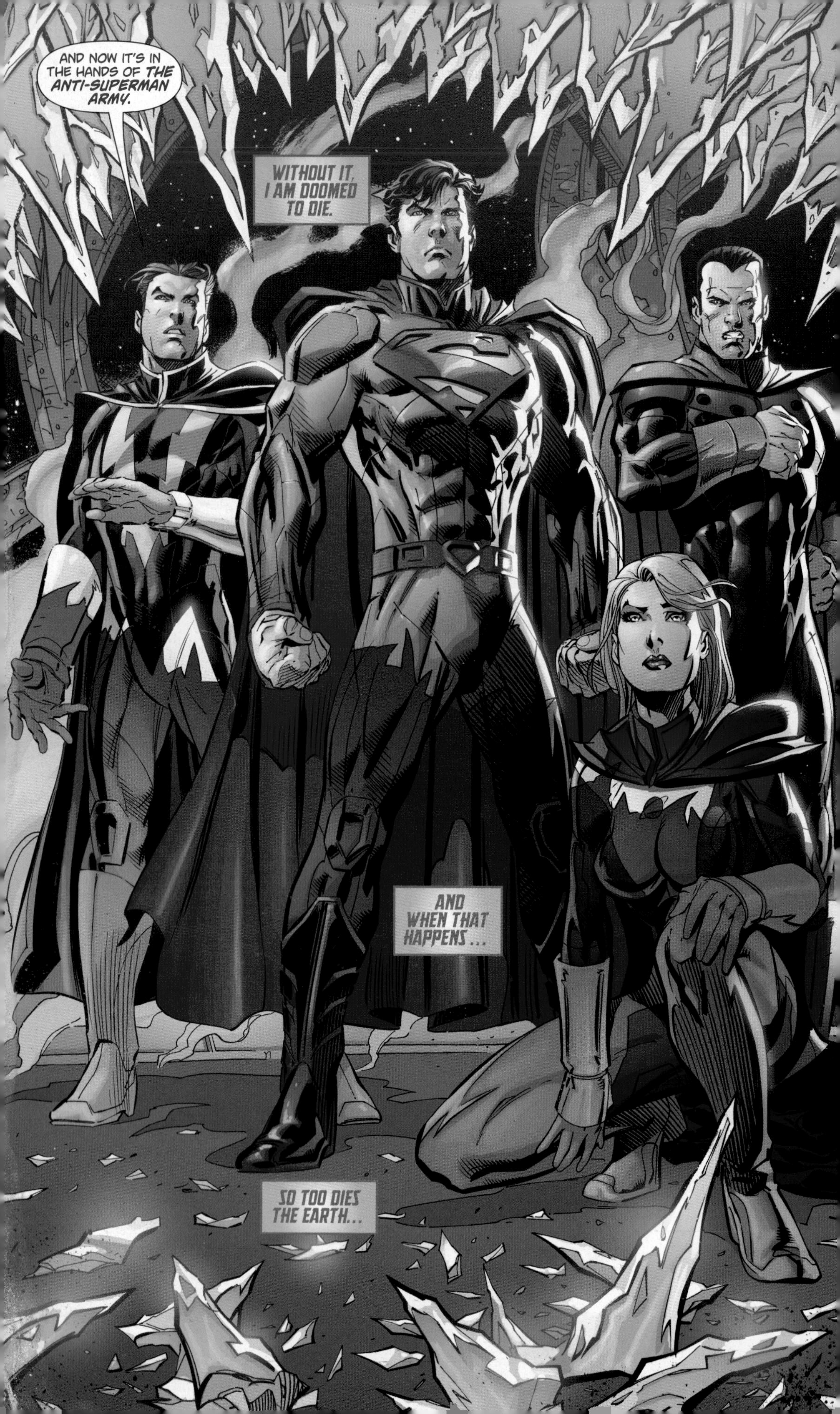

AND NOW IT'S IN THE HANDS OF THE ANTI-SUPERMAN ARMY.
WITHOUT IT, I AM DOOMED TO DIE.
AND WHEN THAT HAPPENS...
SO TOO DIES THE EARTH...

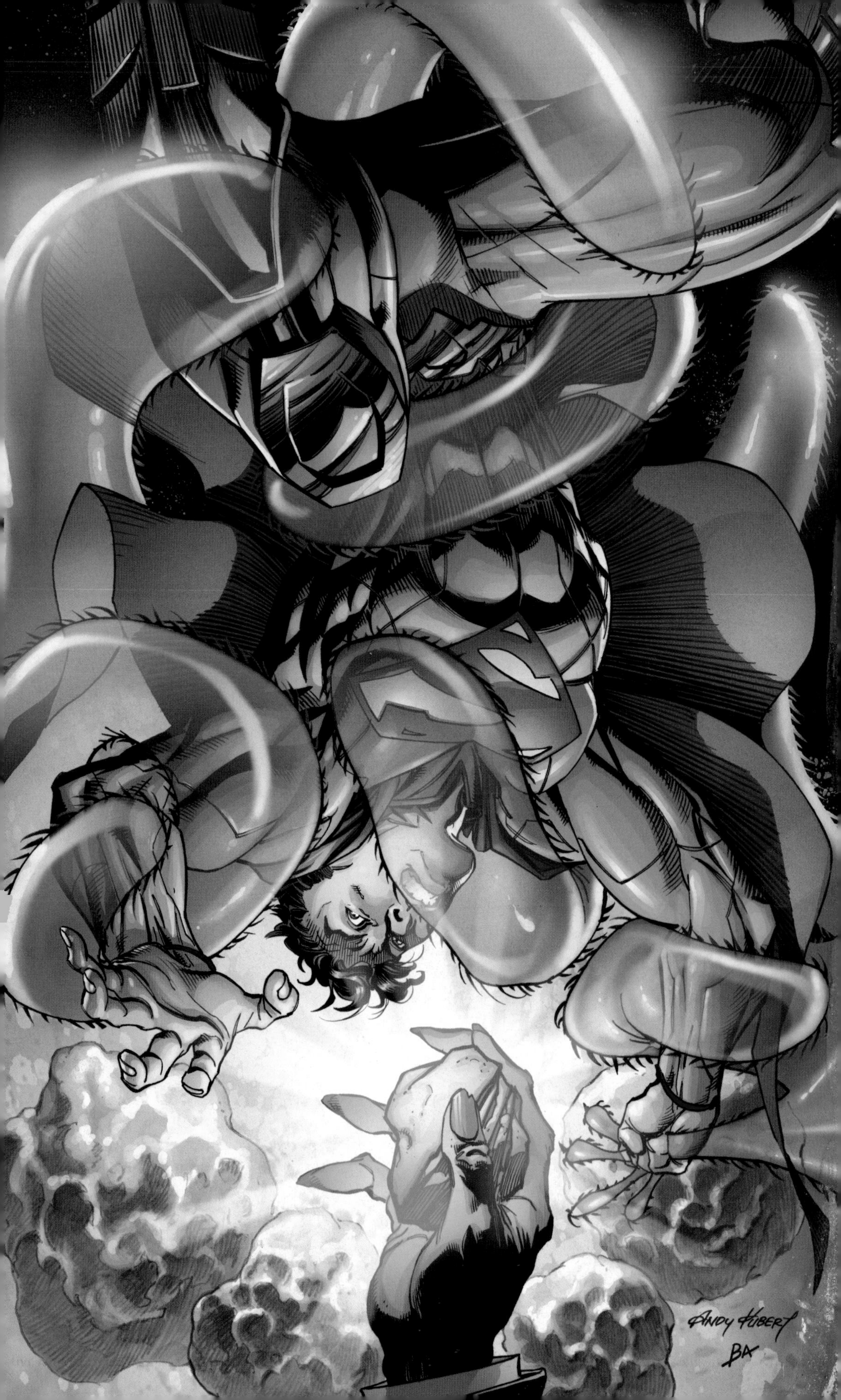
ANDY KUBERT
BA

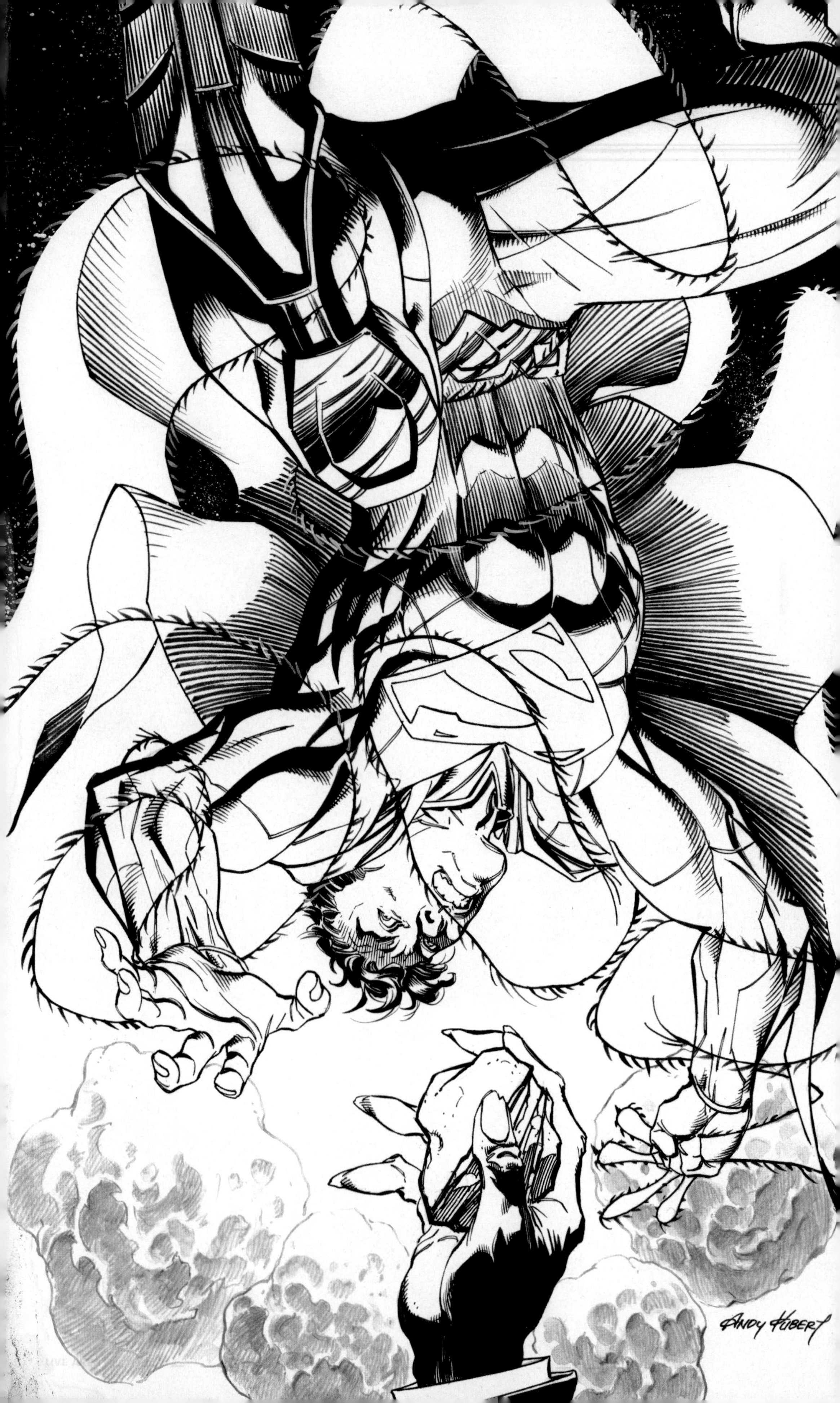
ANDY KUBERT

WHEN SUPERMAN LEARNED TO FLY

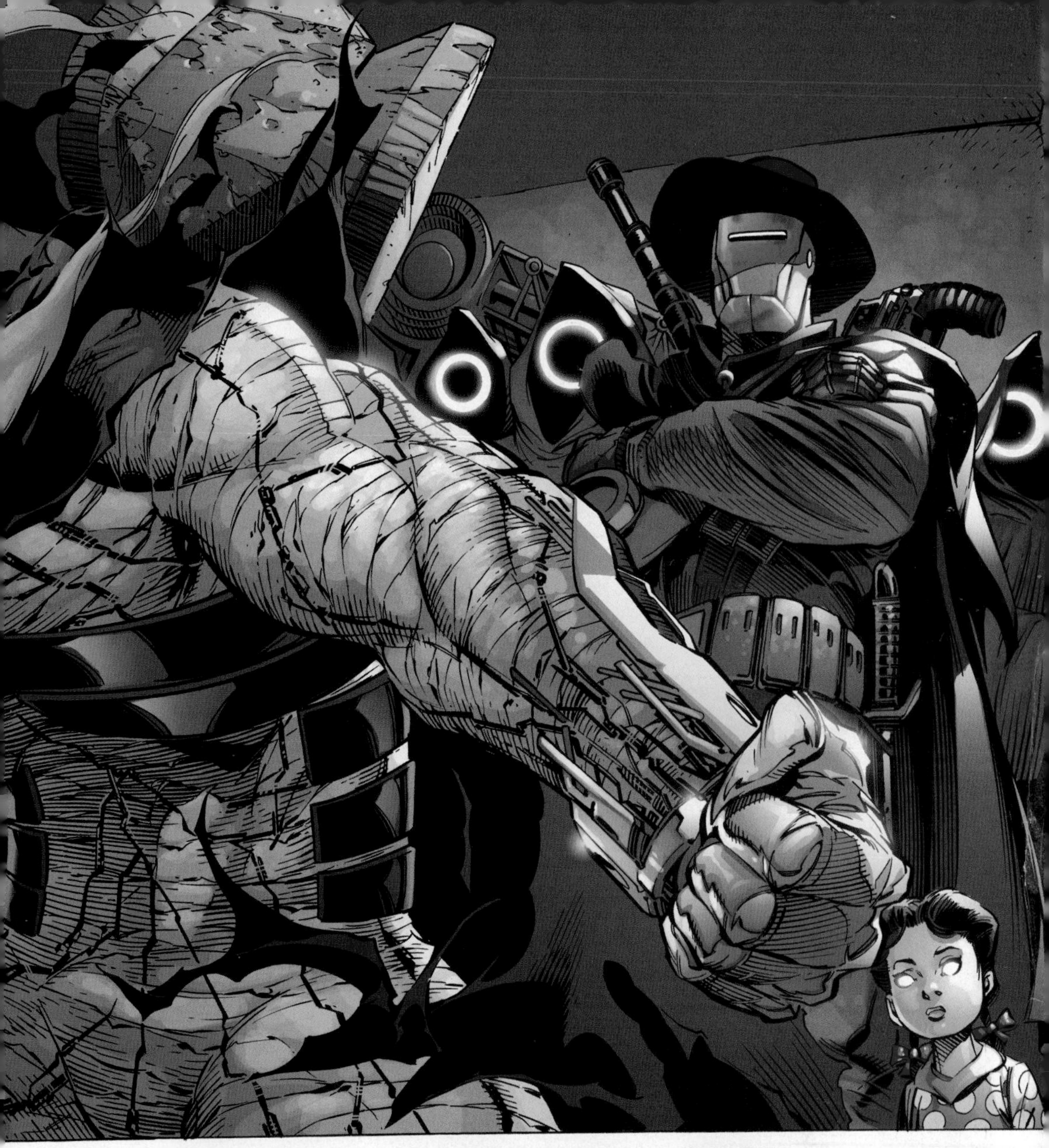

GRANT MORRISON WRITER ANDY KUBERT PENCILLER JOHN DELL INKER
RAD ANDERSON COLORIST PATRICK BROSSEAU LETTERER ANDY KUBERT & BRAD ANDERSON COVER RAGS MORALES & BRAD ANDERSON VARIANT COVER
WIL MOSS ASSOCIATE EDITOR MATT IDELSON EDITOR SUPERMAN CREATED BY JERRY SIEGEL & JOE SHUSTER

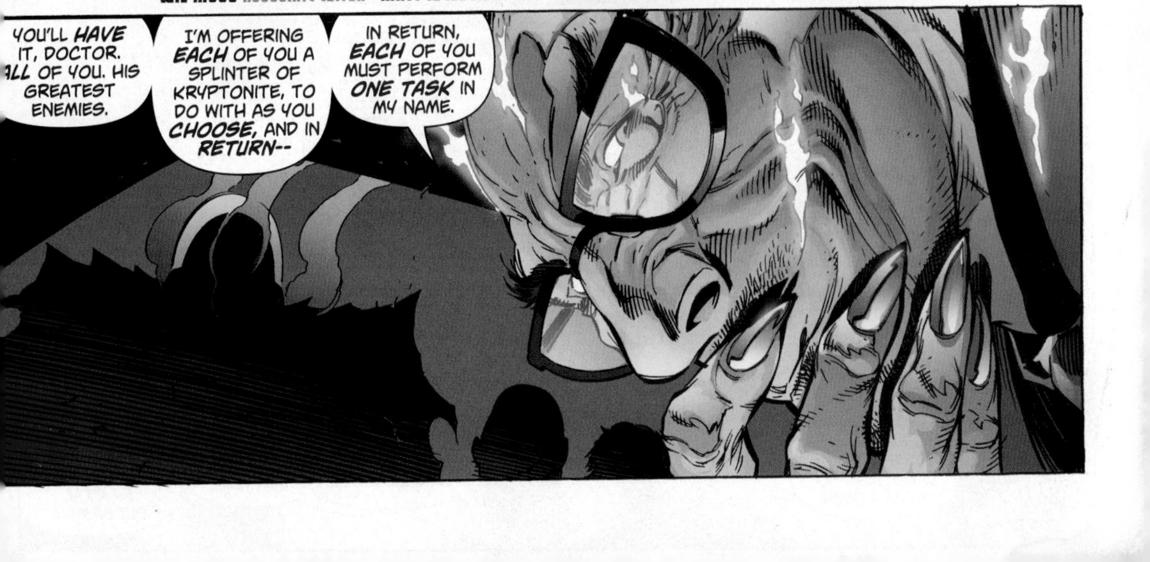
YOU'LL HAVE IT, DOCTOR. LL OF YOU. HIS GREATEST ENEMIES.
I'M OFFERING EACH OF YOU A SPLINTER OF KRYPTONITE, TO DO WITH AS YOU CHOOSE, AND IN RETURN--
IN RETURN, EACH OF YOU MUST PERFORM ONE TASK IN MY NAME.

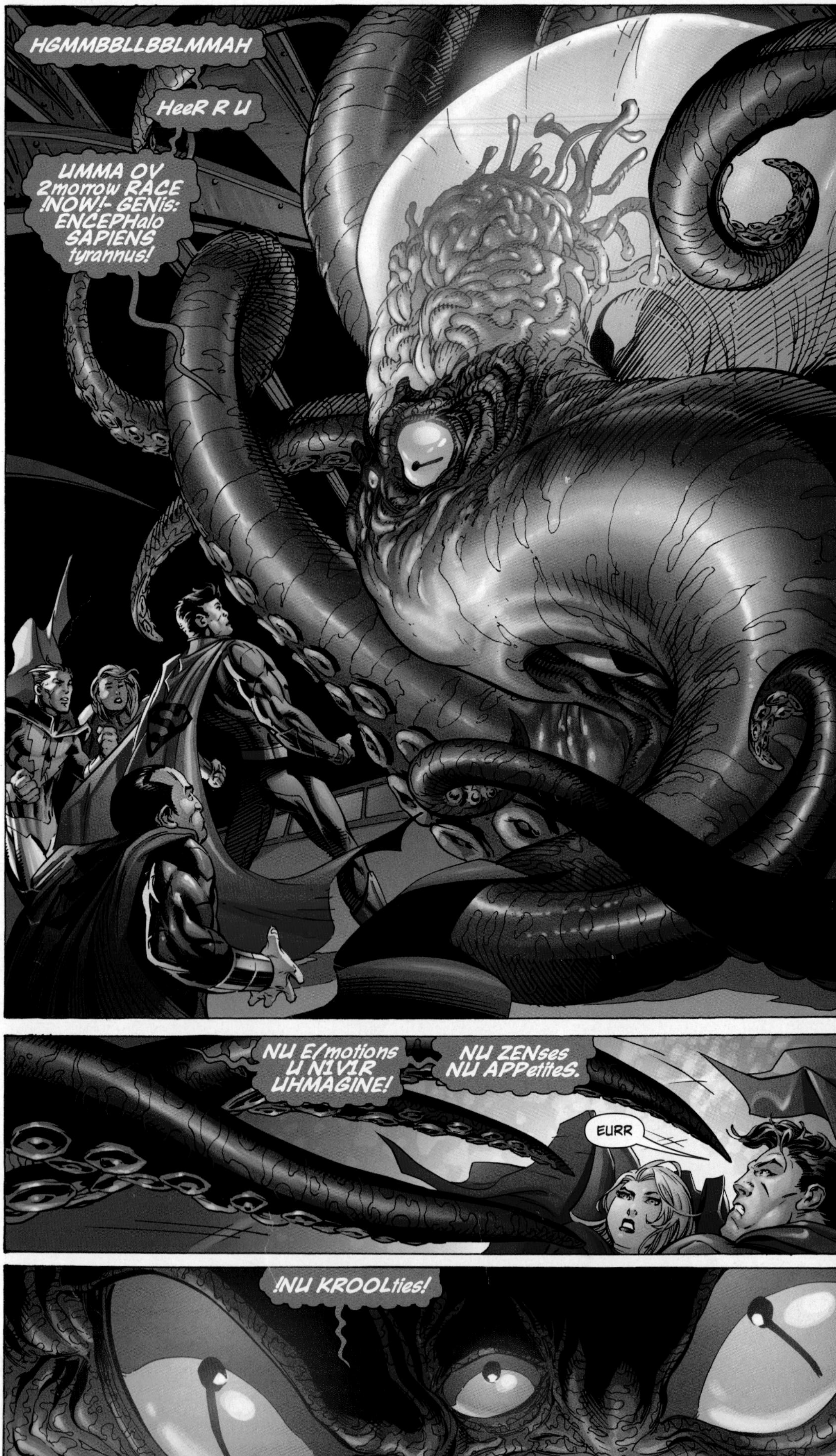
HGMMBBLLBBLMMAH
HeeR R U
UMMA OV 2morrow RACE !NOW!- GENis: ENCEPHalo SAPIENS tyrannus!
NU E/motions U N1V1R UHMAGINE!
NU ZENses NU APPetiteS.
EURR
!NU KROOLties!

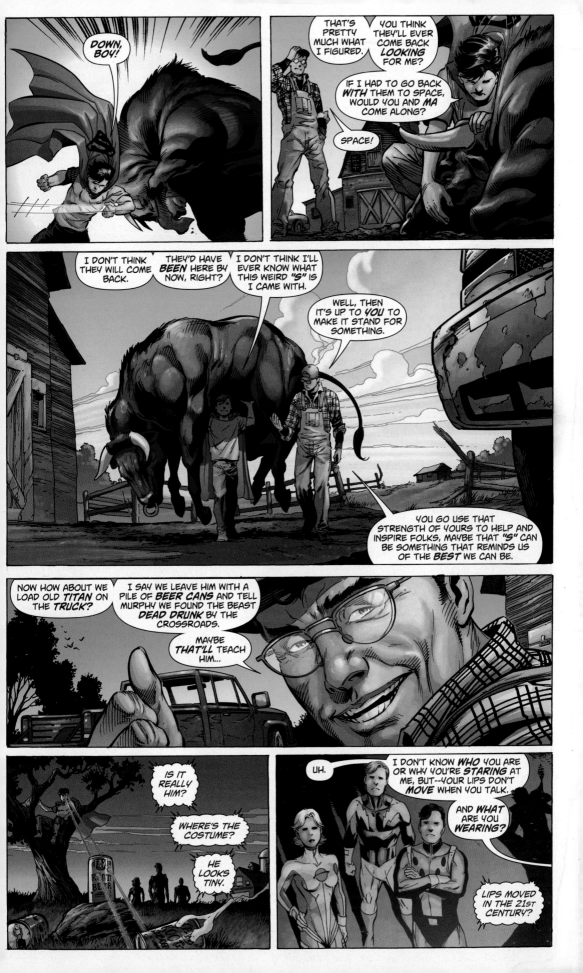

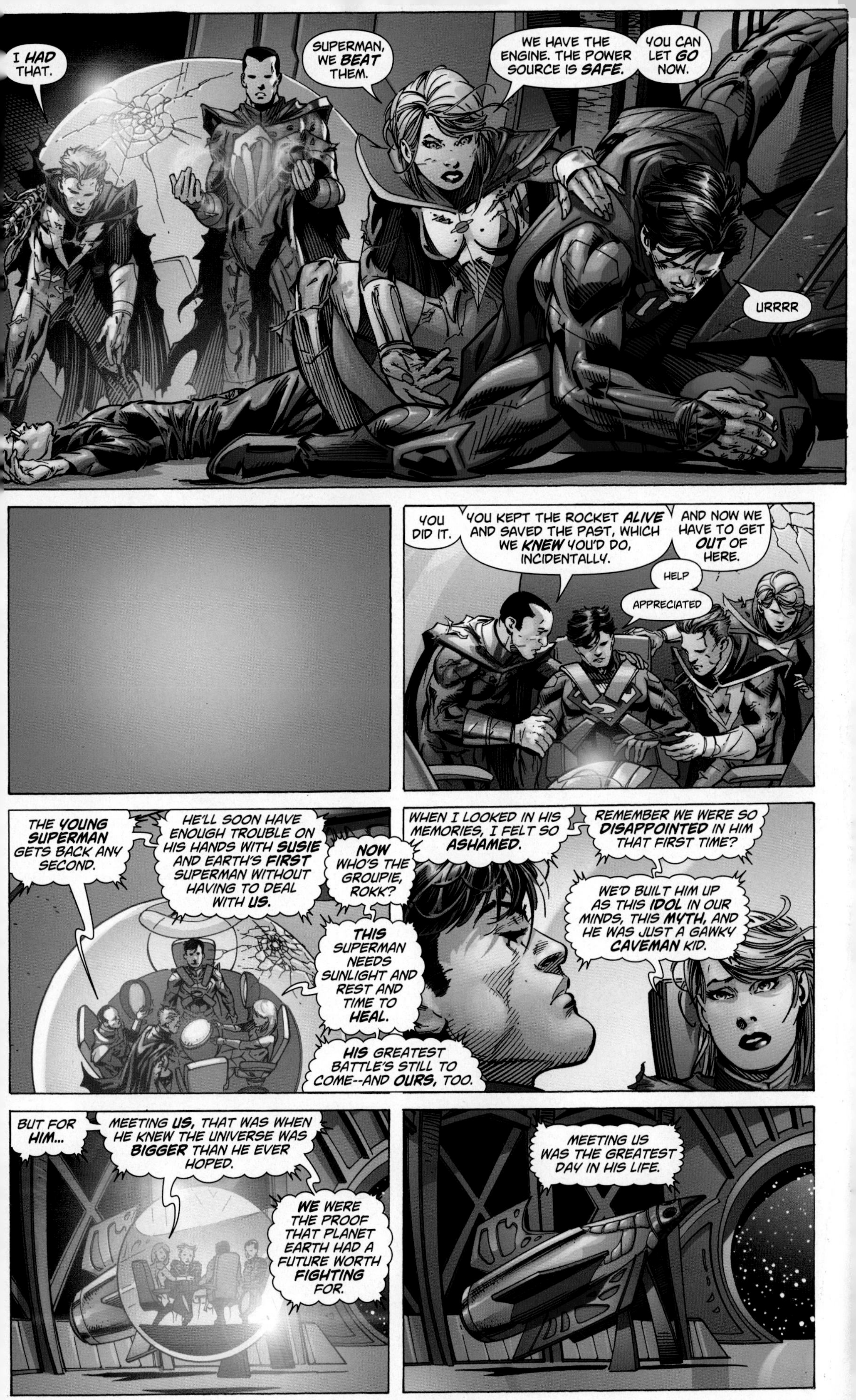

I HAD THAT.
SUPERMAN, WE BEAT THEM.
WE HAVE THE ENGINE. THE POWER SOURCE IS SAFE.
YOU CAN LET GO NOW.
URRRR
YOU DID IT.
YOU KEPT THE ROCKET ALIVE AND SAVED THE PAST, WHICH WE KNEW YOU'D DO, INCIDENTALLY.
AND NOW WE HAVE TO GET OUT OF HERE.
HELP
APPRECIATED
THE YOUNG SUPERMAN GETS BACK ANY SECOND.
HE'LL SOON HAVE ENOUGH TROUBLE ON HIS HANDS WITH SUSIE AND EARTH'S FIRST SUPERMAN WITHOUT HAVING TO DEAL WITH US.
NOW WHO'S THE GROUPIE, ROKK?
THIS SUPERMAN NEEDS SUNLIGHT AND REST AND TIME TO HEAL.
HIS GREATEST BATTLE'S STILL TO COME--AND OURS, TOO.
WHEN I LOOKED IN HIS MEMORIES, I FELT SO ASHAMED.
REMEMBER WE WERE SO DISAPPOINTED IN HIM THAT FIRST TIME?
WE'D BUILT HIM UP AS THIS IDOL IN OUR MINDS, THIS MYTH, AND HE WAS JUST A GAWKY CAVEMAN KID.
BUT FOR HIM...
MEETING US, THAT WAS WHEN HE KNEW THE UNIVERSE WAS BIGGER THAN HE EVER HOPED.
WE WERE THE PROOF THAT PLANET EARTH HAD A FUTURE WORTH FIGHTING FOR.
MEETING US WAS THE GREATEST DAY IN HIS LIFE.

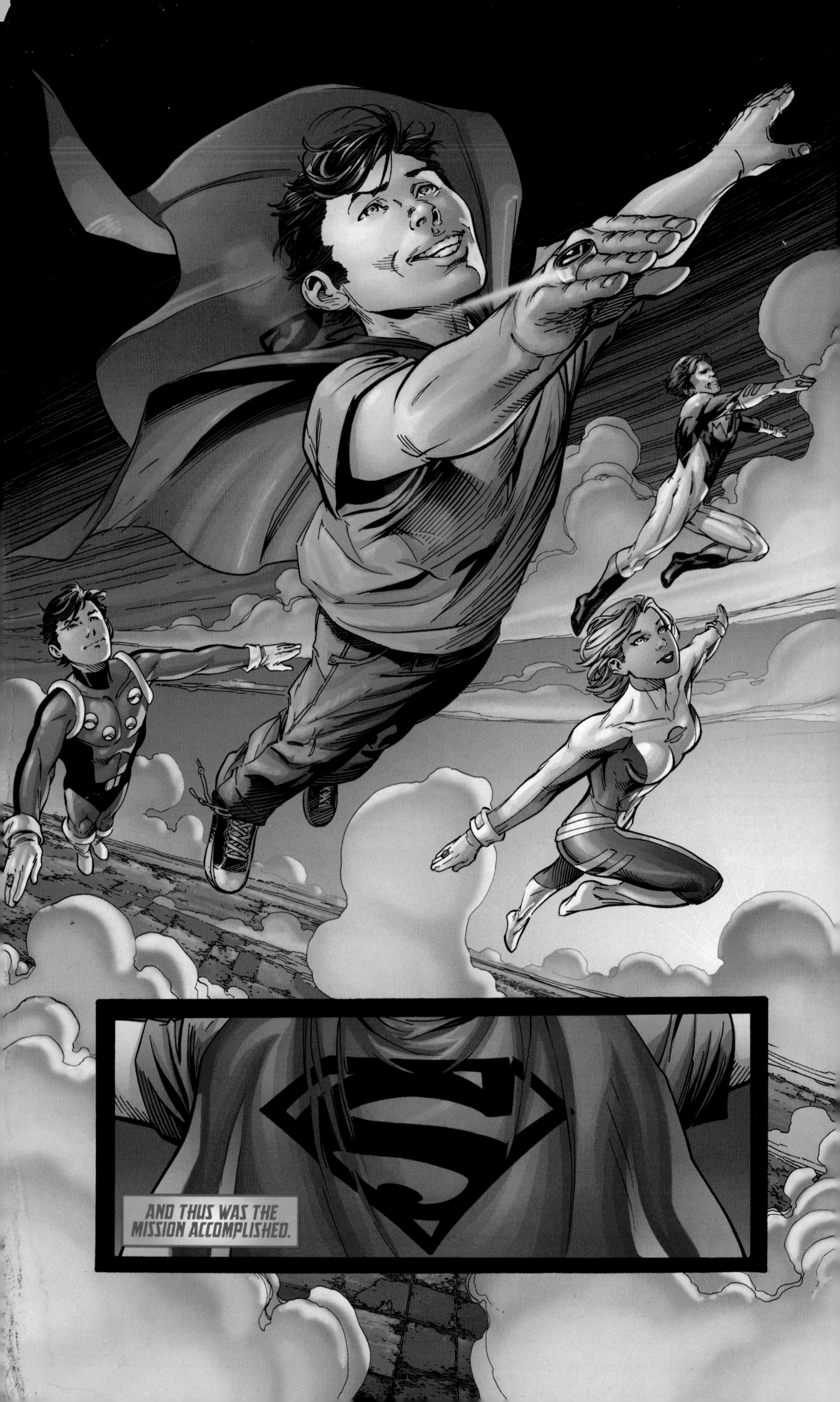
AND THUS WAS THE MISSION ACCOMPLISHED.

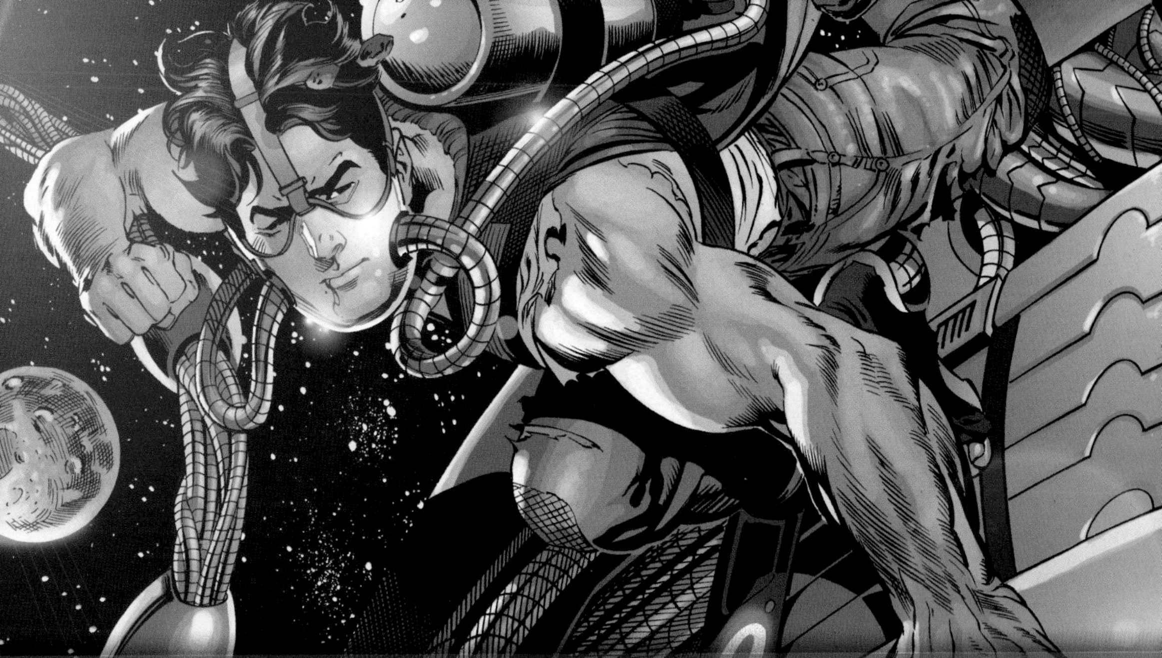

ACTION COMICS BACK-UP ADVENTURES

written by SHOLLY FISCH

HEARTS OF STEEL
Art by BRAD WALKER • Color by JAY DAVID RAMOS

MEANWHILE
Art by BRAD WALKER • Color by JAY DAVID RAMOS with DAVID CURIEL

BABY STEPS
Art by CHRISCROSS • Color by JOSÉ VILLARRUBIA

LAST DAY
Art by CHRISCROSS • Color by JOSÉ VILLARRUBIA

All stories lettered by CARLOS M. MANGUAL

SUPERMAN created by JERRY SIEGEL & JOE SHUSTER
STEEL created by LOUISE SIMONSON & JON BOGDANOVE

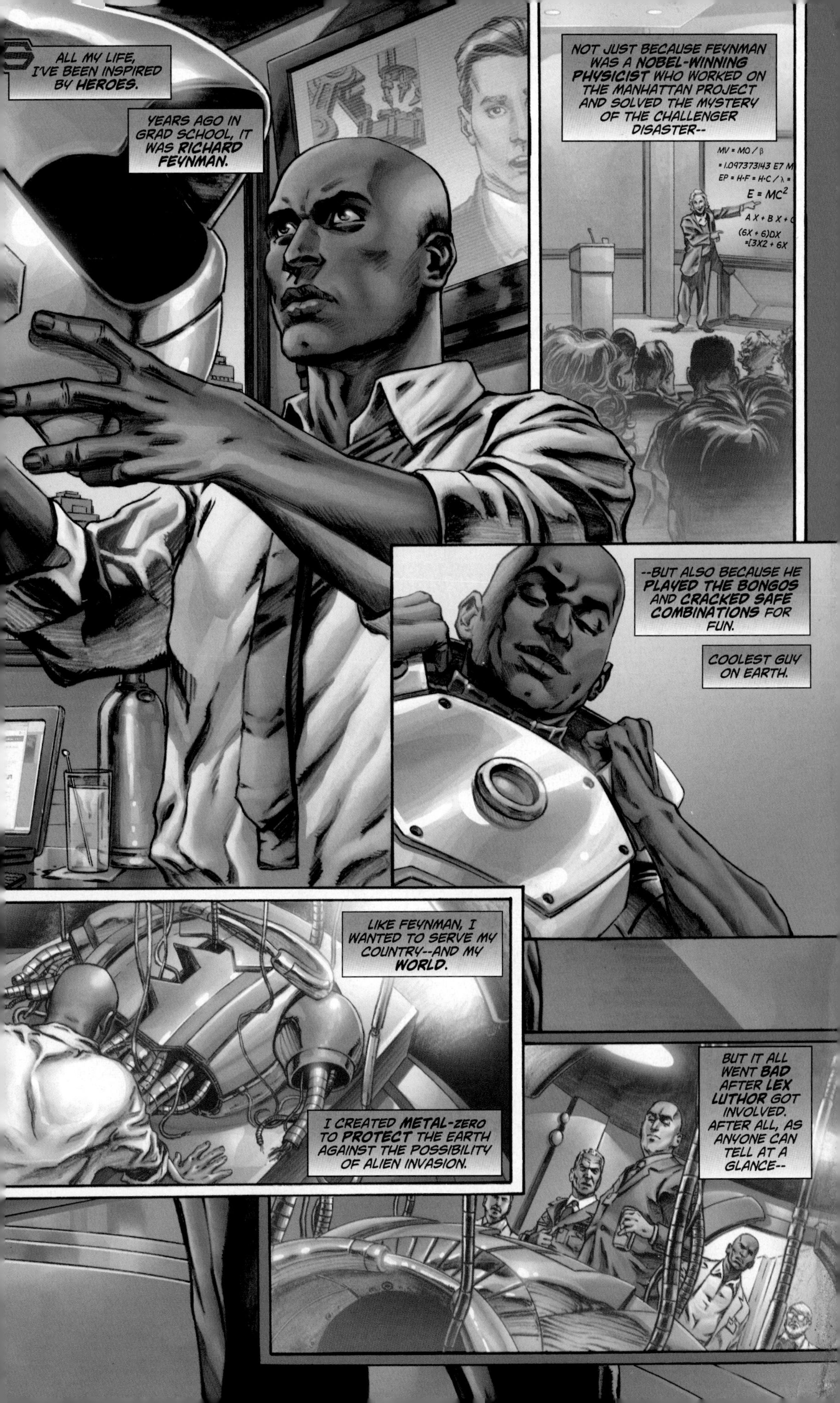

ALL MY LIFE, I'VE BEEN INSPIRED BY HEROES.
YEARS AGO IN GRAD SCHOOL, IT WAS RICHARD FEYNMAN.
NOT JUST BECAUSE FEYNMAN WAS A NOBEL-WINNING PHYSICIST WHO WORKED ON THE MANHATTAN PROJECT AND SOLVED THE MYSTERY OF THE CHALLENGER DISASTER--
MV = MO / β
= 1.097373143 E7 M
EP = H·F = H·C / λ =
E = MC2
A X + B X + C
(6X + 6)DX
=[3X2 + 6X
--BUT ALSO BECAUSE HE PLAYED THE BONGOS AND CRACKED SAFE COMBINATIONS FOR FUN.
COOLEST GUY ON EARTH.
LIKE FEYNMAN, I WANTED TO SERVE MY COUNTRY--AND MY WORLD.
I CREATED METAL-ZERO TO PROTECT THE EARTH AGAINST THE POSSIBILITY OF ALIEN INVASION.
BUT IT ALL WENT BAD AFTER LEX LUTHOR GOT INVOLVED. AFTER ALL, AS ANYONE CAN TELL AT A GLANCE--

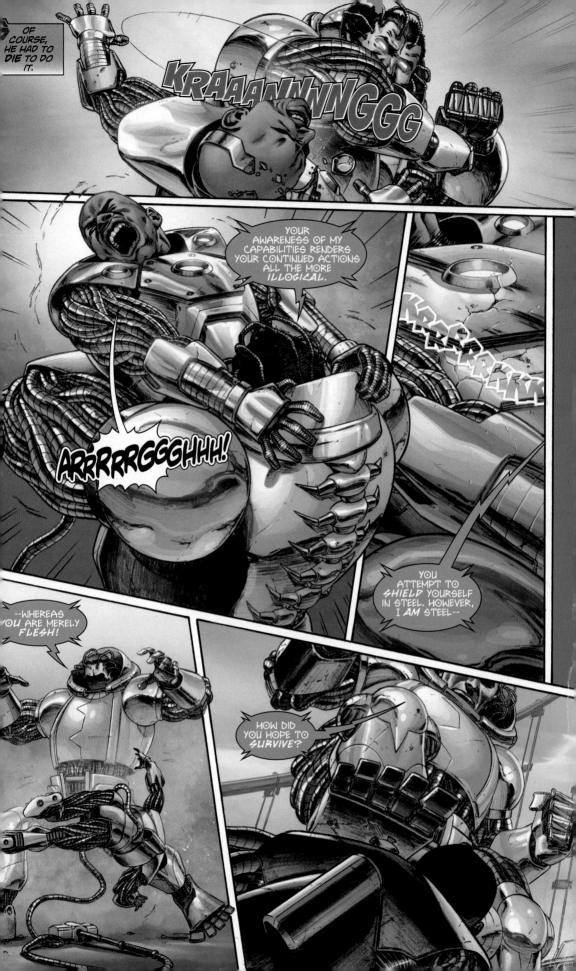

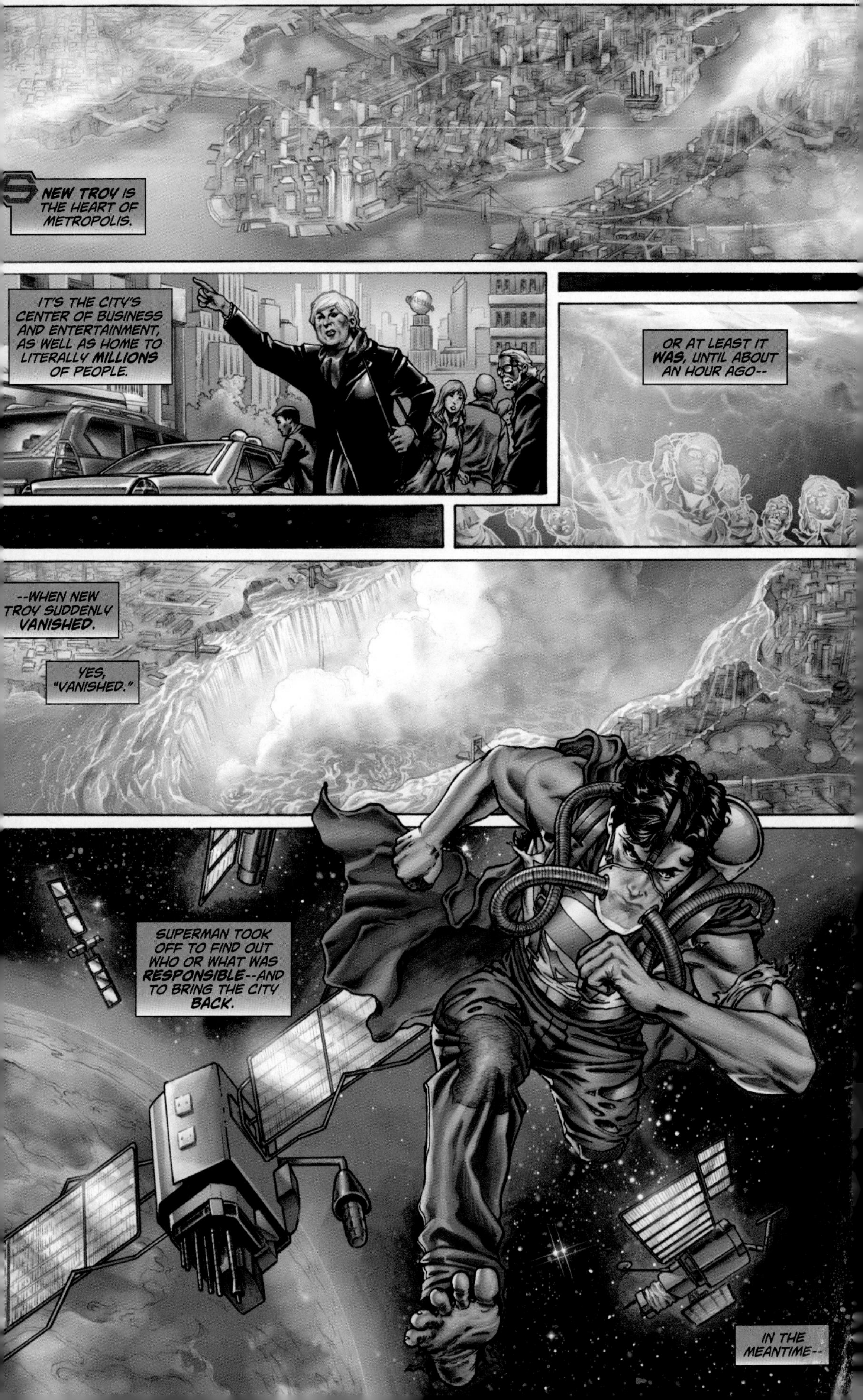
NEW TROY IS THE HEART OF METROPOLIS.
IT'S THE CITY'S CENTER OF BUSINESS AND ENTERTAINMENT, AS WELL AS HOME TO LITERALLY MILLIONS OF PEOPLE.
OR AT LEAST IT WAS, UNTIL ABOUT AN HOUR AGO--
--WHEN NEW TROY SUDDENLY VANISHED.
YES, "VANISHED."
SUPERMAN TOOK OFF TO FIND OUT WHO OR WHAT WAS RESPONSIBLE--AND TO BRING THE CITY BACK.
IN THE MEANTIME--

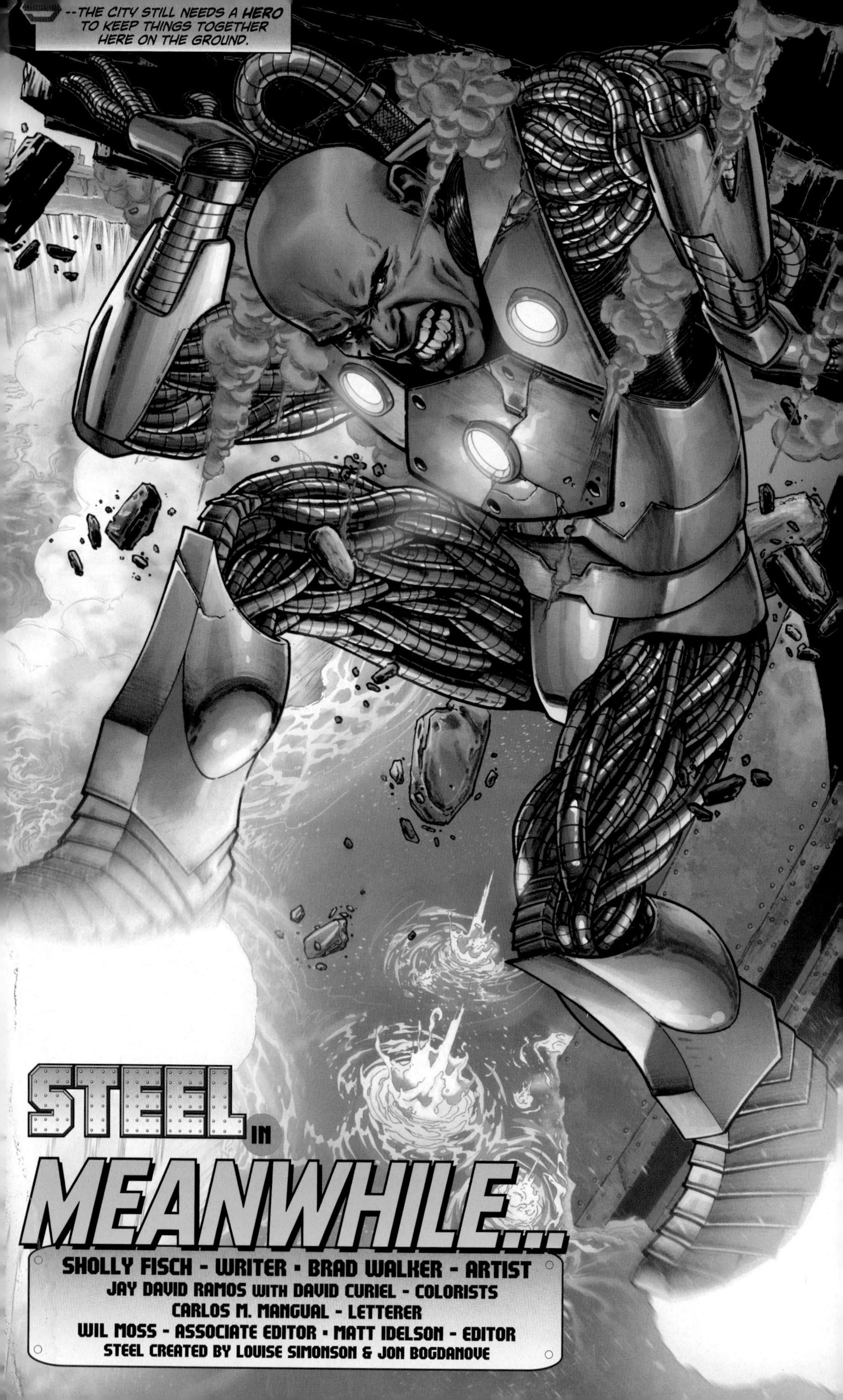

--THE CITY STILL NEEDS A HERO TO KEEP THINGS TOGETHER HERE ON THE GROUND.
STEEL IN
MEANWHILE...
SHOLLY FISCH - WRITER - BRAD WALKER - ARTIST
JAY DAVID RAMOS WITH DAVID CURIEL - COLORISTS
CARLOS M. MANGUAL - LETTERER
WIL MOSS - ASSOCIATE EDITOR - MATT IDELSON - EDITOR
STEEL CREATED BY LOUISE SIMONSON & JON BOGDANOVE

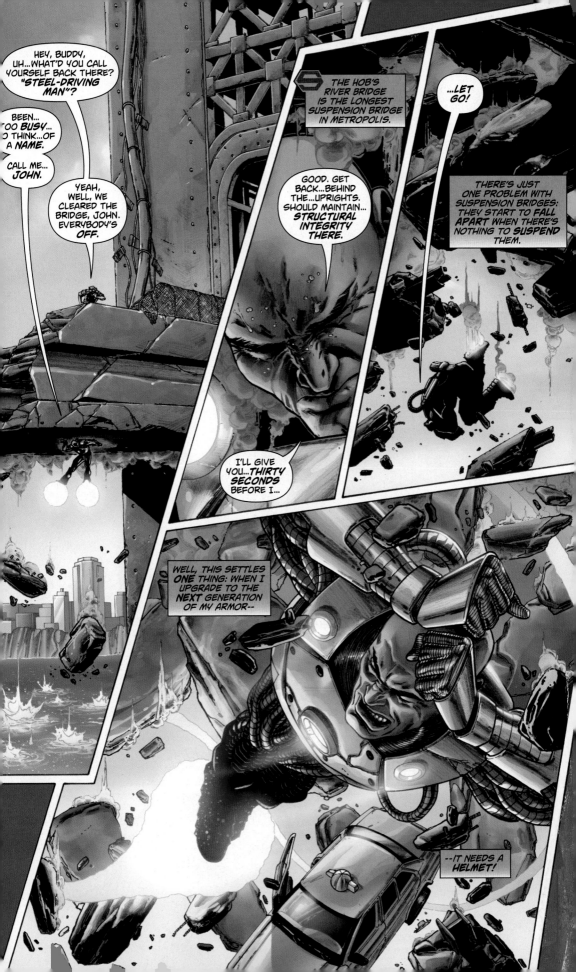

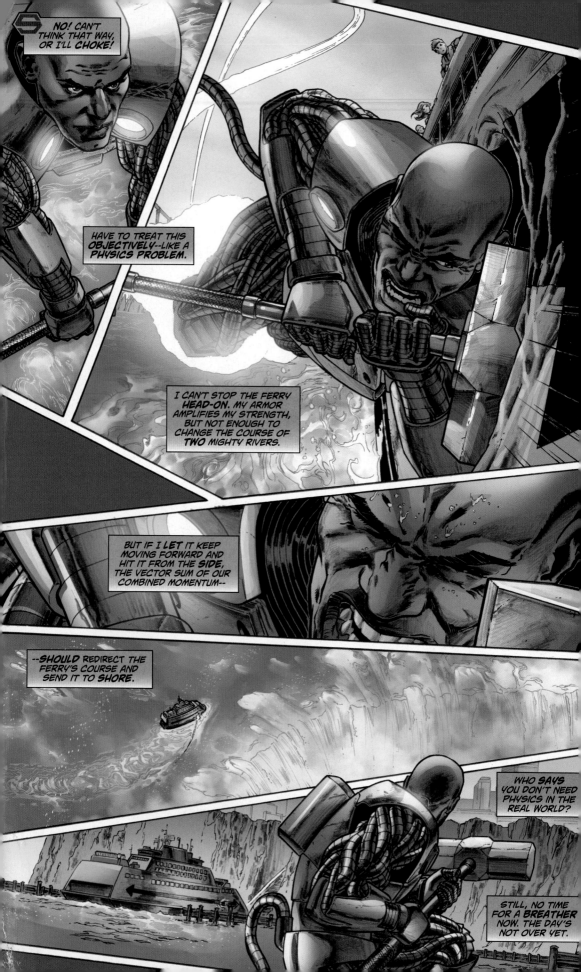

BUT THEN I START LOOKING LESS AT THE *CRISIS* AND MORE AT THE *PEOPLE.*

AND I *REALIZE* SOMETHING.

WHEREVE PEOPLE OF ARE COMIN TO MEET

NOT JL EMERG THE RE

I THOUGHT IT WOULD TAKE A *HERO* TO BRING METROPOLIS THROUGH THIS DISASTER.

I WAS *WRONG.*

IT DOESN'T TAKE *ONE* HERO.

IT TAKES *MILLIONS* OF THEM.

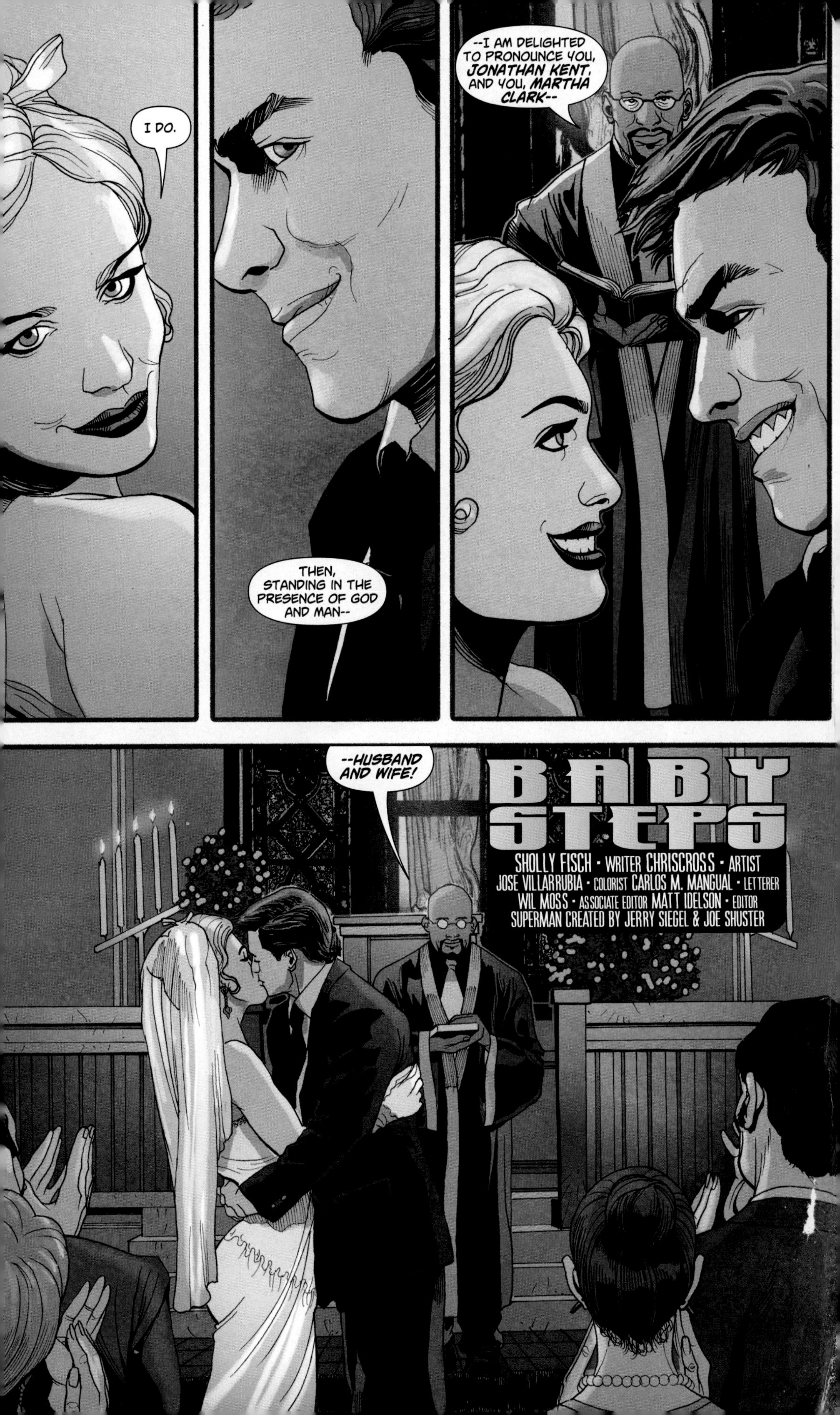
I DO.
THEN, STANDING IN THE PRESENCE OF GOD AND MAN--
--I AM DELIGHTED TO PRONOUNCE YOU, JONATHAN KENT, AND YOU, MARTHA CLARK--
--HUSBAND AND WIFE!
BABY STEPS
SHOLLY FISCH · WRITER CHRISCROSS · ARTIST
JOSE VILLARRUBIA · COLORIST CARLOS M. MANGUAL · LETTERER
WIL MOSS · ASSOCIATE EDITOR MATT IDELSON · EDITOR
SUPERMAN CREATED BY JERRY SIEGEL & JOE SHUSTER

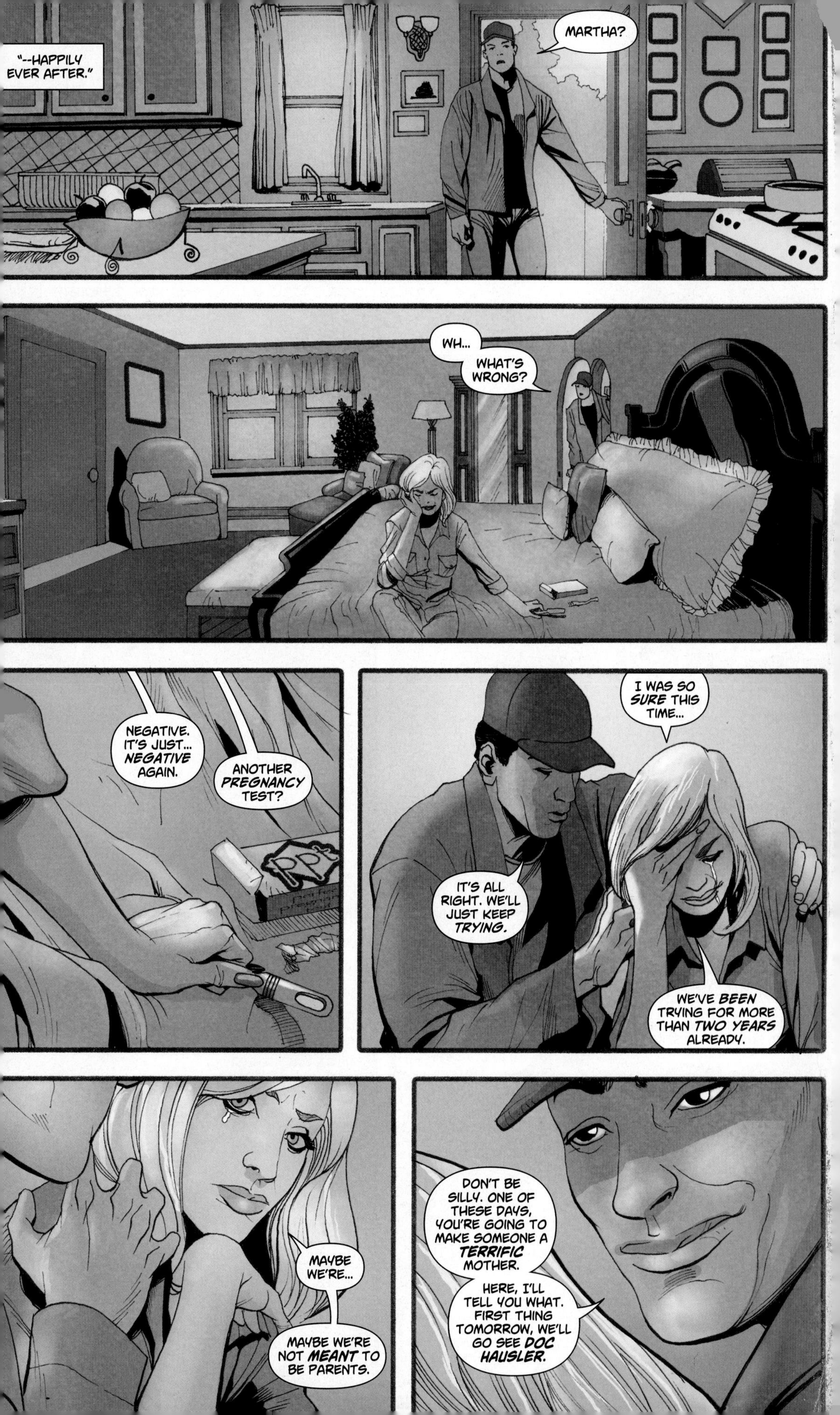
"--HAPPILY EVER AFTER."
MARTHA?
WH... WHAT'S WRONG?
NEGATIVE. IT'S JUST... NEGATIVE AGAIN.
ANOTHER PREGNANCY TEST?
I WAS SO SURE THIS TIME...
IT'S ALL RIGHT. WE'LL JUST KEEP TRYING.
WE'VE BEEN TRYING FOR MORE THAN TWO YEARS ALREADY.
MAYBE WE'RE...
MAYBE WE'RE NOT MEANT TO BE PARENTS.
DON'T BE SILLY. ONE OF THESE DAYS, YOU'RE GOING TO MAKE SOMEONE A TERRIFIC MOTHER.
HERE, I'LL TELL YOU WHAT. FIRST THING TOMORROW, WE'LL GO SEE DOC HAUSLER.

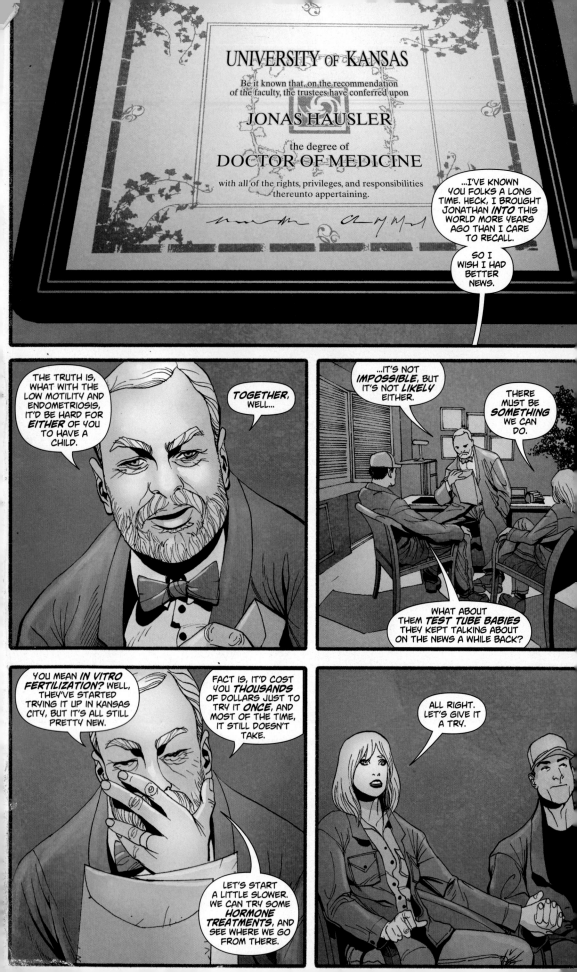

LAST DAY

SHOLLY FISCH · CHRISCROSS · JOSE VILLARRUBIA · SUPERMAN
WRITER · ARTIST · COLORIST · CREATED BY
JERRY SIEGEL
CARLOS M. MANGUAL · WIL MOSS · MATT IDELSON · AND
LETTERER · ASSOCIATE EDITOR · EDITOR · JOE SHUSTER

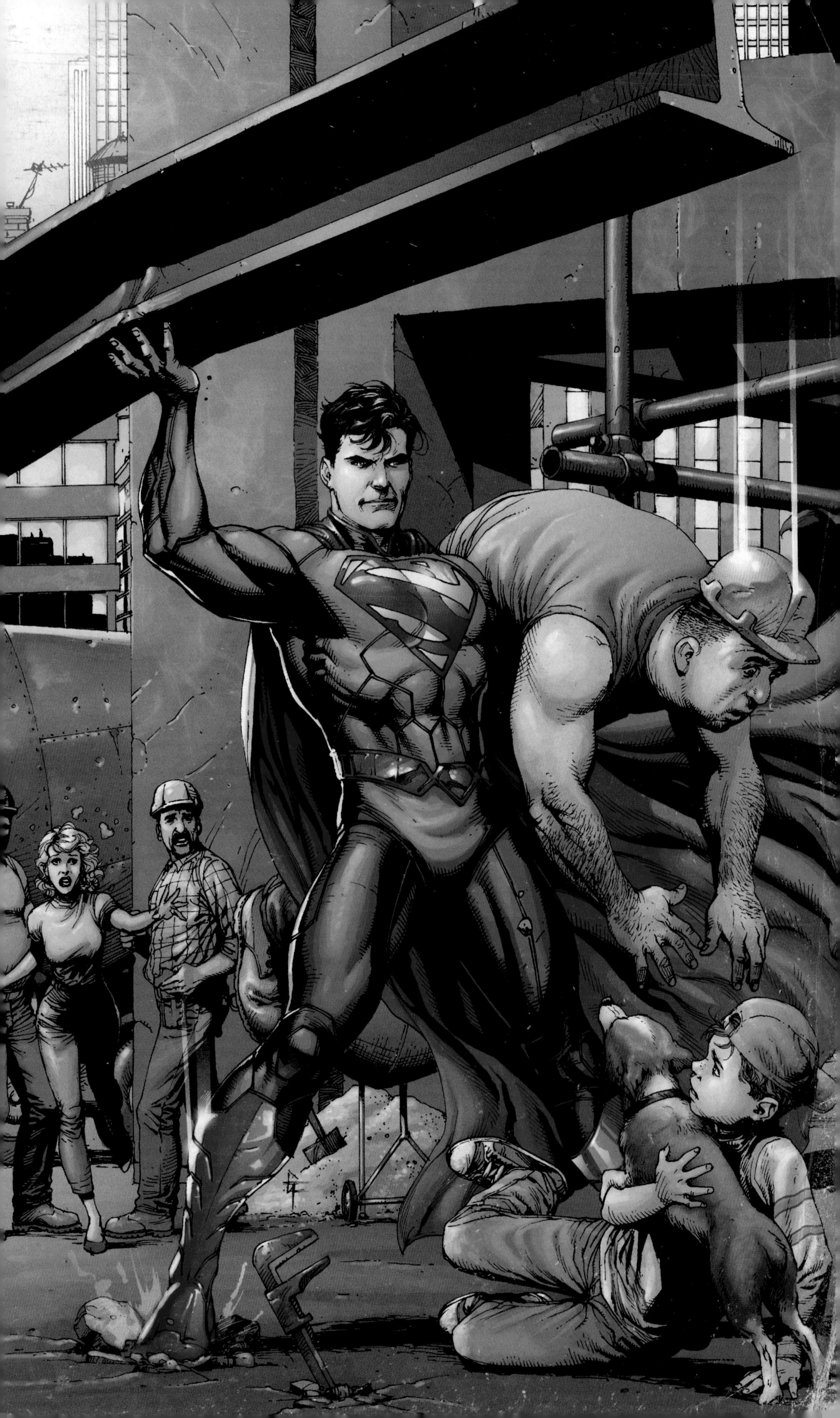

GET AN EXCLUSIVE PEEK BEHIND THE SCENES
OF THE CREATION OF ACTION COMICS #1-2 WITH
GRANT MORRISON AND RAGS MORALES

Rags Morales' cover sketches for ACTION COMICS #1.

ACTION!

GRANT MORRISON: The physical things Superman does came from the first year of ACTION COMICS, where they were doing this nonstop, kinetic, muscular action. I wanted to get that into the actual form and structure of this whole run, that feeling of motion and action. It's called ACTION COMICS — let's do that!

RAGS MORALES: For the first twenty years, flying with that pose I gave him on the first cover — the one bent leg and the one straight leg, and counterbalancing with the arms — was the Superman trademark, and it made him look like he was running. Here I am trying to do an homage to it. It brought it back to the essence of that character.

HE LITTLE MAN

ORRISON: I was thinking of the warf from *Twin Peaks* — a gnome-ke figure, a creepy little elf.

ORALES: I relied more on the Robert lake character from *Lost Highway*. omehow he ended up looking a little it like Elvis Costello, too... [Laughs]

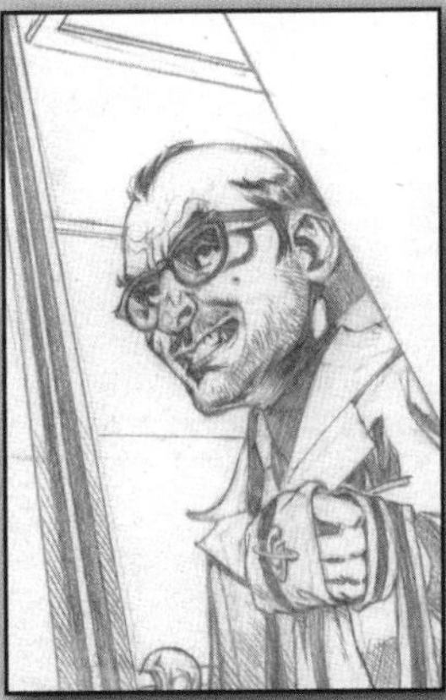

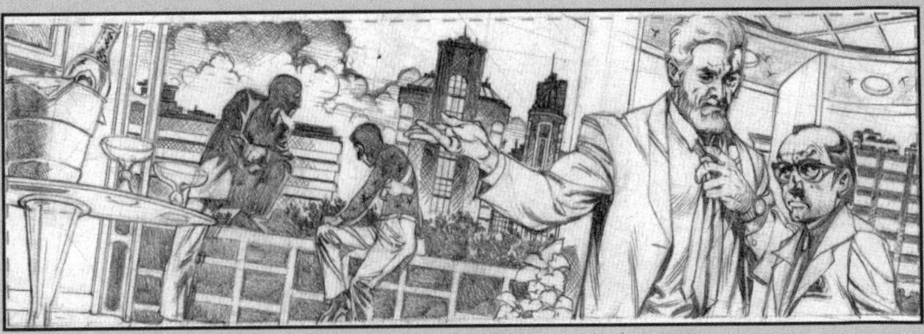

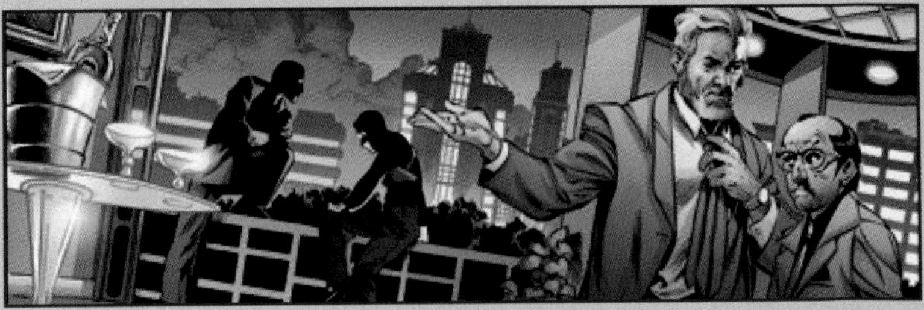

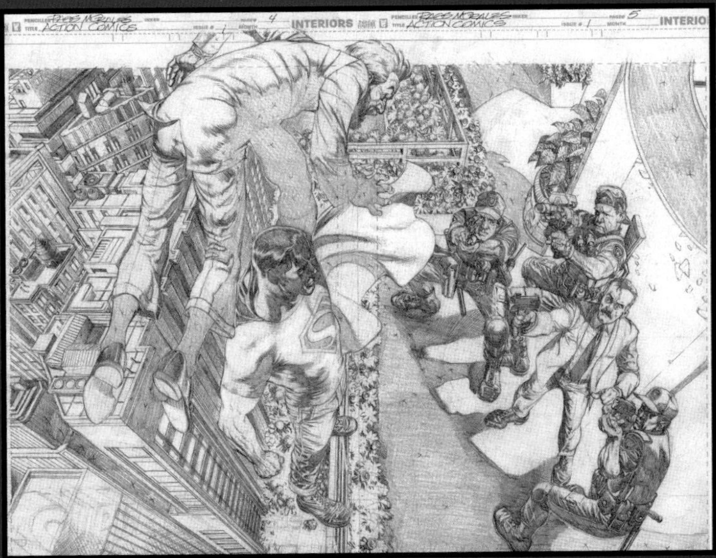

ACTION COMICS
INTERIORS
ACTION COMICS
INTERIO

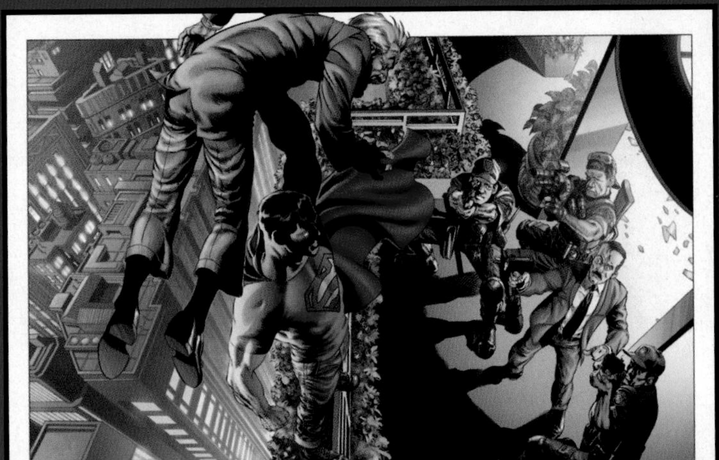

A WHOLE NEW SUPERMAN

MORRISON: Like a guitarist in a band of 17-year-olds, experience doesn't even come into it — he just does it. He's a super hero — he doesn't have to think. He's a kid who's been set free from Ma and Pa Kent. Both of them are dead, and suddenly he thinks, "I'm the most powerful thing on the planet. It's time to start cleaning up!" [Laughs] It seemed like you could get a really good story out of a young man who's not considering what he's doing — he's just doing it because it feels right.

MORALES: Honestly, I could never really get into Superman before. I even had a hard time drawing him, because he'd been done so many times by so many people. I'm glad we're going back to the beginning with him. It's a chance to do it all over again, knowing what we know now.

SUPER-SWAGGER

MORALES: I thought, "What are the two iconic things that Superman would be to me?" He'd be part Steve Reeves and part Elvis. [Laughs] When he's catching the bullet, he's got that Elvis light in the corner of his eye.

MORRISON: That swagger is part of what the rest of the world believes about America. "They're all John Wayne!" [Laughs] I wanted to put that back into Superman, that attitude of "I know what I'm doing, I'm the biggest guy on the block...but lucky for you, I'm a good guy!"

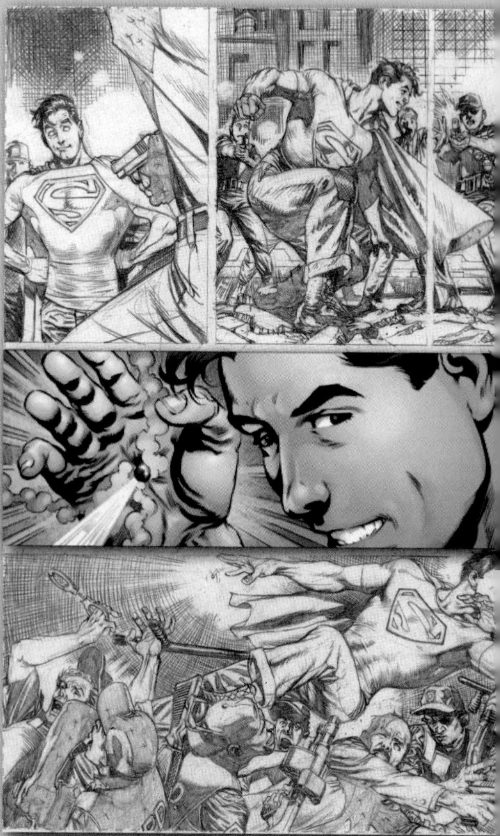

THE LABORS OF SUPERMAN

MORRISON: I constantly put Superman up against very physical objects: a wrecking ball, a tank, a train, solic stone. It was designed for the motion of that muscular, 1938 Superman — to really tie him into physical things, tc big, heavy objects.

MORALES: I love that he's powered down. Love it, love it, love it, love it. I love that he's Herculean again. He's about doing the tasks. Superman back in the '40s was more relevant than Superman of recent years, because things hurt him. There was a danger to that.

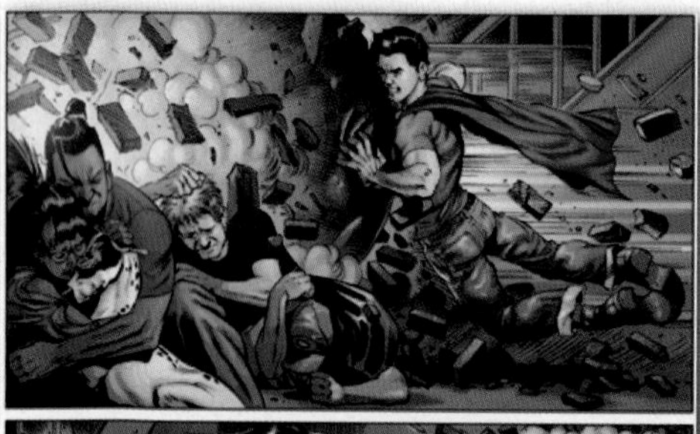

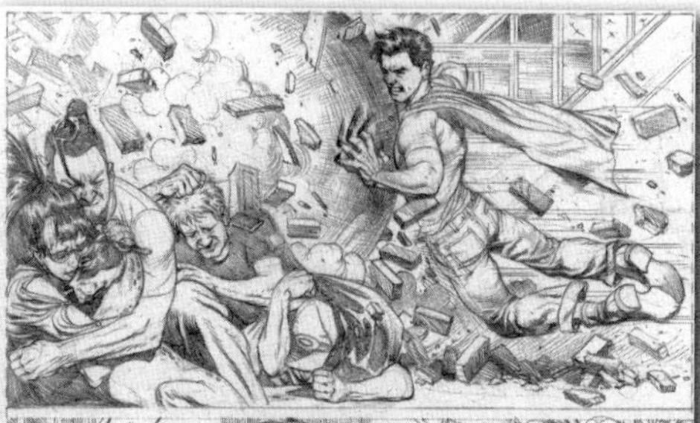

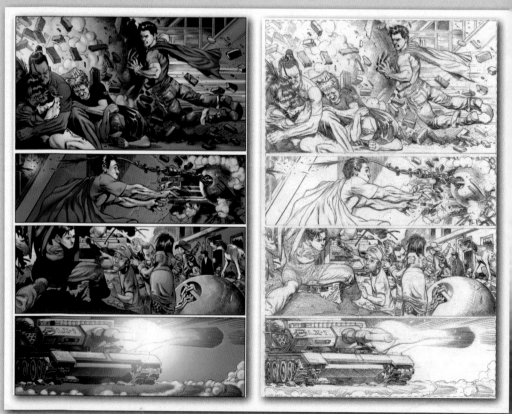

CLARK KENT

MORALES: I put him in baggy clothing to hide his muscles. Maybe stoop his posture a little — make him a little slack-jawed in certain moments so he doesn't look at all like a hero — more like a 12-year-old nerd, which is what he's trying to do. He's a very good actor, which is a super power I don't think many other super heroes have. And I realized that there's a certain amount of thickness to the lenses of his glasses that can help distort the size of his eyes and make them seem larger.

MORRISON: I love Rags's Clark Kent. I think it's great, this Harry Potter Clark Kent. His face is so young and pliable! His eyes get bigger, so he looks more like a kid. That's why Rags is so good to work with — he really thinks about this stuff, and it makes such a big difference to the finished product. When I saw that Clark Kent, it changed the way I wrote the character. He suddenly seemed very young, and he could be a little bit brattish. Clark's obviously this little hardcore farmer's boy who's not taking any crap from anyone.

MORE POWERFUL THAN A LOCOMOTIVE?

MORRISON: When he's hit by a train, he's not the Superman we've seen for the last 25-30 years. This is someone who can be hurt. I wanted to show he has limits. But it's also this upfront connection to the Superman legend — he's actually punched in the chest by the "speeding bullet."

MORALES: Originally, when Superman took off, he was exerting effort. To stop a train was painful. To get electrocuted was painful. He survived it much better than we could, but we forget how impossible these things are to do. I love that he's been brought back down to Earth. That's the way it should be.

X LUTHOR

...erman is us at our best, and Lex is ...but they're both us. He's selfish, he's ...ected, he's greedy, he's egotistical, he ...s to hate Superman but really he wants to ...k like Superman, he's constantly chugging energy drinks, he talks crap...[Laughs] I wanted to make him an embodiment of all of our worst traits. They're what make us human, so that's what makes Lex human and relatable. That's why Lex Luthor's such a great villain: We all recognize those traits.

MORALES: Lex's weight is one of those little subliminal things. It adds a layer of jealousy and feeling insignificant and insecure about yourself. He's this out-of-shape, snide, condescending jerk who we're too mature now to stuff into a locker when we see him, but we still do it every time in our heads. [Laughs] Luthor's that guy from the electronics store who condescends to you when you ask about the difference between a megabyte and a gigabyte.

The following is a panel description from the script of ACTION COMICS #1:
Big pic. Now we cut to a military command center somewhere outside Metropolis. N... center atmosphere with military personnel hunched over computers. Big wall sc... like they have at NASA. All yours, Rags. The picture is dominated by a big screen which we see a GRAPHIC OF METROPOLIS with a pulsing circle in lower midtown where Superman was last seen.

Silhouetted against the screen are two of our principal players — Lois Lane's GENERAL SAM LANE and Superman's arch-villain LEX LUTHOR. Lane is the archet... tough American dad. Luthor, like Superman, is a little younger, perhaps a little hea... and sturdier. I like the idea that he was a little fat until his jealousy of Superman d... him to the gym to become the trim, muscular Luthor of the Silver Age and more re... stories. So he's not obese but he's veering a little more in the visual direction of Luth... heavier build as it appeared in stories from 1941 to 1959.

LOIS LANE, REPORTER

MORRISON: Lois is an army girl, but she's become... crusading journalist to annoy her parents. She's l... Clark Kent: She's crusading, she wants to do good, sh... a hero in her own right. It changes the whole Sup... man dynamic, because Lois isn't tied to any guy. Sh... a party girl, she's smart, she's clever — she's Lady Ga... She's the smartest girl on the planet.

MORALES: I think she has a poster of Woodward... Bernstein on the wall — that's what's important to h... I see her as constantly thinking. She may be saying o... thing, but in her eyes you can tell she's thinking fifte... steps ahead of you.

JIMMY OLSEN, ~~SUPERMAN'S~~ CLARK KENT'S PAL

MORRISON: Jimmy's playing the role of Clark's friend rather than Superman's friend. He's the guy that Clark connected with when he first turned up in Metropolis. The two of them are geeks together, talking about movies and sci-fi. Jimmy's a young kid who's getting into this whole photography thing and is really smart. These are characters who you can imagine all have blogs, and Jimmy has his photographs up on Flickr. They're modern kids.

MORALES: He's Clark's best friend. They're buds. They're on the same level. Initially, he was all, "Well, golly gee, Mr. Kent!" But now he's just kind of like, "Hey, Clark, man — dude." If you want to make Jimmy Olsen cool, stop making him such an obsequious sycophant. You bring Clark down to him — which is perfect for Clark, too. It puts them on equal terms and instantly makes Jimmy cooler.

"THAT BEAT-UP-LOOKING KID...

MORRISON: You can tell he's in danger simp... because he's no longer in motion!

MORALES: All art comes from the center. All y... have to do is remember all the scraps you g... into as a kid...

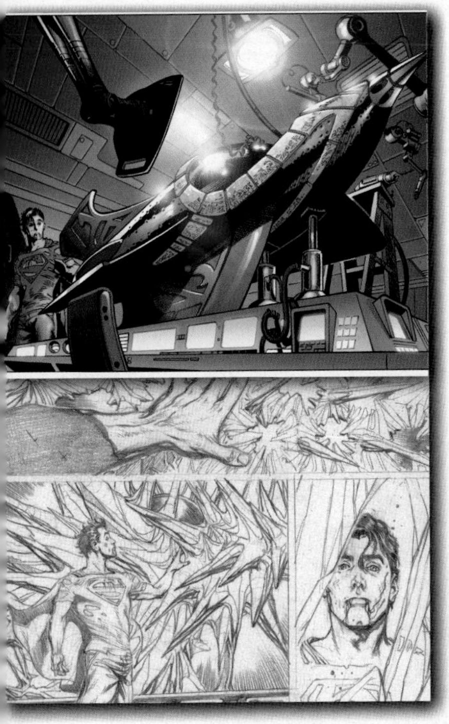

KAL-EL'S ROCKET

MORRISON: The rocket is Moses' basket, the basket that the Hindi hero Karna was placed in — the idea of people putting a child into the river of destiny. The cape, the rocket, the costume, the ship we see at the end of #2 — everything is part of the story and has character arcs of its own. Every little bit of the Superman legend is turned into something meaningful in its own right.

MORALES: Those little squiggles are designed to be hieroglyphs. If you're Kryptonian, you can read them. But it's funny: As I was drawing it, I started seeing things that reminded me of Moses' basket. Then I'm thinking, "Kal-EL— 'El' is a Hebrew word for God. The world's being destroyed, so he's being put into the basket and sent down the Nile." So I made it a little more basket-y.

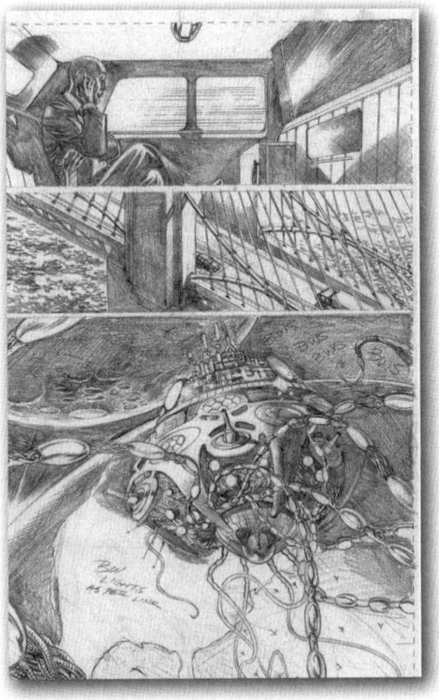

"IT CAME FROM OUTER SPACE"

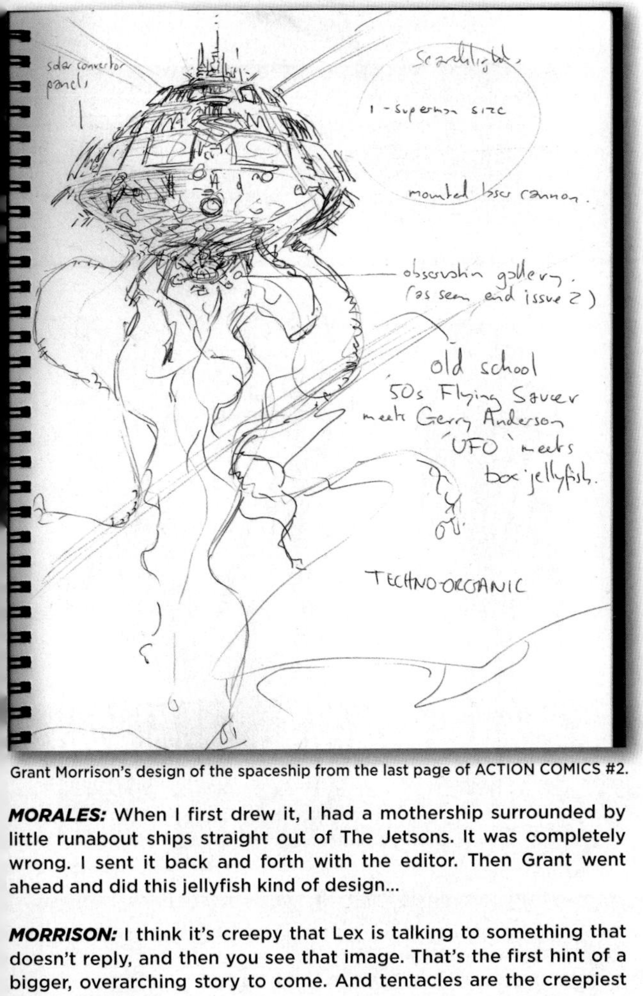

solar convertor panels
Searchlight
1 - Superman size
mounted laser cannon.
observation gallery. (as seen end issue 2)
old school 50s Flying Saucer meets Gerry Anderson 'UFO' meets box jellyfish.
TECHNO-ORGANIC

Grant Morrison's design of the spaceship from the last page of ACTION COMICS #2.

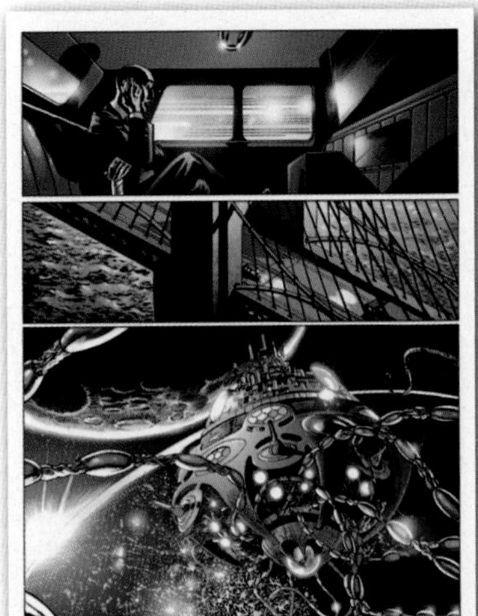

MORALES: When I first drew it, I had a mothership surrounded by little runabout ships straight out of The Jetsons. It was completely wrong. I sent it back and forth with the editor. Then Grant went ahead and did this jellyfish kind of design...

MORRISON: I think it's creepy that Lex is talking to something that doesn't reply, and then you see that image. That's the first hint of a bigger, overarching story to come. And tentacles are the creepiest things! [Laughs]

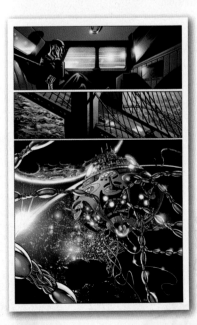

KRYPTON DESIGNS BY GENE HA!

MORRISON: It's the planet of your dreams. A scientific utopia. I wanted to explore Krypton as the world of super people. What would happen if they worked it all out, if they lived for 500 years with amazing technology?

GENE HA: I'm going to vary Kryptonians by standard facial features and hair texture and placement, mixed with very unusual color of hair and skin. A cocktail party of supermodels attacked by a god-child with god-crayons. I see Kryptonian identity as being very tied to their bodies. They always want their bodies to be more perfect, though their concept of perfection can drift into surprising directions.

MORE THAN JUST A LAMP

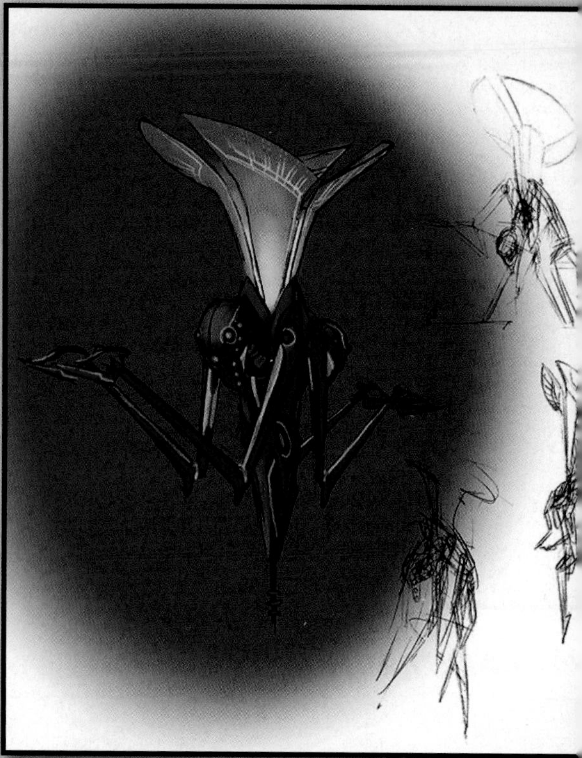

HA: The serving bots are both servants and decorative lamp with figural columns. The lily/insect wing/lampshade is the hover device. The robots are supposed to hint both at manti arms, and also skeletons — lilies and skeletons being metaphor for the briefness of life and the permanence of death.

LIKE SON, LIKE FATHER

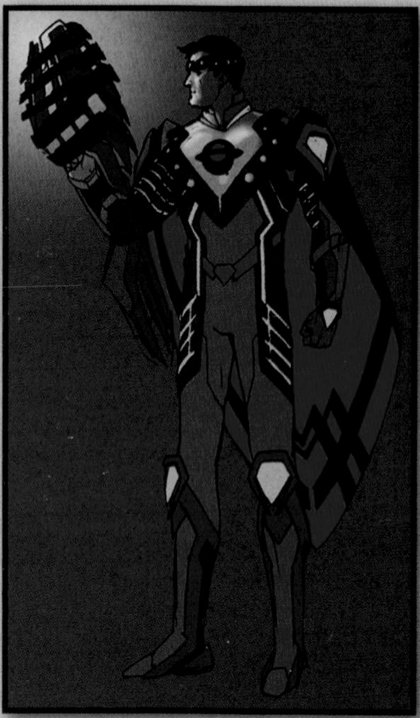

MORRISON: Jor-El looks just like the father of Superman should look. He's wearing an outfit that closely resembles the Jim Lee Superman suit, except in Jor-El's trademark green and red. He has the science guild symbol on his chest — a ringed planet.

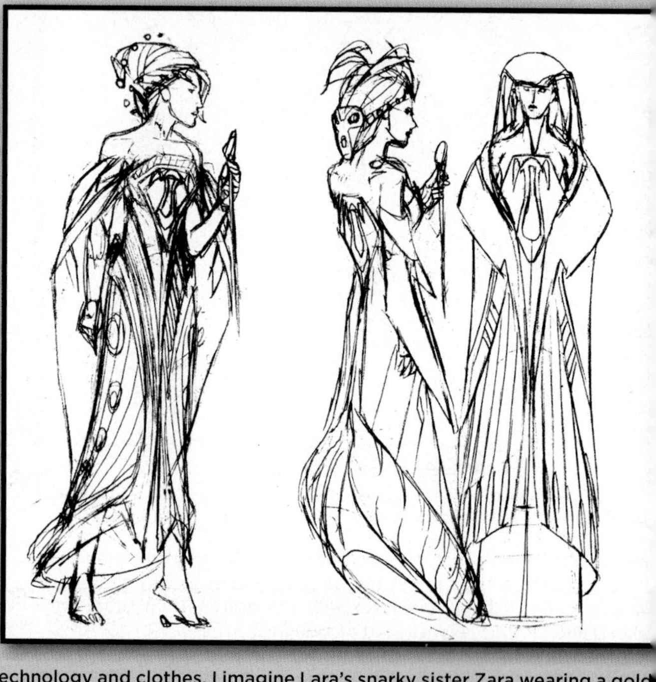

THE NEW FALL (OF KANDOR) COLLECTION

HA: At the basic level, Kryptonians could have body-defying technology and clothes. I imagine Lara's snarky sister Zara wearing a golden face mask on the back of her head, which lets her speak to and see people behind her back. She pretty much only uses her real mouth to emote and eat and drink. Instead of drinking cocktails, they're sniffing from glass tubes. This plays with ideas like sniffing flowers, and sticking your nose into a wine glass before taking a sip. No idea what they get from sniffing: aromatherapy, mild intoxication, or even nutrition.

The party platform
es heavy use of anti-
ity and other hover
nology. Each floor has
nal Kryptonian gravity
ach side, and people are
ing on each side. It has
airs, but instead the sun
al columns also have
own gravity for anyone
hing its surface.

CITY AS
SCIENCE COLONY

HA: I'm imagining Kandor as a
giant science colony. It's a moun-
tain-sized power grid transformer,
transforming and storing voltages,
radiation, dimensional warps, and
perhaps even information and
telepathic memories. The main
administration is in the float-
ing dome at the top of the city,
but various other facilities have
occupant space, too.

al at top
rk at bottom

Interviews by Sean T. Collins
Design by Rob Clark Jr.

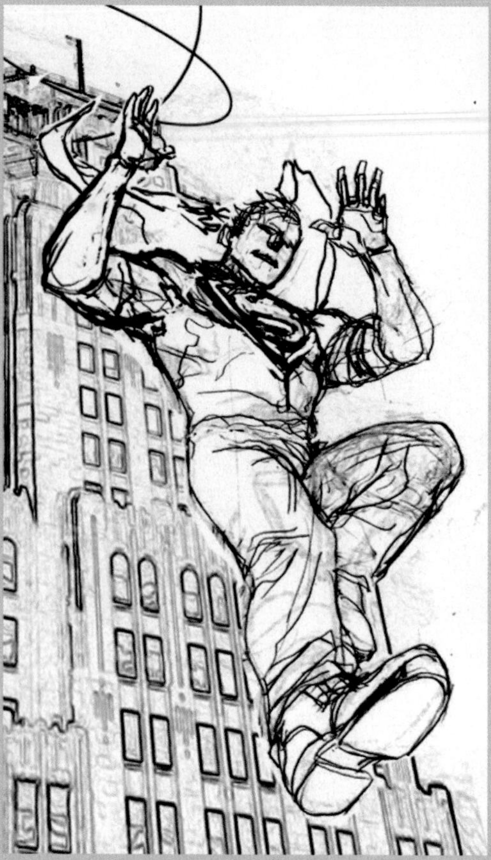

Cover sketches and pencils by Michael Choi.

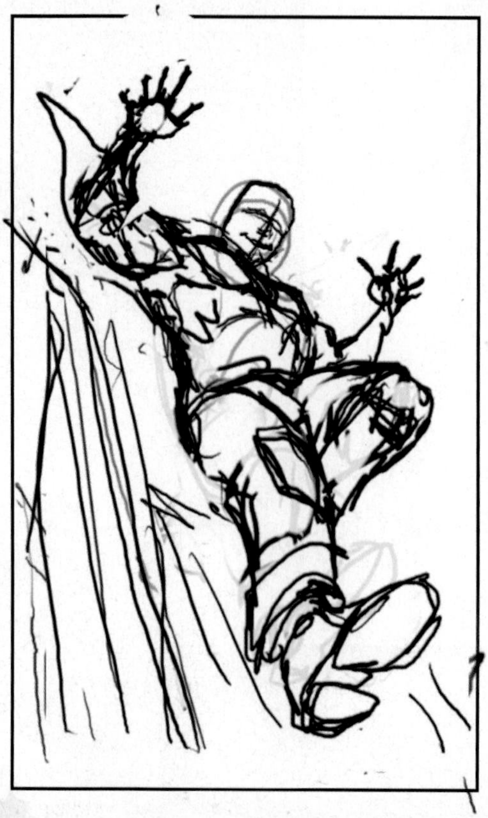

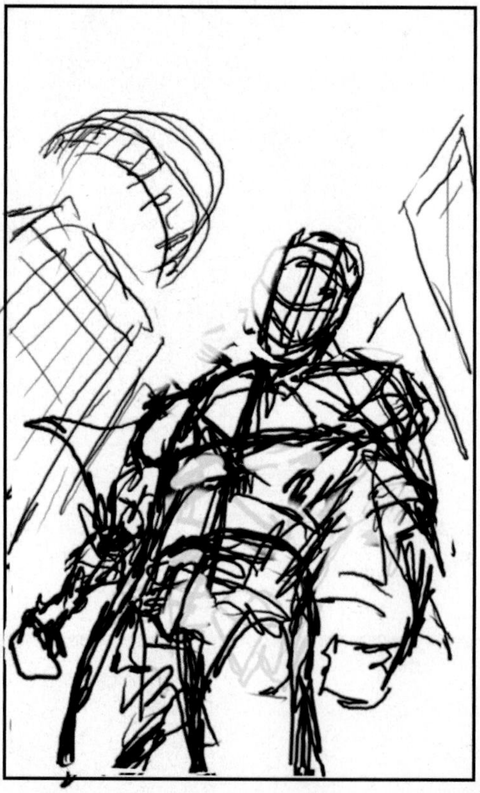

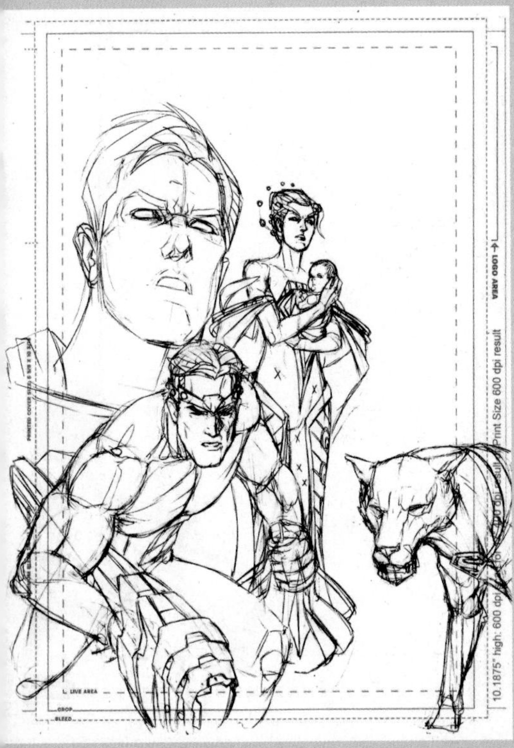
LOGO AREA
LIVE AREA
CROP
BLEED

Cover sketches and pencils by Gene Ha.

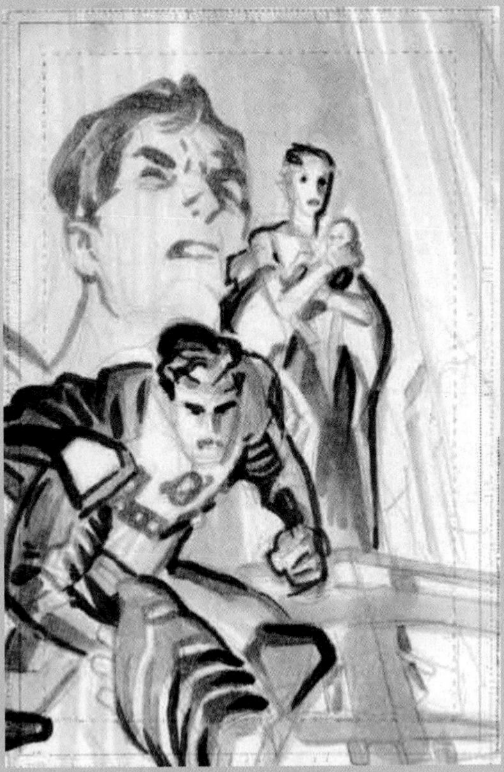

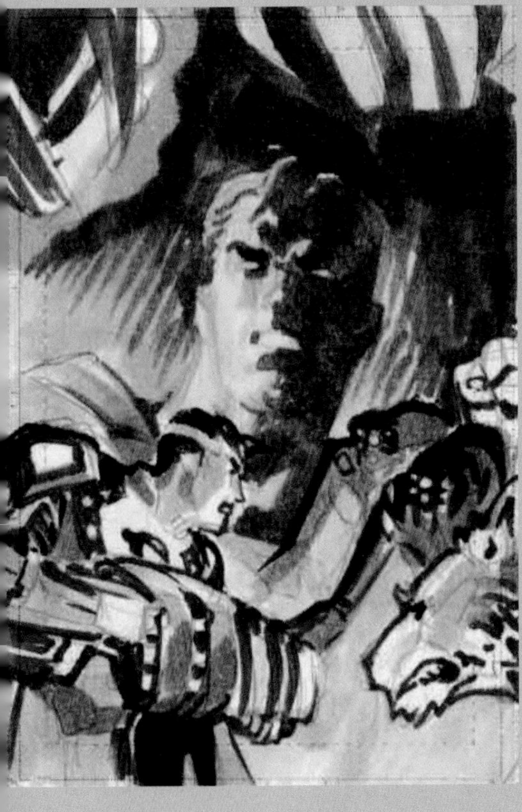

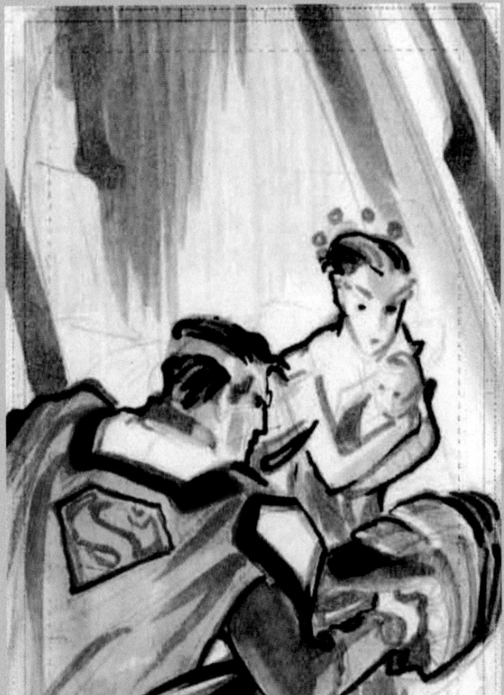

Cover sketches by Andy Kubert.

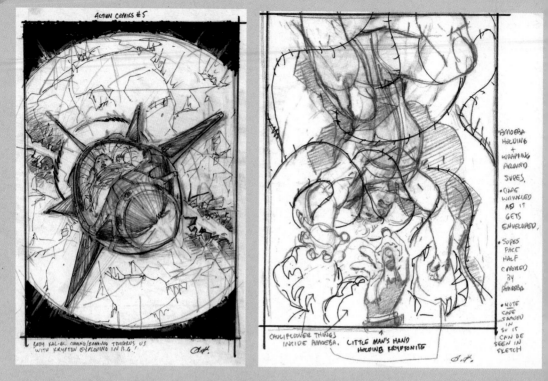

Cover sketches
and pencils by
Chris Burnham.